A Few Good Men

5th Marines Engagements 1914-2000

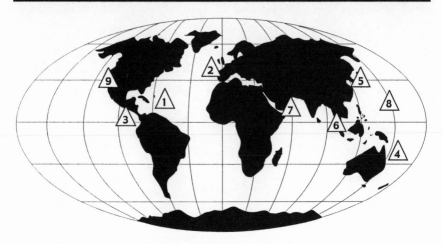

△1 Caribbean (1914)   △4 Southwest Pacific (1942–1944)   △7 Persian Gulf (1991)

△2 France (1917–1918)   △5 Korea (1950–1955)   △8 Western Pacific (1944–45; Present)

△3 Nicaragua (1927–1932)   △6 Vietnam (1966–1971)   △9 Camp Pendleton (Cold War)

A Few Good Men

The Story of the Fighting Fifth Marines

Ronald J. Brown

PRESIDIO

This book, like Robert Roth's award-winning novel Sand In The Wind, *is dedicated to all of the numbers, but most especially the "03's."*

Published by Presidio Press, Inc.
505 B San Marin Drive, Suite 160
Novato, CA 94945-1340

Library of Congress Cataloging-in-Publication Data

Brown, Ronald J.
    A few good men : the story of the Fighting Fifth Marines /
    by Ronald J. Brown.
       p.   cm.
    Includes bibliographical references and index.
    ISNB 0-89141-736-2
    1. United States. Marine Corps. Regiment, 5th—History. I. Title.

    VE23.25 5th .B76 2001
    359.9'631'0973—dc21
                               001021552

All photos courtesy Marine Corps University unless otherwise noted.

Printed in the United States of America

Contents

Foreword

This book tells the story of one of the most acclaimed regiments in the United States Marine Corps. From its service in France during World War I, to its participation in the Gulf War, the 5th Marines has been instrumental in protecting our nation's interests and building our Corps's legacy. The regiment has fought in "every clime and place," always acquitting itself with distinction and bringing honor to our service as "Soldiers of the Sea." But why, given the copious amount of literature available, should anyone want to read this composition? The simple answer is that no other work so thoroughly details this unit's remarkable achievements or provides such insight into the men who made up its ranks. By systematically chronicling its evolution and describing many of the regiment's significant actions in various conflicts of the twentieth century, this history is poised to become the authoritative reference. While such a comprehensive account is useful to a general audience, it is especially beneficial to the military professional who must have a full appreciation of historical antecedents, and understand their potential implications. This book's appeal, therefore, lies not only in its informational construct, but also in its educational value, for, to paraphrase President Harry Truman, the only thing new in the world is the history we haven't learned.

While each of the Corps's eight infantry regiments has a glorious history, the "Fighting Fifth Marines" is unique in that it has earned the most battle honors. Since 1914 this regiment has served at home and abroad during times of war and peace. It was originally formed as a temporary unit that served as a floating reaction force in the Caribbean. Since then, it has participated in the trench warfare of World War I, peacekeeping duties in Nicaragua, four landings in the Pacific during World War II, occupation duty in North China and Guam, every major Marine campaign in Korea, a six-year tour of duty in Vietnam, service afloat and ashore during the Persian Gulf Conflict, and humanitarian intervention in Bangladesh. The regiment's Marines still proudly wear the distinctive *fourragere* awarded by the French Ministry of War for the unit's exceptional performance on the battlefields of France during the Great War. These Marines have, and continue to make, significant contributions to our national security and the Corps's hard-won reputation as a force-in-readiness. As these words are being written, a Navy amphibious ready group somewhere in the Western Pacific is carrying a battalion of the 5th Marines who, just like their heroic forebears, are prepared to take action anywhere trouble should arise. While these Marines perform their mission, the remainder of the regiment trains and waits in readiness at Camp Pendleton, California. These Marines have shaped security policy and written history. This is their story, and it is skillfully told by retired Marine Ron Brown.

I first met Lt. Col. Ronald J. Brown when he reported to my command post at Zakho, a rural village nestled in the Zagros Mountains of northern Iraq, in 1991. The 24th Marine Expeditionary Unit (Special Operations Capable) was there to provide security and humanitarian relief for more than a half million Kurdish refugees seeking asylum from the wrath of Iraqi dictator Saddam Hussein. Ron, at that time a Marine reservist who volunteered to go to northern Iraq after service in Operations Desert Shield and Desert Storm, was there to chronicle Marine participation in Operation Provide Comfort. In many ways he was representative of the dedicated citizen-soldiers who make up America's Total Marine Force. After four years of active service in 1971 he returned to his chosen profession as a high school history teacher and football coach but kept his ties with the Marine Corps alive as a member of the Marine Corps Reserve. With the call to arms to Southwest Asia, he dropped his chalk at Southfield-Lathrup High School and hastily threw his gear into the ALICE pack that would carry his kit halfway around the world. It was there, in a most unlikely spot, that our paths crossed.

Ron Brown is uniquely qualified to write this history. He was an infantry officer with the 5th Marines in Vietnam and then, two decades later, the field historian for the Marine Forces Afloat, which included the 5th Marines during Operations Desert Shield, Desert Storm, and Sea Angel. Ron has been a prolific author with several books, numerous arti-

cles, many book reviews, and an award for fiction among his writing credits. This current work will add to his long list of publications and to the
trove of historical writings that help preserve Marine Corps history. Me-
thodically researched and splendidly written, this book is sure to benefit students and historians alike.

James L. Jones, Jr.
General, USMC

Acknowledgments

Like any lengthy and complex endeavor, this history of the 5th Marines was a collaborative effort, and the author wishes to thank all who helped. Their efforts and contributions were invaluable. Any errors of fact or opinion, however, are the responsibility of the author.

This book contains neither a formal bibliography nor endnotes. Instead, specific sources are cited in compendium endnotes arranged by chapter and section. In addition to research done at the Marine Corps Historical Center at the Washington Navy Yard, where I gleaned much information from documents such as muster rolls, unit diaries, area files, command chronologies, operations plans, after-action reports, and official messages; official histories; and oral history interviews, additional information came from my personal interviews with individuals and my own observations. Comments provided by Ernest Cheatham, Jim Webb, Ken Houghton, Bernard Trainor, and George Clark were very helpful. Materials generously provided by David A. Homscher and John J. Culbertson are also much appreciated. Most artwork, maps, and photographic images included herein are from the Marine Corps University and Marine Corps Historical Center collections, although Dr. Wayne Jens of Presque Isle, Michigan, and J. Douglas Taylor of Farmington Hills, Michigan, did some special photographic work.

My most sincere gratitude goes to the fine staffs at the Alpena Public Library, the Novi Public Library, the Presque Isle Public Library, the National Archives and Records Administration, the Marine Corps Historical Center, the Marine Corps University, and the Marine Corps Research Center. Particularly helpful was an old friend and mentor, eminent Marine Corps historian Charles R. "Rich" Smith. Rich originally encouraged me to tackle this project and then provided assistance above and beyond the call of duty on many occasions. Special thanks also go out to the rest of the staff at the Marine Corps Historical Center, including Director Emeritus Brig. Gen. Edwin H. Simmons (Ret.), Benis M. Frank, Jack Shulimson, Charles D. Melson, Jon T. Hoffman, Danny J. Crawford, Robert V. Aquilina, Anne A. Ferrante, Lena M. Kaljot, Sheila Gramblin, Frederick J. Graboske, Robert E. Struder, Catherine A. Kerns, W. "Steve" Hill, Jack T. Dyer Jr., Evelyn A. Englander, and Patricia E. Morgan. I also wish to salute my comrades in arms from Moblization Training Unit (Historical) DC-7, who shared the Saudi sand and Iraqi dust with me: Cols. Peter M. Gish, Charles J. Quilter II, Dennis P. Mroczkowski, and Lt. Col. Charles H. Cureton. Without a doubt, one of my saviors was Patricia A. Mullen, the custodian of the Marine Corps University archives. She bravely answered the call when I had nowhere else to turn. E. J. McCarthy, the executive editor of Presidio Press, was most helpful and very supportive throughout the publishing process, as was copy editor Dr. Dale Wilson. I would also like to thank Wayne and Dorothy Jens of Presque Isle, Michigan, for all their help and encouragement.

I particularly wish to acknowledge the very special contributions of George B. Clark, the "Sage of Pike, New Hampshire." He is a former Marine whose additional duties now include running The Brass Hat, a publishing and bookselling business that specializes in Marine Corps materials. George is a man with unparalleled knowledge of Marine Corps history and an affinity for the Marines who have populated its ranks. He is a dedicated historian and a great friend who has served as my quartermaster, drill instructor, chief tactician, father confessor, and brother at arms. He not only selflessly shared his unmatched knowledge and treasure trove of materials with me, but he also kept the fire for history burning when my spirits were dampened and the proverbial alligators were snapping at my posterior. Without him, this project would never have come to fruition. Thus, I owe him a greater debt than I can ever repay.

I must also acknowledge the uncounted numbers who have filled the muster rolls of the 5th Marines since 1914. My deepest appreciation goes out to each and every one of them—not for their help with this book, but for Belleau Wood, Soissons, Blanc Mont, the Meuse River, Nicaragua, Guadalcanal, New Britain, Peleliu, Okinawa, Korea, Vietnam, and Desert Storm, as well as the many unmentioned battles that have been lost to the public eye and the ones that are yet to be fought. Once—many, many years ago in a battle-scarred land half a world away—I was one of those numbers and at that time, just like Korean War Navy Cross holder and former U.S. Representative "Pete" McCloskey, it was my honor to "walk with giants" while serving with the Fighting Fifth Marines.

Semper Fi.
Ronald J. Brown

Military Organizations and Abbreviations

I have opted to use standard Marine Corps style conventions in this narrative. The word *Marines* is therefore always capitalized. Additionally, use of this term may be somewhat confusing to the uninitiated reader since it can mean either a group of individual Leathernecks or a single regiment. When identifying a single regiment, Marines is singular. Because the 5th Marines is one regiment, the singular pronoun *it* rather than the plural *they* is grammatically correct.

Regiments are the largest military units made up of subordinate units all from the same arm. During most of its existence, the 5th Marines was composed of three rifle battalions, which in turn were composed of rifle companies and rifle platoons. Conversely, the 11th Marines is an artillery regiment made up of artillery battalions and firing batteries. When a Marine infantry regiment is reinforced for combat operations it is officially designated either a regimental landing team (RLT) for amphibious operations or a regimental combat team (RCT) for extended inland operations. In this narrative, however, I frequently use the term 5th Marines for simplicity even though the regiment was reinforced by combat support units and thus was technically an RLT or RCT at the time. It is also important to note here that a current Marine regiment is similar in size and mission tasking to a modern U.S. Army brigade, whereas a Marine brigade is a much larger entity that invariably includes organic aviation units.

From smallest to largest, the common command levels for Marine infantry units are the fire team, consisting of four enlisted men led by a corporal; the squad, with about a dozen enlisted men led by a sergeant; the platoon, made up of about three dozen men led by a lieutenant; the company, consisting of about 250 men led by a captain; the battalion, with about a thousand men commanded by a lieutenant colonel; the regiment, with about three thousand men commanded by a colonel; and the division, with some twenty thousand Marines commanded by a major general. Regimental and battalion commanders have staff sections to assist the smooth functioning of their units, these include administration, intelligence, operations, logistics, and communications. Medical (doctors and corpsmen) and morale (chaplains) personnel are provided by the U.S. Navy and are attached to Marine units.

Since 1941, the U.S. Marine Corps's operating forces have been organized into divisions, large combined-arms units designed to carry out amphibious operations and capable of sustained independent operations in the field. Marine divisions are divided into three rifle regiments, an artillery regiment, and various service and combat support battalions (tanks, medical, amphibian tractors, etc.). Although some nonmilitary reporters and historians have become confused about correct usage, Marine divisions are never properly referred to using the noun "Marines" (i.e., the 1st Marines is a regiment, not the 1st Marine Division).

The 5th Marine Regiment has almost always mustered three rifle battalions: the 1st, 2d, and 3d Battalions. In the text I often use the military abbreviations 1/5 ("one-five"), 2/5 ("two-five"), and 3/5 ("three-five"). Similar abbreviations indicate other U.S. Marine units (e.g., 1/1 means the 1st Battalion, 1st Marines). During the Korean War, the 1st Marine Division also included a Korean Marine Corps (KMC) regiment whose men were called KMCs and whose battalions are identified as 1/KMC, 2/KMC, 3/KMC, and 5/KMC. The U.S. Marines have often been reinforced by, or worked closely with, U.S. Army units. Reference to a unit called the 23d Infantry, for example, indicates a U.S. Army regiment. Reference to 3-41 ("third of the forty-first") would mean an army infantry battalion.

Since the Korean War, the Marine Corps has deployed units for combat as Marine air-ground task forces (MAGTFs). This organization ensures unity of command by placing all arms under a single commander. Although MAGTFs vary greatly in size and composition, each has a command element, a ground combat element, an air combat element, and a service support element. Modern Marine regiments usually serve with either a division/air-wing-sized Marine expeditionary force (MEF) or a regiment/air-group-sized Marine expeditionary brigade (MEB), but individual battalions or detachments can be assigned to a Marine expeditionary unit (MEU) for independent activities such as unit deployment rotations or for use as special landing forces (SLFs). The 5th Regiment has been assigned to various brigades over the years: the U.S. 4th Infantry Brigade in France, the 2d (Marine) Brigade in Nicaragua, the 1st (Provisional) Marine Brigade before World War II, a similarly named provisional unit in the early days of Korea, and RLT 5 was the ground combat element of the 5th Marine Expeditionary Brigade (MEB) in Southwest Asia. The 5th Marines has usually been part of the 1st Marine Division (1st MarDiv), but not always—the regiment was part of the U.S. Army 2d Division (Regular) during World War I. In Vietnam, the 5th Marines, as an organic unit of the 1st MarDiv, was also part of III Marine Amphibious Force (III MAF), but in Southwest Asia it came under the operational control of I MEF. Battalion landing teams (BLTs) from the 5th Marines were formed into SLFs during the Vietnam era, and they currently form the ground combat nucleus of the 31st MEU in the western Pacific.

Introduction

New arrivals at the 1st Marine Division processing center were told "If you want action, join the 5th Marines." This statement was especially true in 1969, but it also could be applied to almost any American conflict in the twentieth century. The muddy trenches of France in 1918, the steamy jungles of Nicaragua during the Banana Wars, the tropic Pacific islands that lined the road to Tokyo during World War II, the frigid mountains of Korea, and the barren sands of the Persian Gulf are just as familiar to the 5th Marines as are the golden hills of Camp Pendleton and the rocky shores of Okinawa.

The "Fighting Fifth Marines" is neither the oldest nor the most traveled Marine Corps regiment, but this unit has seen more combat service than any similar size unit in the United States armed forces since 1914. The story of the 5th Marines closely parallels the history of the modern Marine Corps and, arguably, no other single American military regiment has played such a crucial role on so many battlefields.

When German invaders cracked the French lines and were headed full steam for Paris in 1918, a crusty old captain of the 5th Marines sounded the turning point of World War I when he boldly announced, "Retreat Hell! We just got here." The German juggernaut was soon thereafter halted in its tracks at Belleau Wood. An anonymous member of the 5th Marines took the first steps to victory when he leaped out of his Higgins boat and onto the sandy beach at Guadalcanal in 1942; the Japanese were on the defensive in the Pacific from that point on.

A badly battered United Nations Command was being hard pressed by the North Korean Peoples Army. Withdrawal from Korea seemed imminent when the 5th Marines "fire brigade" arrived at

Pusan in August 1950, not long thereafter the shattered NKPA was "bugging out." Elite units of the North Vietnamese army slipped into Hue City under the cover of holiday celebrations in 1968. Within two weeks the enemy battle streamer lay in the dusty rubble and it was the Stars and Stripes flapping over the ancient Imperial Palace. Two decades later that very same American flag was raised over the American Embassy after the 5th Marines helped liberate Kuwait City from Iraqi oppressors.

The ranks of the 5th Marines have included some of the most colorful characters in the history of the corps. Henry L. Hulbert was a cashiered British colonial officer who redeemed himself by earning a Medal of Honor at Samoa, then bravely fought at Belleau Wood, Soissons, and St. Mihiel before being cut down leading reinforcements forward through a wall of enemy fire at Blanc Mont. George Hamilton, feted as "bravest of the brave . . . the finest officer in the American Expeditionary Force," should have received the Medal of Honor on two different occasions, but his heroism went unrecognized because John "Black Jack" Pershing refused to approve the nation's highest award to any Marine officer in the American Expeditionary Force. Celebrated artist and popular author John Thomason was renowned as the "Kipling of the Corps" for vivid drawings and salty stories based upon his experiences in World War I. Likewise, his good friend Laurence Stallings's facile pen helped create one of the most popular plays of the Roaring Twenties before he chronicled the exploits of America's "Doughboys" a half-century later.

Gray-bearded Lou Diamond was a gunner without peer who, according to legend, dropped a mortar round down a Japanese warship's funnel at Guadalcanal. Fifty-one-year-old Paul Douglas, an esteemed professor of economics at the University of Chicago, enlisted in the Marine Corps after Pearl Harbor and was often at the forefront of the action being seriously wounded twice; as a congressman he co-authored Public Act 416, the so-called "Marine Corps bill" in 1952. "Silent Lew" Walt distinguished himself by leading units of the 5th Marines in two different wars before commanding all Marine forces in Vietnam. Jim Webb was a highly decorated platoon leader with 1/5 in Vietnam before becoming a best-selling novelist and later gaining notoriety as the outspoken defender of the warrior ethos while secretary of the navy.

Although this incomplete roll of heroes is an impressive one, we must always remember that no man is more important than the unit; as all Marines well know, individuals come and go but the regiment is eternal. Thus, long after most of us are pushing up daisies, the Fighting Fifth Marines will be standing ready to march toward the sound of gunfire at a moment's notice.

1: Genesis

Modern U.S. Marines enjoy a standing second to none as fighting men of the world. The Marine Corps is a unique expeditionary force manned by "the few, the proud"—highly skilled and extremely motivated warriors with a worldwide reputation for physical toughness and steadfastness under fire. The Marine Corps is the largest and best-trained amphibious force in the world. But U.S. Marines are much more than that. In our contemporary lexicon, the word *Marines* is indicative of the best of the best. This high standing was not always the case, however. In fact, at one time the Marines were considered almost superfluous by the Navy Department; they were a force without a mission. It was not until the early twentieth century that the current image of the Marine Corps as a fighting elite began to come into focus.

For more than 140 years, from the creation of the Continental Marines in 1775 until World War I, the Marine Corps was a small organization whose primary function was to serve as a naval constabulary. American Marines enforced discipline on board U.S. warships and fought from the sail tops during ship-to-ship engagements during the first half of the nineteenth century. The coming of the post–Civil War "steel-and-steam" navy virtually ended the necessity for these traditional roles, so the Marines spent several decades searching for a raison d'être. During the doldrums, Marines guarded navy yards, served on board capital ships where they were relegated to basically ceremonial duties, manned secondary batteries, or participated in occasional landing parties to protect American lives and property overseas. The Spanish-American War in 1898 was a watershed for the Marine Corps. After that conflict it became plain that Marines were needed to conduct advanced base

1

operations, specifically the seizure and defense of overseas coaling stations and shore facilities. On a less theoretical level, the Marines became experts in the conduct of small wars when they were repeatedly used to occupy American overseas territories or to prop up shaky governments in Latin America. But it was not until World War I that the Marines achieved their current reputation as a first-class fighting outfit.

The initial opportunities to showcase the "new" Marine Corps occurred in the Philippines and Latin America between the end of the Spanish-American War and the onset of war in Europe fifteen years later.

Caribbean Reaction Force

The history of the modern 5th Marines can be traced back to April 1914, when Pres. Woodrow Wilson's patience and diplomatic acumen were sorely tested by events in the Caribbean during the second decade of the twentieth century. There was civil unrest in Mexico, Cuba, Haiti, and Santo Domingo. Each of these insurrections would eventually require an American military presence during what were later collectively called the "Banana Wars." One such foray occurred when the Mexican government failed to make proper amends for illegally detaining American military personnel at Tampico in 1914. This crisis, and the threat of German intervention in Mexico, caused U.S. military forces—including Marines—to land at the Mexican port of Veracruz, an action that set the stage for the creation of the 5th Marine Regiment.

The 44th, 45th, and 46th Companies were among the Marine units dispatched to Mexico. The 45th Company, organized on 26 April 1914, was composed of Marine Barracks personnel from Portsmouth, New Hampshire; Boston, Massachusetts; Norfolk, Virginia; and the Marine detachment of the USS *Southery*. Concurrently, the 46th Company was formed from barracks personnel stationed at Washington, D.C.; Norfolk, Virginia; Annapolis, Maryland; and Philadelphia, Pennsylvania. Both companies were assigned to the Marine Battalion, Special Service Squadron. The navy's Special Service Squadron was a motley collection of second-line warships and gunboats that cruised Latin America's Caribbean and Pacific coasts during the Banana Wars, a distant progenitor of the modern amphibious ready groups that carry forward-deployed Marine expeditionary units. Together, the two companies sailed on board the armored cruiser USS *New York* for what the muster rolls termed "tropical service beyond the seas." The 44th (Expeditionary) Company was organized at Marine Barracks, Port Royal, South Carolina, on 2 May 1914. The 44th Company, like the other two units, mustered three officers and 125 enlisted men when it departed for the Caribbean aboard the armored cruiser USS *Washington*, the Special Service Squadron's flagship. The *Washington* visited Santo Domingo and Guantanamo, Cuba, then sailed to Veracruz, where the 44th Company debarked on 15 June 1914.

The Marine Corps was an institution in transition at that time. It had only recently expanded its ranks to include a standing expeditionary brigade. Previously, there had been only two types of permanent Marine operational forces: ships' detachments afloat and Marine barracks ashore. Marine companies, then the base units of the Corps, were identified by numbers and usually consisted of several officers and about a hundred enlisted men, but each varied in size according to its location and specific duties. The decentralized nature of the naval guard mission meant there was no need for permanent Marine units larger than companies, so Marine regiments and battalions had always been ad hoc task organizations formed for specific duties without standard tables of organization or equipment and were disbanded once the crisis passed.

This policy changed when the Advance Base Force, the forerunner of the modern Fleet Marine Force, was created in 1913. It consisted of units and personnel specifically allocated for expeditionary duty. This brigade-sized force included permanent infantry units supported by naval gunners, cannoneers, engineers, supply personnel, and communications specialists. Battalion and regimental officers—usually a commanding officer, a second in command, an adjutant, a quartermaster, and a paymaster—were collectively known as "field and staff," but this rudimentary headquarters had not yet adopted the sophisticated staff organization familiar to Marines of the modern era. The two-regiment Advance Base Force was home ported at the Philadelphia Navy Yard on League Island in the Delaware River.

While diplomatic tensions reached the boiling point at Tampico, the two permanent regiments of the Advance Base Force departed Philadelphia and waited at New Orleans, Louisiana, and Pensacola, Florida. President Wilson finally ordered a joint-service force made up of army, navy, and Marine brigades to take Veracruz after he learned a German ship was sailing to Mexico to deliver arms. The 2d Regiment of Marines

landed at Veracruz on 21 April 1914, where it was quickly joined by the
1st Regiment, a newly formed provisional 3d Regiment, and several navy
battalions manned by bluejackets from various ships' companies. Veracruz was safely in American hands within three days, but an American
occupation force was needed to keep the peace. Accordingly, the 1st Provisional Marine Brigade was detached from naval jurisdiction and joined
U.S. Army forces to perform that duty on 1 May.

The situation elsewhere in the Caribbean was so tenuous, however,
that a separate Marine unit was needed to deal with problems in Haiti
and Santo Domingo (a country now known as the Dominican Republic). Such a regiment was formed on 13 July 1914. There were already
three Marine regiments in the Caribbean and a fourth was located at the
Puget Sound Naval Station, Bremerton, Washington. The fledgling unit
was given the next numerical designator and was thereby named the "5th
Regiment of Marines." The Marine Battalion, Special Service Squadron,
was detached from the 1st Marine Brigade at Fort San Juan in Veracruz
and promptly designated the 1st Battalion, 5th Regiment. The 44th,
45th, and 46th Companies and a small field and staff detachment
formed this unit.

The original battalion commander was Maj. Carl Gamborg-Andresen,
who had been breveted to lieutenant colonel for his outstanding performance during the Boxer Rebellion. However, he fell ill and was replaced by Maj. "Lighthorse" Harry Lee in August. The battalion adjutant
was 1st Lt. Clarke H. Wells. The acting sergeant major was 1st Sgt. Pink
H. Stone, a tough no-nonsense NCO who later earned a commission and
commanded a company in France. Captain Arthur E. Harding commanded the 44th Company, Capt. Alexander M. Watson the 45th, and
Capt. Harold C. Snyder the 46th. Most of the 1st Battalion boarded the
armed transport USS *Hancock* for movement to Cuba on 15 July and arrived at Guantanamo's Deer Point four days later. However, the detachment on board the *Washington,* consisting of Captain Snyder and sixty-
seven enlisted Marines, sailed for the troubled shores of Hispaniola,
where a revolution was brewing in Haiti.

The 2d Battalion and regimental headquarters were formed at Norfolk, Virginia, during the latter half of July. Colonel Charles A. Doyen
was detached from Marine Corps headquarters to become the regiment's first commanding officer. The fifty-three-year-old Doyen was typical of many Marine officers in that his early career included appointment from the Naval Academy, serving with Marine detachments

aboard ship, duty at various Marine barracks, and expeditionary service. Doyen was atypical in that he had already commanded the 2d Regiment and the 1st Provisional Marine Brigade, the latter twice. Colonel Doyen brought with him a small staff composed of Lt. Col. Ben H. Fuller (who had commanded his own regiment in 1911) as second in command, Capt. Russell H. Davis as the quartermaster, Capt. Davis B. Wills as the paymaster, and Charles L. Eichmann as the regimental sergeant major. Major Charles S. Hatch commanded the 2d Battalion, with 1st Lt. Edwin N. McClellan as adjutant and 1st Sgt. Walter J. Eddington Jr. as the senior enlisted man. The 2d Battalion line units included the 37th, 47th, and 48th Companies. Captain William Hopkins commanded the 37th Company, which only recently had returned from China. The 47th and 48th Companies were made up of Marines from East Coast duty stations. Captain William L. Redlee commanded the 47th but was later replaced by Capt. Robert Y. Rhea. Captain Edward A. Greene commanded the 48th. This contingent sailed from Norfolk for Cuba on board the *Hancock* on 30 July. The 5th Regiment was united for the first time at Guantanamo on 4 August 1914. Thus began the history of the unit that would later become famous as the "Fighting Fifth Marines."

On 12 August 1914, the 5th Regiment boarded the *Hancock* at Deer Point and began sailing the Caribbean waters off Hispaniola to fulfill its first mission as a standby force. The *Hancock* moved from point to point along the coast to help quell unrest. Meanwhile, Captain Snyder's *Washington* detachment went ashore as part of the Puerto Plata occupation force. Things gradually settled down and the situation in Santo Domingo promised to remain stable. This did not, however, mark the end of the 5th Regiment's Caribbean duties. Turmoil in nearby Haiti shook President Wilson, so the 5th Regiment was dispatched to the capital city of Port-au-Prince and arrived there on 31 October. This crisis soon ebbed and the 5th Regiment, still embarked aboard the *Hancock,* returned to Guantanamo on 15 November. Eight days later, the Marines of the 5th Regiment once again packed their sea bags and set sail for Haiti. After about three weeks at sea the situation ashore quieted down and the *Hancock* turned north and headed for Philadelphia.

The 5th Regiment landed and was disbanded at League Island on Christmas Eve, 1914. The 37th and 45th Companies were detached to East Coast naval stations and the other units were dissolved. Individual Marines returned to their original duty stations insofar as was practical.

Postscript

Colonel Doyen became commanding officer of the Marine Barracks at Washington, D.C., upon his return but his association with the 5th Regiment was not over. Three years later he again took command of the regiment and led it to France. The 5th Regiment had been active for only a little more than five months, but that short service must have been a good training ground because three of the six company commanders during that period—Snyder, Greene, and Rhea—later commanded the regiment. "Uncle Ben" Fuller commanded Marine brigades in Latin America during and after World War I and eventually became commandant at the height of the Great Depression (from 1930 to 1934). While serving as a major assigned to headquarters, Edwin McClellan wrote the official history of the Marines in World War I, and penned the most comprehensive history of the Marine Corps to date in the 1920s. Hal Snyder and Davis Wills were plank holders in the Marine Corps Association (MCA), which was formed at Guantanamo on 25 April 1913. They, along with the most promising young officer in the Corps—Lt. Col. John Archer Lejeune—were members of that organization's first executive board. The MCA's purpose was to inform Marines worldwide about developments that affected the Corps and to provide a sounding board for new ideas. Its magazine, the *Marine Corps Gazette,* is still going strong and is one of today's most respected professional military journals.

Although the 5th Regiment was no longer on the Marine muster rolls, its name had been established. Within a few years the unit would be recognized around the globe for its valor and military achievements, and by the dawn of the twenty-first century would be America's most decorated twentieth-century regiment.

After the 5th Regiment of Marines was disbanded, virtually all Marine expeditionary troops were committed to the Caribbean in support of the "Roosevelt Corollary" to the Monroe Doctrine. Under this modification of a century-old cornerstone of U.S. foreign policy, the United States would intervene anywhere in the Western Hemisphere where anarchy or fiscal problems threatened order. This happened so often that the Marines quickly gained a reputation as being "State Department" troops. They were so efficient that news correspondent Richard Harding Davis wrote, "The Marines have landed and the situation is well in hand." Between 1914 and the declaration of war with Germany in 1917, Marine brigades occupied Haiti and Santo Domingo, and a floating battalion was home ported at Guantanamo. The scale of these deployments left no units for the Advance Base Force, so stateside Marines either stood guard at various barracks or were members of the supporting establishment. That was the situation as ominous war clouds began wafting across the Atlantic.

2: World War I

While the 5th Regiment was keeping a watchful eye on Hispaniola in 1914, what should have been a minor event, the assassination of an obscure Balkan prince, provided the spark that ignited the flames of a European war. The conflagration soon spread across the continent and began to engulf the entire world. The people of the United States, traditionally an isolationist nation, overwhelmingly wanted to stay out of what they saw as a strictly European affair. President Wilson echoed the sentiments of the American public when he promised to keep the United States out of the war and proclaimed neutrality. In 1914 the United States was content to concern itself with protecting its borders and shielding its citizens from the ravages of armed conflict. World War I quickly settled into a bloody stalemate on the ground, but the German submarine menace briefly became a "hot button" issue after the sinking of the British liner *Lusitania,* which was carrying American passengers. Germany quickly promised to attack only military ships in the future, and America resumed its comfortable isolationist stance. In the Western Hemisphere, there was trouble in Latin America. Haiti and Santo Domingo still seethed with resentment. The hottest spot, however, was Mexico. The bulk of the U.S. Army was sent south of the border to chase down outlaw Poncho Villa after his men murdered American citizens in Mexico and burned Columbus, New Mexico, in 1916. Indeed, armed conflict with Mexico seemed much more likely than did fighting overseas at that time. Meanwhile, the Marines were spread across the Caribbean keeping local insurgents in line and, at the same time, protecting the Panama Canal. Two international incidents in early 1917 dramatically changed America's diplomatic calculus. First, Germany resumed unrestricted submarine warfare in a desperate attempt to starve Britain into submission, and, second, a secret German entreaty for Mexican assistance against the United States became public knowledge. These outrageous actions by Germany forced the president to take action.

First to Fight

On 2 April 1917, a reluctant President Wilson requested a formal declaration of war against Germany. Congress assented and the United States entered the Great War on 6 April. A few weeks later, Wilson promised Marshal Joseph J. C. Joffre, the head of a special French military mission to Washington, that he would send an American expeditionary force to France within a month. This was not an easy promise to keep because the United States was woefully unprepared for war, but Wilson's solemn vow set the wheels of American mobilization into high gear.

On that fateful April morning the U.S. Marine Corps had only 13,725 men, including 511 officers, on its rolls. With war looming, however, the Corps's statutory strength was increased threefold on 22 May. A curious mix of farm boys, factory workers, college students, and adventurers was drawn to the previously little known Marine Corps by recruiting posters proclaiming "Tell That to the Marines" and "Be First to Fight." An unexpectedly large number of enlistees overwhelmed existing Marine Corps facilities, so temporary recruit depots were opened at Philadelphia and Norfolk in an effort to relieve pressure on the overloaded recruit depots at Paris (it was not spelled "Parris" until 1919) Island, South Carolina, and Mare Island, California. Six thousand acres of land hastily leased near the sleepy town of Quantico, Virginia, located on the Potomac River about fifty miles south of Washington, D.C., became the primary Marine overseas staging base.

When Secretary of the Navy Josephus Daniels offered a regiment of Marines for European service on 19 May 1917, the Marine Corps already had four regiments in active service, so the new unit was designated the 5th Regiment. Ready to depart for France just three weeks later, the regiment mustered seventy officers and 2,187 enlisted men. This amounted to almost one-sixth of the entire strength of the Marine Corps, and Marines made up one-fifth of the American Expeditionary Force (AEF) that sailed for Europe in June. The rapid and efficient mobilization of the 5th Regiment and its inclusion in the first American contingent to arrive in France was no accident. It was the product of considerable forethought and preparation. Major General Commandant George Barnett was determined that a Marine unit must be included in the initial forces sent to France to keep the Marine pledge to "be first to fight." Accordingly, he coordinated with various War Department agencies and began to lobby behind the scenes for Marine representation in the AEF. His efforts bore fruit. Secretary of War Newton D. Baker accepted the offer of "a Marine regiment, equipped as infantry, for duty in France" on 23 May 1917.

Prior to receiving Baker's official blessing, General Barnett began recalling selected overseas units to the United States so they could be quickly organized into expeditionary battalions to form a regiment "for duty beyond the seas." One battalion had been organized at Quantico by 25 May, and eight expeditionary companies were en route to Philadelphia from the Caribbean. Commandant Barnett realized that travel space would be at premium, so he wisely got the navy to agree to let the Marines sail to France on board naval vessels instead of nonfleet transport ships by offering Marines as watch standers, lookouts, gun crews, deck parties, and colliers.

Secretary Daniels officially directed Commandant Barnett "to organize a force of Marines to be known as the Fifth Regiment of Marines for service with the Army as part of the first expedition to proceed to France" on 29 May. The 5th Regiment—which would serve under the War Department, not the Navy Department, in France—was organized in accord with U.S. Army tables of equipment and organization with a headquarters company, a supply company, three machine-gun companies, and nine infantry companies. The Marines, normally outfitted in woolen forest-green uniforms, would instead sail wearing tropical attire consisting of cotton khaki uniforms with canvas leggings and green felt field hats. They were armed with M1903 Springfield bolt-action rifles and dependable Lewis light machine guns.

The 1st Battalion, 5th Regiment, was formed at Marine Barracks, Quantico. It was commanded by lanky, mustachioed Maj. (later Brig. Gen.) Julius S. Turrill, an experienced and popular leader. The battalion was composed of the 15th, 49th, 66th, and 67th Companies. The 15th (Machine Gun) Company, commanded by Capt. Andrew B. Drum, moved to Quantico from Pensacola. The 66th (Capt. George K. Shuler) and 67th (Capt. Edmund H. Morse) Companies were formed using prospective battleship guards at Norfolk barracks, then moved north to Quantico. Included in the 67th Company was 2d Lt. (later Lt. Gen.)

Keller E. Rockey, who commanded the 5th Marine Division at Iwo Jima three decades later. The 49th Company, commanded by aggressive former star football player 1st Lt. George W. Hamilton, was formed using recruits and Marines from the USS *New Hampshire*. This unit joined the 1st Battalion at Quantico a few days after the 66th and 67th Companies arrived. The 1st Battalion departed Quantico on 7 June and traveled by rail to Philadelphia. The Marines were greeted along the route by well wishers who cheered after reading "Berlin or Bust" and other patriotic slogans scrawled in chalk on the sides of the railway cars.

The units that would soon form the 2d and 3d Battalions were sailing north as the 1st Battalion was gathering at Quantico. The 23d (Machine Gun) Company, commanded by Capt. George H. Ousterhout Jr., sailed to Philadelphia from Haiti. The 43d (Capt. Joseph D. Murray), 51st (Capt. Lloyd W. Williams), and 55th (Capt. Henry M. Butler) Companies came to Philadelphia from Cuba. These units combined to form the 2d Battalion on 30 May under the command of Lt. Col. Frederic M. Wise, who preferred the nickname "Fritz" to his alternate sobriquet "Dopey." Wise was a heavyset ("He looked like he was seven months pregnant" according to future Commandant Lemuel C. Shepherd Jr., a second lieutenant assigned to the 55th Company) martinet who ruled with an iron fist. He was feared, rather than loved, by his junior officers—but his orders were obeyed without question or hesitation. This would prove to be both a blessing and a curse in France.

The 8th, 16th, 45th, and 47th Companies also arrived at Philadelphia on 30 May. They were earmarked for the 3d Battalion. The 16th Company (Capt. Edward W. Sturdevant) came in from Haiti, while the 8th (Capt. Holland M. Smith), 45th (Capt. Benjamin S. Berry), and 47th (Capt. Frederick A. Barker) Companies arrived from the Dominican Republic. Major Charles T. Westcott Jr. commanded the 3d Battalion. The fiery-tempered and outspoken Holland Smith later become known as "Howlin' Mad" during his tenure as the senior Marine in the Pacific during World War II, and he was destined to become one of the most notable Marines of all time. Captain Berry eventually led the 3d Battalion at Belleau Wood, commanded the 5th Regiment in Nicaragua during the Banana Wars, and retired as a brigadier general. Captain Sturdevant was soon promoted to major and command of the 3d Battalion. He subsequently commanded the regiment in 1931.

When the 5th Regiment was reactivated at the Philadelphia Navy Yard on 7 June 1917, a familiar name—Col. Charles A. Doyen—was atop the muster list. By seniority and field experience, Doyen, an unattached line officer at Marine Corps headquarters serving as an unofficial assistant commandant, was the obvious choice. Of course, the fact that he was a Naval Academy classmate and good friend of Commandant Barnett may have played a part in his being named to this prestigious command as well. The regimental adjutant was Maj. Harry R. Lay (who later commanded the 5th Regiment in 1925), the paymaster was Capt. Davis B. Wills (another familiar name on the muster rolls), and the quartermaster was Capt. Bennett Puryear Jr. Lieutenant Colonel Logan Feland, the regimental second-in-command designate, was on detached duty with U.S. Army Gen. John J. Pershing's staff. Feland was one of only two Marine officers allowed to go to France to observe the fighting. The intelligent and hard-working Feland, a forty-eight-year-old former National Guard lieutenant who saw action in Cuba, was slated to join the 5th Regiment when it arrived in June. A liberal sprinkling of recruits from Paris Island and Philadelphia brought the line companies of the 5th Regiment up to around two hundred men each. About two dozen old salts and highly trained specialists led by 1st Lt. Alphonse DeCarre assembled at Washington, D.C. They formed the nucleus of the 5th Regiment's Headquarters Company. However, most Marines assigned to Headquarters Company were raw recruits carefully selected for their high intelligence and special skills by Marine gunner James McCoy. Captain Puryear, the regimental quartermaster, also served as the Supply Company commander. The regiment's Base Detachment, made up of personnel for whom there were no berthing spaces, remained at Quantico when the rest of the regiment departed. This unit—composed of a small headquarters and the 7th, 17th, 18th, 20th, and 30th Companies—assimilated new arrivals earmarked to be combat replacements in France. On the Base Detachment's muster rolls were Capt. (later Brig. Gen.) Robert L. Denig, 2d Lt. LeRoy P. Hunt, and 2d Lt. Albert P. "Bert" Baston (an All-America football player who led a three-hundred-man recruit contingent of student-athletes from the University of Minnesota, among them future general Merwin H. Silverthorn).

Commandant Barnett was smugly informed by the War Department that there would not be enough room on the army troop transports to carry the Marines overseas in early June 1917. Undaunted, he calmly replied that transport space would not be necessary because the Marines had previously made other arrangements: RAdm. Albert Greaves, commander of the U.S. Atlantic Fleet cruiser and transport force, had already agreed that a regiment of Marines could be embarked in naval vessels for transportation to France. Three navy ships, all assigned as part of the convoy escort, carried the 5th Regiment across the Atlantic. They were the venerable (but slow moving) *Hancock,* which had carried the original 5th Regiment around the Caribbean, the brand-new armed transport USS *Henderson* (the "Hendy Maru" was the first purpose-built troop transport ship and was later given the naval vessel registry number AP1), and the USS *DeKalb* (actually the former German ship *Prinz Frederich Eitel,* which was at Norfolk for repairs when the United States declared war on Germany; U.S. Customs seized the ship and it was promptly refitted as an American military transport ship and renamed to honor Prussian Baron de Kalb, who fought with the Continental Army during the American Revolution).

Embarkation began on 7 June when Headquarters and Supply Companies started boarding the *Hancock* at League Island. When he found out the *Hancock* was assigned to the last convoy to leave, Colonel Doyen ordered selected members of his staff, Supply Company, the 43d Company, and the regimental band to move to the speedier *Henderson.* After three days under canvas at League Island the 1st Battalion boarded the *DeKalb* on 11 June. Twenty officers and 790 enlisted men then waited on board for two weeks before sailing for France from New York Harbor.

The 2d and 3d Battalions moved to New York by rail and water. The 2d Battalion headquarters and the 23d and 51st Companies boarded the USS *St. Louis* at Philadelphia, sailed down the Delaware River to New York Harbor, and then transferred to the *Henderson* on 14 June. The 3d Battalion moved to New York by rail and embarked from the Ninety-sixth Street Pier. The 3d Battalion was at first split between the armored cruisers USS *Seattle* (8th and 16th Companies) and USS *Charleston* (45th and 47th Companies), but was reunited on board the *Henderson* for the voyage to France. Interestingly, the *Seattle* was the same ship that carried Captain Snyder's detachment in 1914. The former Special Service Squadron flagship had been renamed for a city (instead of the state of Washington) in accordance with new naval vessel registry regulations issued in 1916.

When final loading was complete, the *Henderson* carried Colonel Doyen's regimental headquarters staff, the 2d and 3d Battalions, and the band; the *DeKalb* carried the 1st Battalion; and Headquarters Company was aboard the *Hancock.* The *DeKalb* was assigned to the first transport group, the *Henderson* to the second, and the *Hancock* to the final group.

The first two convoys slipped out of Ambrose Channel for France with-out fanfare on 14 June. The *Hancock*'s convoy departed three days later.

Life on board the ships was not exactly a pleasure cruise. It was the first sea voyage for most of the new Marines, many of whom had never seen an ocean before. Much to the amusement of the "old salts," it took these seasick neophytes several miserable days to become accustomed to the ships' pitching and yawing as they cut through the never-ending swells. A number of the newest Marines on board the *Hancock* saw little during the voyage except for the torrid engine rooms, where they la-bored in twelve-hour shifts to feed coal into the ever hungry boilers. Other Marines pulled less arduous but still demanding duty as gun crews and lookouts. Compulsory shipboard drills and endless chow lines marked the passing days. Free time was devoted to target practice, main-tenance of clothing and equipment, and daily inspections of living spaces.

The trans-Atlantic crossings were not without incident, but there was no loss of life to enemy action. The ships carrying the Marines were es-cort vessels, not part of the convoy, so their crews had to be vigilant and ready for action at a moment's notice. At about 2015 on the evening of 22 June, the *Seattle* sounded the alarm after it cut through the wake of a German submarine. A few seconds later, the *DeKalb* maneuvered to avoid two torpedoes. The U-boat disappeared below the waves amid a hail of gunfire from the *DeKalb* and USS *Havana*. The second convoy, including the *Henderson,* was spotted by two U-boats off the coast of France on 26 June, but neither submarine chose to engage the Ameri-can ships because French destroyers had sailed out to meet them. The *DeKalb* arrived at the port of Saint-Nazaire on the southwest coast of France on the twenty-sixth, but the 1st Battalion remained on board overnight. The *Henderson* made port the next day and moored along-side the *DeKalb*.

Colonel Doyen went ashore, met with Lieutenant Colonel Feland, and then reported to Maj. Gen. William L. Sibert, commander of the U.S. Army's 1st Division, on the twenty-seventh. At that time the 5th Regiment was detached from naval jurisdiction for service with the army by direc-tion of the president. This change meant the Marines were now oper-ating under War Department rules rather than naval regulations. When they finally came ashore, the Marines were enthusiastically greeted by the citizens of Saint-Nazaire, who showered them with candy, cookies, and cigarettes. The 5th Regiment was finally "over there," ready to repay a debt owed since the French sent much-needed help to the colonies during the American Revolution.

Training

The 1st Battalion (less the 15th Company) disembarked from the *DeKalb* and moved into quarters ashore. The 2d and 3d Battalions landed briefly to conduct a practice march on the 28th. The next day work parties erected tents at a regimental camp located about three miles southeast of the port. The late-starting *Hancock* finally arrived at Saint-Nazaire on 2 July, and the entire 5th Regiment was ashore living under canvas in France on the evening of the third.

High hopes that action would soon follow were quickly dashed by reality. The first task was to unload the ships, so Marines were pressed into service as stevedores. Unfortunately, they were neither trained nor equipped for this job. Unloading the ships was backbreaking work accomplished by labor alone. In a postretirement interview Lt. Gen. Merwin H. Silverthorn, a Marine enlisted man in 1917, recalled, "We didn't have little hand trucks [or] cargo hooks . . . we didn't even have gloves." He went on to explain that there was a reward for the men assigned to this thankless task: "We did quite a bit of pilfering." Candy and cigarettes, neither of which was free at that time, were favorite targets. These prizes were hard to get because they came in tin-lined boxes, but "judicious use of a bayonet or pocket knife" provided the Marines entry. Another forcibly impressed stevedore, Ben Finney, opined that the Marines brought back "so many chock-full packs . . . the powers to be decided they wouldn't need us again."

The 3d Battalion was temporarily detached to guard the dock area, supply depots, and lines of communication on 12 July. The 45th Company moved into billets in Saint-Nazaire and was assigned to guard the docks. The 47th Company, under Major Westcott, became the guard force at Permanent Camp Number One. It protected the Remount Station and assumed provost duties inside the port city. The 16th Company moved to Nevers for provost duty and guarded the medical depot there. In September, individual Marines throughout the regiment were detached to attend schools, to serve as couriers, or to act as military police.

These were not duties the Marines wanted or trained for, but they were necessary jobs. As an "additional" regiment (the 1st Division already mustered four Regular Army regiments), as well as belonging to a "foreign"

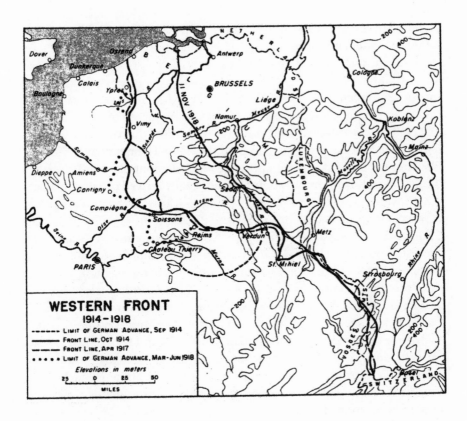

WESTERN FRONT
1914–1918
------- Limit of German Advance, Sep 1914
——— Front Line, Oct 1914
——— Front Line, Apr 1917
• • • • Limit of German Advance, Mar–Jun 1918

Elevations in meters

25   0   25   50

MILES

service, the Marines were expendable. General Pershing, the AEF commander, justified his decision to break up the Marine regiment in a letter to Commandant Barnett. Pershing lauded the Marines' "excellent standing . . . good conduct . . . high state of discipline and excellent soldierly appearance," but noted that the 5th Regiment lacked organic transportation and fighting equipment. He explained that the need for service and provost troops required him to scatter the Marines in order to keep the 1st Division intact. General Pershing concluded by promising to assign the Marines to a fighting division as soon as sufficient service and rear-area troops were at hand.

Despite this setback every effort was made to train the officers and men. Close-order drill, the manual of arms, and practice marches filled the days at Saint-Nazaire. Marines of the 5th Regiment not assigned other duties trained with the 1st Division at Gondrecourt beginning on 15 July. Regimental headquarters, Supply Company, the 1st and 2d Battalions, and the 8th (Machine Gun) Company crowded into infamous "Forty-or-Eight" (so called because some spatially challenged sadist decided these small conveyances could actually carry forty men or eight horses) railway cars and proceeded to Menaucourt and Naix-les-Forges. These towns were located in eastern France at the rear of what later became the American defense sector.

The 6th Groupe de Chasseurs Alpins of the French Army was assigned to train the Marines on 21 July. The elite *chasseurs* (French light infantry), like the Marines, were a separate service branch and wore distinctive dark-blue uniforms, hence their nickname "Blue Devils." The 30th Battalion, Alpine Chasseurs, worked with the 1st Battalion, 5th Regiment, at Naix; the 115th Battalion trained the 2d Battalion; the One-Pounder (37mm) Gun Section, Headquarters Company's Pioneer Section, and the 8th (Machine Gun) Company trained with the 70th Battalion at Menaucourt; and the Headquarters Company's Signal Section was with the French 8th Battalion at Horville. The Blue Devils taught offensive and defensive tactics, trench construction, grenade throwing, bayonet fighting, and chemical protective measures. The Marines were treated to live-fire demonstrations by airplanes and artillery. Colonel Doyen also set aside time for physical fitness, sanitation, close-order drill, and small-arms marksmanship. The latter was a Marine Corps specialty. The French were impressed by the ability of individual Marines to hit long-range targets, but they were skeptical about whether such skills could ever be put into use on the modern battlefield.

The Marines enjoyed excellent relations with local townspeople. Because there were few barracks available, many Marines lived in nearby barns, sheds, or haylofts. City-bred Americans with sensitive olfactory organs were dismayed to discover that the local people took great pride in the manure piles ("French banks" according to some wags) kept close by the living quarters. The gigantic flies that inhabited those questionable measures of wealth bothered everyone. The Marines cleaned up the villages where they were stationed and entertained the local people with band concerts and impromptu (usually off-key) songfests. French women washed and sewed the Marines' clothing, sold fresh milk and eggs, and cooked wonderful meals. The ever hungry Marines soon developed a taste for fried potatoes cooked in the inimitable French style. The words *Vin Blanc* and *Vin Rouge* also became staples of Marine lingo. There was, at any rate, little free time because Colonel Doyen believed in "training, training, and more training."

General Pershing inspected the 1st and 2d Battalions at the towns where they were quartered on 1 August. Two weeks later, General Sibert inspected the 5th Regiment. General Pershing and Gen. Henri P. Pétain, the French commander in chief, inspected the entire 1st Division on 19 August. After the latter inspection, the general staff reported the Marines were "the finest body of men under our command." General Pétain was so impressed that he congratulated Colonel Doyen on the splendid appearance of the Marines and praised the cleanliness of the towns. Gaining such recognition was no small feat. In fact, the hard-to-please Pershing, known as the "Iron General," relieved the 1st Division commander when other units failed similar inspections.

Despite this impressive performance, some Marine units were broken up and temporarily assigned to the Service of Supply. The 8th Company finished training and returned to guard Camp Number One at Saint-Nazaire on 22 August. Major Turrill and the 67th Company were detached for provost and courier duty in England the same day. They were assigned to police the American rest camps at South Hampton, Winchester, and Romney. The detachment did not rejoin the regiment until March 1918. Lieutenant Colonel Feland became acting commander of the two-company (49th and 66th) 1st Battalion and Captain Hamilton assumed temporary command of the battalion when Colonel Feland was detached for duty at Bourmont on 24 October. Newly promoted Maj. Edward Greene assumed command of the 1st Battalion on 18 February 1918, a position he held until Major Turrill returned from England on 12 March 1918.

The regiment suffered its first loss in France when 2d Lt. Frederick Wahlstrom of Headquarters Company was killed in a motorcycle accident near Menaucourt on 20 August 1917.

The 5th Regiment was scheduled to join the soon-to-be formed U.S. Army 2d Division (Regular) and was reassigned to Bourmont. Elements of the regiment available for instruction moved to Haute-Marne and Vosges on 24 and 25 September 1917. The 1st Battalion was billeted in Adrian barracks, mass-constructed wood and tar-paper buildings that were the World War I equivalent of World War II–era Quonset huts, on a hill next to the Breuvannes-Morrey road. The 2d Battalion, Supply Company, and Headquarters Company were located about three kilometers away at Damblain. Unfortunately, Commandant Barnett's desire that the Marines be "first to fight" did not pan out, as the U.S. 1st Division came under enemy fire while assigned to the front in the Toulon sector.

Colonel Doyen was promoted to brigadier general and was promptly "dual hatted" as the commander of both the 5th Regiment and the 4th Infantry Brigade on 23 October. Although officially designated an infantry brigade, the latter unit was universally referred to as the "Marine Brigade." The 4th Brigade at first included only the 5th Regiment, but later added the 6th Marine Regiment and 6th Machine Gun Battalion. Three days later, on 26 October, General Doyen temporarily added the 2d Division to his list of commands, becoming the first Marine officer to command an army unit of that size. He held that post until 8 November, when army Major General Omar Bundy replaced him. The 2d Division included the 3d Infantry Brigade (9th Infantry, 23d Infantry, and 5th Machine Gun Battalion), the Marine Brigade, the 2d Field Artillery Brigade, and 2d Division support troops (2d Engineers, 4th Machine Gun Battalion, 1st Field Signal Battalion, 2d Headquarters and Military Police Battalion, 2d Supply Train, 2d Ammunition Train, 2d Engineer Train, and 2d Sanitary Train).

This reorganization led to changes within the 5th Regiment. Lieutenant Colonel Hiram I. Bearss became the regimental commander on 30 October, a position he held until Col. Wendell C. ("Buck") Neville arrived on 1 January 1918. Buck Neville was a highly regarded Naval Academy graduate and one of the most decorated Marine officers of his day. He was a colorful campaigner who saw action in Cuba, the Philippines, and the Boxer Rebellion before receiving the Medal of Honor for his actions at Veracruz. His gruff style and booming voice soon led to the nickname "Whispering Buck," a title ironically bestowed because his staff claimed his blaring pronouncements could be heard all the way back at the general staff headquarters without the use of a telephone.

It was a very hard winter. The Adrian barracks proved to be drafty, chilly hovels whose inadequate stoves did not generate much heat but often filled the flimsy structures with soot. The Marines, by then training under the tutelage of the French 151st Infantry Regiment, occupied mock trenches during the bitterest weather to hit Europe in several decades. They practiced raids and reliefs in addition to defensive tactics in the snow. During the late winter and early spring of 1918, brigade and regimental maneuvers became biweekly events. Saturdays were devoted to sanitation and barracks inspections. The veteran company commanders and battle-hardened NCOs were demanding taskmasters who cut the men little slack. Occasional leaves or liberties were granted, so only a lucky few ever enjoyed the pleasures of "Gay Paree" or strolled the streets of nearby Aix-les-Bains. The winter training period was a difficult time, but it hardened the Marines and gave them time to develop all-important unit cohesion before being thrust into combat.

The 8th Company at Saint-Nazaire was cited for its outstanding performance in a letter of commendation on 8 January 1918. Its first commanding officer, Capt. Holland Smith, was the first Marine officer to be assigned to the army's General Staff School. Captain John H. Fay succeeded him in late November 1917. The 8th, 45th, and 47th Companies moved from Saint-Nazaire to Colombey-les-Choiseul on 9 January 1918. Major Westcott commanded the reunited 3d Battalion there until 26 March, when Major Sturdevant relieved him.

As Marines began trickling back from their Service of Supply duties, the 5th Regiment was reorganized to newly adapted army standards. General Doyen issued a memorandum on 30 January stating that "due to unforeseen conditions it is . . . necessary to abandon distinctive [Marine] uniforms." Gone were wide-brim Marine field hats, khaki leggings, and forest-green uniforms. Fore-and-aft "overseas" caps, British-style wraparound puttees, and U.S. Army–issue olive-drab uniforms, replaced these traditional items.

As part of a general reorganization, the machine-gun companies were detached from their parent units and replaced by infantry companies to create "square" battalions. The 8th (Machine Gun) Company became a regimental asset and the 15th and 23d Companies were transferred to the 6th Machine Gun Battalion. A critical shortage of airplane machine guns caused General Pershing to recall all of the Marines' Lewis machine guns in March. French Hotchkiss heavy machine guns and Chauchat automatic rifles replaced the lightweight, reliable, and familiar .30-caliber Lewis guns. The Chauchats were inaccurate and temperamental pieces that were detested by the Marines and army infantrymen who used them.

In accord with army structure, all Marine infantry companies were "squared" with four platoons. The new companies included six officers and 250 enlisted men. To do this the Base Detachment at Bordeaux was disbanded on 23 January 1918, and its men were then used to bring the ranks of the 5th Regiment up to strength. Base Headquarters and Supply Company personnel were reassigned throughout the regiment. The 30th Company, commanded by future Marine Corps historian Capt. Clyde H. Metcalf, was detached for courier service. The 17th and 18th Companies replaced the recently detached machine-gun companies in the 1st and 2d Battalions respectively. The 1st Battalion was reinforced by the 12th and 26th Companies, which were dissolved to bring the rest of the infantry companies up to strength. The 16th Company, previously the 3d Battalion's machine-gun company, was reorganized as an infantry company. The 20th Company from the Base Detachment was also added. In its final organization for combat the 1st Battalion included the 17th, 49th, 66th, and 67th Companies; the 2d Battalion had the 18th, 43d, 51st, and 55th Companies; and the 3d Battalion was composed of the 16th, 20th, 45th, and 47th Companies. The Marine companies were also assigned letter designations to conform to army standards at that time, but the practice was so seldom followed that even army clerks listed Marine companies by their numbers instead of letters.

The entire 4th Marine Brigade was first assembled on 10 February 1918 when the 6th Regiment and the 6th Machine Gun Battalion finally joined the 5th Regiment at Bourmont. Many observers commented that the 4th Brigade was the finest body of troops in the AEF. Both regimental commanders were Medal of Honor recipients, and many of the officers were former enlisted Marines who were well versed in the ways of the Marine Corps and had seen previous combat action. More than one-third of the enlisted men in the 5th Regiment were combat veterans with more than four years service. All of the enlisted Marines were fine physical specimens and well-qualified marksmen. Fritz Wise recalled that he accepted no Marines who were not expert shooters, and rejected men with even the slightest physical flaw (to include those wearing eyeglasses). A friendly rivalry between the Marines and the army regulars in the 3d Infantry Brigade assigned to the 2d "Indianhead" Division soon caused them to be called the "race horse brigades" because they were always racing to outdo each other.

At the Front

Although originally slated to undergo a three-month training cycle before being sent to the front, the 2d Division was ordered into the lines much sooner because of an unexpected German offensive. The 4th Brigade was at Bourmont when it was ordered to Les Esparges in the quiet Toulon sector on 12 March. The 2d Battalion entrained at Breuvannes the next night and arrived at Dugny the following afternoon. The 18th and 51st Companies were assigned to Camp Nivolette and the 43d and 55th Companies were at Camp Douzaines. The 8th (Machine

Gun) Company and Headquarters Company arrived by train during the night of 14 March.

The 5th Regiment suffered its first "casualties" when German artillery ranged the railroad station and a shell fragment holed the regimental drum and destroyed several other instruments as the bandsmen took cover nearby. Luckily, most German shells whistled harmlessly over the Marines' heads as they marched to Camp Nivolette. The 3d Battalion arrived at Lemmes (instead of Dugny, which was under enemy observation) on the sixteenth. The 1st Battalion detrained on Saint Patrick's Day, then moved into billets vacated by the 2d Battalion, which had replaced the French 9th Infantry Regiment at the front.

The regiment occupied trenches around Les Esparges, located just twelve miles southeast of the bloody battlefield of Verdun. Colonel Neville used a system whereby the battalions rotated duties about every six days. One battalion manned the trenches facing the German lines while the other two improved and repaired existing fortifications, dug new trenches, and strung barbed-wire entanglements. The energetic brigade commander, General Doyen, inspected all six miles of the lines on a daily basis. Although it was a quiet sector, the 5th Regiment was the first Marine unit to meet the enemy and its men got their first bitter taste of life at the front. After their baptism of fire, the Marines could differentiate the sounds of incoming and outgoing artillery. They also became intimately acquainted with the huge rats, "cooties" (lice), and putrid mustard gas associated with trench life.

The regiment moved into the Bonchamp Line in early April. It was there that the regiment suffered its first man killed in action: Cpl. John L. Kuhn. This sad event occurred during a night raid on 17 April. It also marked the first time awards for valor were given to members of the regiment. Second Lieutenant Max D. Gilfillan and Sgt. Louis Cukela received the French Croix de Guerre for their actions. Undeterred by the loss of Corporal Kuhn, the Marines launched another raid on the Grusson trench the following night. The Germans responded with a tremendous barrage that hit the 18th Company sector, killing one man.

The Germans also launched a raid to find out what all the commotion was behind the Allied lines. The raiders were repulsed by a determined 45th Company, which held Saint-Privat Hill. About seventy-five of the enemy penetrated the Marine lines and then spread out, bombarding various dugouts and bunkers as they went. One German officer and several others were cut down by Marine fire as they reached the company command post. At that point, the raiders pulled back under the cover of a box barrage. One wounded German was left behind. The Marines lost two killed and twelve wounded (one of whom later died) during the hectic fifty-minute firefight. Navy Lt. Comdr. Alexander G. Lyle, the regimental dentist, rushed forward through a heavy barrage and administered such effective surgical aid that he saved the life of a badly wounded Marine corporal on the night of 23 April. Commander Lyle's heroic actions resulted in him receiving the navy Medal of Honor, the first such award bestowed upon any member of the 5th Marines. Separate navy and army Medals of Honor were awarded at that time, and most—but not all—Marines in France were given both medals for the same act. The Navy Department invariably opted to similarly honor naval personnel cited by the AEF, so two medals were usually given out. The same was true for naval personnel awarded the army Distinguished Service Cross (DSC) in France; they were retroactively given Navy Crosses. Dual Medals of Honor were later officially consolidated into single medals from the recipient's parent service. Only two Marines, Dan Daly and Smedley Butler, neither of whom served in the 5th Regiment, hold Medals of Honor for two different actions. Commander Lyle's Medal of Honor citation did not pass through General Pershing's headquarters because U.S. Navy personnel in France were governed by navy regulations rather than under army jurisdiction, as were the Marines. An army Medal of Honor thus was not recommended for him. This engagement, the regiment's first face-to-face encounter with the enemy, made it clear the Marines had learned their lessons well during the previous winter's training.

The 4th Marine Brigade lost its commander when General Doyen was invalided home on 7 May. Doyen vehemently protested what he considered to be an unfair, politically motivated reassignment. Many Marine officers felt that way as well, and some made it clear they considered this act a bare-faced ploy by the headstrong AEF commander to keep the Marines in line. Some historians, in fact, now believe Pershing's action was actually intended to quash Commandant Barnett's attempts to get a full Marine division to France. Regardless of the reason, Doyen's relief had immediate repercussions. Junior officers were admonished to keep quiet, and several brigade staff members were placed under arrest for continuing to question the relief after being told to shut up. Holland Smith listed staff majors Bennett Puryear, Maurice E. Shearer, and Henry N. Manney Jr. as members of the Marine cabal opposed to

Doyen's ouster. Fortunately, most likely at the insistence of Doyen's successor, all charges were dropped in the interest of interservice harmony.

Doyen's replacement was Brig. Gen. James G. Harbord, USA, a dashing cavalryman and former enlisted soldier who had most recently been General Pershing's chief of staff. Harbord was described as likable and an excellent administrator. Strangely missing from Harbord's record, however, was command of troops. By his own admission, Harbord had never led more than a hundred or so men, and he further asserted he had never even seen a full regiment on parade. He had been an enlisted quartermaster clerk prior to receiving his commission, and he served as the 10th Cavalry's quartermaster rather than as a line officer during the Spanish-American War. The fact that he was John Pershing's tent mate in Cuba certainly did not hurt his career, but he also gained a reputation as an excellent administrator. He spent more than ten years with the Philippine Constabulary before General Pershing picked him to be the AEF chief of staff. Although lack of troop-leading experience did not make Harbord unique in the rapidly expanding AEF, there is cause for speculation about the underlying reasons for Doyen's sudden dismissal and Pershing's selection of his replacement. The technical reason given was his health, but no Marine who served with Doyen noticed any obvious ailment. General Bundy, his division commander, in fact recommended Doyen for promotion despite the results of his physical exam.

Colonel Neville still commanded the regiment. Captain Fay had the 8th (Machine Gun) Company. Major Turrill commanded the 1st Battalion. Captain Roswell Winans, who had been awarded the Medal of Honor while a first sergeant in the Dominican Republic, commanded the 17th Company. Athletic, aggressive, and a crack shot, Capt. George Hamilton led the 49th Company. Captain William L. Crabbe commanded the 66th Company. Captain Keller Rockey should have been in command of the 67th Company, but he was serving as the battalion adjutant, so 1st Lt. Orlando C. Crowther filled that role after 23 May. Fritz Wise's 2d Battalion included the 18th (Capt. Lester S. Wass), 43d (Capt. Joseph Murray), 51st (Capt. Lloyd Williams), and 55th (Capt. John Blanchfield) Companies. Major Benjamin Berry—who replaced Major Sturdevant on 1 May—commanded the 3d Battalion, which included the 16th (Capt. Robert Yowell), 20th (Capt. Richard N. Platt), 45th (Capt. Peter Conachy), and 47th (Capt. Philip T. Case) Companies.

The 5th Regiment departed the Toulon sector for the Gizors training area in mid-May to undergo ten days of open warfare exercises. Gizors, located between Paris and Beauvais, was a most pleasant place. The training was not particularly arduous, the surroundings were beautiful, the weather was perfect, the mademoiselles were charming, and Marine spirits were high. During the last week of May 1918, the Marines finished brigade maneuvers. They then underwent normal postexercise inspections and looked forward to a short break before moving up to support the 1st Division at Cantigny.

Decoration Day, 30 May, was supposed to be a day of rest before returning to the front. Things were so quiet that Fritz Wise slipped away to meet his wife near Paris, General Harbord went for a long horseback ride, and Lt. Lem Shepherd wiled away the afternoon looking forward to a delicious home-cooked meal with a French family. Some of the troops went into town for a hard-earned liberty, the first such break since arriving in France. Most spent the morning at memorial services and the afternoon watching unit athletic contests or visiting the YMCA hut to write letters home.

This refreshing interlude came to a screeching halt after headquarters received word the Germans had launched a massive attack that ruptured the French lines near Chemin des Dames. The broken French army was streaming from the battlefield in full retreat. Telephones buzzed, whistles screeched, and runners went out to gather up Marines on liberty. Lieutenant Shepherd was disappointed to learn he would be unable to keep his rendezvous. Colonel Wise was enjoying a very pleasant candlelit dinner with his wife and friends when he was called away to answer the phone. Second Lieutenant James H. Legendre, the battalion adjutant, told him: "We've been ordered up to the front at once. The *camions* [French trucks] will be here at five o'clock in the morning." Fritz Wise immediately commandeered an ambulance and sped back to his battalion. The 5th Regiment was about to keep its rendezvous with destiny.

Belleau Wood

The French 43d Division was torn apart by the unexpected Ludendorff Offensive, and the Germans poured through a four-kilometer-wide gap in its lines. A feeling of doom, unknown since the dark days of 1914, overcame the French. The outlook was so bad that the government began to evacuate Paris after Château-Thierry fell on 1 June. Amid the uproar at French headquarters following the sudden collapse of the front, Maj.

Gen. Jean Degoutte asked Col. Preston Brown, the U.S. 2d Division chief of staff, if the Americans could be counted on. Brown's reply was one for the history books: "General, these are American regulars. In a hundred and fifty years they have never been beaten. They will hold."

The U.S. 2d Division was assigned to the French Sixth Army's XXI Corps, and the Marine Brigade was ordered to move east up the Paris-Metz highway to stem the flow of onrushing Germans threatening Paris. While hasty plans were being made at headquarters, the Marines fell out into the streets in full marching order. Rations and ammunition were hurriedly issued as the regimental baggage trains and field kitchens limbered up. The 1st and 2d Battalions boarded *camions* at 0600 on 31 May and began moving toward the sound of the guns just after dawn.

Motor movement soon became impossible because so many dejected soldiers and panicky civilians choked the roads. The American convoy passed through Meaux (about twenty-five miles northeast of Paris) and then proceeded to the village of May-en-Multien, where the weary Marines dismounted and continued their journey on foot. Lieutenant Colonel Wise ignored French advice to return to Meaux and instead ordered his 2d Battalion to move east toward Montreuil and Château-Thierry. It became an arduous movement as the day wore on. The Marines were sporting heavy transport packs, the temperature was rising, the roads were steep and dusty, and canteens were empty. Even long-service veterans later admitted it was a difficult march. The 4th Brigade eventually took up reserve positions near Marigny on 1 June. The 6th Marines filled a gap between Triangle Farm and Hill 142, with the 5th Regiment in support near Pyramides Farm to the south.

Not long after settling in, Major Turrill was ordered north to close a gap between the French on the left and the Marines to the right, but this was not possible with the few troops the 1st Battalion had at hand. Buck Neville therefore ordered Lieutenant Colonel Wise to move the 2d Battalion into the line north of Champillon. Not accurately portrayed on the aged and inaccurate French maps, the area actually covered almost two miles, a disposition that left the 2d Battalion dangerously overextended. From right to left, Captain Williams's 51st Company defended Champillon Wood southwest of Hill 142, Captain Blanchfield's 55th Company was at Les Mares Farm, and Captain Wass's 18th and Captain Murray's 43d Companies were strung out on the battalion left as far as Veuilly Wood. Much of the 2d Battalion line was in open country with little concealment and no cover, so the Marines hollowed out shallow protective ditches. These small depressions soon became known as "foxholes," a name that stuck and has since become standard military terminology for individual fighting positions. Actually, Wise's official report was the first military document to use the name foxhole, although most military historians now agree the term was probably informally used to describe individual fighting holes during the American Civil War.

The 5th Regiment was disposed in an elongated L when darkness fell on 2 June. On the left (west) flank, Wise's 2d Battalion was spread from Veuilly Wood to the Champillon-Torcy road. To the right, Turrill's 1st Battalion manned centrally located defensive lines in Saint-Martin Wood. Headquarters Company occupied a small area immediately behind the 1st Battalion. Major Berry's 3d Battalion was in the woods south of the 1st Battalion. Unfortunately, Colonel Neville did not control the latter unit, which was the XXI Corps reserve and could not be committed without General Degoutte's permission. Regimental headquarters was located in a quarry about five hundred meters northwest of Marigny, quite a way from the likely battlefield considering the primitive state of communications in those days. Captain Fay's 8th (Machine Gun) Company and Major Puryear's Supply Company finally arrived by rail that evening. Some machine gunners were quickly sent forward to support the 2d Battalion. Headquarters Company's Sapper and Bomber Sections also rushed up when it was discovered the French had departed without notifying anyone, leaving the 2d Battalion's left flank dangerously exposed.

That the situation was desperate was indicated by General Harbord's admonition "to hold at all costs." Between 2 and 5 June, repeated German assaults were beaten back by artillery, mortar, machine-gun, and rifle fire. Particularly telling was the effect of well-aimed fire from American Springfield rifles. Marine marksmen, working their bolts at a furious pace, thinned the advancing gray ranks until the attackers fell back. It turned out that Colonel Doyen's insistence upon rifle marksmanship was not the waste of time that the skeptical French had asserted it to be. The most important of these attacks occurred on 3 June 1918 when the German 273d Regiment, 26th Division, tried to overrun the 2d Battalion near Les Mares Farm. During this action Lieutenant Shepherd of the 55th Company took a bullet in the neck but stayed in the fight. One of the rocks of the 55th Company was GySgt. Herman Tharau, who calmly strolled along the lines pointing out targets and correcting men's shooting techniques as German bullets whizzed by. Thirty-nine-year-old "Babe"

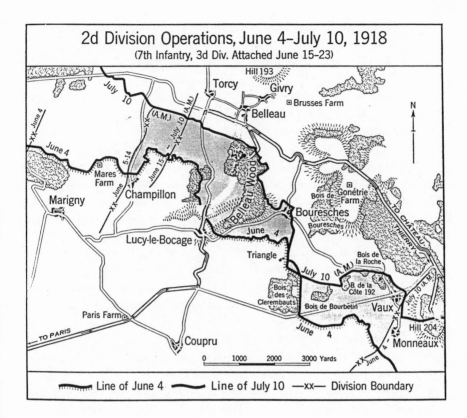

2d Division Operations, June 4–July 10, 1918
(7th Infantry, 3d Div. Attached June 15–23)

Line of June 4 — Line of July 10 —xx— Division Boundary

Tharau—his nickname derived from his solid frame, which reminded people of Paul Bunyan's mythical blue ox—was fearless and steady under fire, exuding both courage and a sense of humor. Colonel Wise later recalled, "Our rifle fire seemed to take the heart out of the Germans . . . suddenly [those still alive] broke and ran." It later turned out that this was the farthest advance by the German army. The fearsome German juggernaut that had panicked the French government and put thousands of civilians to flight was stopped by a few resolute Marines a mere thirty-nine miles from Paris. Just as Colonel Brown promised, the American regulars held.

Remnants of the tired French army flooded through the Marine lines throughout the day and night. Many *poilus* had lost their weapons, and all were too demoralized to care about stopping the Boche. Captain William O. Corbin, the 51st Company's second in command, stopped a fleeing French staff officer on the road north of Champillon and asked for information. The reply was a vague one to the effect that "all was lost" and the Marines should fall back at once. Captain Corbin ignored this suggestion and continued supervising Marine defensive preparations. When Corbin paid no heed to verbal instructions, the French major scribbled a written order giving permission for the Marines to pull out. Message in hand, Corbin returned to the command post and dutifully presented the Frenchman's note to his company commander. Captain Williams read the message and disgustedly exclaimed, "Retreat Hell! We just got here!" Captain Williams's less colorful written message to Colonel Wise stated: "[A] French major ordered Captain Corbin to retreat. . . . I have countermanded this order . . . please ensure the artillery does not shorten its range." Williams's courageous reply fired Marine imaginations, and Leatherneck pride swelled as word of his response spread through the ranks. This dramatic incident set the stage for a pivotal battle that would capture the imagination of the American people like no other single event of the war and consequently changed the course of Marine Corps history.

Sixth Army ordered XXI Corps to attack on 6 June. Two attacks by the 2d Division were planned. The first would straighten the line in the north, while the second would reduce a German-held salient southwest of the town of Belleau. The 4th Marine Brigade was assigned the area north of the Paris-Metz highway, a zone of action that included Hill 142, Belleau Wood, and the town of Bouresches. The enemy lines were believed to run from Bouresches to Belleau village, and the main line of resistance was centered along a raised railway bed to the east. Retreating French units reported that the wood itself was only thinly held, but the lateness of the hour prevented the Marines from scouting its dark recesses.

The Marine Brigade held a doorstep-shaped line that stretched west from Triangle Farm to Lucy-le-Bocage, north along the Lucy-Torcy road, then bent west past Champillon. Most of the terrain consisted of rolling hillocks covered by a checkerboard of woods and open fields filled with red poppies and green wheat. An irregular patch of forest, Belleau Wood, was sandwiched between Hill 133 on the north and Hill 181 to the south. This key terrain feature fronted the American lines and screened German movements. A former hunting preserve, Belleau Wood was covered by thick underbrush, dotted with moss-covered boulders, cut by deep ravines, and topped by thick hardwood trees. In short, it was a nearly impregnable natural fortress. Unfortunately, the exact terrain and true size of the zone were unknown because Marine tactical maps misrepresented it.

The French reports that the woods were empty were also inaccurate. Belleau Wood was actually defended by the elite 1,169-man 461st Regiment and the 2d Battalion, 40th Fusilier Regiment. Preregistered artillery fires ringed the wood, and German spotters in sausage-shaped observation balloons hovered overhead ready to call for fire as soon as they spotted movement. The Germans had constructed three defensive lines across Belleau Wood's narrow waist to block expected attacks from the south. There were numerous cleverly concealed, mutually supporting light and heavy machine-gun positions among the boulders, behind the woodpiles, and in the ravines that crisscrossed the woods.

At 1500 on 5 June, General Bundy ordered General Harbord to mount the planned attacks the next day. At the time it was believed that neither Hill 142 nor Belleau Wood were heavily defended, so seizing them should require only minor actions. In reality, the fight for Belleau Wood would become the biggest American battle since the Civil War, as well as the largest engagement with foreign troops to that point in American history.

General Harbord's plan was to attack north and consolidate with the French 116th Infantry near Torcy in the morning. To do that, the Marines needed to capture a rectangular area about two hundred yards deep and four hundred yards long northeast of Hill 142 as a jump-off point. Actually, the Hill 142 designation was a misnomer. It was technically a battle position located on a downward-sloping ridge, a wood-covered finger that ran from Hill 176 inside Saint-Martin Wood and pointed northward in the general direction of Torcy. The limit of advance was a dirt cart path that fronted the woods until it joined the main road near Torcy Bridge. Major Turrill's 1st Battalion was ordered to undertake this mission.

The problem with Harbord's plan was not its concept but its timing. Brigade did not issue its orders until about 2230, seven hours after Harbord was first alerted. It must be recalled that during that time commanders often had to use runners because the telephones of the day were so unreliable. This inordinate delay (variously attributed to the desire for secrecy or overly fastidious attention to creating a "perfect" plan) meant that Buck Neville was not able to issue his orders until half-past midnight. The tardiness of the staff work left Major Turrill only about an hour to formulate his own plan, assemble his scattered battalion, and issue the attack order. Two companies were at hand, but the other two were still in the lines awaiting relief that had been scheduled for the previous evening. At every level this was woefully inadequate preparation for what promised to become the largest battle in Marine Corps history to date.

One of the most disastrous command decisions made that night was to forego a heavy artillery barrage. General Harbord did not want to alert the enemy of his intention to attack, so he ordered only a cursory preparation. Half of the 1st Battalion went over the top at 0345 on 6 June after roughly five minutes of raking artillery fire on the objective. The assault units were separated by the spine of Hill 142, with the 67th Company on the left and the 49th Company on the right. The 23d (Machine Gun) Company and the 2d Artillery Brigade provided limited fire support. Turrill's bobtail battalion advanced only fifty yards into the gray, predawn darkness before Maxim machine-gun fire tore through the ranks as the Marines emerged from Saint-Martin Wood into an open wheat field. The 67th and 49th Companies stepped out in four neatly dressed assault waves and advanced at a walk, just as they had been taught by the Blue Devils at Gondrecourt. Unfortunately, those Napoleonic tactics were ill suited to modern warfare, where automatic weapons controlled the forward edge of the battlefield. The attack temporarily foundered. In a matter of moments the assault waves lost cohesion and went to ground. The officers, wearing Sam Browne belts, made conspicuous targets and suffered grievous losses. The 67th Company was left leaderless when Lieutenant Crowther and 1st Sgt. Daniel A. "Pop" Hunter were both cut down. Crowther single-handedly took out a machine-gun nest and was engaging a second when he met his fate. He was posthumously awarded the Navy Cross. Hunter was struck down as he led the advance forward toward the woods.

Captain Hamilton of the 49th Company—described by battalion adjutant Keller Rockey as "a fine leader respected by his men, his contemporaries, and his seniors"—rose to the occasion and led the Marines forward in a series of rushes. Most Chauchat automatic rifles were quickly knocked out of action and the Marines had few grenades, so they took the enemy trenches using hand-to-hand combat. It turned out the objective was much more heavily defended than originally thought. Instead of only a few scattered remnants of the Les Mares assault force that were expected, three fresh German machine-gun companies were in place on the nose of Hill 142.

Hamilton's Marines broke out of the woods then surged six hundred yards past the limit of advance. The lead platoon actually moved as far forward as Torcy Bridge. Three Marines made it into Torcy, but they were cut off and only one escaped. The remains of the other two were discovered during a well excavation more than fifty years later. German airborne spotters lurking above the battlefield were alerted by this movement in the open and quickly ordered up an accurate artillery barrage. This fire, coupled with flanking machine-gun fires coming from the right and left, soon made the narrow Marine salient untenable. Captain Hamilton realized the danger and led his Marines back to the relative safety of Hill 142 through a wooded ravine. En route, the gallant company commander killed four Germans in close combat. Back on Hill 142 he organized hasty defensive lines that he later described as "a confused mix of the 49th, 66th, and 67th Companies" in his report to headquarters.

Captain Winans's 17th and 1st Lt. Walter T. H. Galliford's 66th Companies had missed Zero hour because they had not yet been relieved in place as promised. As a result, these orphan units did not arrive at the line of departure until after the assault was already under way. Of course, the gods of war operate in strange ways, and the fortuitous late arrival of these unscathed units actually lent some much-needed depth to the attack. Major Turrill sent elements of the 8th (Machine Gun) Company and Ros Winans's 17th Company into action after about an hour. First Lieutenant Bert Baston, shot in both legs while leading his platoon of the 17th Company forward into the woods near Hill 142, refused to be evacuated until his men were under cover and in good firing positions. Baston was evacuated (and later retired) due to his injuries, but eventually received the DSC and the Navy Cross for his bravery that day. Lieutenant Galliford's 66th Company moved into the woods by bits and pieces over a period of time. One of the heroes of the 66th Company was Marine Gunner Henry Hulbert, who led his platoon forward through intense fire. Hulbert was, arguably, the one of the most colorful Marines of all time. Born in England, he was fired as a colonial official for having had an illicit affair. Exiled from the British Empire, he joined the U.S. Marine Corps and was awarded the Medal of Honor in Samoa. His conduct under fire, professional demeanor, and impeccable dress made him the first Marine selected as a warrant officer. He was, in his day, a "Marine's Marine."

Captain Keller Rockey, who later received the Navy Cross for his actions that day, reported that the high ground had been taken and Major

Turrill was on his way to the front at 0537. Turrill reported that although the 1st Battalion was on the objective, his left flank was weak and his right was completely uncovered. This was disturbing news because it implied Major Berry's supporting attack had been delayed. In fact, there was no sign of the 3d Battalion. The first hints of real trouble began to filter back to headquarters at about 0900 when emergency pleas for ammunition and stretchers arrived at Neville's command post. Captain Hamilton actually sent back a mix of good and bad news. His report stated that he held the woods, but all of his officers were out of action. Lieutenant Colonel Feland, the battle-tested 5th Regiment second in command, hurried forward to join Turrill at his command post. Once he learned of the situation, Feland ordered the 51st Company (2d Battalion) and 45th Company (3d Battalion) moved up on the 1st Battalion's left and right flanks respectively. The defensive lines were thus shored up, but the first step to capture Belleau Wood had been a costly one. The 1st Battalion lost nine officers and 325 enlisted men before noon.

The badly mauled 1st Battalion (most platoons had been reduced to about squad size and were led by corporals) then endured intense artillery fire and a series of German counterattacks. Most of the day the Marines had to duck incoming nine-inch shells called "sea bags" and 77mm direct-fire "whiz-bangs." Gunnery Sergeant Ernst A. Janson (serving under the alias Charles F. Hoffman) spotted an enemy machine-gun platoon trying to infiltrate Marine positions using heavy brush for concealment. He warned his platoon and then fearlessly mounted a one-man bayonet attack that stunned the enemy. Without his quick action, the 49th Company would most certainly have been dealt a fatal blow by five German machine guns. Hoffman's heroism at Hill 142 resulted in the first Medal of Honor awarded to a Marine during the Great War. The 1st Battalion held these positions against numerous attacks over the next two weeks.

On 8 June, a lanky new lieutenant from Texas, John W. Thomason Jr., led some replacements into the line. The aristocratic young officer spent his spare time jotting copious notes and drawing sketches on any scrap of paper handy, much to the amusement of the enlisted men in his platoon. These scorned etchings and derided musings later made the 5th Marines famous in the decades following World War I. Of course, once that happened, many of the men who had secretly laughed at their lieutenant's bizarre behavior then claimed they were the role models for Thomason's characterizations.

An unfortunate pattern that would be often repeated in the next few weeks was set at Hill 142. The initial messages from observers were overly optimistic and gave staff officers far from the battlefield an inaccurate picture of what was really happening at the front. It appeared everything was going splendidly from the quiet safety of the command posts, when at the front the battle was actually a close-run affair. The repeated failure of senior commanders to personally inspect the front (neither Harbord nor Neville visited their units at any time during the battle) needlessly added to the problems.

General Harbord, satisfied with reports of progress in the north but without firsthand knowledge of the battlefield, issued Field Order No. 2 in the early afternoon on 6 June. The next Marine attack would be a two-stage affair to clear Belleau Wood and capture the town of Bouresches. The 6th Regiment and Major Berry's 3d Battalion would conduct a pincer attack to take the railway station at Bouresches, seize Hill 181, and clear southern Belleau Wood. Concurrently, the 1st and 2d Battalions, 5th Regiment, commanded by Lieutenant Colonel Feland, were to launch coordinated attacks to take Hill 133 and clear the northern end of Belleau Wood. Unfortunately, the plan for the 3d Battalions of both regiments to attack side-by-side while Feland's task group carried the northern wood was totally unrealistic and never came to fruition. What actually occurred was a disjointed assault carried out by separated units attacking into the teeth of the enemy defenses.

The 6th Regiment was at Triangle Farm and the 5th Regiment was in the woods west of the Lucy-Torcy road, too far apart for mutual support or to adequately coordinate the attack. Major Berry's three 5th Regiment companies were strung out, and his 45th Company was still attached to the 1st Battalion at Hill 142. Berry was supposed to attack southeast out of Saint-Martin Wood, cross an open field, and hit the German extreme west flank. This disposition placed the 3d Battalion in the center of the planned assault. Turrill's 1st Battalion was to keep pace with the French attack on the far left (north) and move forward until reaching Hill 126 near Torcy Bridge. Ironically, the lead elements of the 1st Battalion had carried that objective earlier in the day but had been forced to abandon it in the face of heavy enemy fire. This earlier failure did not bode well for the latter attack.

The 3d Battalion's disastrous assault inexorably unfolded like a Greek tragedy due to circumstances beyond Major Berry's control. For the second time that day, seemingly sensible orders ran into practical difficulties. Southern Belleau Wood was well defended, not thinly held as General Harbord had assumed. Additionally, his order did not reflect the true situation at Hill 142, where the 1st Battalion was fighting for its life, not mopping up enemy stragglers. That embattled unit would not be able to attack as ordered because there was no way the depleted 1st Battalion could mount effective offensive action.

The main Marine attack was about to jump off without any idea of exactly where the enemy was or in what numbers or with what weapons. French suggestions that the Marines advance in small groups using infiltration tactics were ignored. General Harbord wanted Belleau Wood taken by storm, not by stealth. In hindsight, it is obvious this decision was a flawed one. To make matters worse, Harbord again opted not to use a lengthy artillery preparation. The Marines had neither hand grenades nor Stokes mortars with which to subdue enemy machine-gun nests. This lack of adequate fire support was compounded by the fact that the tactical maps of the battle area were based on an 1834 survey and were grossly in error with regard to terrain and scale. They showed Belleau Wood to be much smaller than it actually was and misrepresented the ground found therein. The lack of adequate command preparation and failure to scout the objective were about to inflict many needless casualties.

Major Berry blew his whistle and led the 3d Battalion forward at 1700 on 6 June 1918. Three platoons of Captain Conachy's 45th Company were on the left, Captain Platt's 20th Company was in the center, and Captain Case's 47th Company was on the right. Captain Yowell's 16th Company was in support. As had happened earlier at Hill 142, the neatly dressed assault waves were soon shattered by deadly machine-gun fire. Along the way, an anonymous gunnery sergeant energized the faltering Marine line when he yelled, "Come on you sons-of-bitches, do you want to live forever?" The attack continued after that, but at a terrible cost. Sergeant Merwin Silverthorn of the 20th Company later recalled, "In my platoon there were 52 people; only six got across the first 75 yards." The reserve 16th Company was sent in, but it too was cut to pieces trying to cross the fire-swept fields. Major Berry took a bullet that shattered his arm, but he got up and continued into the woods. *Chicago Tribune* war correspondent Floyd Gibbons was hit three times and lost an eye while moving forward to assist Berry. Sergeant Silverthorn went down with a bullet in the ankle about fifty yards away. A few Marines actually made it into the woods, but it was obvious the main attack was a costly failure.

Casualties were heavy; nearly two-thirds of the 3d Battalion lay dead or wounded among the poppies and wheat. With Major Berry seriously wounded, Capt. (later Lt. Gen.) Henry L. Larsen assumed temporary command of the 3d Battalion.

The hard-pressed 1st Battalion at Hill 142 and the battered 2d Battalion in Saint-Martin Wood did not try to take the northern portion of Belleau Wood. Lieutenant Colonel Feland wisely held the battalions in place when the French failed to advance rather than needlessly expose his men to devastating flanking fire. When his decision was later questioned, Feland replied that such an attack would have gained nothing but the senseless slaughter of the attackers. He correctly deduced that there was too much open ground and too few men to carry the position without French support.

General Harbord belatedly called off the futile assault at 2115, but it was a moot point. By that time the Marines on the scene had already either dug in or fallen back. The 6th Regiment possessed a small toehold inside Belleau Wood, and a handful of Marines were inside Bouresches, but the railway station had not been captured. With his left stalled and the center pinned down, Harbord had no choice but to consolidate his positions and reorganize his units. Rather than repeat the day's failure, Harbord sagaciously decided to postpone follow-up attacks until Belleau Wood had been softened by several days of artillery bombardment. Sadly, the first day of fighting at Belleau Wood cost the Marine Corps more men killed in action than it had cumulatively lost since 1775.

That night, Wise's 2d Battalion linked up with the battered remnants of the 3d Battalion, but it was a confused and costly move. The men had to hold on to each other in the inky darkness as they marched clear across the regimental zone. The 2d Battalion's lead elements unexpectedly emerged into the open, came under immediate fire, and had to hastily reverse course. Caught in a cross fire between the Germans in Belleau Wood and the survivors of the 3d Battalion dug in along the east edge of Saint-Martin Wood, confused Marines milled around unsure if they should move forward or backward. Lem Shepherd recalled that he received the order to pull back as he lay on the open ground with bullets hitting all around him. Leery about such an order, he called out for further instructions. In reply, he was told the order came directly from Fritz Wise. This loud confirmation initiated a hasty pull back. Lieutenant Legendre repeatedly exposed himself in order to rescue wounded men unable to move out of the line of fire. Tragically, Capt. John Blanchfield's premonition of death that he had earlier shared with Lieutenant Shepherd came true. Blanchfield was struck down that night and later died of his wounds. His place in the ranks was quickly taken over by his stalwart second in command, but within a matter of moments Shepherd was hit and had to be evacuated. Second Lieutenant Lucius Q. L. C. Lyle temporarily took command until an army officer, 1st Lt. Eliot D. Cooke, could be transferred from the 18th Company to assume command of the 55th Company. Although the idea of an army officer commanding Marines may seem strange, at that time it was not unusual for U.S. Army officers to serve with Marine units (or vice versa). More than fifty Army Reserve officers served with the 4th Brigade during the war, and many notable Marine officers (among them John Lejeune, Hiram Bearss, Fritz Wise, and artilleryman Robert H. Dunlap) commanded army units.

The battered 3d Battalion was pulled out of the lines the next day and returned to Maison Blanche Wood, where it became the 4th Brigade reserve. Major Maurice Shearer—former commander of the 1st Battalion, 6th Regiment—took over, and Captain Larsen reverted to being the 3d Battalion's second in command. Two days later, the rebuilt 3d Battalion was sent back to Triangle Farm. General Harbord told Major Shearer to go over and familiarize himself with Bouresches because the 3d Battalion was going to relieve those elements of the 6th Regiment holding the ruins of that village on 9 June. Among the replacements assigned to Captain Case's 47th Company of the 3d Battalion was 2d Lt. Laurence T. Stallings Jr., an eager twenty-three-year-old intellectual not long removed from college. Within two weeks, Stallings—the senior surviving officer—would be leading the 47th Company back into Belleau Wood.

After a two-day artillery bombardment it was time to attack Belleau Wood one more time. General Harbord's Field Order No. 4 was issued at 1745 on 10 June. In it he called for Fritz Wise's 2d Battalion to attack the northern end of Belleau Wood with Hill 133 as the main objective. This attack would be supported by artillery and machine guns. Colonel Wise was to refuse his left flank along the Lucy–Château Belleau ravine when he reached the objective. Lieutenant Colonel Harry Lee's 6th Regiment was to attack north and link up with the 2d Battalion. Unfortunately, this was yet another case of mistaken assumptions at headquarters. Harbord's order assumed the 6th Marines was much farther into Belleau Wood than was actually the case. The 2d Battalion flank would be exposed to intense flanking fire from the right as it moved over open ground because the 6th Regiment had really cut only a small niche out of the south end of the woods (far short of its objective at the juncture of Belleau Woods's narrow neck and the southern edge of the northern copse designated "Line X"). Zero hour was set for 0430.

Had the actual situation been as Harbord imagined it, this would have been a sound plan. The Marines would strike the enemy from the flank at his weakest point to capture dominant terrain that would allow the French freedom of movement in their zone. The Germans inside Belleau Wood thus would be caught in a Marine vise pressing in from north and south, and the enemy's supply lines could be severed by massed machine-gun and observed artillery fires. With the Germans outnumbered and isolated from reinforcement or resupply, Belleau Wood should thereafter fall like a ripe fruit. Unfortunately, due to still-debated circumstances, the attack did not come off as planned. Rather than a flanking maneuver to take the northern third of the wood, the 2d Battalion wound up making a frontal assault near its center, covering almost exactly the same ground that Major Berry's men had been slaughtered on only a few days before. The 2d Battalion thus became pinched between two enemy forces with its supply routes under German observation rather than vice versa. Hence, instead of the hoped for coup de main, the Americans actually became bogged down in a bloody two-week slugfest to clear what was soon dubbed "Hellwood."

Lieutenant Colonel Wise and Colonel Neville held a commander's conference in the evening to go over the plan of attack. Documentary evidence points to a scheme of maneuver whereby the 2d Battalion was to move through a gap in the woods south of Hill 169, hug the southern edge of the northern copse, push rapidly into the forest, pivot north, and use one company to clear the northern woods and one company to take Hill 133. The 6th Regiment was to launch a diversionary attack in the middle of Belleau Wood. Like Harbord's earlier plans, this scheme of maneuver seemed to be a good one that used speed of movement to hit the enemy at the weakest spot. Had it been properly executed, the attack would have struck while northern Belleau Wood was defended by only a single demoralized German company. There can be little doubt such an attack would have succeeded. But, alas, we shall never know because the planned assault was not the one that was carried out. Instead, the 2d Battalion marched directly into hell on earth.

The 2d Battalion was holding the wooded ridge just west of the tree-lined Lucy-Torcy road. All hands were tired and hungry. They had been under continuous fire since 2 June, and most had not eaten a hot meal since Decoration Day. The 2d Battalion had repeatedly repelled ground assaults, been strafed by German airplanes, and suffered several gas attacks. In fact, Colonel Wise had lost more than one-fourth of his personnel due to illness, injury, and sundry duties. Despite these problems, the 2d Battalion jumped off on time and crossed the line of departure in good order. Sometime after that, however, things began to go awry.

Colonel Wise lost control of the attack as soon as his Marines disappeared into the heavy morning mist that shrouded the freshly plowed fields between the Saint-Martin and Belleau Woods. The assault waves stepped off smartly, but they inexplicably headed southeast toward Hill 181 instead of hugging the south side of Hill 169 in the north. Some have speculated that the Marines became disoriented and misread the unfamiliar terrain in the early morning mist or that the men were naturally drawn to the sound of gunfire to the south. There is no definitive answer as to why the attack became so misdirected, but this simple directional error resulted in the death of many good men. Unfortunately, such is the fog of war. To this day there is much controversy over what historians call "the missing order." In his book written several years after the war, Wise denied responsibility for this fiasco. He asserted he was prepared to use a flanking attack that would enter Belleau Wood north of Hill 133, but he could not because he was overruled by written orders that arrived at his command post at the last moment. Unfortunately, there is no documentary evidence or corroborating testimony that such a plan existed. No such order is in the official records, and two officers present when the final order arrived contradict Wise's account. The battalion intelligence officer, 1st Lt. William R. Matthews, claimed the last-minute order was merely confirmation of Field Order No. 4, and company commander Eliot Cooke later explained the battalion officers rejected a flanking maneuver because they wanted to "keep it simple." Ironically, support units and reinforcements that moved up in accord with the original plan met no resistance and were confused about why they could not locate the 2d Battalion in the nearly unoccupied northern woods.

Artillery preparation of Belleau Wood began promptly at 0330 on 11 June. A fortuitous dense fog clinging to the open ground limited visibility and dulled sounds. The Marines used this cover to sweep across the road and move silently through the wheat in a box formation. Captain Williams's 51st Company led on the right with Lieutenant Cooke's 55th Company moving in trace. Captain Charley Dunbeck's 43d Company was on the left with Captain Wass's 18th Company in support. No liaison with the 6th Regiment had been established, so the 2d Battalion assault began without its promised support from the right. Twelve guns from the 6th Machine Gun Battalion laid withering fire to fill the void as soon as the artillery barrage began to roll forward across Belleau Wood.

The 2d Battalion came under increasingly heavy fire from the right flank as it neared the woods, and a tough fight in the center of Belleau Wood soon ensued. The battle raged throughout the morning. The attackers, probably moving toward the sound of guns, veered into the lower portion of the woods, where a battalion of the 40th Fusiliers was fighting the 6th Marine Regiment. The Marines had to sweep the treetops with gunfire to eliminate snipers, every brush pile and depression had to be carefully searched so the Marines would not be taken from the rear, and enemy machine-gun nests had to be cleared by hand-to-hand fighting. The Marines lacked the implements to properly fight trench warfare; there were no tanks, trench mortars, or direct-fire artillery weapons, and few grenades. Instead, the assault units had to rely upon small arms and bayonets. Command and control were difficult in the heavy underbrush and during close-quarters combat. The contest was reduced to a series of isolated small fights, random bantam battles to the death raging on without rhyme or direction. Sweating men grappled in individual combat armed with knives, guns, bayonets, and shovels. By noon the Marines held about five hundred square yards in the narrow neck of the woods.

Williams's 51st Company rolled up the enemy flank, reached the far side of the wood, and stopped to regroup. Cooke's 55th Company likewise crossed the woods, then joined Dunbeck's 43d Company on its left (north) flank. The 18th Company was sent farther north after Captain Dunbeck noticed how open that flank was. During the action, support and assault companies merged into a tangled mess and the true situation inside the wood was skewed by the confusion of combat. As at Hill 142, the first reports painted a rosy picture. They indicated that all was going well, many prisoners were coming in, and the Germans were retreating. The initial hints of trouble came when Captain Williams reported his company was suffering from machine-gun fire and asked for help. Captain Dunbeck soon thereafter reported all objectives were taken, but his stated losses were heavy. Captain Wass reported the enemy was preparing a counterattack from the Bouresches-Belleau road and requested immediate artillery support.

Small-unit leaders went down rapidly during the attack. Only one of the 2d Battalion company commanders and only one first sergeant made it through the battle unscathed. Second Lieutenant (later Maj. Gen.) Samuel C. Cumming of the 55th Company was evacuated after a 77mm shell shattered his ankle. Captain Williams was cut down by machine-gun fire and his second in command, Captain Corbin, was also knocked out of action. Army Second Lieutenant Robert H. Loughborough, the only officer left, assumed command of the 51st Company (by then reduced to only sixteen men) until he was replaced by 1st Lt. Percy D. Cornell. Captain Dunbeck also was wounded and had to be evacuated. Soft-spoken 1st Lt. Drinkard B. Milner, a mild-mannered minister's son, took over the 43d Company much to the chagrin of his battalion commander. Luckily, first impressions can be deceiving; Milner proved himself to be a first-class combat leader.

The Germans tried to hit the Marine positions from the far side of the railway track during the afternoon. This assault force was repelled as it crossed an open area. Timely American artillery, as well as accurate rifle and machine-gun fire from Major Shearer's 3d Battalion holding Bouresches, and small-arms fire from the dug-in 2d Battalion combined to do the trick. About 150 infantry replacements rushed into the woods, and more than a hundred combat engineers were pressed into service to fill gaps in the Marine lines as the day wore on.

Not long thereafter, the 2d Battalion's intelligence officer, Lt. Bill Matthews, met GySgt. Michael Wodarczyk escorting some prisoners to the rear. The muscular noncommissioned officer (NCO) had cleared part of the woods almost single handed, and he reported the northern woods was occupied by only a few Germans manning some hasty defensive positions. Intrigued, Matthews surveyed part of the area in question without encountering any Marines or Germans before he returned to central Belleau Wood. There, he linked up with the 2d Battalion company commanders who were holding an impromptu council of war. Matthews was incredulous to discover the assault units were so far out of position. When asked why, one commander pointed to Bouresches and insisted it was Belleau, he then pointed to Belleau claiming it was Torcy (a directional error of about ninety degrees). Matthews could not convince them of the true direction, and he was equally unsuccessful persuading them that the left (north) flank was completely uncovered. Angry that his concerns were being ignored, Matthews returned to the 2d Battalion command post. He reported his alarming findings to Lieutenant Colonel Wise, who summarily dismissed them. Instead of taking note, Wise wrongly berated Matthews, denigrated his efforts, questioned the validity of his information, and eventually relieved Matthews based upon this confrontation. It was not Wise's finest hour as a commander, and many innocent Marines would pay with their lives. Some of his detractors later mused that Wise's stubbornness that day may have confirmed the veracity of his despised nom de guerre, "Dopey."

Fritz Wise sent word to Colonel Neville that the 2d Battalion held all its objectives, but also mentioned that his left flank was weak and he feared a German attack from that direction. This message, unfortunately, presented a very misleading account of the true picture. Wise knowingly covered up the fact that his attack had gone astray. He should have realized by then that the Marines did not actually hold all of Belleau Wood as he inferred. Instead, just as Matthews had told him, the 2d Battalion was bunched up in the center of the woods. Regrettably, Wise's erroneous report set off a series of acrimonious felicitations that have not stood the test of time. Not long after Wise's communiqué was forwarded to division headquarters, General Harbord relayed hearty praise to Colonel Neville. Lieutenant Colonel Wise, in turn, received a message stating, "The division commander . . . sends [his] congratulations." This laudatory memo was, to say the least, a premature one that would later become an embarrassment to all parties.

The potential success of a properly executed attack on the northern woods was brought to the fore by an unusual incident. Captain Alphonse DeCarre, the Headquarters Company commander, led an eighty-man support party carrying supplies and tools forward along the route delineated in the original attack plan. This party moved out of its assembly area and crossed into Belleau Wood near Hill 169 as specified by Colonel Neville. It entered Belleau Wood unopposed, but DeCarre became worried when he could not locate the 2d Battalion. Prudently, he ordered the column to halt and prepare hasty defensive positions. He then led a small scout party forward. They quickly encountered a German machine-gun nest. The Germans, believing they faced an overwhelming force, surrendered after a brief firefight. Three German officers and 169 enlisted men were captured. The Marines suffered only two killed and four wounded. This action made it obvious the northern woods had been ripe for plucking that morning. But, alas, it was a missed opportunity.

It eventually became apparent at 4th Brigade headquarters that the Marines did not hold all of Belleau Wood. Confronted with this belated revelation, Lieutenant Colonel Wise reluctantly admitted the facts but assured General Harbord and Colonel Neville that the 2d Battalion could capture the rest of Belleau Wood after extensive artillery preparation. Accordingly, the 2d Artillery Brigade pummeled the northern woods most of the day on 12 June. The 2d Battalion pivoted north, fanned out, and continued its attack to dislodge the enemy that afternoon. An intense two-and-a-half-hour artillery barrage directly preceded the assault. Unfortunately, most of that fire hit too far north to be of much use. This time the Marines changed tactics. They infiltrated the German lines with small combat teams composed of two or three men instead of charging forward in vulnerable, hard-to-control assault waves. The 2d Battalion surged forward in a variety of places but was still unable to advance in others.

For the drive north, the 55th Company was on the right (at the edge of the woods), the 43d Company was in the center, and the 18th Company was on the left. The shattered remnants of the 51st Company, which remained about the size of a reinforced platoon until replacements arrived and Capt. Francis Fisk took over on 17 June, was in support. The Marine attack penetrated the German main line of resistance, and the 43d Company reached a hunting lodge being used as a command post. There, a captured Prussian officer revealed that fresh German troops were on the way to conduct a night counterattack. This information, plus the heavy losses suffered already, caused the Marines to stop. All companies were digging in by 2135. The day's attack yielded mixed results. The Marines took many prisoners and captured some machine guns and trench mortars, but they still failed to clear the entire woods. The Marine defensive front inside the woods looked not unlike a fishhook. It stretched from the eye near Hill 169 in the west with the stem running south along the east side of the woods to the hook's apex located near the hunting lodge. Wise's 2300 report indicated his lines were weakly held and the 2d Battalion was being heavily shelled.

Colonel Neville decided to send reinforcements into northern Belleau Wood. The only available unit was the 1st Battalion's 17th Company located in Saint-Martin Wood east of Hill 142. First Lieutenant Robert Blake led his platoon ahead to scout the planned route in the early morning darkness on the thirteenth. Blake's patrol entered the woods near Hill 169 and ran into a few Marines who had been isolated there for two days. They returned to the company post of command. Captain Ros Winans accepted Blake's report at about 0700, requested reinforcements, then led his men across the gap between the two woods at about

0800. Like DeCarre earlier, Winans discovered the 2d Battalion was still not where it was reported to be. When a low-flying German reconnaissance plane spotted the Marines, Winans ordered his men to immediately pull back, and the vacated area exploded in a furious barrage just as the last Marines were making their exit. These actions on 12 and 13 June made it obvious that Belleau Wood was well defended and had been zeroed in by German artillery. It was also apparent that Wise's optimistic messages to headquarters could not be reconciled with the more realistic assessments of Captains Winans or DeCarre.

General Harbord belatedly realized the attack was stalled and no longer had sufficient momentum to clear Belleau Wood. The 5th Regiment had suffered grievous casualties. The 2d Battalion was too worn out to continue, the 3d Battalion was overdue for relief at Bouresches, and the 1st Battalion still had its hands full defending Hill 142. Harbord had no choice but to send in the already hard-hit 6th Regiment. Once again, things did not go according to plan. Colonel Wise's Marines repulsed a determined attack at about 0130 on 14 June, then were bombarded by mustard gas as they awaited relief. Future Commandant Thomas Holcomb's 2d Battalion, 6th Regiment, suffered heavy casualties and became disoriented as it moved forward to relieve Wise's tired men during the gas attack. Only about one-third of the relief force actually arrived. The 6th Regiment survivors were not strong enough to effect the planned relief, so they were instead integrated into Wise's defensive lines. Lieutenant Colonel Feland (Neville's second in command) came forward to take charge of the composite force inside Belleau Wood, which included the 2d Battalion, 5th Regiment; 1st and 2d Battalions, 6th Regiment; and Companies D and F, 2d Engineers.

Resupply and medical support were major problems throughout the battle. Most Marine units held exposed positions that could only be reached after dark. Daylight resupply attempts were uniformly unsuccessful. Several such attempts resulted in heavy casualties among Headquarters and Supply Company personnel who vainly tried to bring ammunition, water, and hot chow to their comrades on the firing line. Water was so scarce inside Belleau Wood that the men took to drinking unpurified water from muddy shell holes. Most had to satisfy their hunger with meager French-supplied "iron rations" consisting of hardtack biscuits and nearly unpalatable canned Madagascar beef with vegetables. The Marines scornfully called this smelly, foul-tasting, sometimes tainted food "Monkey Meat."

Navy medical personnel (doctors and hospital apprentices) were understaffed and overworked. Their numbers were supplemented by the regimental bandsmen, who assumed the traditional role of stretcher bearers in combat. German prisoners were put to work carrying Marine casualties on makeshift stretchers as they moved to the rear. The dressing stations at Champillon, Lucy-le-Bocage, and La Voie Châtel were continually under fire. The station at Lucy was shattered by a direct hit on the eleventh that killed several men inside and started a fire. Sailors and Marines working there calmly donned gas masks and went inside the blazing building to recover precious medical supplies and remove the wounded. Navy lieutenant Orlando H. Petty, the regimental surgeon, was awarded the Medal of Honor for his actions that day. Petty's operating area was hit by artillery and gas then caught fire. While working furiously to save Capt. Lloyd Williams, Petty was wounded and his gas mask was ruined. The regimental surgeon refused to seek safety until Williams was loaded onto an ambulance. Unfortunately, the heroic Williams, whose "Retreat Hell!" comment has become part of Marine lore, later died. Petty was not the only Navy medic to earn the respect of the Marines at Belleau Wood. Hospital corpsmen fearlessly went "over the top" with Marine combat units to provide first aid and stabilize the wounded for evacuation. In the words of a contemporary account of the battle, "There were many [unnamed navy] heroes who wore the Red Cross at Bois de Belleau."

The 3d Battalion inside Bouresches was hard pressed to hold on. The Germans bombarded the battalion's line from 0323 to 0350 on the thirteenth and then launched a ground assault. During the action General Harbord received an incorrect report stating that the enemy had taken Bouresches. He sent an inquiry at 0410. Major Shearer replied, "Have not given up one inch of ground." The enemy did briefly penetrate the Marine lines but was quickly thrown back. The only Germans still at Bouresches when Harbord's Marines arrived were the dead that littered the streets and nearby fields. Still, defending the town was costly. Captain Peter Conachy was wounded, and 1st Lt. Raymond E. Knapp took his place as 45th Company commander. A prolonged gas barrage hit the town the next morning. Major (later Maj. Gen.) Ralph S. Keyser, temporarily in command of the 3d Battalion, pleaded for reinforcements claiming his Marines were holding on to Bouresches by nerve alone. This call for help was answered when the army's 1st Battalion, 23d Infantry Regiment, arrived. The 3d Battalion then moved back to become the 4th Brigade reserve at Montgivrault Wood.

Belleau Wood was subjected to more gas and heavy artillery fire on the fourteenth, but the hard-hit 2d Battalion had to remain in place. Captain Winans and Lieutenant Colonel Feland conducted a hazardous reconnaissance of northern Belleau Wood before meeting with Major Turrill at the 1st Battalion command post. Winans voiced the opinion that his company could seize the northwest corner of the woods and pinch out the Germans located there if he was well supported by machine guns, one-pounder guns, and artillery. Feland and Turrill concurred. The 17th Company then moved into north-central Belleau Wood, where it joined the 2d Battalion's left flank after a sharp fight in which Captain Winans was seriously wounded. Captain Thomas Quigley came over from the 49th Company to command the 17th for about a week. Lieutenant Blake then served as company commander from 22 June until the arrival of Capt. LeRoy P. Hunt on the twenty-fifth. It turned out that Captain Winans's assessment had been correct. The Marines pushed the remaining Germans into the northern tip of the woods. The plan was to hold those positions while artillery isolated the area, shutting down approach routes to keep German reinforcements and additional supplies from coming in. Steady pressure would thereafter be applied until the Germans capitulated. The flaw in this plan was that the Marine units were too exhausted to mount a final attack.

General Harbord was given tactical control of the army's 7th Infantry Regiment for six days and told to effect the relief of his units in Belleau Wood on a battalion-for-battalion basis over the next two nights. Wise's 2/5 was replaced in the early hours of 15 June. By that time, the 2d Battalion had killed or captured more than four hundred Germans, and had taken fifty-nine machine guns (many of which were then used against their former owners) and ten trench mortars. But it had been a very costly three-day fight: When the 2d Battalion arrived at the Mery-sur-Marne rest area on the sixteenth it numbered only seven officers and 350 enlisted men; nineteen officers and 615 enlisted men had been killed or wounded at Belleau Wood. Luckily, more than 300 men arrived from the Marine replacement camp at Saint-Aignon in the Loire Valley. The newcomers were hurriedly integrated into the ranks and underwent a week of intense training. The 2d Battalion lost its commanding officer when Lieutenant Colonel Wise was relieved after a vociferous disagreement with General Harbord. Wise was officially "detached to attend school," but was actually hospitalized for shellshock. He briefly returned to the 5th Regiment after Harbord left the 4th Brigade. He was promoted soon thereafter, transferred, and given command of the army's 59th Infantry Regiment. Major Keyser assumed command of the 2d Battalion after Wise's relief. The 1st Battalion was replaced by the 7th Infantry on the night of 17–18 June and proceeded by foot march to Montreuil, where it mounted trucks for the ride to Mery, the former station of the 3d Battalion, 7th Infantry. General Harbord also directed that 5th Regiment bandsmen be relieved of duty as stretcher bearers and be kept with the rear echelon until the Marines returned to action.

Predictably, the untested soldiers of the 7th Infantry were unable to advance and could not clear Belleau Wood as ordered. After questioning an enemy prisoner who reported that the Germans held the northern woods in strength, Lieutenant Colonel Feland made another dangerous personal reconnaissance on 22 June. This daring effort confirmed that the American lines were almost unchanged. In fact, Feland discovered the Germans had been reinforced and were more firmly entrenched than before. General Harbord therefore ordered the battered 3/5 back into Belleau Wood with orders to clear it no later than 2000 on 23 June.

The 47th Company rushed back into action on 22 June. Captain Philip Case, who had been leading the 47th Company with one arm in a sling since the eighth, was hit in the other arm and evacuated. Lieutenant Stallings temporarily replaced him and led the company assault until Capt. Gaines Moseley arrived later that night. The 2d Battalion was also put back into the lines that night near Hill 142 with orders to take the "Double Tree" road (the Torcy-Lucy road) west of Belleau Wood using small assault groups. To reduce casualties, Major Keyser was instructed to keep only minimal forces at the forward edge of the battle area and to retain at least two full companies in reserve.

The 3d Battalion tried daylight infiltration tactics to clear the way. Two- and three-man sniper teams roved in front of the Marine lines to locate enemy strong points and gun down any Germans who exposed themselves. The first assault to clear Belleau Wood began at 1900 on the twenty-third. Major Shearer launched this attack without artillery support hoping to catch the enemy off guard as darkness settled in. Unfortunately, the ploy did not work. Captain Yowell's 16th and Captain Platt's 20th Companies were repulsed with heavy losses. The Marines pulled back at midnight so artillery could thoroughly pulverize what remained of Belleau Wood. The entire next day was devoted to intermittent artillery fire. The same was true on the twenty-fifth until a continuous two-hour heavy barrage started at 1500. The 47th and 20th Companies moved out at 1700 closely following a rolling barrage that advanced at the rate of a hundred yards every three minutes. The 2d Battalion likewise moved out after an intense barrage lifted at 1755. The Marines finally cleared the trenches east of Hill 142, secured the Torcy-Lucy road, and had captured all their objectives by 2100. Two platoons were then detached to support the 3d Battalion's 16th Company, which was in bad shape. That unit was pinned down at the northern edge of Belleau Wood and was being commanded by GySgt. Walter Sweet because all of its officers had been killed or wounded. Sweet was given a battlefield commission and later received the DSC and Navy Cross.

During the fighting Lieutenant Stallings led a squad forward to reinforce an endangered platoon. They ran into a nest of Germans. The Marines went down in a hail of gunfire that ripped Stallings's leg open from the knee down and left him unconscious. He was the only survivor of the ten-man relief force. In true Marine fashion, after being rescued the seriously wounded lieutenant dutifully reported the situation to Major Shearer before being carried to the aid station under the bridge at Lucy. Stallings first became aware of the seriousness of his wounds when Colonel Neville, alarmed at losing one of his most promising junior officers, blurted out "Oh Laurence, your fighting days are through!" Contrary to the surgeons' dire predictions at the time, Stallings survived the war. However, his foot had to be amputated and his wounds troubled him for the rest of his life.

Twice that night the Boche launched desperate attacks to dislodge the Marines. Both were repulsed. Major Shearer was finally able to truthfully report, "Woods entirely U.S. Marine Corps" at 0700 on 26 June. The last Marine push netted 309 German prisoners and 23 machine guns, but cost the 3d Battalion another 260 casualties. Thus ended the largest and most important battle in Marine Corps history to that point in time.

It had been a costly five weeks at Belleau Wood for the 5th Regiment. Four hundred and ninety-three Marines were killed in action or later died of wounds, another 44 officers and 1,510 Marines were wounded and evacuated, 8 men were captured, and 54 were missing. The casualties the 3d Battalion suffered at Belleau Wood almost equaled its entire strength three weeks before. The other two battalions had been reduced to about half strength. One Marine would later be awarded the Medal of Honor, but many others had proved their bravery under fire. Of particular note was Lieutenant Colonel Feland's leadership. A contemporary account stated he was seen daily at the forward edge of the battle-field "encouraging the officers and men and improving the situation with wise suggestions" and "on several occasions [he took the place of] tired battalion commanders [so they could] rest."

The 5th Regiment was sent to a quiet sector near Villers-sur-Marne to recover. The 1st Battalion held lines at Crouttes and the 2d Battalion was at Villers. The 3d Battalion left Bois Gros Jean on 5 July and returned to Bois de Chaumont. The next day it completed its march and joined Headquarters Company and the 8th (Machine Gun) Company at Crouttes. Although trenches and machine-gun emplacements were dug and watches were stood, the main purposes of this respite were to rest, relax, and train replacements.

The 5th Regiment at Villers-Crouttes was a much different regiment than the one that entered Belleau Wood a scant month before. Many long-service veterans had fallen, and most of the survivors took on new responsibilities. Newly promoted Major General Harbord took over the 2d Division on 11 July. Colonel Buck Neville was promoted to brigadier general and replaced Harbord as commander of the 4th Brigade. Logan Feland was promoted to colonel and took command of the 5th Regiment when Neville departed. Of the three original battalion commanders, only Major Turrill retained his command. Almost all of the original company commanders were gone, and most companies mustered only one or two officers and a few senior NCOs. The fallen veterans had to be replaced. To fill the officer ranks it was decided to promote from within the enlisted ranks. Promising youngsters like Sergeant Silverthorn received field commissions and were soon commanding platoons, while some senior NCOs and warrant officers became temporary captains and were given companies.

Although the tired veterans of Belleau Wood were not aware of it at the time, their exploits made the Marines the toast of the town across the United States as a result of flamboyant Floyd Gibbons's vivid descriptions of the actions at Les Mares Farm and Belleau Wood, which appeared on the front pages of virtually every major American newspaper. The Marine Brigade became the first AEF unit mentioned by name when a sympathetic censor, believing Gibbons had been killed, let his "last dispatch" go out unedited. This publicity coup was a double-edged sword for the Marine Corps. It led to a dramatic upsurge in volunteers and made the previously unknown Corps famous, but it also garnered the long-lasting enmity of jealous army officers—including the commanding general of the AEF and a National Guard battery commander named Harry Truman who later became president. Accolades poured in from various headquarters, including telegrams from Marshal Foch and Generals Pershing, Degoutte, and Bundy. The 4th Brigade's heroism was officially recognized on 9 July when General Degoutte ordered that Belleau Wood should henceforth be referred to as the "Bois de la Brigade de Marine" on all maps and in official documents. The 5th Regiment was also cited in French army orders, an honor that resulted in a red and green fourragère battle streamer being added to the regimental colors and award of the Croix de Guerre to Colonel Neville. Official letters of appreciation were received from all the mayors of the Meaux District. Recognition of Marine bravery also came from the enemy. Rumor had it that captured German dispatches reported the Marines fought like *Teufelhunde,* the mythical canine guardians of the underworld, and the Marines thereafter adopted the nickname "Devil Dogs," an appellation that remains in use to this day.

Soissons

Dreams of liberty in Paris and the raucous celebration to follow did not pan out for most Marines. In fact, only a select few (chosen it was rumored for the appearance of their uniforms) were tapped to parade during the Fourth of July gala in the city of lights. When the expected two-week furloughs in "Gay Paree" did not materialize, the Marines had to be happy with daily swims, flirting with local maidens, and sampling local vintage *vin blanc and vin rouge.* According to Laurence Stallings, Pvt. Henry P. Lenert of the 3d Battalion, who captured an entire German machine-gun company using a daring bluff, was sent to Paris to be decorated. However, the brash Lenert decided he would rather see the sights, drink champagne, and meet some Parisian beauties, so he took what came to be known as "French Leave." Lenert returned to the 3d Battalion after his unauthorized absence escorted by military police and without the Croix de Guerre, but word of his noncombat exploits quickly spread through the ranks and made him a living legend among rank-and-file Marines.

The 5th Regiment, still part of the U.S. 2d Division, was assigned to Maj. Gen. Charles E. Mangin's XX Corps in the French Tenth Army after eleven blissful days in reserve. The XX Corps was scheduled to conduct an Allied counterattack to cut the vital railway junction near Soissons, northwest of Belleau Wood, as part of a general Allied offensive to reduce a German salient that bulged as far forward as the Marne River. This would isolate the bulk of the German forces and compel the rest to retire to the Hindenburg Line at the German border.

The first inkling most Marines had that they might be returning to the front occurred when they noticed what appeared to be ever increasing thunder claps and lightning flashes in the vicinity of Reims on Bastille Day. All liberties were canceled, and the Marines were told to stand by for further orders after Crouttes was shelled on the fifteenth. Companies were assembled in full marching order an hour after midnight, then waited in ranks for most of the day on 16 July. There was no noon chow because the mobile kitchen units had already departed for an unknown destination and iron rations were not authorized. By then it was obvious to even the lowest-ranking private that something big was afoot. This was confirmed when the first *camions* arrived. As more than one old salt remarked, "they ain't sending trucks for liberty parties." The 5th Regiment was headed back into action.

The 1st Battalion departed Saacy-sur-Marne at about 2000 and rode all night. The 2d Battalion left Villers at about 1600 and marched to Crouttes, where it loaded onto waiting trucks early that evening. The 3d Battalion left Citry at about 2000 and arrived at Morienval thirteen hours later. The Marines motored and marched generally west, then north, to the gigantic forest near Villers-Cotterêts. The 8th (Machine Gun) Company and the regimental combat trains joined the rest of the outfit at the assembly area near Taillefontaine at about 1300 on the seventeenth. There was no hot food, few rest stops, and no sleep to speak of during the march. The men were hungry, thirsty, and tired after being crammed into the tiny truck beds like sardines in a tin. This deprivation had an interesting side effect: The Marines were spoiling for a fight by the time they reached the Fôret de Retz.

The 2d Division was placed on XX Corps's right flank and assigned a narrow eight-mile sector that ran west to east in a mild dogleg from the Fôret de Retz to the Château-Thierry road. The French 12th Heavy Tank Groupement (a mix of thirty light and heavy tanks), a ten-plane French aviation squadron, and XX Corps artillery were earmarked to assist the 2d Division's advance. The 4th Brigade was on the 2d Division's left flank, tied in with the 1st Moroccan Division to the north (left) and the 3d Infantry Brigade to the south (right). The 5th Regiment would lead the assault with the 6th Regiment in support. There were three intermediate objectives: Verte Feuille Farm at the edge of the woods, Beaurepaire Farm on the Chaudun road, and Vierzy Ravine. The final objective was the high ground near the town of Tigny, which dominated the Château-Thierry road. The battlefield included a corner section of the Fôret de Retz and then became fairly open country dotted with strongly built stone farms, occasional villages, and several deep-wooded ravines. Waist-high wheat fields covered most of the attack zone.

The Marines met considerable misfortune while en route to the attack position. The approach march was so difficult that many veterans considered it harder than the actual fighting. Sheeting rain, crowded roads, and confusion over the location of jump-off positions delayed movement to the line of departure. The Marines spent the stormy night of 17–18 July trying to move through a jumble of stalled traffic, cursing humanity, and frightened horses. Most vehicles and artillery pieces were mired in the sticky mud covering the roadway. It was so dark that each Marine had to hold on to the man in front of him during most of the five-mile march, still some Marines got lost or were injured in the confusion. They arrived so late that the already tired units at the rear of the assault battalions had to double-time to get into position for the attack. As the 49th Company slid into its final positions on the far left flank, Lt. John Thomason ordered the passing men to "Fix Bayonets!"

The 1st and 2d Battalions were selected to lead the assault and the 3d Battalion was in support. Major Keyser's 2d Battalion was arrayed with the 18th, 43d, and 55th Companies on line from right to left, and the 51st Company was detailed to maintain liaison with the 9th Infantry on the right flank. Major Turrill's 1st Battalion was arrayed with the 66th and 17th Companies forward, the 49th serving as liaison, and the 67th in support. A German barrage hit while the Marines awaited the signal to move out, and the 1st Battalion's jump-off was briefly delayed as a result.

The American artillery barrage began just as the last Marines reached the line of departure. The tired and hungry men were given no time to rest or organize before platoon leaders were blowing their whistles and shouting "Forward!" at 0435. The assault forces were confused because the attack had been launched without proper notification or adequate preparation time. The 2d Battalion's 55th and 43d Companies were too far north as Zero hour approached. Captain Murray's 43d Company was able to recover in time to jump off, but Lieutenant Cooke's 55th Company was pinched out by the 1st Battalion's 66th Company and could not join the advance until about 0600.

The Marine lines moved forward through the darkness at the edge of the Fôret de Retz. They carefully stepped through barbed wire interlaced with thick underbrush before encountering vigorous opposition. German snipers fired from trees, but sharp-shooting Marines quickly eliminated them. Machine-gun positions dotted the woods so close-in fighting was required. Acting GySgt. Louis Cukela of the 66th Company crawled through intense enemy fire to outflank a German position, then cleared three machine-gun emplacements using rifle fire, his bayonet, and captured grenades. He later received the Medal of Honor for his actions.

Most resistance ceased when the French tanks clanked forward. (The defenders in the Fôret de Retz were less resolute than the ones at Belleau Wood.) Cries of *"Kamaraden"* soon echoed through the woods and several hundred Germans emerged with their hands held high. The rest of the enemy scurried over the dim skyline seeking shelter in nearby villages and tree lines. The advancing Marines cleared the woods before the sun was high and progressed rapidly across the rolling wheat and beet fields. The 2d Battalion, working closely with the French tanks, soon held Verte Feuille Farm. Conspicuous by his bravery was Babe Tharau, the hero of Les Mares Farm, who captured several enemy positions by himself. All intermediate objectives were in Marine hands by 0900 despite some fierce resistance in Capt. William Corbin's 51st Company zone and the loss of Captain Murray of the 43d Company.

In the 1st Battalion zone, Captain Hunt's 17th Company advanced on the left with Captain Crabbe's 66th and Capt. Frank M. Whitehead's 67th Companies to the right. Lieutenant Thomason's 49th Company liaison party hugged the division boundary, moving behind the 17th Company and maintaining contact with the Moroccans on the left.

At about 0800, Captains Platt and Yowell of the 3d Battalion led their companies (the 16th and 20th respectively) forward to join the attack. Each man carried three extra bandoliers of ammunition.

The 3d Battalion occupied reserve positions in the trench line at the jump-off point at about 0530, but was broken up to support other units by midmorning. Major Shearer parceled out all four of his line companies to the assault units or for support duties until his command was reduced to a single squad at Verte Feuille Farm and a platoon-sized provost detachment in the rear. Captain Yowell's 16th and Captain Platt's 20th Companies were attached to the 1st Battalion, and Lieutenant Knapp's 45th Company was attached to the 2d Battalion at 0800.

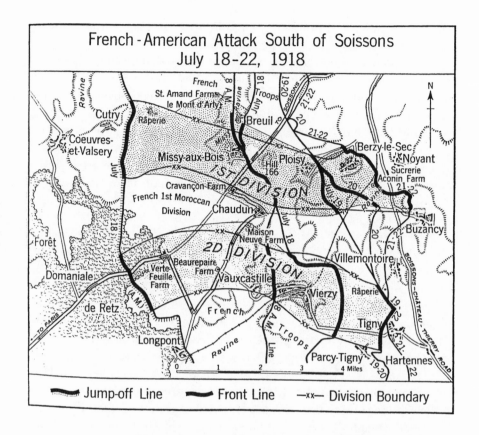

French - American Attack South of Soissons
July 18-22, 1918

Jump-off Line   Front Line   —xx— Division Boundary

The major enemy point of resistance for the 1st Battalion was near Chaudun. During the advance some Moroccans and a few Doughboys from the 18th Infantry Regiment strayed too far south. They became mixed with the Marines in the vicinity of Le Translon Farm. With no other Allied units visible to the north and intense fire coming from that direction, Captain Hunt elected to cross the division boundary. He led a bold forty-five-minute attack to carry Chaudun, then had his men occupy a trench line about a hundred yards southeast to wait for the rest of the assault force to catch up. The 66th and 67th Companies passed through and moved into the Vauxcastille Ravine that delineated the first objective and made contact with the 2d Battalion at about noon.

About an hour and a half later Captain Moseley's 47th Company was detailed to escort prisoners to the rear and return with ammunition. Major Shearer remained in charge of the provost detail guarding the division headquarters at Verte Feuille Farm until 0300 on 20 July, when that unit was dissolved. Shearer was then told to report back to the 5th Regiment at its assembly area in the Fôret de Retz.

Austrian-born Sgt. Matej Kocak of the 66th Company was separated from his unit during the fighting but advanced alone, uncovered by supporting fire, and destroyed a German machine-gun emplacement. That done, he rallied a lost Senegalese platoon from the 1st Moroccan Division and led a bayonet attack on additional enemy positions. Sergeant Kocak thus became the second Marine from the 66th Company to earn the Medal of Honor that day at Soissons. Lieutenant Thomason of the 49th Company led a small party forward to eliminate a machine-gun position and killed thirteen enemy gunners. Thomason, who was wounded in the process, was later awarded the Navy Cross.

The second attack of the day was directed at the town of Vierzy on the far right. Vierzy was a key objective, but it was strongly held and the Germans were firmly entrenched on the high ground surrounding it. Both American brigades and a French unit were slated to conduct the attack under the leadership of Brig. Gen. Hanson E. Ely, USA, the 3d Brigade commander. The 2d Battalion, 5th Regiment, was attached to the 9th Infantry Regiment for the attack on Vierzy. This came as a surprise because the Marines were hoping to rest and eat after capturing all of their objectives. This was not to be. Instead, Major Keyser received verbal instructions to attack at about 1650. He was to approach Vierzy from the northwest in conjunction with the Moroccans under the tactical control of the 3d Brigade. This late notification left Keyser little time to warn his units. He moved from Verte Feuille Farm to the ravine to notify his company commanders, but only three companies were in position when Zero hour arrived. The 18th, 43d, and 51st Companies, supported by tanks, moved down the ravine and went over the top on schedule. The 55th Company, which had not been warned of the impending attack until the last minute, followed in support.

The Americans moved out on time, but the French did not. The Doughboys were soon pinned down by heavy machine-gun fire. After that pocket of resistance was eliminated, the advance resumed until the 51st Company came under more heavy machine-gun fire about six hundred yards farther ahead. The 51st and 18th Companies and six tanks reduced the enemy positions. When the tanks withdrew through the Marine lines to rearm and refuel, they drew intense artillery fire. The results were tragic. The Marines suffered many casualties and four tanks were destroyed. This barrage mortally wounded doughty Captain Wass of the 18th Company. Dusk found the 2d Battalion once again under heavy fire from Maxim machine guns hidden in wheat fields to the front and sides, until the assault units were forced back. The Marines took cover in an old trench about two kilometers short of the objective and remained there until moving to new positions overlooking the main road in the early morning darkness the following day.

Major Turrill of the 1st Battalion did not receive his orders until 1715, less than fifteen minutes prior to the attack. While hastily leading a motley mixture of 150 1st Battalion Marines forward via Beaurepaire Farm and Vauxcastille, he met Capt. John Fay, who was bringing up the 8th Company's machine guns and ammunition, which had only recently arrived with the supply train. The machine gun company and the 1st Battalion pushed forward together in the dusk. The 1st Battalion, reinforced by the 16th and 20th Companies of the 3d Battalion and supported by American and French tanks, took about four-fifths of the town during a sharp fight. The 23d Infantry then moved in to finish the job. The 5th Regiment was firmly in possession of the ridge running from Chaudun to Vierzy when darkness closed in. By 2000, the Americans held the Vierzy Plateau but were done in by a full day's fighting and seventy-two hours without hot food or sleep. Colonel Feland moved his regimental command post to Vauxcastille that night.

The Marines had taken about four miles of enemy territory, captured numerous prisoners, and seized many enemy weapons and much equipment on 18 July. The next morning, regimental headquarters occupied a large tunnel near Vierzy. Captain DeCarre was ordered to bring up mobile kitchen units, the supply train, and men previously held out of the fighting. (After Belleau Wood the Marines adopted the British practice of holding 10 percent of each company back to form an experienced cadre in case of heavy losses or to be used as an immediately available emergency reserve.) Low-flying German aircraft repeatedly strafed this column during its move forward. This was no surprise because enemy aircraft had been active throughout the battle despite losing two of their number to Marine fire.

The 6th Marine Regiment took over the attack on the nineteenth. It gained about a mile against heavy resistance, withstood two counterattacks, and forced the Germans to withdraw. The 5th Regiment made no advance that morning, but was intermittently bombed and strafed. Major Turrill and a reconnaissance party moved into the tunnel occupied by the 5th Regiment headquarters during the afternoon. While there, he was informed the rest of the 1st Battalion was being shelled and bombed so he ordered Captain Hamilton, his second in command, to bring the rest of the battalion to the tunnel. This was accomplished before dark without loss. Major Keyser was ordered to move the 2d Battalion into the line between the French and the 6th Regiment that night and was hit by enemy high explosive and gas shells.

The regiment began pulling back the next day. The 8th (Machine Gun) Company was relieved in place and returned to the regimental assembly area inside the Fôret de Retz on the nineteenth. The 1st Battalion pulled back to the assembly area at about 0200 on the twentieth. The French relieved the 2d Battalion at about 0400, and that unit moved back into the assembly area as well. When the reserve unit arrived at the assembly area it was split up and the Marines returned to their parent units. The 5th Regiment began moving to an intermediate rest area on 21 July. The last units arrived at Silly-le-Longue five days later. The 2d Division was then reassigned to the French Eighth Army and was ordered to move to the vicinity of Nancy (about 175 miles east of Paris) for replenishment, rest, and reorganization on 29 July. The Marines spent four days at Silly-le-Longue cleaning up and conducting light drill before boarding trains for Nancy on the thirty-first.

The Soissons Offensive pushed the Germans back from the Marne River to the Vesle River and forced them to begin a general withdrawal. Some historians consider this victory the turning point in the war. The 5th Regiment lost 5 officers and 38 enlisted men killed, 18 officers and 360 enlisted men wounded, and 34 enlisted men missing in a little more than forty-eight hours of combat. Company commanders were particularly hard hit with Captain Wass (18th) dead and Captains Crabbe (66th), Hunt (17th), and Murray (67th), and Lieutenant Cooke (55th) wounded and evacuated.

The Marbache Sector

Brigadier General (later Major General Commandant) John A. Lejeune briefly commanded the 4th Brigade from 26–29 July 1918. On the latter date he became the commanding general of the 2d Division when Major General Harbord departed to take over the troubled AEF Service of Supply. Harbord's good nature and excellent organizational skills served him well, and by all accounts his was a very successful tenure. He subsequently put these traits to good use as the chief executive officer of the Radio Corporation of America (RCA) after leaving the army. General Lejeune and Colonel Neville were belatedly notified they had been respectively promoted to major general and brigadier general to date from 1 July. Both men thereafter continued to command the same units (the 2d Division and 4th Brigade) until the Armistice.

The 5th Regiment began to depart on a two-day railway journey of more than a hundred miles to the Marbache sector in the vicinity of Nancy in the Moselle Valley on 31 July. This long-distance move was actually part of a grand deception to draw German attention away from the site of the next big push: Saint-Mihiel. Allied intelligence was well aware the German high command considered the Marines to be "shock troops," so enemy intelligence officers closely monitored Marine movements because they were certain the American Devil Dogs would spearhead any new Allied offensive.

Nancy was a relatively quiet sector. The Regimental Field and Staff, Headquarters Company, Supply Company, and 1st Battalion were located at Villers-les-Nancy; the 2d Battalion was at Vandoevre; and the 3d Battalion and 8th (Machine Gun) Company were at Heilcourt. Each of these was on the outskirts of Nancy. The 5th Regiment was finally granted a true rest period and morale soared. Many deserving men were granted liberty and were allowed to sightsee and relax in the town. Assistant Secretary of the Navy Franklin D. Roosevelt inspected the Marines on 5 August. The future president asked General Neville if there was anything he could do to assist the Marines. Buck Neville replied that it was difficult to tell Marines from the 3d Brigade soldiers because both units wore the same uniforms, and he asked that enlisted Marines be allowed to wear the Marine Corps' eagle, globe, and anchor emblem. Roosevelt immediately agreed and authorized the Marines to obtain the collar devices immediately. Ironically, the emblems procured were stamped on round buttons very similar to army collar devices rather than the distinctive insignia discussed by Roosevelt and Neville so recognition remained a problem, as did the fact most Marines did not receive them until after the Armistice. Previously, the unofficial practice of wearing eagle, globe, and anchor devices on field hats was strictly against army regulations, but most Marine officers turned a blind eye when enlisted men did so.

Colonel Feland continued to command the 5th Regiment. Captain George K. Shuler (until 8 August) and Captain Fay (transferred from the 8th Company) served successively as regimental adjutant. First Lieutenant James A. Nelms succeeded Captain Fay as commander of the 8th

Company. Recently returned Lieutenant Colonel Wise and Major Shearer respectively commanded the 2d and 3d Battalions. Major Turrill was promoted to lieutenant colonel on 16 August and temporarily turned over the 1st Battalion to Capt. Raymond F. Dirksen, who was in charge until Lt. Col. Arthur J. O'Leary assumed command on 28 August. Lieutenant Colonel Wise was replaced by Maj. Harold L. Parsons as commander of the 2d Battalion on 19 August, and transferred to an army division for the duration.

The Marbache sector at Pont-à-Mousson was a quiet but vital area that protected the major railways and highways between Nancy and Metz. The Marines began relieving the French 64th Division on 6 August and completed this task on the ninth. The 2d Battalion manned forward positions along the Moselle River on the outskirts of Pont-à-Mousson, the 1st Battalion was in the position of resistance, and the 3d Battalion was in support behind the second position.

Upon arrival, Fritz Wise arrayed the 18th, 55th, and 43d Companies across the front and placed the 51st Company in reserve on Mousson Hill. A German raiding party targeted these positions on the night of the eighth. The German presence was announced by a rather loud explosion that resulted when a bangalore torpedo exploded prematurely and scattered the unlucky raiders. As the Germans fled the storm of Marine machine-gun and rifle fire unleashed after the explosion, their own artillery hit them. Unfortunately, the same fire caught the 18th and 55th Companies. The German barrage blew up an ammunition dump and inflicted several casualties, including one man killed. No other action was encountered by Marine patrols and the sector was so quiet that local farmers tended their fields without concern. General Lejuene ordered the 5th Regiment relieved of responsibility for Marbache on 14 August. All movements had to be made at night, however, so the relief took two days. The regiment lost two men killed and seven men wounded while in the Marbache sector. One of those men was the beloved GySgt. Babe Tharau, his life cut short in a so-called quiet sector by flying stone shaken loose during a fierce enemy bombardment. In the words of his company commander and good friend, Lem Shepherd, "Babe's death was mourned by all."

The 5th Regiment proceeded to Govillers between Toul and Nancy where the Camp Bois L'Eveque training area was made available so the Marines could prepare for the next battle. Lieutenant Colonel Turrill, now the regimental second in command, established and supervised a rigorous and effective training program. Line battalions spent three to five days at the rifle range honing their marksmanship skills. Additional weapons training included grenade throwing, automatic-rifle operations, and combat-firing techniques. The rest of the time was devoted to practicing offensive tactics, and each battalion was able to conduct field exercises. Headquarters Company's One-Pounder and Bomber Sections alternated days at the range, the Pioneer Section trained to construct and destroy barbed-wire obstacles, and the Signal Section attended technical school at Colombey-le-Belle. A final regimental review and awards ceremony was held on 25 August, then it was time to move back up once again.

Saint-Mihiel

The first days of September were devoted to moving to the Saint-Mihiel sector. Regimental Field Order No. 62 was issued on the second. It directed the 5th Regiment to move to Maron the first day and Aingeray the second day. The distance was covered in easy stages. Headquarters and the 1st Battalion left Govillers at 2100 on 2 September and marched until 0420 the next morning. From there they continued on to the Bois Ropage near Aingeray and stayed at that designated rest area until the ninth. The 3d Battalion also left on the second and arrived at Limey on the tenth. The 2d Battalion departed on 4 September and reached its destination six days later. Major Robert E. Messersmith replaced Major Parsons as 2d Battalion commander on the eleventh. The 8th (Machine Gun) Company moved into its reserve positions on the sixth. Colonel Feland opened the regimental command post at 1500 on the tenth at Manoncourt. The last elements of Headquarters Company were in place the next morning. The 3d Battalion received 204 replacements as it moved into its support positions. The 2d Battalion moved into its attack position on the night of the eleventh.

The Saint-Mihiel Offensive was the AEF's first independent operation. Its purpose was to reduce a salient that had been a constant thorn in the French side since the early days of the war. The 2d Division, as part of I Corps, was to advance by a series of rushes along the Remenauville-Limey axis to capture Thiaucourt and the Jaulny-Xammes Line within two days. The first day's attack would jump off from trench lines near Limey, seize the Bois de Heiche, and then continue to the northern edge of the Bois du Fey. The final objective was Thiaucourt. Zero hour was set for 0500

Plan of Attack of First Army, September 12, 1918

Legend:
- ┄┄┄ Jump-off Line Sept. 12 (A.M.)
- ▬▬▬ Front Line Actually Reached
- —xxxx— Army Boundary
- —xxx— Corps Boundary
- Numerals indicate divisions   Arrows indicate direction and weight of attacks

on 12 September. The 2d Division's 3d Brigade would move out after a four-hour preparatory barrage and advance behind a rolling barrage moving forward one hundred yards every four minutes. The 4th Brigade was in support and would follow behind the 3d Brigade with the 5th Regiment moving up on the right in a column of battalions.

The promised barrage began promptly at 0100. The regulars in the 3d Brigade stepped off on schedule at 0500 and the Marines followed at about 0540. Little opposition was encountered by the first wave. The 3d Battalion led the regimental line forward through the barbed wire and advanced against virtually no resistance because the 9th Infantry was very thorough as it cleaned out enemy strong points. The 16th and 20th Companies were in the vanguard, with the 45th and 47th in support. The day's intermediate objectives fell like a row of toppling dominoes; Remenauville was taken by 0900, the Bois du Fey was occupied by

1230, and Thiaucourt was captured at 1500. The attack timetable was speeded up and the army objective of Jaulny fell at 1600. Evening found the 3d Battalion just east of Thiaucourt and the 2d Battalion was just north of Bois de Heiche. The assault forces covered nine kilometers and the army objective was taken a day early. The 1st Battalion's 16th and 20th Companies were ordered to move up and were attached to the 9th Infantry in anticipation of an enemy counterattack. The expected attack never developed, so the companies rejoined their parent battalion at about 2100.

The 5th Regiment was to relieve the 9th Infantry before midnight on the thirteenth. The 2d Battalion moved into the lines and replaced elements of the 9th Infantry at the Bois du Fey at 1910. The 1st Battalion moved north of Jaulny and occupied defensive positions overlooking the Rupt de Mad. Not long after the 2d Battalion moved into its new positions, Major Messersmith was ordered to send patrols forward and establish a strong combat outpost line in the Bois de Hailbat. The 45th and 47th Companies moved up opposite banks of the river until they made contact with the 3d Battalion, 6th Regiment. They encountered no enemy but had some difficulty negotiating the wire obstacles strewn across their paths. These Marines moved ahead of the 6th Regiment's lines in small groups to occupy the forward edge of the Bois de Montagne. The area was plastered by an enemy barrage and hit by a counterattack on the evening of the fourteenth, but Captain Moseley's 47th Company repelled the Germans with deadly rifle and machine-gun fire.

The 1st and 2d Battalions held these positions for the next few days. The 3d Battalion was broken up and its units were attached piecemeal to the 1st and 2d Battalions. There were no further enemy ground attacks, but all units were strafed by enemy airplanes and subjected to intermittent artillery fire. The 2d Battalion brought down a Boche aircraft on the fourteenth, and a 37mm gun attached to the 1st Battalion scored eight direct hits on enemy positions at a range of more than a thousand yards. The 77th Division's 309th Infantry Regiment relieved the 5th Regiment on the night of 15–16 September. The great Saint-Mihiel Offensive was over for the 5th Regiment. Its losses in four days of fighting were twenty-three killed and 113 wounded.

The Marines moved into the Bois de Heiche to consolidate at noon on the sixteenth, then marched to Minorville the next day. From there, the 5th Regiment moved to a training area near Toul. Newly promoted Maj. George Hamilton replaced Lieutenant Colonel O'Leary as commander of the 1st Battalion on 22 September. The regiment trained at Dom Germain as an unending stream of Allied aircraft droned overhead, artillery fire flashed over the horizon, and the dim sound of gunfire echoed in the background from 25–28 September.

Blanc Mont

The final American campaign of World War I included two major combat operations by the 5th Regiment: the Battle of Blanc Mont Ridge and crossing the Meuse River on the eve of the Armistice. Blanc Mont was the most significant of these actions because it cracked the Hindenburg Line wide open and included the 5th Regiment's single most costly day of fighting in France. Crossing the Meuse was the regiment's final act of the Great War.

Blanc Mont, located in the Champagne sector, was considered so important an objective that the best American unit, the 2d Division, was pulled out of the First Army and loaned to the French Fourth Army to take it during a massive Allied offensive to clear out the Germans located on the banks of the Meuse River south of Sedan and in the Argonne Forest. On 26 September, Maj. Gen. Henri Gouraud—a French colonial infantryman commanding the Fourth Army—asked General Lejeune to move his division forward from Toul to capture the vital high ground north of Somme-Py known as Blanc Mont Ridge.

The 5th Regiment boarded *camions* on the twenty-ninth and proceeded to the town of Suippes in the Champagne sector. The Marines found the area dark and foreboding, an eerie wasteland created by four years of warfare. The once-lush vineyards had long since disappeared, and most of the fertile topsoil had been blown away by incessant bombardment to reveal a chalky limestone subsurface that gave Blanc Mont ("White Mountain") its name. Blanc Mont (which should not be confused with towering Mont Blanc in southern France) was a 210-meter-high hill on a massif about twenty-five miles from the city of Reims, close enough that its famous cathedral spires could be spotted from the top of White Mountain. The Germans had occupied this position since 1914, and by the late summer of 1918 it was a defensive masterpiece that had broken many a French attack. German fortifications included intricate, well-constructed fighting trenches and concrete emplacements protected by barbed wire. Of particular importance to the Marines were a series of interlaced trenches on the front of the ridge. These were known as the Krefeld, Prussian, Essen, and Elbe trenches. The forward area was defended by the German 51st Division, with the 200th Division in reserve. The Essen Hook was a particularly worrisome center of resistance formed by a curved section of elevated trench studded with pillboxes and bunkers. Although the Essen Hook was inside the French zone of action, fires from there could easily enfilade the Marine zone and threaten the American advance. Thus, the success of the American advance would depend upon the ability of the French to keep pace with the Marines and secure their left flank.

Major Earl H. "Pete" Ellis, the 2d Division's brilliant adjutant, devised a complex attack plan. It called for General Lejeune to split the 2d Division during the initial assault in order to bypass a German stronghold known as "Viper Woods." The Marine Brigade on the left would attack due north to capture most of the western section of Blanc Mont Ridge while the 3d Brigade, attacking diagonally from the right, would move behind Viper Woods to capture the eastern ridge. The French would come in from the left flank to seize Blanc Mont's far western slope. This done, the 2d Division main attack would then continue north to capture the town of Saint-Étienne-à-Arnes. The Marine Brigade would attack in column with the 6th Regiment leading the assault and the 5th Regiment in support during the first phase. The regiments would reverse that order of march for the second phase. Colonel Feland planned to move his regiment forward in a column of battalions, leapfrogging them ahead as the attack progressed. The 8th (Machine Gun) Company reinforced the 1st Battalion, the 23d (Machine Gun) Company reinforced the 2d Battalion, and the 77th (Machine Gun) Company reinforced the 3d Battalion.

The 5th Regiment had to conduct some preliminary operations to seize the assigned jump-off line. Major Hamilton's 1st Battalion, Major Messersmith's 2d Battalion, and Lieutenant Nelms's 8th (Machine Gun) Company moved up to Somme-Py on the night of 1–2 October and relieved the French 61st Division. It was a difficult relief conducted on a dark, rainy night in unfamiliar terrain without prior reconnaissance or experienced guides. Once the Marines were in place, the 1st Battalion was assigned to the forward line, the 2d Battalion was in support, and Maj. Henry Larsen's 3d Battalion remained in reserve south of Somme-Py.

The main attack went off as scheduled on the third. The 6th Regiment moved out at 0550 after a short bombardment to capture its portion of

Blanc Mont (Hill 210). The Marines closely followed a rolling barrage and were supported by twenty-four French light tanks. The 2d Battalion went over the top to lead the 5th Regiment advance after the last elements of the 6th Regiment passed by. The 3d Battalion and the 1st Battalion followed, maintaining five-hundred-yard intervals. There was little opposition until the attackers were raked by fire from the Essen Hook. Luckily, this fire was from relatively long range, so the advance continued unchecked. The 2d Battalion guided on the Somme-Py railway line to protect the division left boundary. Captain David T. Jackson's 18th and Capt. James Keeley's 51st Companies moved ahead on the left and right respectively. They were followed by Capt. DeWitt Peck's 55th and Capt. Charley Dunbeck's 43d Companies. The 3d Battalion followed behind the 2d, and the 1st Battalion hugged the 2d Division's left boundary in an effort to maintain contact with the French.

The attack ran into trouble almost immediately. The French failed to carry the Essen Hook, so this difficult assignment was given to the 17th Company. Captain Hunt used one of Headquarters Company's one-pounders, some heavy machine guns from the 23d Company, and a couple of French tanks to take out several Maxim guns at about 0830. The Marines then made an enveloping attack and cleaned out the remaining positions in close combat. This difficult work was done before 1100, and more than a hundred enemy prisoners of war were turned over to the French. Unfortunately, the Germans launched a determined counterattack and recaptured the position. This loss disrupted the 4th Brigade's scheme of maneuver and threatened the Marines' left flank by mid-afternoon. The 6th Regiment held the lower slopes of Blanc Mont by 1030, but was under heavy fire and needed support. Therefore, at about 1300, Colonel Feland was ordered to pass his regiment through, continue the attack, and take Saint-Étienne Heights that evening.

However, the French failure at the Essen Hook considerably affected the 5th Regiment's ability to carry out this order. Colonel Feland had been forced to deploy his battalions on a line facing west to cover the gigantic gap between the rapidly advancing American units and the static French line. The 2d Battalion became so strung out that the 51st and 55th Companies lost touch with headquarters. The 1st Battalion moved forward but soon had to swing left to help fill the gap as well. The 3d Battalion, in echelon to the left rear, took up support positions in the Passau and Augsburg lines. Communications thus were tenuous at best. Colonel Feland therefore had to delay the attack toward Saint-Étienne

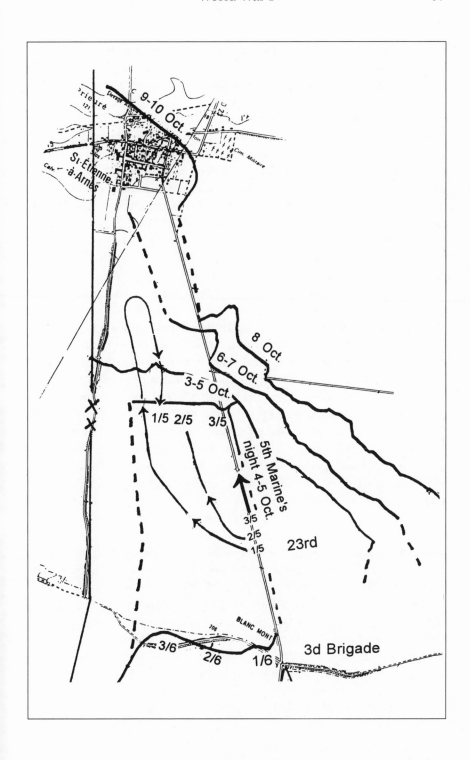

until his subordinate units could disengage and reorganize. He set Zero hour for 0600.

The next day, 4 October 1918, was fated to become "the bitterest day in the history of the 5th Regiment in France" according to a contemporary official history. The Marines were pounded by shellfire as they moved to the jump-off line and mounted the attack across open ground without artillery or tank support. It progressed without resistance for a couple of kilometers, but the Marines were actually moving into a clever trap. They drove only a narrow wedge into the German lines before being stopped cold by fire from three sides: Ludwig's Rucken (sometimes called Saint-Étienne Heights) to the front, Blanc Mont Ridge to the left rear, and Petersburg Hill on the left flank.

Machine-gun fire and a mix of high-explosive and gas shells simultaneously hit the assault force. Trapped in a cross fire coming from three sides, Major Larsen was unable to move his men forward or back. Boxed in and cut off, he called for help as soon as his battered battalion was able to creep back and take shelter in some scrub pines behind a low ridge. The 2d Battalion tried to help, but it too was soon reeling under fire and was forced to give ground. Things were so bad that the battalion commander and at least one company commander were in the process of falling back when George Hamilton arrived on the scene. He led the 1st Battalion—still on the far left flank—to the rescue. Major Hamilton and Lieutenant Nelms shored up the 2d Battalion's lines, then Captain Hunt's 17th Company cleared a lane through the German lines to the besieged battalions by midafternoon. This action, conducted under withering enemy fire, stabilized the front line and stopped a potential disaster.

Still, things were not going well and casualties were high. All three battalions were reduced to less than half strength as they manned a thin line in a small wooded rectangle known as "the Box," which was under constant enemy fire as night fell. A German attack was repulsed with great difficulty before elements of the 6th Regiment were able to come forward. All of the 3d Battalion company commanders (Yowell, Platt, Davies, and Quigley) were out of action. Among the other wounded was Second Lieutenant Silverthorn, who took a bullet in the heel. Fifty-one-year-old 1st Lt. Henry Hulbert, the Medal of Honor holder for actions in Samoa, was killed bringing supplies forward. A second Medal of Honor man, Sgt. Matej Kocak, who had earned his at Soissons, was also killed that day. Captain Whitehead of the 67th Company went down, and

Capt. Francis S. Kieren became the new company commander. Captain Charley Dunbeck, once again in command of the 43d Company after being bayoneted and shot in both legs at Belleau Wood, was shot in the head and had to be dragged to safety. Corporal William E. Campbell, a clerk in the 43d Company, left the relative safety of the command post to assist the wounded and fought off a German attack despite suffering two wounds.

A German counterattack punched through the newly established but thinly held Marine lines at about 2000. It was repelled by "Lyng's Comanches," a thirty-man reserve force created on the spur of the moment by GySgt. Arthur S. Lyng and Sgt. Robert Stover of the 49th Company. First Lieutenant Francis J. Kelly's 66th Company of the 1st Battalion later reinforced this small force. Kelly earlier had replaced Captain Dirksen, who had been gassed and evacuated. Major Hamilton took command of all the survivors and tried to sort out the thoroughly mixed-up units under heavy fire. Somehow he got a headcount, and soon thereafter reported there were not enough men left to conduct the attack scheduled for the following morning. Only about a hundred of the more than four hundred men who entered the Box that morning were still in action that night. Faced with difficult circumstances, General Neville turned the attack mission over to the 6th Regiment, but Hamilton was ordered to hold his ground at all costs.

Dawn on 5 October revealed a panorama of abandoned German equipment, including several machine guns and field pieces. These items served as mute testimony to the effectiveness of the Marine defense, but the 5th Regiment was so reduced in strength that it was no longer combat effective. John Thomason recalled that on 6 October the 49th Company's two dozen survivors received enough rations to feed the 234 men who had jumped off three days earlier. The hungry Marines ate their fill of foul-tasting Monkey Meat and sour bread, and then put the remaining ration boxes to use as a protective bulwark. Writing about the 5th Regiment's time at Blanc Mont after the war, Thomason concluded, "We were shot to pieces in the Champagne Sector" and lamented that "war was no longer an adventure" after that.

Captain David T. Jackson's 18th Company was temporarily attached to the 23d Infantry at 1000 on the fifth, but the rest of the regiment pulled back to defensive positions on Blanc Mont Ridge and remained there until relieved by the U.S. 36th Division on the ninth. The Marines suffered numerous casualties from enemy artillery fire during the four days they occupied those positions. Among the wounded was Lt. Lem Shepard, commander of the 55th Company. He received his third wound stripe in as many months and was evacuated. It was his last combat action in France, although he would later return to the 5th Regiment in Germany after the Armistice.

Marshal Henri Pétain called Blanc Mont "the greatest single achievement of the 1918 campaign" in a congratulatory message. The 5th Regiment eventually received its third citation from the French army for its actions there. Blanc Mont was, however, a costly victory. The 4th Brigade suffered 726 killed and more than 3,500 wounded between 2 and 10 October. The 5th Regiment's losses for that period were 61 officers and 1,059 enlisted men killed or wounded—about 60 percent of its strength.

Crossing the Meuse

The battered 5th Regiment moved south to a rest area around Sousain, about fifteen miles from the front. There it absorbed several replacement drafts and rested before moving farther south to Chalons on 14 October. The Marines moved to Leffincourt five days later. After several false starts and some tiring countermarches, General Neville was informed the 4th Brigade would be detached from the French Fourth Army and reassigned to the 2d Division to spearhead an attack by the U.S. First Army. The target was the German V Corps, which was to be pushed out of its fortifications and forced back across the Meuse River. A factor surmised by a few armchair strategists, but viewed as a pipedream by most frontline veterans, was that crossing the Meuse River would be the 5th Regiment's final combat action of the Great War.

The 4th Brigade launched its attack from Buzancy on 1 November. Resistance was light as each of the 5th Regiment's battalions took its turn leading the advance. Major Hamilton's 1st Battalion was first in the line of march, followed by Captain Dunbeck's 2d and Major Larsen's 3d Battalions. The attackers moved out promptly at 0530 after a two-hour barrage with Capt. Francis Fisk's 49th and Lt. Robert Blake's 66th Companies leading the assault and Captain Hunt's 17th and Capt. Harry K. Cochran's 67th Companies in support. The artillery did a superb job, so few enemy machine guns were encountered. Hand grenades and automatic-rifle fire quickly dispatched those that were left. Unfortunately, Captain Cochran was cut down leading an attack. Popular and well-respected Capt. Frank Whitehead, who had recovered from the wounds he suffered at Blanc Mont, replaced Cochran. The twin towns of Landres and Saint-Georges were reduced to rubble and no enemy were encountered there.

The 2d Battalion assumed the point at about 0810. The Marines encountered some stiff fighting at Landreville. One particularly stubborn position was located inside a château where the Germans used a Red Cross insignia to lure the Marines close before opening up with hidden Maxim guns. The bloody fighting there ended after about a hundred of the enemy surrendered; a like number were later found dead. Captain Charley Dunbeck, healed from his head wound at Blanc Mont, was now commanding the 2d Battalion by virtue of being the battalion's senior surviving officer. Dunbeck sent army 1st Lt. Charles D. Baylis's 55th Company on a flank attack to clear Hill 299. Thirty machine guns, two eight-inch guns, twelve howitzers, and several trench mortars were captured when the position was cleared at about 1130. Major Larsen's 3d Battalion then took over the lead and pushed forward to Hill 300. The 3d Battalion encountered little resistance, but captured six artillery pieces and 112 prisoners along the way. Captain John R. Foster's 18th Company was detached from the 2d Battalion and placed under Major Larsen's control to bridge a huge gap that had opened between the Marines and the U.S. 89th Division. During the next two days the entire 2d Battalion was attached to the 9th Infantry, and the rest of the 5th Regiment was in support of the 3d Brigade. Captain Nathaniel H. Massie, commanding the 43d Company, was gassed and evacuated on 4 November, but he returned to serve as the 2d Battalion second in command for the Meuse River crossing. Captain Gilder D. Jackson Jr. took his place in the line. The 5th Regiment was reunited on the fifth when it took over positions in the front lines.

Strong reconnaissance patrols moved ahead of the general advance to scout the Meuse River. General Lejeune wanted to cross that barrier at two points about five miles apart. One point was near Mouzon and the other was at Letanne. Unfortunately, the Germans had destroyed or removed all bridges across the Meuse in the designated areas and were keeping a close watch on all likely crossing areas. However, the German side of the river was not fortified, and Lejeune believed it was held by only skeleton units of the German 31st and 88th Divisions, which could be easily reduced by artillery fire and then quickly overcome once the Marines were on the far shore. Later events proved this estimate to be somewhat optimistic.

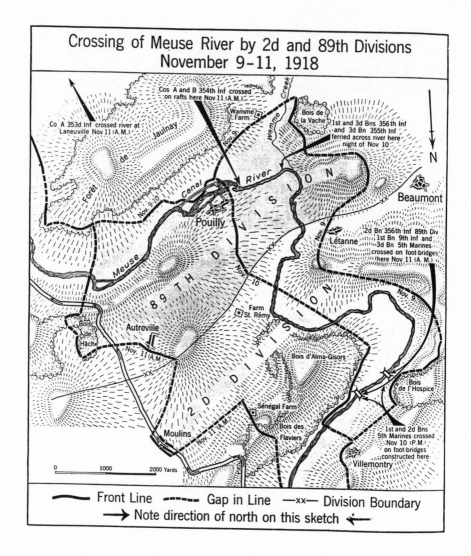

Crossing of Meuse River by 2d and 89th Divisions
November 9–11, 1918

It was originally planned to cross the Meuse on the night of 9–10 November, but difficulty obtaining bridge-building materials delayed the crossing until the next day. The 6th Regiment, reinforced by the 3d Battalion, 5th Regiment, was slated to make the main crossing at Mouzon. The rest of the 5th Regiment, attacking in conjunction with a battalion from the U.S. 89th Infantry Division, would cross near La Sartelle Farm just north of Letanne. The 17th Artillery Regiment of the 2d Artillery Brigade and the 8th, 77th, and 23d (Machine Gun) Companies would provide fire support. The Marine assault units were to rapidly cross the river in order to secure a bridgehead by taking the Bois de Flaviers and linking up near Mouzon. The army unit would capture Alma-Gisors Hill and then drive east to link up with other army units.

Major George Hamilton commanded the Letanne assault force, which consisted of Capt. Roy Hunt's 1st Battalion and Capt. Charley Dunbeck's 2d Battalion. Hamilton issued his orders at about 1700 on the tenth. The crossing was supposed to be a supporting attack to draw enemy attention away from the main crossings. As things turned out, however, it became the main attack. Hamilton wanted his Marines to cross over the northernmost bridge with the 2d Battalion in the lead and the 1st Battalion in support. The army battalion would use the southern bridge and then advance to link up with army units crossing the Meuse near Pouilly. The assault would be launched under the cover of darkness after an hour-long artillery preparation. This plan, however, had to be changed. When the designated army unit failed to show up, Hunt's battalion was pressed into service to lead the assault across the southern bridge.

The two Marine operations had mixed results: One was successful; the other was not. Regardless, it was a miserable night for everyone. Freezing rain pelted the Marines as they moved forward. Heavy enemy artillery and accurate machine-gun fire at Mouzon kept the bridges from being built so that the attack was called off at dawn on the eleventh. The 3d Battalion returned to the Bois du Fond, where Major Larsen learned the Armistice had been signed and was to go into effect later that day.

At Letanne, Major Hamilton ordered his "supporting" attack to begin at about 2130. Captain Charley Dunbeck dismissed rumors of a cease-fire. He told his men, "I am going across that river, and I expect you to go with me." German artillery and machine-gun fire churned up the west bank and disrupted the Marine advance. A thick fog and the moonless night concealed the Marines' movements and minimized the effectiveness of enemy flares, but John Thomason recalled the route to the river was still lined with dead and wounded engineers.

The ink-black darkness made movement across the flimsy bridges at Letanne difficult. The 1st Battalion crossed the southern footbridge (a grandiose term for what was actually little more than some floating drums strung together by unevenly spaced duckboards) over the Meuse despite heavy casualties. Hamilton could only muster about a hundred men on the far side and only one machine gun of the 23d Company was in action. The undaunted major quickly organized the survivors into a provisional company and then led them toward a three-tier machine-gun emplacement dug into the side of Alma-Gisors Hill. Eventually, about three hundred Doughboys from the 89th Division's 356th Infantry and a hundred or so Leathernecks from the 8th (Machine Gun) Company made it across to bring Hamilton's force up to about six hundred men just before dawn.

The 2d Battalion's bridge was temporarily put out of action just after Captain Dunbeck's lead elements got across. This interrupted the northern crossing for almost two hours and fragmented the 2d Battalion. Captain Sam Cumming, the senior officer on the west bank, was forced to hold the rest of the 2d Battalion on the far side of the river until the engineers could repair the damaged span. The 51st, 43d, and 55th Companies finally made it across at about 2330. The number of Marines at that site was about two hundred. Unfortunately, Captain Cumming was unable to locate his battalion commander because Dunbeck and part of the 2d Battalion had already joined Hamilton's assault force to the south. Cumming, acting on his own initiative, decided to lead the bulk of the 2d Battalion downriver to make the planned linkup with the 6th Regiment. It was a tough fight. Captain Cumming personally took out a key machine-gun position along the way, but only two officers and a handful of enlisted men were still standing when the 2d Battalion reached its objective.

As the first rays of light began to filter through the open door of his command post, General Lejeune was told of a radio report that hostilities would end at 1100, less than five hours away. He was officially informed of the impending cease-fire via a dispatch from Marshal Ferdinand Foch at 0845. Lejeune immediately ordered Colonel Feland to expedite getting the word to Major Hamilton. This was not easy because the 1st Battalion's command post was at Senegal Farm on the far side of the Meuse. By midmorning, the 49th and 67th Companies were entrenched atop the ridge and the 66th was already on the outskirts of Moulins. Concurrently, most of the 2d Battalion was pushing toward Bellefontaine. This force included two companies: Captain Jackson's 43d and 1st Lt. Sydney Thayer Jr.'s 55th. Captain Cumming's 51st Company held an isolated position at Mouzon, vainly awaiting the arrival of the 6th Regiment. There was one final burst of artillery fire just before 1100, and then the front suddenly began to quiet. Major Hamilton's Marines had not yet received word of the Armistice and continued to engage the enemy. Captain Hunt was finally informed of the Armistice at about 1145, but Captain Cumming remained unaware of the cease-fire until the enemy notified him about three hours later. Luckily, no casualties were suffered after 1100, but the last night of the war had been a costly one. The 5th Regiment lost thirty-one killed and 148 wounded while crossing the Meuse in the final hours before the cease-fire.

In his final report, General Lejeune commented: "In the face of heavy artillery and withering machine gun fire, the 2d Engineers threw two footbridges across the Meuse, and the 1st and 2d Battalions of the 5th Marines crossed resolutely and unflinchingly to the east bank and carried out their mission." The 2d Division report claimed that "Heroic deeds were done by heroic men" during the closing hours of the war. General Pershing's report noted that the Americans had forced a crossing of the Meuse east of Beaumont and gained the commanding heights that completed control of the Meuse line. General Lejeune was privately less than enthusiastic about the last night of the war when he wrote to his wife: "We fought our last battle . . . it was pitiful for men to go to their death on the eve of peace."

The 1st and 2d Battalions dug in where they were but remained ready for action after receiving the cease-fire order. The 3d Battalion and regimental headquarters crossed the Meuse later that evening. The cease-fire announcement evoked a variety of reactions. In some places both sides joined in jubilation by sharing drinks and handshakes; in other areas only an eerie stillness marked the end of the bloodiest war in history. Most Marines simply acknowledged the end by lighting previously forbidden bonfires to dry their soaked clothing and warm their chilled bodies for the first time in days. All men on both sides, except those on watch, soon fell into an exhausted sleep. Losses during the final days of the World War had been heavy. The 5th Regiment suffered 125 dead, 415 wounded, and 90 missing (most of them presumed drowned while crossing the river) after 1 November.

Watch on the Rhine

A new formation, the U.S. Third ("Occupation") Army, was created to occupy a sector between Luxembourg and the Rhine River near the German town of Koblenz. The 2d Division was one of the American units ordered to move into Germany for occupation duty. The 5th Regiment was relieved of its responsibility for defending the Meuse at 1100 on 14 November. The 1st and 2d Battalions then marched to Pouilly, and the 3d Battalion went to Letanne for a brief rest prior to the march into German territory. It must be remembered that the Armistice was only a temporary cease-fire and no peace treaty or formal surrender had yet been signed, so although the German army had been defeated in France, some renegade pockets of resistance or diehard individuals inside Germany might still cause trouble. There was a distinct possibility that hostilities might resume without warning. Accordingly, the movement of Allied forces into Germany would be a tactical, not an administrative, one. The tired and footsore 2d Division was selected to be the vanguard of the American advance through France, Belgium, Luxembourg, and into Germany.

The march to the Rhine started at 0500 on 17 November. The 5th Regiment and Company C, 2d Engineers, led a massive procession. The 1st Battalion was in the lead, the 2d Battalion protected the flanks, and the 3d Battalion, Headquarters Company, the 8th (Machine Gun) Company, and the supply trains comprised the main body. There was a brisk chill in the predawn darkness and each Marine was burdened with heavy marching orders. Freezing rain and snow flurries filled the air as the column snaked its way northeast toward the German border some sixty miles away. The entire march lasted about a month and covered almost two hundred miles before it was over. The distance was covered in steps of about ten miles each day, with one day's rest each week. This slow pace was necessary because of a lack of motor transport and the poor condition of the pack animals that made up the supply trains. Newly issued boots caused much discomfort and bloody blisters were the price of being forced to march in poorly fitted footwear.

The initial movement to Villes-Moiry-Montmédy went smoothly. The Marines marched ten hours each day with stops at Margut and Fromy in France, and Saint-Marie and Arlon in Belgium. Despite poor weather and heavy packs, it was a generally pleasant move through France. Grateful villagers showered the Marines with small gifts, victory arches graced almost every town, and cheering inhabitants lined the streets to enjoy the spectacle. The Marines entered Luxembourg at 1320 on the twenty-second and then marched through Usseldange, Colmar-Berg, Reichslang, Gilsdorf, and Medernach before moving into defensive positions in the vicinity of Eppeldorf on the Saar River on 25 November.

The Marines who arrived at Saint-Nazaire in 1917 had boasted they would dance at the Kaiser's doorstep sometime in the future. This dream was finally realized when the 5th Regiment crossed into Germany on 1 December 1918. The 2d Battalion was in the vanguard with the 43d Company leading. The 1st and 3d Battalions were on the flanks. That night, an outpost line was established from Lauperath to Uttfield. The 6th Regiment took the lead on 5 December and the 5th Regiment was part of the main body until the column reached Zissen four days later. The Marines remained there until the thirteenth and then crossed the Rhine over the Remagen Bridge at noon that day. The 4th Brigade briefly manned an outpost line near Leutesdorf and the 5th Regiment was billeted in the town of Honningen for three days. Thereafter, the regiment established permanent winter quarters in the Wied River Valley.

The 4th Brigade occupied the front of the 2d Division sector with the 5th Regiment on the right and the 6th Regiment on the left. The 3d Battalion occupied the outpost line near Waldbreitbach, the 1st Battalion was at Niederbreitbach, the 2d Battalion was at Segendorf and Rodenbach, and Headquarters and Supply Companies were at Altwied. Regimental headquarters was located in a magnificent castle on a high hill overlooking the Wied Valley at Schloss Von Rapes. The Germans greeted the Americans with a mixture of scorn, trepidation, and curiosity. Those Germans afraid for their lives or expecting their towns to be looted were pleasantly surprised to find the Marines treated them with courtesy and respect. Soon, most of the local people went out of their way to make the Army of Occupation as comfortable as possible.

The Marines quickly settled into normal garrison routine when no overt threat developed. A rigorous training schedule was carried out, although it was briefly interrupted by a severe influenza epidemic. Rifle ranges were constructed, schools were started, and weekly maneuvers were held. Mess halls were built and each man was assigned a comfortable billet. Liberties to Paris, Nice, and Aux-les-Bains were granted and the Marines were encouraged to sightsee along the Rhine. Athletics and amateur shows also relieved the boredom. One highlight was a long-awaited gridiron clash between the Marines and army regulars from the

2d Division's Race Horse Brigades at Koblenz, an affair so bloody that German war veterans who watched their first American football game denounced the sport as "barbaric."

General Pershing, Secretary of the Navy Daniels, and Assistant Secretary of the Navy Roosevelt reviewed the 2d Division at Hausen on 21 March 1919. During the ceremony Lieutenant Cukela was presented the Medal of Honor and the regimental colors were decorated with the Croix de Guerre for the second time, an achievement that entitled members of the 5th Regiment to wear a red and green shoulder cord known as a fourragère in perpetuity. These "pogey ropes," as they are irreverently known, are still worn by present-day members of the 5th Marines to honor the combat achievements of their military forebears. However, serving members of the regiment must doff this ornamental braid when they are transferred. "Pogey" was once a derisive term for candy, and it has evolved into a derogatory soubriquet applied to anyone perceived to hold a soft or cushy job while others are toiling away. One of the longest-running practical jokes in the Marine Corps regularly occurs when jealous members of other regiments secretly inform naive civilians that the pogey rope signifies its wearer possesses either limited mental capacity or is infected by a virulent social disease.

In April 1919, Col. Harold C. Snyder, who had commanded the 46th Company during the Caribbean intervention of 1914, became the regimental commander after Logan Feland was promoted to brigadier general. Major Pete Ellis replaced Snyder as the regiment's second in command. About a hundred men from the 5th Regiment were transferred to a special ceremonial regiment composed of representative units from the U.S. Third Army. Future Commandant Clifton B. Cates Jr. of the 6th Regiment commanded the Marine contingent, Company E. First Lieutenant Merwin Silverthorn of the 5th Regiment was his second in command.

German representatives to the Versailles peace conference became obstinate in May 1919 and refused to accept Allied terms of surrender. International friction over this issue and domestic dissatisfaction inside Germany threatened to spark civil unrest, so the Occupation Army activated its emergency plan. The 2d Division marched east under arms beginning on 17 June. This show of force continued until the Germans finally agreed to terms on the twenty-third. The 5th Regiment's advance to Hartenfels was the deepest penetration into Germany by a Marine unit. The rest of the Marine occupation tour was uneventful.

The 5th Regiment departed Germany in late July 1919 for Brest, France, after participating in Independence Day and Bastille Day ceremonies. The 5th Regiment joined the 4th Brigade headquarters and elements of the 6th Regiment on board the transport *George Washington* and sailed for the United States. The *George Washington* arrived amid great celebration at New York Harbor on 3 August. The Marines debarked at Hoboken, New Jersey, then moved into quarters at Camp Mills on Long Island. The 5th Regiment joined other elements of the AEF in a victory parade down New York City's famous Fifth Avenue five days later. The twenty-five-thousand-man 2d Division stretched for several miles and required more than an hour to pass in review. The parade ended at 110th Street, but the Marines marched on to Hoboken where they caught transportation south.

The 4th Brigade moved to Quantico by train where it was formally returned to the Naval Service. The Marines were hurriedly issued forest-green uniforms to replace the army-issue uniforms they had worn overseas. President and Mrs. Wilson reviewed the 4th Brigade in Washington, D.C., on 12 August 1919. The president penned a note to Commandant Barnett after the review that said, "The whole nation has reason to be proud [of the Marines]." Demobilization became the order of the day on 13 August and the regiment was disbanded at Quantico.

Second Division General Order No. 37 dated 25 April 1919 enumerated Marine battle actions during World War I. It listed the Toulon Sector (15 March–13 May 1918), the Aisne Defensive (31 May–5 June 1918), Château-Thierry (6 June–9 July 1918), Aisne-Marne Offensive (18–19 July 1918), Marbache Sector Defense (9–16 August 1918), Saint-Mihiel Offensive (12–16 September 1918), Meuse-Argonne (Champagne) Offensive (1–10 October 1918) and the Meuse-Argonne Offensive (1–11 November 1918). The 5th Regiment's colors bore silver bands on its staff to recognize four major campaigns: the Aisne Defensive, the Aisne-Marne Offensive, the Saint-Mihiel Offensive, and the Meuse-Argonne Offensive.

Postscript

The members of the 5th Regiment met mixed fates after the war. Some stayed in the military and rose to great heights within their chosen profession: Buck Neville and Lem Shepherd both went on to become Commandant; LeRoy Hunt retired as a four-star general after commanding the 5th Marines at Guadalcanal; Merwin Silverthorn became a lieutenant general, all of his children served in the Marines Corps, and his son commanded a battalion of the 5th Marines in Korea; much-respected Logan Feland never became Commandant, but he did rise to major general—the highest Marine rank of the day—and commanded the 2d Marine Brigade in Nicaragua; Col. Robert Blake commanded the 5th Marines on the eve of World War II and retired as a major general; Eliot D. Cooke, USA, also became a major general, and he published several excellent articles about his time with the Marines at Belleau Wood; Brig. Gen. Bennett Puryear served as the assistant quartermaster general of the Marine Corps during World War II; and Brig. Gen. Alphonse DeCarre commanded the 2d Marine Division at Guadalcanal.

Charley Dunbeck, the baby-faced "mustang" (Marine slang for a man commissioned from the ranks), was the only 2d Battalion company commander at Belleau Wood to survive the war. He was wounded four times, once badly enough to be medically retired, but was recalled for service during World War II. During that time he was cited for meritorious service before his second retirement in 1946. Bert Baston, the Minnesota football captain who became a war hero at Belleau Wood, was recently selected as an end on the "Big Ten All Time Football Team"—more than eighty years after his playing days ended.

Fate was not kind to General Doyen. Upon his return to the United States, he assumed command at Quantico. He had a reputation as an outstanding trainer, and his recent experience in France was quickly put to use in the rolling hills of Virginia. Unfortunately, he contracted influenza—the deadly Spanish flu that most likely worked its way across the Atlantic on board American troop ships—and died of bronchial pneumonia on 6 October 1918. Shortly thereafter, his wife was presented the first Distinguished Service Medal awarded to a Marine by the Navy Department. The citation lauded Doyen's high training standards and described their effect upon the fine performance of the 4th Brigade in France.

A most tragic fortune also awaited George Hamilton. Generally recognized as the finest Marine officer in France, he was admired by his men (memoirist Elton Mackin described him as tall, athletic, and "movie-star" handsome), respected by his peers, and had the complete confidence of his superiors. On at least three different occasions—the assault at Hill 142, stemming the near-rout at Blanc Mont, and crossing the Meuse on the last night of the war—his valorous actions probably deserved the nation's highest military award, but no Medal of Honor was bestowed upon any Marine officer serving with the AEF. The reasons for this anomaly have been buried by the sands of time, but many historians suspect the causes were interservice jealousy and the animosity of General Pershing, who was no friend of the Marine Corps. Pershing went out of his way to keep Marine units away from the front lines because he allegedly felt Marines were "glory hounds." One Marine officer was given a Navy Medal of Honor for heroic actions in the air, but aviator Ralph Talbot was flying with the navy's Day Bombardment Wing (under British operational control), so his award was granted outside of AEF channels and was not subject to review by General Pershing. Major Hamilton—feted as the "best of the best," a fearless hero called the "finest officer in the AEF" by his commanding officer in France—was treated little better by his own service. He was unceremoniously returned to his permanent rank of captain in 1919. Like so many other officers who had repeatedly proven themselves on the field of battle, he was abruptly informed that service in France would carry no special benefits (i.e., promotion preference) in the peacetime Marine Corps. The result was a large number of retirements and resignations by officers, including Hamilton, who had served so well with the 4th Brigade. It must have been galling to a proud man like Hamilton to be shunted aside when others with far less distinguished records (in particular one of the men Hamilton reported for fleeing the battle line at Blanc Mont) kept their rank or were given plum assignments. George Hamilton, the scion of a wealthy family, left the Marine Corps to take up the family business in 1920. Despite success as an executive, Hamilton craved more action than he found sitting behind a desk, so he returned to the Marine Corps as a student aviator in 1921 only to die a tragic death the following year.

Although the gallant 5th Regiment had been struck from the Marine Corps's muster rolls, the valor of its Marines during the Great War would become the subject of popular histories, stage plays, moving pictures, novels, and short stories in the postwar period. The most notable of these were coauthor Laurence Stallings's play *What Price Glory?* whose stark realism took Broadway by storm in the mid-twenties before becoming a popular movie of the same name, and the stirring postwar short stories and moving illustrations by John Thomason, which offered brilliant portrayals of Marines in action in publications like *Scribner's Magazine,* the *Saturday Evening Post,* and *American Mercury.*

Laurence Stallings did not let the loss of a foot at Belleau Wood keep him down. Instead, he became a literary personage of great achievement after the war. He was a prolific writer whose credits included the widely acclaimed books, *The First World War: A Photographic History* and *The Doughboys*, in addition to his famous stage play. He eventually left the cosmopolitan life of New York for the bright lights of Hollywood. His screenplays included the popular silent movie *The Big Parade* and the classic western *She Wore A Yellow Ribbon*. During World War II, Stallings returned to active service with the U.S. Army, holding the rank of lieutenant colonel while assigned to the U.S. Army Air Forces as a liaison officer.

John Thomason, at the urging of his good friend Stallings, embarked on a part-time literary career after the war, but unlike Stallings he remained on active duty until 1944. Thomason published numerous articles, several books, and a vast array of art while a serving Marine officer. His work was so popular that he enjoyed a reputation as the "Kipling of the Corps." His most vivid tales of his time with the 5th Regiment in France were told in *Fix Bayonets!*—a literary masterpiece that is still in print.

There were others who drew upon their experiences with the 5th Regiment to make a mark as well. Former corporal "Wild Bill" Campbell, who was awarded the French Croix de Guerre, the army DSC, and the Navy Cross for his actions at Blanc Mont, wrote the novels *Company K* and *The Bad Seed* using the pen name William March. The first was critically well received, and the latter was a best-seller. A bitter Fritz Wise (he had been passed over for general's stars, which he attributed to a malicious "whispering" campaign) gained a measure of lasting notoriety when he told his story in the book *A Marine Tells It to You*. This memoir is still in print after almost three-quarters of a century. It offers an excellent general overview of life in the "Old Corps," but modern historians view many of its details with skepticism. Wise often got names and chronology wrong, made several outrageous claims, and his versions of controversial actions (e.g., his ill-fated frontal assault on Belleau Wood) did not jibe with historical documents or contemporary eyewitness testimony. Interestingly, despite his relief from command by General Harbord after Belleau Wood, Wise was still promoted to colonel. He was then transferred to the U.S. 4th Division where he successfully commanded the army's 59th Infantry Regiment and later the 8th Brigade.

Two of the most colorful enlisted men in the Corps, GySgt. Mike Wodarczyk and Sgt. Louis Cukela, served with the 5th Regiment. Both were typical of many of the eastern European immigrants who chose the service as a career. Although the popular media after the war portrayed Marine NCOs as hulking Irishmen with hearts of gold under their tough-as-nails exteriors (e.g., William Boyd as Sergeant Quirt in the play *What Price Glory?*), serving Marines were far more familiar with the accented tongue lashings of their Slavic sergeants. Cukela and Wodarczyk were two of these legendary characters, and both men were undoubtedly role models for fictional NCOs played on film by actors like Wallace Beery and Victor McLaglen.

Wodarczyk was already a Marine hero before he sailed for France. In 1914 he had been recognized for bravery while fighting a warehouse fire in Norfolk. He was eventually awarded the DSC and Navy Cross for his actions at Belleau Wood. He was so severely wounded at Blanc Mont that he was forced out of the Marine Corps for medical reasons in 1919. He was, however, able to return to active duty when the Corps expanded in 1920. This time around he chose to specialize in aviation. His fine work as a mechanic earned him an officer's warrant, and Gunner Wodarczyk was one of the first flying Leathernecks to earn the Distinguished Flying Cross (DFC). Strangely, Wodarczyk was not authorized to wear the golden wings of a naval aviator until after he had been at the controls for seven years because of strict peacetime limits on the number of pilots authorized by Congress. The Marine solution was to let warrant officers and enlisted men fly under the rubric "student aviator" without drawing flight pay or wearing wings. Wodarczyk was such a student, and he did not officially become a naval aviator until after his combat service in Nicaragua. He often joked that he got his wings and the DFC at the same ceremony. Although this was not true, it has become part of the lore of the Corps. The "Polish Warhorse" was one of the few Marines to be decorated for heroic actions on the ground and in the air. He was called out of retirement for World War II, was decorated for meritorious service, and was wearing the silver leaves of a lieutenant colonel when the war ended.

Louis Cukela is probably the most highly decorated Marine of World War I. In addition to earning the Medal of Honor at Soissons, he was the first Marine enlisted man to receive the French Croix de Guerre. He later added another one, along with the French Legion of Honor and Medal Militaire. He also received the Italian Croce al Merito de Guerra and the

first foreign decoration awarded by the newly formed country of Yu-
goslavia. Cukela, who was born in Serbia in 1888, came to the United
States in 1913. He served with the U.S. Army from 1914 to 1916 and then
enlisted in the Marine Corps in 1917. He was wounded in action twice
and received several "spot promotions" in recognition of his bravery. He
finished the war as a temporary lieutenant, was awarded a regular commission in 1919, and became a captain in 1921. He continued his career
as a fighting Marine during the Banana Wars—serving overseas in Haiti,
Santo Domingo, the Philippines, and China. After a tour of duty with
the Civilian Conservation Corps and quartermaster duties at Norfolk and
in Washington, D.C., he retired in 1940 as a major, but was recalled to
active duty after America declared war in 1941. He served at Norfolk and
Philadelphia during World War II and finally ended his active service on
17 May 1946. His most famous exploit, however, did not occur on the
field of battle. He will forever be remembered by the Marines for his
malapropian quote, "Next time I need some damn fool for a mission,
I'll go myself."

3: Between the World Wars

The immediate postwar years were ones of turmoil. In the wake of the Great War, the Marine Corps was reduced to less than a quarter of its wartime strength. As part of that reorganization, the number of Marine officers was cut to less than a thousand men. Commandant Barnett appointed a board to determine who should be retained and to formulate future promotion policies. This commission determined that service in France should carry no special weight and ruled that prewar promotions policies should be retained. The result was that most "temporary" officers, those who had been hurriedly promoted from the enlisted ranks in 1917, would lose their commissions and most regular officers would be reduced in rank. The board's findings led to a spate of resignations by college-educated officers and created resentment among the NCOs who had to forfeit their commissions.

The appointment of a new Commandant in 1920 ushered in the "Age of Lejeune." Major General John A. Lejeune was a farsighted "progressive-traditionalist" who revitalized and modernized the Marine Corps during his nine-year stint as commandant. He reversed the personnel decisions made by his predecessor, a decision that brought many fine officers back into the Marine fold. He also stressed the importance of military education, embraced the use of Marines as a naval expeditionary force, and placed the Marine Corps squarely in the public eye throughout the 1920s.

During most of the first decade after the war the Marines were busy in Latin America, where small wars in familiar places like Haiti, Santo Domingo, and Nicaragua remained troublesome. After 1920, however, the Marine Corps was given a new strategic focus and assigned a new mission. With Germany's war machine dismantled and the rest of Europe undergoing social and economic problems, the United States began to look to the west, where Japan was an emerging potential foe. Accordingly, War Plan Orange—a contingency plan for armed conflict with Japan that called for an island-hopping drive across the central Pacific—dictated a new mission: amphibious assault. Although the Marines continued to put out brushfires in Latin America, the underlying emphasis of Marine Corps efforts became developing the tactics and techniques of seizing defended beachheads.

Quantico

When the dust settled after World War I and the United States began its return to normalcy in 1920, John Archer Lejeune was appointed Major General Commandant of the Marine Corps. His tenure transformed the Marine Corps into a modern military force, and his forceful leadership sowed the seeds for Marine amphibious success during World War II. Lejeune instituted programs that increased readiness, kept the Marines in the public eye, and made the Marines the world's experts in amphibious warfare. The resurgent 5th Regiment played an important role in the creation of General Lejeune's "new" Marine Corps.

The Advance Base Force was manned in only skeleton strength in 1919 because America's armed services were pared to the bone during the hasty demobilization after the war. However, increased Marine Corps strength authorizations in 1920 allowed for the reactivation of the 5th Regiment (albeit at reduced manning levels) on 8 July. Despite severe fiscal restraints, the Advance Base Force of 1920 actually became a larger and more flexible organization than its predecessor. This new unit was renamed the Marine Corps Expeditionary Force (MCEF) when it moved from League Island to the more spacious Quantico. The MCEF's infantry units were the 5th and 6th Regiments, artillery was provided by one battalion of the 10th Regiment, the 1st Regiment was composed of various technical and support detachments, and a small aviation squadron was stationed at Quantico's Brown Field. This integrated combined-arms combat team was the forerunner of modern Marine air-ground task forces.

The 5th Regiment at first consisted of Headquarters Company and the 8th, 17th, and 49th Companies with Col. (later Maj. Gen.) Frederic L. Bradman in command, but the regiment gradually increased strength by adding Supply Company on 1 August, the 18th Company on 6 August, the 20th and 43d Companies on 27 August, the 16th Company on 3 September, the 66th Company on 1 October, the 51st Company on 23 October, and the 45th Company on 20 November. In 1921, the 5th Regiment was assigned to the East Coast Expeditionary Force when the 6th Marines departed for California to become the nucleus of the West Coast Expeditionary Force. The 5th Regiment added a Stokes Mortar Company (redesignated Howitzer Company in May) on 29 April, the 23d and 77th Companies on 4 May, and the 73d (Machine Gun) Company on 14 May. The 8th Company, which had been temporarily detached for duty at Norfolk, rejoined the 5th Regiment on 4 May. Headquarters Company was dissolved and its men were reassigned to either regimental headquarters or the 1st, 2d, or 3d Battalion headquarters on 17 May.

The second building block in Lejeune's program to create a new Marine Corps was to establish a favorable public image. He appointed colorful Brig. Gen. Smedley D. Butler as commanding general at Quantico with orders to turn it into the showplace of the Marine Corps. The energetic Butler did this with relish. He used Marine labor for construction projects to modernize and expand the base as he mixed military training and individual educational programs. Officers received advanced military training while enlisted Marines learned job skills that could be applied in the civilian labor market. The Quantico Marines football team became a nationally recognized powerhouse that played the best college teams, and Marine baseball teams were of near-professional caliber. Additionally, Marine marksmen routinely carried off most awards at the national rifle matches, and Marine teams won an unprecedented five consecutive national matches. Marine shooters, among them 1st Lt. Merritt A. "Red Mike" Edson of the 5th Regiment, soon became the ones to beat at national rifle and pistol competitions. The most successful of the publicity pushes occurred when Marine units stationed at Quantico conducted a series of high-profile maneuvers at Civil War battle sites near Washington, D.C., in the early 1920s.

Commandant Lejeune also used the power of his office to reestablish stronger ties with the navy. He envisioned the Marine Corps not as a small naval guard, but as a modern combined-arms amphibious assault force assigned to the U.S. Fleet. To this end, former 5th Regiment second in command Maj. Pete Ellis wrote Operation Plan 712-D, "Advanced Base Operations in Micronesia," which delineated the Corps's role in War Plan Orange. Ellis then went on a spy mission to the western Pacific and died mysteriously in the Palau Islands in 1923. To increase amphibious capabilities to implement War Plan Orange, Marine units participated in fleet landing exercises and tested equipment in the field while the Marine Corps Schools developed doctrine at Quantico. Unfortunately, this already slow process was interrupted by operational deployments and was hampered by a lack of funding from a parsimonious and isolationist Congress.

During the early 1920s an operational pattern emerged. The Marines of the 5th Regiment spent each summer or fall on annual large-scale ground maneuvers in the eastern United States, the winters saw fleet landing exercises in the Caribbean, and the rest of the time was devoted to training and construction projects at Quantico. The regiment underwent several organizational changes and some familiar names—including Edward Greene, Harold Snyder, and Robert Rhea—appeared on the list of regimental commanders during that time.

The 5th Regiment took part in the East Coast Expeditionary Force fall maneuvers from 26 August to 4 October 1921. This was the first of four so-called Civil War maneuvers held at the Wilderness in 1921, Gettysburg in 1922, New Market in 1923, and Antietam in 1924. These activities shrewdly used field exercises to garner favorable publicity for the Marine Corps. The maneuvers were attended by national dignitaries, drew huge crowds, and were favorably reported about in newspapers across the country.

The Wilderness maneuvers did not attempt to re-create the Civil War battle. Instead, they showcased modern tactics, weapons, and techniques. This exercise was the largest Marine war game to that time. The exercise forces included the 3d (1st and 10th Regiments) and 4th (5th and 6th Regiments) Marine Brigades. The Marines left Quantico and proceeded south to Aquia Creek on 26 September then moved to the Fredericksburg fairgrounds the next day. The five-mile column that filled the Washington-Richmond highway was described in contemporary press reports as "a very inspiring spectacle." The Marines conducted a tactical approach march to Wilderness Run on the twenty-eighth. Thereafter, all territory to the west was considered an ocean while the Marines simulated an amphibious assault. As part of the simulation, they seized a defended beach, consolidated to defend the "island," constructed fortified positions, and repelled a counterattack. President Warren G. Harding arrived at the "Canvas White House" on 1 October, then he and his cabinet officers observed the maneuvers and reviewed the troops before returning to Washington the next day. The exercise was described as "a sensational demonstration of the fitness of the Marine Corps and its readiness to take the field in any emergency."

The 5th Regiment was called into action twice during the latter half of 1921. The first was an incident in Latin America. A border dispute between Costa Rica and Panama threatened U.S. interests, and Marines were needed to calm the situation. The 3d Battalion was hurriedly organized for expeditionary duty on 19 August. The 8th, 16th, and 20th Companies and a headquarters detachment sailed for Panama on board the battleship USS *Pennsylvania* on the twentieth. The battalion arrived at Balboa ten days later and transshipped to the USAT *St. Mihiel.* This demonstration of force did the trick, and the unit returned to Quantico on 20 September after a month-long Caribbean sojourn that demonstrated the Marine Corps's readiness and flexibility.

The second contingency was an internal one. An outbreak of lawlessness during the era popularly known as the Roaring Twenties required an unusual Marine domestic response. The U.S. Post Office Department was unable to protect itself against a rash of mail robberies and requested military help. President Harding ordered Secretary of the Navy Edwin Denby "to detail as guards for the United States mails . . . officers and men of the United States Marine Corps" on 7 November 1921. Secretary Denby, a no-nonsense former Marine, gave explicit orders that the mail guards should shoot to kill if attacked. More than twenty-two hundred Marines, including most of those assigned to the 5th Regiment, were armed with shotguns and submachine guns and then parceled out across the United States in small detachments to guard postal depots and trains carrying the mail. The robberies stopped immediately. Their unusual domestic mission accomplished, all of the 5th Regiment's Marines returned to Quantico by March 1922.

Colonel Bradman departed in May 1922. The regiment was briefly commanded by Lieutenant Colonels James K. Tracy and Raymond B. Sullivan before Lt. Col. Harold Snyder took over on 3 October. He remained in command until 15 March 1924. The only organizational change in 1922 was the redesignation of Supply Company as Service Company in April.

The training highlight of 1922 was the recreation of Pickett's Charge at Gettysburg, Pennsylvania. The 5th Regiment left Quantico by barge for Haines Point, Maryland, and marched from there into Washington, D.C. That evening the regiment passed in review for the president and his guests. It was the first time a large military unit had paraded on the White House grounds since the Civil War. The march through Maryland included stops at Bethesda, Gaithersburg, Rockville, Frederick, and Thurmont. The Marines reached the Gettysburg battlefield on 26 June. There they constructed another canvas White House, surveyed the battlefield, conducted field maneuvers, and rehearsed the reenactment of Pickett's Charge. The president, living veterans of that 1863 fight, and more than a hundred thousand spectators were thrilled as the Marines acted as both Union and Confederate forces on 1 July. On 3 July, the sixtieth anniversary of the famed assault, the Marines conducted a mock attack over the same ground to show how the objective would be taken using modern weapons. Among the distinguished guests that day was Mrs. Helen Longstreet, the widow of the Confederate corps commander who ordered the charge.

Tragically, a brilliant career ended and the Marine Corps lost one of its most promising officers when George Hamilton, who had successfully commanded the 49th Company and the 1st Battalion in France, was killed when his plane crashed during an aerial demonstration of the latest dive-bombing techniques. During that segment of the reenactment, Hamilton's DH-4B biplane came screaming out of the clouds in a steep dive, a daring exhibition that brought the enthralled audience to its feet. Suddenly, the plane began to shudder as Hamilton desperately tried to regain control, but the aircraft hit the ground in a fiery crash that killed both him and his observer. The investigation report lauded Hamilton for the way he attempted to recover and blamed a faulty altimeter setting for the mishap. The Marine Corps thus lost one of its most promising young officers. One cannot help but wonder what Hamilton might have accomplished had he lived. A saddened 5th Regiment returned to Quantico on 12 July.

Colonel Snyder commanded the regiment throughout 1923. There were several organizational changes in January. The 8th Company transferred from the 1st to the 3d Battalion, the 23d Company transferred from the 3d to the 1st Battalion, and the 77th Company transferred from the 3d to the 2d Battalion. The 43d Company was assigned special temporary duty from 4 March to 1 June at East Camp, Naval Operating Base, Hampton Roads, Virginia, to salvage building materials that were then used for Quantico construction projects. The 3d Battalion headquarters and the 45th Company were part of the honor guard at President Harding's funeral ceremonies in Washington, D.C., on 8 August.

The 1923 maneuvers focused on the Battle of New Market at Fort Defiance, West Virginia. Although not the prestigious national event that the previous two maneuvers were, this one still generated a lot of local interest. Marines wearing dress-blue jackets represented the North, and gray-clad cadets of the Virginia Military Institute (VMI) portrayed the Southern forces. Actually, the students were re-creating one of the greatest moments in their school's history: the heroic stand of the cadet corps at New Market in 1864, when the entire VMI student body volunteered for active service to defend the Shenandoah Valley. The 5th Regiment departed Quantico on 27 August and marched more than three hundred miles in the next forty days. More than 150,000 people watched the battle reenactment on 20 September. The Marines then marched to Lexington in the rain, where they cheered in vain as VMI shut out the footsore Quantico eleven 6–0 on a water-covered gridiron. The rest of the year was devoted to preparation for the upcoming winter maneuvers.

The U.S. Fleet maneuvers of 1924 occupied the first two months of that year. Exercises were conducted in the Panama Canal Zone and at Culebra Island. Colonel Snyder and the 5th Regiment embarked on the *Henderson* at Quantico on 2 January. They landed at Coco Solo in the Canal Zone on 16 January and proceeded to Balboa on the eighteenth. The 5th Regiment participated in shore maneuvers from 19–23 January and received high praise for the simulated destruction of the vital locks that prevented the opposing battle fleet from moving through the canal. The 5th Regiment then boarded the *Henderson* and sailed for Culebra. The men tented at Camp Cole from 31 January to 4 March and conducted a month of maneuvers, including live-fire exercises. This field training was followed by well-earned liberties at San Juan, Puerto Rico, and Saint Thomas in the Virgin Islands before returning to Quantico on 10 March.

Annual fall maneuvers were held at Sharpsburg, Maryland, from 24 August to 19 September 1924. The three-thousand-man MCEF moved from Quantico to Haines Point by barge and then marched to Frederick using the same route it had taken to Gettysburg in 1922. The force made a twenty-three-mile motor march to the Antietam battlefield after three days at Frederick. A crowd of about forty thousand watched as the Marines conducted a modern combined-arms attack using infantry, artillery, tanks, and aircraft to maneuver over the same ground where the armies of Confederate Gen. Robert E. Lee and Union Maj. Gen. George B. McClellan fought to a bloody standstill sixty-two years earlier. The

Marines returned via Washington and passed in review for Pres. Calvin Coolidge on their way back to Quantico. This event brought the Civil War maneuvers of the 1920s to a close.

Lieutenant Colonel Edward A. Greene and Colonel Snyder alternated command in early 1924 until Col. John F. McGill took over as regimental commander on 23 May. McGill's tour lasted about a year. The regiment's top slot became a revolving door throughout the second half of 1925 until the regiment deployed to Nicaragua in early 1927 as Col. Harry R. Lay (who served as adjutant with the original 5th Regiment), Lt. Col. Robert Y. Rhea, and Col. (later Maj. Gen.) Louis M. Gulick alternated in command. The regiment was detached from the 4th Brigade on 15 March 1925, and the 16th, 20th, and 43d Companies left Quantico for duty at the Philadelphia Sesquicentennial celebration during various times between May to November. The regiment's Howitzer Company was disbanded on 10 December.

Elements of the 5th Regiment returned to Guantanamo twelve years after it first assembled there when Marine expeditionary battalions began rotating from Quantico to Guantanamo Bay for five months at a time beginning in 1926, thus instituting a training concept not unlike modern-day Okinawa unit deployment programs. The 1st Battalion, 5th Regiment (Headquarters, 17th, 23d, 49th, and 66th Companies), was the first to deploy. The unit departed on board the *Henderson* on 3 March 1926 and disembarked in Cuba seven days later. The tour was uneventful and the 1st Battalion returned to Quantico on 27 September without incident. The 2d Battalion (Headquarters 18th, 51st, and 77th Companies) embarked on board the USS *Cormorant* at Quantico then transshipped to the transport USS *Chaumont* at Cedar Point, Maryland, and arrived at Guantanamo on 3 October.

Two events interrupted the regiment's training schedule late in the decade. First, the Marines were once again ordered to guard the mail, and members of the regiment performed this duty in eastern, midwestern, and southern states. Again, as in 1921, the robberies stopped as soon as the Marines were on the job. The assignment also kept the regiment from participating in the annual fleet maneuvers that winter.

The second event was international in scope: The regiment was sent to Nicaragua as a peacekeeping force. Nicaragua had long been an area of interest for the United States. Strategically, it offered the only alternative for a canal joining the Atlantic and Pacific oceans other than the Isthmus of Panama. There were also compelling financial reasons (several leading American banks had floated loans to the government), and U.S. mining and fruit-growing companies had outlets up and down the Caribbean Mosquito Coast. By the mid-'20s, Nicaragua was a typical unstable "banana republic." Over the years, Nicaraguan Liberals and Conservatives had violently vied for power, but neither side could provide peace or security once in office. Banditry and civil disorder became so rampant that U.S. landing forces had to come ashore on several occasions to protect American lives and property. Marine landing parties had gone ashore there in 1852, 1854, and 1899. In 1909, the leader was a corrupt Liberal strongman. The United States, on the other hand, supported the Conservatives and sent a provisional Marine regiment to straighten the situation out. The Marines departed within a few months, but another regiment had to be committed until the situation was once again "well in hand." This time a residual Legation Guard remained to show the flag until 1924. The following year, Conservative Emiliano Chamorro Vargas chased out the Liberal government and named himself president. He abdicated in 1926, and Adolfo Diaz took over. Rebel bandits began pillaging the Mosquito Coast, particularly American-owned assets, in December. This set the stage for full-blown American intervention.

Nicaragua

Located in Central America between Honduras and Costa Rica, Nicaragua has been described by Allan R. Millett as a country of "four peoples [Spanish, mestizo, Caribbean, and Indian] and three regions [the prosperous west coast, the rugged central highlands, and the isolated eastern Mosquito Coast]." In 1926 the Conservatives were in office with U.S. blessings, but the Liberals—backed by foreign arms and money, primarily supplied by the Soviet-sponsored Comintern—were in revolt. The Liberal army, commanded by Gen. Jose Maria Moncada, rampaged down the Mosquito Coast, killing an American citizen and threatening U.S. business interests that December. Marines from the ships of the Special Service Squadron landed and established several neutral zones, but these ad hoc landing forces from the *Cleveland, Denver, Galveston,* and *Rochester* were inadequate to ensure future peace, so a call for reinforcements was sent.

Closest to the trouble was the 2d Battalion, 5th Regiment, at Guantanamo commanded by Lt. Col. (later Brig. Gen.) James J. Meade. The

THE U.S. MARINES IN NICARAGUA

battalion boarded the transport ship USS *Argonne* and sailed for
Nicaragua on 7 January 1927. Upon arrival, it was assigned to the Marine Force, Special Service Squadron. Meade's Marines debarked at Bluefields on the east coast. Most of the men immediately marched inland
to Rama to forestall a battle between well-armed Liberal and Conservative forces on 11 January. The crisis at Rama passed about a week later,
so the Marines marched back to the coast. The 51st Company, however,
boarded the Cuyamen Fruit Company tug and barge at Bluefields and

moved upriver to Rama to become the permanent garrison force there on the eighteenth.

The bulk of the 2d Battalion reboarded the *Argonne* and sailed through the Panama Canal to Corinto on Nicaragua's Pacific coast. The 18th Company debarked on 31 January, and Casual Company (a temporary organization that included the "sick, lame, and lazy" in addition to new arrivals and those about to be detached) came ashore on 1 February, followed by Headquarters Company and the 77th Company on the second. Once assembled, the bobtailed 2d Battalion rode the narrow-gauge railway from Corinto to the capital city of Managua to reinforce a Legation Guard that had been hastily formed from the 195-man Marine detachment on board the cruiser USS *Galveston*. Lieutenant Colonel Meade assumed responsibility for the defense of Managua at the request of Pres. Aldolfo Diaz. Despite the Marine presence in the capital, the Liberals were able to cut the railway, ravage Matagalpa Province, and attack U.S. diplomatic personnel there. In response to this crisis, RAdm. Julian L. Latimer, commander of both the Special Service Squadron and Naval Forces Ashore, wired Washington for reinforcements. A Marine air-ground combat team was formed when Marine Observation Squadron 1 (VO-1M) under Maj. Ross E. "Rusty" Rowell arrived in Nicaragua with six DeHavilland DH-4B biplanes on 26 February.

The 2d Battalion was soon joined by the rest of the regiment, which at the time was commanded by Lieutenant Colonel Rhea. Its scattered units had been recalled to Quantico from mail guard for expeditionary duty on 14 February. Headquarters Company, Supply Company, the 1st Battalion, the 43d Company, and the 3d Battalion boarded the *Henderson* at Quantico on 23 February and sailed down the Potomac River for Nicaragua. The *Henderson* made landfall at Corinto on 7 March and the 5th Regiment was thereupon attached to the Naval Forces Ashore. The 3d Battalion landed first, followed by Headquarters Company, Supply Company, the 43d Company, and the 1st Battalion. The debarkation was completed on the tenth.

What had started as a minor landing developed into a full-blown overseas expedition, so the 2d Marine Brigade was activated on 26 March. Brigadier General Logan Feland, the much-respected hero of Belleau Wood and former regimental commander, took over the thousand-man brigade. It included VO-1M, the 5th Regiment, and a provisional battalion composed of landing forces from the Special Service Squadron and the separate 51st Company. The 2d Brigade was a decentralized command with Marine forces of varying sizes distributed to fourteen different towns.

The Marines separated the Liberal and Conservative forces in Matagalpa Province while Pres. Calvin Coolidge's personal envoy, Henry L. Stimson, negotiated a peace treaty that was signed on 4 May. Under the provisions of the treaty, the Conservatives would retain temporary power. The Marines would supervise weapons turn-ins by both sides and then would set up, train, and command a native constabulary as had been done in Haiti and the Dominican Republic. Elections were scheduled so the Nicaraguans could select their own political leaders and enjoy the fruits of democracy at long last. To ensure the latter occurred, an American occupation force would remain until the situation was stable and peace prevailed.

Colonel Gulick arrived in Managua on 1 April and once again took the reins of the 5th Regiment. The 1st Battalion manned lines between the warring factions and supervised the cease-fire. Other units were located in key towns and protected lines of communication. The regiment also supplied six officers to the Constabulary Detachment, a small unit commanded by Lieutenant Colonel Rhea. Its mission was to create, train, and oversee the Guardia Nacional de Nicaragua. Things went very well and both sides cooperated except for Liberal general Augusto Cesar Sandino, a thirty-two-year-old nationalist who rabidly opposed outside intervention in Nicaragua's affairs. He refused to stack arms and instead led 150 rebels into the rugged Neuvo Segovia Mountains in the north. From his mountain hideaway, Sandino spurned diplomatic overtures and vowed to overthrow the existing government. He promised to fight on until the American "imperialists" withdrew and renounced all interest in Nicaragua. This ultimatum left the Marines no choice but to mount a military expedition to bring in Sandino.

Captain Gilbert D. Hatfield led a thirty-eight-man 3d Battalion patrol to Ocotal in the wilderness of the rugged northern highlands. A newly minted forty-eight-man Guardia company eventually reinforced these Marines. At first, Hatfield and Sandino were content to exchange verbal barbs. During one such exchange Sandino invited the Marines to come for a visit, but to make out their wills beforehand. Hatfield replied, "If words were bullets and phrases were soldiers, you would be field marshal instead of a mule thief." This war of words became a shooting conflict when Sandino's gang attacked Ocotal. The outnumbered Marines held city hall against several assaults beginning at about 0100 on 16 July. When extremely accurate Marine rifle and automatic-weapons fire took a heavy toll of the attackers, Sandino disingenuously resorted to negotiation. This ploy failed when Captain Hatfield bravely replied, "Marines do not know how to surrender!" Fortuitously, two Marine biplanes—one flown by none other than Gunner Michael Wodarczyk of Belleau Wood fame—spotted the trouble while flying overhead on routine patrol. Wodarczyk immediately strafed the attackers while his Spanish-speaking wingman landed to discern what the problem was. Alerted about the critical situation when the planes returned to base, Rusty Rowell led a five-plane flight back to the fray. Each plane was loaded with four twenty-pound bombs and all the machine-gun ammunition it could carry. The ensuing dive-bombing attacks killed more than fifty Sandinistas, wounded double that number, and sent the rebels fleeing into the safety of the jungle-covered mountains. Marine losses at Ocotal were one killed and five wounded. Ironically, news of this defeat made Sandino a revolutionary hero among radical groups in the United States opposed to American intervention. The Nicaraguan insurgents were lauded as heroes, anti-imperialist protest marches abounded, the radical left inundated the U.S. news media with atrocity stories, and individual Marines were sometimes castigated as war criminals upon their return to the United States.

Unfortunately, the Marines were unable to exploit their success at Ocotal. They could not put the revolt to a quick end because diplomatic problems in China required an increased U.S. presence in the Far East. The Commandant had to "rob Peter to pay Paul" to come up with an expeditionary force, so the number of Marines assigned to Nicaragua was reduced. Accordingly, the 5th Regiment's strength dropped by about a third when the 2d Battalion's Headquarters, 18th, 43d, and 77th Companies left Nicaragua on 1 July. The battalion sailed from Corinto aboard the *Argonne*, debarked at Piney Point, Maryland, on the twelfth, and was officially disbanded at Quantico on the twentieth. The 51st Company did not sail with its parent battalion, but was instead assigned independent duty in eastern Nicaragua and became the 51st Company, 5th Regiment, on 1 August.

With this pullout, the combat load was shifted from the U.S. Marines to the Guardia Nacional, a force led by American junior officers and NCOs but primarily manned by local volunteers. In the first major test of this concept, 225 Marines and Guardia recruits searched the Neuvo Segovia Mountains for Sandino's secret hideout, called El Chipote. Concurrently, elements of the regiment's 1st and 3d Battalions fought the

Sandinistas east and southeast of Ocotal. Patrols engaged "Lobo's Band" in a running gunfight on the night of 7–8 September, and another fair-sized fight occurred at Telpaneca on the nineteenth. The largest engagement took place on 8 October when a rescue force searching for a downed plane killed about sixty rebels near Telpaneca. Unfortunately, the rescue mission was unsuccessful. John Thomason subsequently wrote a fact-based fictional account about the fate of the two American fliers who were tortured and hanged by Sandino in the popular short story "Air Patrol."

A carefully planned offensive to destroy El Chipote, which was finally located not far from the village of Quilali, was launched on 19 December. Two large patrols commanded by Capt. Richard Livingston of the 3d Battalion and 1st Lt. Merton A. Richal of Headquarters Company, 1st Battalion, were formed for the assault. The patrols were to proceed separately and then rendezvous at Quilali before launching the final attack. Unfortunately, all did not go well. Livingston's 140-man column was ambushed on the banks of the Jicaro River about a mile south of Quilali on the thirtieth. The Marines managed to hold off the attackers and drove them back with a vigorous counterattack, but five Marines and two Guardia troopers were killed. Captain Livingston and twenty-two other Marines were wounded during the engagement.

Lieutenant Richal's patrol encountered a sizable Sandinista force six miles north of Quilali on 1 January 1928. A hail of machine-gun fire and several dynamite bombs caught the Marines by surprise. Lieutenant Richal was hit early, but GySgt. Edward G. Brown rallied the men. They were able to storm a nearby height, where they dug in and waited for a relief column to arrive. In the interim, some Marine aircraft located and pursued the bandits while others air-dropped supplies to their beleaguered comrades on the ground. Richal's force was thereafter able to make it to Quilali without further incident. But the battle was not over. Sandino laid siege to Quilali. It was during this action that Marine aviator Christian F. Shilt was awarded the Medal of Honor for evacuating eighteen seriously wounded Marines during repeated trips under fire. The siege was finally lifted when Marine reinforcements arrived on 10 January.

Marine patrols were soon beating the bush again in search of the elusive Sandinistas. The Marines and Gardia mounted a battalion-sized combined force to pursue Sandino and seal off his mountain bastion. A strong patrol led by Maj. Archibald Young entered El Chipote and discovered that Sandino had fled to Honduras. There was a temporary lull in the fighting, but the *insurrectos* had not been decisively defeated. In his absence, Sandino's men continued to wage guerrilla warfare. The most serious incident occurred on 27 February when a pack train escort led by 1st Lt. Edward F. O'Day lost five killed and seven wounded in a running battle with the Sandinistas.

The 5th Regiment underwent several changes in 1928. Lieutenant Colonel Ben Berry, who was wounded leading the futile charge by the 3d Battalion at Belleau Wood on 6 June 1918, temporarily took over on 31 January and commanded until Col. Rush H. Wallace replaced him on 25 February. Belatedly realizing that Nicaragua had not yet been pacified, Washington finally sent badly needed reinforcements, including the 11th Regiment, which was specifically formed at Quantico for duty in Nicaragua. This increased strength allowed General Feland to divide the country into three military districts. The northern area was assigned to the newly arrived 11th Regiment, the 5th Regiment garrisoned and patrolled the southern area, and a provisional regiment composed of the 51st Company and the Special Service Squadron landing forces was assigned to the east coast.

The regiment's 2d Battalion was reconstituted on 25 March, primarily using troops already at hand and ships' detachments. The 18th Company was formed at Managua, the 43d Company at Corinto was created using Marines from Guantanamo and the USS *Arkansas*'s Marine detachment, the 48th Company was composed of detachments from the USS *Camden* and USS *Florida* at Chinandega, the USS *Utah*'s Marine detachment became the 77th Company at Granada, and Headquarters and Headquarters Company was organized at Granada from the USS *Oklahoma*'s Marine detachment.

The influx of new Marines forced Sandino to shift his area of operations to the far reaches of the already remote eastern provinces. The 51st Company at Bluefields was then reinforced to counter this threat. Major Harold H. Utley came ashore to take charge at Bluefields. His composite force consisted of the 51st Company and units from the 11th Marines, although ships' companies occasionally lent their support as well. The Marines relentlessly pursued the *banditos* and forced them to stay continuously on the move by cutting them off from base camps inside Honduras. Sandino was so crippled by lack of supplies, heavy casualties, and numerous desertions that the rebels were on the brink of defeat by the summer of 1928.

The pacification campaign was going so well that the 1st Battalion could be safely pulled from the field to be trained for supervisory duties in conjunction with the upcoming November elections, and the entire 5th Regiment had been schooled for these tasks by the end of October. The Marine presence had such a calming effect on the countryside that the Nicaraguan populace was undeterred by Sandino's empty threats to disrupt the elective process. The elections on 4 November 1928 saw a huge turnout that removed the Conservatives from power. Liberal leader José Moncada became the new president after what both sides agreed had been a fair and honest election. Happily, the lull in the fighting continued after the ballots had been counted and serenity reigned in Nicaragua for the rest of the year.

The 2d Battalion was once again disbanded in January 1929. Headquarters and Headquarters Company and the 43d and 48th Companies were dissolved on 4 January when those Marines returned to their ships. The 18th Company at Masaya and the 77th Company at Granada were deactivated the following day. Still, the situation in Nicaragua continued to improve despite these reductions. Guerrilla activity came to a near standstill after 1st Lt. Herman H. Hanneken, a veteran of many small wars who gained fame when he killed Haitian rebel leader Charlemagne ten years earlier, captured rebel leader Manuel Jiron. This loss forced Sandino to leave Nicaragua to recruit new followers and raise funds. With Sandino gone, rebel activity was so reduced that only a few individual acts of banditry were reported.

The year 1929 saw a further reduction in Marine forces and several reorganizations of the 5th Regiment. The dormant 2d Battalion was once again called to the colors on 14 February 1929. Headquarters and Headquarters Company was reactivated that day. The reactivation of the 2d Battalion allowed the 11th Regiment to depart in August. Marine strength in Nicaragua was reduced to only about two thousand men at that time. Lieutenant Colonel Lauren S. Willis commanded the 5th Regiment from 17–30 April, and Col. Theodore E. Backstrom arrived and took command on 1 May. The 5th Regiment was reorganized into a "triangular" organization with three battalions of three line companies each that summer. The 3d Battalion's 45th Company was disbanded at Jinotega on 9 August, as was the 1st Battalion's 66th Company at Managua the next day. The 2d Battalion added the 43d and 77th Companies, and the 51st Company was once again welcomed into its ranks. When the dust settled on 4 September, the 5th Regiment had a regimental

Headquarters and Headquarters Company; Supply Company; the 1st (17th, 23d, and 49th Companies), 2d (43d, 51st, and 77th Companies), and 3d (8th, 16th, and 20th Companies) Battalions; and a new commander, Col. James T. Buttrick.

The Guardia Nacional was expanded to offset Marine departures as political pressure to bring the Americans home increased. New tactics were also tried. A program to deny the rebels food, supplies, and intelligence was instituted. Local peasants were forcibly removed from their homes and relocated into carefully monitored concentration areas. Unfortunately, this unpopular program was a dismal failure because dissatisfaction with the corrupt operation of the program and the resentment of those forcibly moved actually increased the number of rebels. The government cause received another setback when Sandino, fresh from courting international support, returned with his pockets stuffed with cash raised by left-wing activists in the United States. Sandino's return did not, however, stop the American withdrawal.

The 5th Regiment was reduced to a single six-company battalion in April 1930. Regimental headquarters was deactivated at Managua on 11 April and the 2d and 3d Battalions followed suit the next day. Both battalion headquarters companies were disbanded. The 77th Company (2d Battalion) and the 8th and 16th Companies (3d Battalion) were also eliminated. The 2d Battalion's 43d and 51st Companies and the 3d Battalion's 20th Company were transferred to 1st Battalion. A new 66th Company was formed at Matagalpa, and a temporary Casual Company was formed at Managua on 12 April then dissolved ten days later. The 20th Company was disbanded at Puerto Cabezas on 15 May. When the reorganization was complete, the 5th Regiment, now commanded by Lt. Col. Franklin B. Garrett, consisted of the 17th, 23d, 43d, 49th, 51st, and 66th Companies. The regiment was called on four times to assist the Guardia, but thereafter conducted only routine security duties during the rest of the second Nicaraguan campaign.

The 5th Regiment was further reduced in size in 1931. The 51st Company was disbanded on 30 April, the 66th Company on 1 May, and the 43d Company on 5 May. The 5th Regiment was officially redesignated the 5th Marines and numbered companies were given letter designations in June. The 17th Company became Company A, the 23d became Company C, and the 49th became Company B. This dual number-letter system, a confusing joint-service bureaucratic throwback used during the Great War, was retained until 1 January 1933. Lieutenant Colonel Edward W. Sturdevant, a name familiar from World War I, commanded the 5th Marines from 8 September to 15 November. He was succeeded by Maj. Anderson C. Dearing, who held that billet until Lieutenant Colonel Willis once again became commanding officer on 4 February then served in that position until 14 November 1932.

Supervising the 1932 national elections was the final task for the 5th Marines in Nicaragua. As before, the men were well schooled as to their duties and the election went smoothly. Again, despite Sandino's best efforts to disrupt it, another honest and tranquil election day passed. Doctor Juan Sacasa took the presidential oath of office at Managua on New Year's Day 1933. This cleared the way for the long-awaited Marine withdrawal. Major Frederick R. Hoyt's 1st Battalion, 5th Marines, moved to Corinto and was disbanded there on 2 January 1933. The Marines sailed for Quantico the next day on board the transports *Henderson* and *Antares*.

The Marines had participated in more than 150 engagements and lost 136 men over six years in Nicaragua. During that time the regiment successfully accomplished the tasks assigned to it. The country was stabilized, democratic elections were held and elected officials took office as scheduled, and possible foreign intervention had been prevented. Sandino was still at large when the Marines left, but the rampant banditry and lawlessness that previously plagued the country had been obliterated. When the 5th Marines finally departed for home, the citizens of Nicaragua were, for a while at least, able to enjoy the comforts of peace and security. Although the Nicaraguan intervention may have had little positive impact on long-term U.S. interests in Latin America, the military lessons learned by the regiment during the second Nicaraguan campaign were carefully catalogued for inclusion in the Maine Corps's *Small Wars Manual,* a document whose major tenets are still usefully applied to military operations other than war that are so prevalent in the post–Cold War era.

While the regiment was busy in Nicaragua, there was a change of Commandants. General Lejeune's successors, Buck Neville and Ben Fuller, were both former members of the 5th Marines. After inheriting Lejeune's mantle, each essentially continued his far-sighted polices throughout the early 1930s.

The Fleet Marine Force

During the decade of the 1930s, the 5th Marines played a major role in the development of Marine Corps amphibious expertise. President

Franklin D. Roosevelt's Good Neighbor Policy quieted Latin America and China was well in hand, so the Marine Corps could devote more time and resources to developing the amphibious readiness necessary to implement War Plan Orange. To do this, the Marine Corps Expeditionary Force was renamed and reorganized, a manual for amphibious warfare was published, research and development of amphibious equipment was seriously undertaken, and field testing of equipment was given a high priority from 1934–41.

The MCEF was renamed the Fleet Marine Force (FMF) in 1933. This event was much more than a simple name change. The FMF was a naval "type command" permanently assigned to the U.S. Fleet. This gave Marine commanders coequal status with their navy counterparts. The new FMF included two brigades: the 1st Brigade on the East Coast and the 2d Brigade on the West Coast, were assigned to the Atlantic and Pacific Fleets respectively, to conduct advanced base operations. This reorganization resulted in the reactivation of the 5th Marines at Quantico, where the 1st and 2d Battalions, FMF, were redesignated the 1st and 2d Battalions, 5th Marines, on 1 September 1934. This woefully understrength two-battalion regiment, commanded by Lt. Col. (later Maj. Gen.) Charles F. B. Price for the next year, was the infantry regiment assigned to the 1st Brigade.

Concurrently, the Marine Corps Schools used historical research and lessons learned in the fleet maneuvers of the 1920s to write the *Tentative Manual For Landing Operations*. This document, first published in 1934, established a comprehensive new amphibious doctrine that included detailed descriptions of command relationships, naval gunfire, air support, ship-to-shore movement, communications, and logistics. This doctrinal guidebook was reworked and expanded over the years and served as the bible for the conduct of American amphibious operations during World War II. It remains the basis for American amphibious doctrine to the present day. The navy formally adopted this work as *Fleet Training Publication 167* in 1938 and the army published it as *Field Manual 31-5* in 1941. Several prominent former members of the 5th Regiment participated in the formation of this seminal work, including Lt. Col. Bennett Puryear Jr. and Majs. Allen H. Turnage, Robert Blake, LeRoy Hunt, and Alexander A. Vandegrift.

The new amphibious doctrine and the developmental equipment needed to put it into practice were tested and improved during a series of fleet landing exercises (FLEXs) held each year from 1935 to 1941. Most FLEXs took place at Puerto Rico's Culebra and Vieques Islands, but one was held at California's San Clemente Island. Each exercise became more complex as time passed and were used as building blocks for expanding doctrine and perfecting amphibious techniques. Writing after World War II, Lt. Gen. Holland Smith noted: "The Japanese bases in the Pacific were [first] captured on the beaches of the Caribbean where [tactical] problems . . . were worked out in Marine maneuvers." The 5th Marines was usually the landing force during these exercises and thus became the primary testing organization for infantry equipment. Among the innovations mentioned in 5th Marines exercise reports were suggestions regarding improved individual uniforms and equipment, and the need for specifically designed troop transport ships, self-propelled ramped landing craft, and armor-plated troop-carrying amphibious vehicles.

A pair of cadre regiments—the two-battalion 5th Marines and the one-battalion 10th Marines—plus various support units, and a 12-plane observation squadron comprised the 1st Marine Brigade during FLEX 1 at Culebra from 19 January to 22 February 1935. Headquarters Company and the 2d Battalion were embarked on the battleship USS *Wyoming* and the 1st Battalion sailed on board the squadron flagship USS *Arkansas*. The operational emphasis was on field problems ashore, but everyday the Marines climbed down gangways and loaded into ships' boats for movement to the beach. There was one full-scale landing exercise. Among the lessons learned by the 5th Marines and reported by Colonel Price in his exercise summary were that battleships were not well suited to the transport role (it too long to get down the gangways and into the landing boats) and existing navy small craft were too few in number and poorly configured to support landing operations. These recommendations resulted in testing new types of landing boats, the use of cargo nets instead of gangways, and the conversion of World War I–era "four-pipe" destroyers into APD high-speed assault transports.

Fleet Landing Exercise 2, held from 4 January to 24 February 1936, was a more elaborate undertaking. The 1st Marine Brigade (composed of the 5th and 10th Marines, various support elements, and Aircraft One) conducted eight landings. This time the Marines went over the side using cargo nets to board whaleboats and motor launches. Each battalion conducted at least one daylight landing, a daytime landing covered by a smoke screen, and a night landing. Battalion exercises were followed by a regimental rehearsal, and a full-brigade landing culminated the maneuvers.

Although these landings were far better than the ones the year before, there were still many teething pains. A forty-foot motor launch carrying two rifle platoons almost broached on a coral reef during a special test and required most of the day to free itself. The 2d Battalion encountered difficulty during its night landing. The landing boats got lost on their way to the ships in the dark, so the Marines could not implement the landing plans. Then some coxswains became confused during the ship-to-shore movement and made landfall considerable distances from the intended landing areas. The 1st Battalion had more success with its night landing as a result of lessons learned the previous night. It was a good thing Col. Harold L. Parsons held a regimental rehearsal prior to the final brigade exercise, because the same mistakes were made during the rehearsal. Boats got lost in the dark, circled in confused groups until daylight, failed to leave the line of departure on time, and landed at the wrong beaches. The brigade landing was smoother, but was still marred by confusion on the beaches. Colonel Parson's postexercise report noted that the ships had insufficient troop and cargo space and too few organic landing boats. He recommended that assault transport ships be designed, built, and earmarked to support the FMF.

Colonel Charles J. Miller's 5th Marines ventured through the Panama Canal to California's San Clemente Island for FLEX 3 in 1937. This exercise, the largest amphibious landing to date, reunited the 5th and 6th Marines for the first time since the Civil War maneuvers more than a decade before. An army regiment joined the two Marine regiments for daytime, smoke-screened daylight, and night landings. Five landing boats foundered in the heavy Pacific surf, and Colonel Miller reported that "Navy standard boats [are not] tactical vehicles . . . [they lack] speed and maneuverability and are extremely difficult to handle in the surf." He deemed them inadequate as landing craft because they did not permit rapid debarkation of troops at the water's edge. The breakdown of the *Arkansas* forced the 5th Marines to be transported piecemeal, and this incident once again reinforced the inadequacy of warships used to transport troops for amphibious operations.

Night landings were tried again during FLEX 4 in 1938, but this time some new wrinkles were added. Two rifle companies transferred from transports to troop-carrying destroyers to act as an advance force. They landed about six hours before the rest of the regiment came ashore and secured the landing areas. This part of the exercise went very well and led to further experiments that were so successful the 1st Battalion became a specially organized, destroyer-mounted landing force in 1941. The 5th Marines's night landing was less successful. Landing boats struck uncharted reefs or landed in the wrong place, and units became hopelessly mixed as they came ashore. Although night landings were conducted in subsequent exercises, it was generally conceded after FLEX 4 that large-scale night landings were impractical under combat conditions. (Only two relatively large-scale night landings were conducted during World War II: one by the 2d Raider Battalion at Makin, and the other by the 1st Parachute Battalion at Tanambogo. The results were mixed at best, and no further night amphibious operations were attempted.) Fleet Landing Exercise 5 was held at Culebra in early 1939. This time Col. Julian C. Smith commanded the 5th Marines.

The regiment was also called on to perform several high-profile ceremonial missions during the decade. Several companies were present at the Century of Progress Exhibition in Chicago in 1934; the 1st Battalion stood guard over the blackened hulk of the German zeppelin *Hindenburg* after its tragic immolation at Lakehurst, New Jersey, in 1937; and the regiment furnished men for the Marine detachment at the New York World's Fair in 1939. The 5th Marines also participated in three more Civil War reenactments: the Chancellorsville Pageant in 1935, the First Manassas in 1936, and the Petersburg Crater in 1937. Battalions of the 5th Marines provided shooters and rotated duties as support personnel for the annual national rifle matches at Camp Perry, Ohio. The regiment also provided cadres to assist summer reserve training at Quantico.

There were few organizational changes during this time. The 5th Marines continued to be a two-battalion regiment mustering a Headquarters Company (including 37mm gun and 81mm mortar sections), Service Company, six rifle companies (A, B, C, E, F, and G) and two machine-gun companies (D and H). Among the more notable commanders of this period were Col. Samuel M. Harrington, the primary author of the *Small Wars Manual*, and Lt. Col. Henry Larsen, who had commanded the 3d Battalion in France in 1918. Lieutenant Colonel (later General) Allen Turnage briefly commanded the regiment in 1938.

The year 1940 was one of change. The outbreak of war in Europe in 1939 pointed out the need for American preparedness. This, in turn, led to an expansion of the Marine Corps. In April 1940, after returning from the Caribbean where it participated in FLEX 6, the 5th Marines added a third rifle battalion by breaking up its existing units. These units were divided into equal parts, but commanders were not told who would be selected to lead which detachment until after the rosters had been submitted. This simple solution ensured an equitable allocation of men and prevented favoritism in the selection process. Both old and new units were then brought up to strength by adding old hands culled from various posts and stations throughout the Corps, recently activated Marine reservists, slick-sleeve privates from Parris Island, and shiny-bar second lieutenants fresh out of Quantico. This process was so successful that it was later used to create the 7th Marines in 1940, the 1st Marines in 1941, and a new 1st Battalion in 1942. The 5th Marines was commanded during this time by Col. Charles D. Barrett (August 1939–May 1940), Col. David L. S. Brewster (May 1940), and Col. Alfred H. Noble (May 1940–March 1941). Lieutenant Colonel Graves B. Erskine, one of a handful of Marine mustangs who rose from private to four-star rank, stood in as acting regimental commander for Noble from 7–10 November 1940.

By the end of 1940 the war in Europe was heating up, and it was obvious America would most likely be dragged into it sooner or later. This resulted in constant expansion and frantic preparations throughout the next year. Although the United States was not officially involved in the ongoing European war, several emergencies arose that required Marine attention. After Adolf Hitler's Nazi legions engulfed the European continent it became increasingly likely the Marines on the East Coast would soon be called into action. Among the contingencies faced by the 5th Marines were the possible seizure of the French island of Martinique in 1940 and the occupation of the Portuguese Azores in 1941. It was also obvious U.S. Army units would have to be trained to conduct amphibious operations and that Marines would have to serve as instructors.

The 1st Marine Brigade, led by former 8th Company commander Brig. Gen. Holland Smith, moved from Quantico to "Gitmo" (Guantanamo) for winter maneuvers in the late fall of 1940. Thereafter, as one chronicler of the 1st Marine Division noted, the Marines never really came out of the "boondocks" until the end of World War II—except for a brief sojourn in Melbourne, Australia. On 1 February 1941, while participating in FLEX 7, the 1st Marine Brigade became the 1st Marine Division. However, this eight-thousand-man unit remained a division in name only until it returned stateside.

Fleet Exercise 7 was the last one before the United States entered World War II. The 5th Marines, less one separate company on board an APD destroyer, was embarked on board the USS *McCawley* (formerly the SS *Santa Barbara*). This exercise provided a good test of the Higgins landing craft, vehicle, personnel (LCVP) thirty-six-foot, front-ramped landing boats. They passed with flying colors. The Marines reported these new landing craft were excellent and recommended their immediate adoption. The 5th Marines also explored using machine guns to fill the fire-support gap created when naval gunfire shifted from the landing area to inland targets, a technique later put to good use in the South Pacific.

The year 1941 was a time of upheaval and expansion. The 5th Marines was in a state of constant turmoil. It continually lost talented individuals and had to break up trained units to create new organizations as the Marine Corps tripled its size. Lieutenant Colonels Charles T. Brooks and Robert C. Kilmartin alternated command of the regiment until the arrival of Col. Robert Blake on 27 May. Blake, a lieutenant in World War I, earned the Navy Cross, DSC, and two Silver Star citations while serving with the regiment in France. The 5th Marines was split into three groups after FLEX 7. The 1st Battalion returned to Quantico to become a special test unit. The other two battalions went to Parris Island and Norfolk to absorb new recruits and conduct small-unit training. Detachments from the 5th Marines were sent to New River, North Carolina, in late May to erect Tent Camp One in the scrub pines and swamps near Onslow Beach. This desolate 112,000-acre post, later named Camp Lejeune, became the 5th Marines's home base from September 1941 until the regiment shipped out for the Pacific in May 1942.

The 1st Battalion received a new commander, Lt. Col. Merritt A. Edson, in June. Red Mike became famous throughout the Corps after leading the Coco River patrols in Nicaragua and distinguished himself as a member of the Marine rifle team while serving with the 5th Regiment in the twenties. Edson was handpicked to take over the 1st Battalion in order to turn it into a unique Marine unit. Although it remained an organic 5th Marines battalion and retained its normal structure in garrison, the 1st Battalion was task organized into six 120-man reinforced rifle units for embarkation on APD high-speed transport ships. These outdated, flush-deck destroyers (the *Manley, Calhoun, Gregory, Little, McKean,* and *Stringham*) were converted into transports by removing two boilers and using the empty space for troop compartments. Although they were short on creature comforts and cargo space, these ships were fast enough to keep up with a combat task force and could provide their own naval gunfire support. The APDs mounted a few landing craft, but the primary ship-to-shore transportation mode was rubber boats. Consequently, the 1st Battalion became proficient in their use and specialized in night landing operations. It was envisioned that the entire battalion or any combination of its six rifle units could land either as part of a conventional regimental landing force or be used independently to conduct amphibious raids, deceptions, or advance force operations.

The 5th Marines, as part of the 1st Marine Division, was assigned to the 1st Joint Training Command (later Amphibious Corps, Atlantic Fleet) in the summer. It provided training cadres to the U.S. Army's 1st Infantry Division, and the entire regiment participated in joint landing exercises in June, July, and August that were actually rehearsals for a proposed joint army-Marine landing in North Africa. Edson's 1st Battalion returned to Quantico and effectively became an independent organization at the end of these maneuvers. The unit was formally separated from the 5th Marines in late January 1942 when it was renamed the 1st Raider Battalion. The 2d and 3d Battalions, 5th Marines, were carved up to create a new 1st Battalion in February.

The complexion of the 5th Marines, like that of all other Marine units, changed with the outbreak of World War II. This was true for both the structure of the regiment and the Marines that filled its ranks. The regiment was reorganized to conform with the wartime D-series tables of equipment and organization, and its units were as fully manned as possible. Marine divisions used a triangular structure with three infantry regiments. The new 3,168-man rifle regiments consisted of a headquarters company and three 933-man rifle battalions each consisting of a headquarters company, a weapons company, and three rifle companies. Rifle companies had three rifle platoons and a weapons platoon. Weapons companies included 81mm mortar and machine-gun sections. Platoons mustered three nine-man rifle squads and one eight-man Browning Automatic Rifle (BAR) squad. A regimental weapons company armed with halftrack-mounted 75mm guns and 20mm dual-purpose guns for antitank defense and antiaircraft use was added in April. By that time, the "Old Corps" veterans were far outnumbered by fresh-faced volunteers who signed on only for the duration of the war and did not intend to make the service a career. Old salts who preferred to lament the loss of professionalism rather than change to accommodate the needs of the armed forces found this transition particularly hard to take. Fortunately, the newcomers—like their World War I predecessors—quickly adapted to military life and soon could not be distinguished from the long-service regulars.

New tables of equipment and organization brought about a new way of doing things as well. Regimental commanders could call upon division headquarters to provide combat and service-support specialists and equipment. These combat support assets included the 75mm and

105mm howitzers of the 11th Marines, navy Seabees and Marine pioneers and combat engineers of the 17th Marines, M3 light tanks of the 1st Tank Battalion, navy doctors and corpsmen from the 1st Medical Battalion, and amphibious vehicles and drivers from the 1st Amphibian Tractor Battalion. Detachments from these units were assigned to the 5th Marines to create a tactical unit called a combat group (a designation later changed to regimental combat team) composed of three transport units called combat teams (later changed to battalion landing teams).

The appearance of the 5th Marines changed as well. Gone were the khaki field uniforms and dishpan-shaped helmets. They were replaced by green-herringbone dungaree and rounded M1 steel helmets. There would be no chance of mistaking World War II Marines for army Doughboys, as had happened in France during World War I, because the letters *USMC* as well as an eagle, globe, and anchor emblem were stenciled in black ink on the left-breast pocket of Marine uniforms. Marine small arms, with minor exceptions (e.g., the ill-fated Reising guns), were the same ones that had served so well for the past three decades: the M1903 Springfield rifle, the M1911A1 .45-caliber semiautomatic pistol, the .30-caliber BAR, the M1917A1 .30-caliber water-cooled medium machine gun, and the M1919A4 .30-caliber air-cooled light machine gun.

Postscript

Although many interwar Marines served with the regiment, two went on to particularly distinguish themselves in the Pacific campaigns. One, fatherly Julian Smith, took over the 2d Marine Division after Guadalcanal, led it at the bloody battle of Tarawa in the Gilberts, oversaw planning for the seizure of the Palaus as a provisional corps commander, and served as the deputy commander of FMF Pacific. He was one of the most popular and respected senior Marines when he retired after World War II. Colorful Red Mike Edson was arguably one of the most versatile Marine officers of all time. He was already a crack shot, a spit-and-polish seagoing Marine, a courageous combat leader, a meticulous planner, and a fine staff officer. His World War II service added even more luster to his star. He ultimately sacrificed his career to save the Marine Corps and suffered an untimely end. But as will be seen, Edson's service with the 5th Marines was far from over.

4: World War II

Japan was a latecomer to the world stage. That long-isolated island empire in the Far East managed to avoid major contact with the West until the arrival of Commodore Matthew Perry's American squadron in 1854. The Japanese, however, quickly adopted Western ways and successfully merged modern technology with the ancient ways of Samurai warriors to create a first-class military system. In the late nineteenth century Japan tossed China out of Korea, annexed Formosa, and made inroads into Manchuria. Early in the twentieth century, Japan stunned the Western world when it humbled Russia's cumbersome war machine. The burgeoning Japanese Empire obtained vast new territories when it was granted mandates over former German territory in the Pacific in the wake of World War I. Unfortunately, Japan's relations with the United States continuously declined from that point forth. American Marines got a preview of the next decade when they witnessed Japanese aggression firsthand during a series of incidents in China during the 1930s. An economic blockade that involved cutting shipments of raw materials from the United States and an oil embargo by European colonial powers to protest Japan's heavy-handed methods used to create the Greater Far East Co–Prosperity Sphere forced that nation's hand in late 1941. The result was the surprise attack on Pearl Harbor and Japan's quick capture of every major Allied outpost and colony in the Far East. Spurred on by success throughout the Pacific, the Japanese decided to move on Australia. That offensive was halted by the Battle of the Coral Sea in May 1942, but American lines of communication were still at risk and the outcome of the war was far from certain that summer.

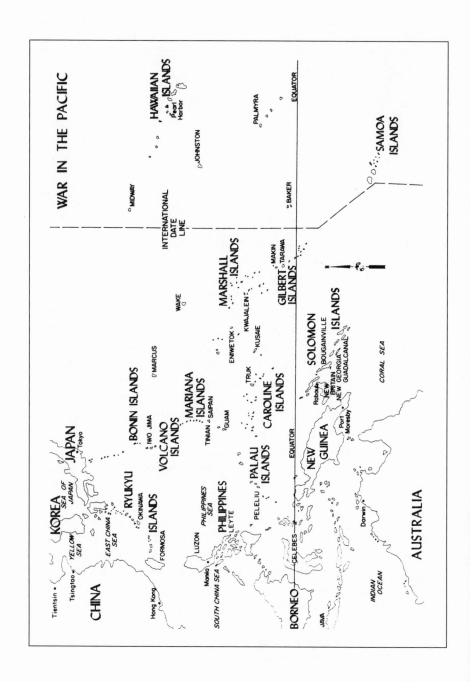

Call to Arms

The United States was propelled into its second major war of the twentieth century when the Japanese launched a surprise attack on U.S. military bases on the island of Oahu in the Hawaiian Islands on 7 December 1941. After that fateful morning—a date that still lives in infamy—the United States began its transformation from a blissful isolationist refuge into the most powerful belligerent in the most devastating armed conflict in history. The war in the Pacific was one that the United States had planned for but did not expect precisely at that moment. The Marine Corps, like all of the other U.S. services, was caught short of men, supplies, and equipment. It was a hectic few months before these shortfalls could be rectified and the United States could finally strike back. In the meantime, outmanned and outgunned, Americans took a beating. Small Marine outposts at Guam and Wake Island were overwhelmed. In the Philippines, a Marine regiment was ordered to surrender—the only time that has happened in American history. Because these far-flung units could not be reinforced, their only choice was to delay the enemy to buy time for America's armed forces to build strength for the fight.

The 5th Marines spent the last days of peace in 1941 and the early months of 1942 at New River's tent camp. The attack at Pearl Harbor brought a sudden influx of recruits who enlisted for the duration, and they began arriving at New River in unprecedented numbers at the beginning of the new year. The 1941 fall maneuvers consisted of field problems and practice landings. The Marines used ships and landing craft for amphibious practice when they were available, but most of the time wooden ship mock-ups on the beach had to suffice. The 5th Marines moved to Solomons, Maryland, for advanced amphibious training in January and February 1942. These exercises were originally scheduled to be conducted at New River's Onslow Beach, but they had to be moved inside the safety of the Chesapeake Bay because German submarines were sinking Allied ships at will along the Atlantic Coast. In fact, the area off North Carolina was so dangerous it became known as "Torpedo Junction."

Bob Blake turned over the reins of the 5th Marines to old friend and World War I comrade Col. LeRoy Hunt—the fearless and charismatic leader who had commanded the 5th Regiment's 17th Company and 1st Battalion during the Great War—on 9 April 1942. The regiment trained with a sense of urgency because the men were certain they would soon see action. It was far from certain, however, exactly where or when this action might take place. In the spring of 1942, the European theater seemed to be the place where the East Coast–based 1st Marine Division would most likely be used. The long-anticipated call to action finally came in May. It turned out, however, that the 5th Marines was not headed for North Africa as expected but was instead shoving off for the South Pacific to implement War Plan Orange. The 5th Marines moved to Norfolk, boarded the transport USS *Wakefield* (formerly the SS *Manhattan*), and set off on the longest ocean voyage in regimental history on 20 May. It would be a long time before the 5th Marines returned to the United States.

By the time the Marines arrived in the South Pacific, the Japanese had been stymied. Their drive south ended in the Coral Sea, and efforts to take Hawaii and the Aleutian Islands were stopped cold at the Battle of Midway. Although it was not exactly obvious at the time, the Japanese Empire had reached its zenith and would be on the defensive from then on. On 2 July 1942, the U.S. Joint Chiefs of Staff directed the Southwest Pacific (Gen. Douglas MacArthur) and South Pacific (VAdm. Robert L. Ghormley) theater commanders to mount offensive actions to neutralize the Japanese stronghold at Rabaul on the island of New Britain. Three tasks were envisioned: (1) seizure of bases in the Solomon Islands chain, (2) seizure of New Guinea, and (3) clearing the rest of the Bismarck Archipelago. The timetable had to be significantly speeded up when Allied intelligence became aware of Japanese movements in the Solomons. This set the stage for an epic battle, one that soon rivaled Belleau Wood's place in the history of the Marine Corps.

Guadalcanal

The *Wakefield* arrived in Wellington, New Zealand, on 14 June 1942. The men of the 5th Marines, like those of the 5th Regiment at Saint-Nazaire in 1917, were promptly put to work unloading supplies and equipment. This round-the-clock toil in the chilly winter rain (the seasons are reversed south of the equator) was necessary because civilian dock workers were on strike. Actually, the hard labor had a very real benefit: it worked the grumbling Marines—softened by the long ocean voyage— back into shape. Once the ships had been unloaded, the regiment moved about thirty-five miles north of Wellington to Paekakariki Training Camp at McKay's Crossing in the mountains. Major General Alexander A. Van-

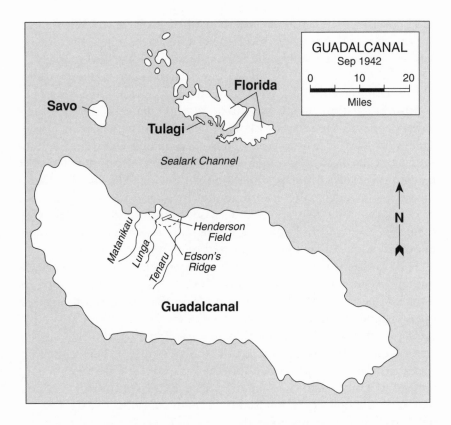

degrift, the 1st Marine Division commanding general and veteran of service in the 5th Marines, was sure he would need all the promised time until January 1943 to turn his division into a cohesive fighting force. Among his problems were that divisional elements were scattered across the Pacific from California to Samoa, stateside training had left much to be desired because of constant turnover of personnel and the large number of new Marines, and civilian cargo ships carrying vital supplies had to be unloaded and that material stowed aboard assault transports for combat operations. At a routine commanders' meeting, General Vandegrift was mildly surprised to learn there was soon going to be an American landing in the Solomons, but he was flabbergasted to find out his division was to be the assault unit. Despite many previous high-level assurances that the Marines would not be committed to combat for at least six months, Vandegrift was abruptly informed that he had less than two weeks to prepare for the division's first combat operation.

The reason for such haste was that Allied intelligence officers had just discovered that the Japanese had occupied an excellent harbor and were building an airfield in the Solomons, a South Pacific island chain located about three-quarters of the way between Hawaii and Australia. These enemy positions threatened Allied lines of communication in the Southwest Pacific. To end that threat an immediate amphibious campaign was needed to seize the island of Tulagi along with nearby Guadalcanal and Gavutu. The offensive was code-named Operation Watchtower, but the hasty planning and perceived lack of support led to it being unofficially known as "Operation Shoestring." Information about the area was sketchy; there were neither firm estimates as to Japanese forces nor detailed maps of the area. As General Vandegrift said in his memoirs, "We did not know how strong [the enemy] was, nor did we know his plans . . . [we] knew only that he had to be stopped."

The 1st Marine Division was at only about two-thirds strength because one of the three infantry regiments (the 7th Marines) and its support units had been detached to guard American Samoa. But with combat operations about to begin, the 2d Marines (of the 2d Marine Division), the 1st Raider Battalion, and the 3d Defense Battalion were attached to bring Vandegrift's division up to full combat strength. The reinforced 1st Marine Division was split into two task groups for Operation Watchtower. Task Force Yoke was to capture Tulagi and Gavutu, which were nestled in the shadow of Florida Island on the north side of Sealark Channel. Task Force Xray was to seize and defend a patch of the northern Guadalcanal coast that included an airfield on the far side of Sealark Channel.

Colonel LeRoy Hunt commanded the 5th Marines. His executive officer was Lt. Col. William J. Whaling. Both men were popular, highly decorated officers who had proven themselves in the heat of battle on many occasions. The regimental staff included personnel officer Capt. Donald L. Dickson (an accomplished artist whose popular sketches and paintings were used to raise morale on the home front after he returned to the United States), intelligence officer Capt. Wilfred H. "Bill" Ringer Jr., operations officer Maj. William I. Phipps, and logistics officer 2d Lt. William L. Williams. Lieutenant Colonel William E. Maxwell commanded the 1st Battalion, Lt. Col. Harold E. Rosecrans led the 2d Battalion, and Lt. Col. Frederick C. Biebush commanded the 3d Battalion. The 5th Marines was reinforced for Operation Watchtower by the 2d Battalion, 11th Marines; Company A, 1st Tank Battalion; Company A,

1st Engineer Battalion; Company A, 1st Pioneer Battalion; 1st Platoon, Battery A, 1st Special Weapons Battalion; Company A, 1st Medical Battalion; Company A, 1st Amphibian Tractor Battalion; and the 1st Platoon, 1st Scout Company. Combat Group A was composed of the regimental headquarters and Combat Teams 1 (1st Battalion, reinforced) and 3 (3d Battalion, reinforced). Combat Team 2, composed of the 2d Battalion and a few combat support detachments, was assigned to Combat Group B.

Combat Group A was assigned to Task Force Xray. Combat Team 2 joined the 1st Raider Battalion, the 1st Parachute Battalion, and elements of the 2d Marines in Task Force Yoke. General Vandegrift would lead the bulk of the division ashore at Guadalcanal's Red Beach, while Brig. Gen. William H. Rupertus, the assistant division commander, would command the Tulagi-Gavutu landings.

The 5th Marines made its way down from Camp Paekakariki, hastily boarded the assigned ships, and sailed for Fiji on 22 July 1942. The convoy from New Zealand rendezvoused with arriving navy and Marine units at Fiji's Koro Harbor four days later. Final plans were talked over and rehearsals were held from 28–31 July before the convoy wove its way west to the Solomons. Luckily, the movement to Guadalcanal went undetected.

On the night of 6 August 1942, the convoy broke into two assault groups, which then slipped past Savo Island and took up offshore assault positions in the predawn darkness of the seventh. On the eve of battle, Colonel Hunt reminded his men that they need not worry because they were Marines and their training and spirit would carry the day. He then performed an impromptu "buck and wing" dance in the wardroom to relax his officers. Similar talks, less the "buck and wing" and in far saltier language, were concurrently made by many veteran NCOs speaking to green troops in the sweaty troopship holds. These speeches probably went something like "Aw right you people, listen up! When we hit the beach tomorrow git outta them boats fast and keep moving straight inland for the 'O-1' Line. Don't bunch up, don't move parallel to the beach, and don't wait for orders. And above all else, remember you're United States Marines and no [expletive deleted] little [racial epithet deleted] is gonna show us up. Remember Wake Island!"

The Marines were roused from fitful sleep during the early morning hours, ate beans for breakfast, then returned to the sweltering troop compartments until ordered topside. Loudspeakers blared "Marines to your embarkation stations!" at 0600. A quarter of an hour later the Marines divided into thirty-six-man boat teams and began to climb down the cargo nets into their assigned landing craft, vehicle, personnel (LCVPs). The convoy's night approach had been so successful that the enemy was unaware of the American presence until the first salvos broke the morning calm. As naval gunfire pummeled the shore, boat groups circled in the transport area until ordered to "Land the Landing Force." The little Higgins boats then formed into landing waves for the rough ride to the shore.

Captain William L. Hawkins's Company B, 5th Marines, landed on Red Beach at 0909, one minute before the scheduled H-hour. There was no enemy opposition as the 1st Battalion fanned out to the right, and the 3d Battalion did likewise on the left to clear the way for the 1st Marines. It went so well that Colonel Hunt opened his command post ashore at 0938. The 1st Battalion was ordered to cross the Tenaru (actually the Ilu) River and occupy positions along Alligator Creek before dark. Contemporary maps were inconsistent about place names, so the place names used herein are those found on a 1942 sketch map used by the 5th Marines with current designations appearing in parentheses upon first citation for clarity. The 3d Battalion manned a defensive arc that stretched about fifteen hundred yards from the east branch of Ilu Creek (actually the Tenaru River) to the beach. The landing and consolidation on Guadalcanal, except for an ever-growing pile of supplies at the beach, had gone much smoother than expected. In fact, the first casualty of the day was a careless Marine who cut himself trying to open a coconut.

On the far side of Sealark Channel, the 2/5 stormed ashore through heavy surf at Tulagi's Blue Beach in the wake of Edson's Raiders at 0916. Colonel Rosecrans established his command post just west of the beach then parceled out his battalion to accomplish a variety of tasks. Company F swept across the northwest section of the island, but reported no enemy. Company E operated in support of Raider Company B, and elements of Company H (the battalion weapons company) supported Raider Company C's attack against Hill 208. Present for duty with Company H was fifty-two-year-old MGySgt. Leland Diamond. Vociferous and profane, eccentric "Lou Diamond" was considered a mortarman without peer and was a living legend in the Corps. He had been a railroad man prior to joining the Marine Corps at age twenty-seven, but by 1942, he was an expert with 60mm and 81mm mortars. Although respected by all as an outstanding fighting man, he was—by his own admission—not a "spit-and-polish" Marine. Lou Diamond was an old China Hand and veteran of the Great War who sported a goatee, seldom saluted officers, disdained the use of a helmet in combat, and perpetually wore dungarees regardless of uniform-of-the-day regulations. When questioned by a general officer about why he was wearing dungarees to a formal awards ceremony, Lou Diamond testily replied, "I made the landing wearing them, so they're good enough to get a commendation in." Lou Diamond was also known as "the Honker" because of his booming voice, which was so loud that he allegedly drowned out the air-raid sirens on the "Canal." Among the many sea stories told about Lou Diamond is one about him putting a mortar round down the smokestack of a careless Japanese destroyer when it wandered too close to shore at Guadalcanal. Although this particular story is probably apocryphal, Lou Diamond was certainly one of the most colorful Marines in the Corps's history.

Company G reported for duty at Colonel Edson's command post at about 1300. Not long thereafter, Colonel Rosecrans relocated his battalion command post closer to the action. The 2d Battalion occupied positions behind the Raider lines and supported Edson's Marines by fire as they repulsed a series of Japanese counterattacks that night. Companies E and F maneuvered into positions on the northeast slopes of Hill 281 on the morning of 8 August and swept forward. This action forced the enemy to take cover inside a small ravine. Company H then used Lou Diamond's mortars and plunging machine-gun fire to reduce enemy resistance until assault teams could take this final pocket. Company G joined the Raiders to clear this troublesome area in the midafternoon. All organized resistance ended within a couple of hours, and Red Mike Edson declared Tulagi secure before nightfall on D-plus-1.

General Vandegrift assessed the situation on Guadalcanal before he turned in on D day night. Fortunately, there had been no serious enemy opposition. Less fortunately, progress inland had been laboriously slow, and it was painfully obvious existing maps were inaccurate. This meant the proposed scheme of maneuver was impractical. Colonel Hunt was informed of Vandegrift's impending change in plans at about 2200 on the night of the seventh. Instead of capturing Mount Austen as previously planned, the 1st Marine Division would take the airfield and then establish a defensive perimeter at Lunga Point. The 5th Marines (less the 2d Battalion on Tulagi) would make the attack along the beach while the 1st Marines conducted an inland flanking movement. The 5th

Marines would then assume defensive positions along the west bank of the Lunga River once the airfield was safely in American hands.

The attack went about as planned on D-plus-1. The 1st Battalion, reinforced by M3A1 Stuart light tanks from Company A, 1st Tank Battalion, crossed Alligator Creek and moved out with its right flank on the beach. This advance was made without serious incident, although Lt. Col. "Wild Bill" Whaling chafed at the slow progress of the assault units. The Marines encountered only scattered resistance and captured several prisoners along the way. Field interrogations and captured documents revealed the Japanese had been so surprised that they established no organized resistance and had as yet formulated no viable counterattack plan.

Colonel Hunt was ordered to continue the attack to Lunga Point before the enemy could recover. Regimental Weapons Company halftracks led the way at about 1430, and Colonel Hunt personally led the 5th Marines into Kukum village about a half-hour later. This hastily organized attack turned out to be a coup de main. The Marines discovered large quantities of food and ammunition. Particularly treasured were canned delicacies and bottles filled with rice wine or Japanese beer. Valuable abandoned communications gear and engineer equipment was also taken intact. Captain Gordon D. Gayle (the 1/5 operations officer) wisely ignored orders to destroy an enemy communications suite, and the Japanese radios he saved were put to good use later on. It was not known at the time, but this unexpected bounty of food and equipment would become the margin of victory during the close-fought battle for what the Japanese eventually called "Starvation Island."

Japanese aircraft sank an American destroyer and set fire to a transport ship on the afternoon of the eighth. To make matters worse, General Vandegrift received disturbing confirmation that all American aircraft carriers were going to be withdrawn the following day in spite of his strenuous objections. This unhappy situation was compounded by a naval disaster at Savo Island that night in which four Allied cruisers were sunk by an undetected Japanese task force. As a result, the American transports and supply ships sailed from Guadalcanal with virtually all heavy cargo and most supplies still in their holds the following morning. Thus, as the Japanese closed in on Guadalcanal, the 1st Marine Division was left to fend for itself with no naval support or air cover and without vital supplies and equipment.

All alone, the Marines had no choice but to dig in and impotently endure repeated air and naval bombardments. Major offensive action was out of the question because of personnel shortages and the necessity to strictly ration food and ammunition. The main enemy threat was believed to be a counterlanding, so General Vandegrift had to use the bulk of his forces to protect the vulnerable coastline. The Guadalcanal coast was dotted with strong points where heavy machine guns and 37mm antitank guns were placed to repel enemy landings. The tanks and 75mm self-propelled guns (SPMs) were organized as mobile reserves. The lengthy inland flank was outposted but could not be protected by an unbroken line due to the lack of men.

The 5th Marines was assigned the far left flank. Colonel Hunt's command post was located at Kukum village. The 3d Battalion defended the western defensive zone along the beach, with its left flank dangling in the thick inland jungle. The 1st Battalion defensive area extended along the beach from Kukum to the east bank of the Lunga River. The orphaned 2d Battalion, still part of Task Force Yoke, remained on Tulagi until the end of August.

Most useful intelligence about Japanese tactical dispositions on Guadalcanal came from either passive observation or extensive patrolling. The 5th Marines mounted daily patrols and some of these developed into major actions. A twelve-man patrol encountered a similar Japanese force several miles southwest of Kukum, but both sides hurriedly broke off the action. The next day, a stronger patrol was denied a crossing at the mouth of the Matanikau River by an unidentified enemy force. These two meeting engagements, combined with lack of contact by other patrols, indicated the enemy main force was located in the Matanikau area. As it turned out, the regiment was frequently involved in operations to clear this area during the remainder of its stay on Guadalcanal.

To confirm the extent of enemy presence Lt. Col. Frank B. Goettge, the division intelligence officer, planned to mount a daylight patrol to search the coast toward Point Cruz. This combat mission, however, was changed to a humanitarian one after a Japanese warrant officer captured by the 1st Battalion led Goettge to believe the enemy was weak and wanted to surrender. Lieutenant Colonel Whaling disbelieved the report and warned Goettge not to land anywhere between Point Cruz and the Matanikau River. He also told Goettge that under no circumstances was he to remain ashore after dark. Despite Bill Whaling's strenuous objections, the patrol included Capt. Bill Ringer and part of the 5th Marines intelligence section. Also included were two navy officers: regimental surgeon Lt. Comdr. Malcolm L. Pratt and Lt. Ralph Cory, a skilled linguist who had previously translated intercepted coded Japanese radio messages. The wisdom of including such irreplaceable men was questioned at the time by Colonel Whaling and by military historians ever since. Goettge should have listened more closely, because "Wild Bill" Whaling was the most experienced jungle fighter in the 1st Marine Division. He was a skilled woodsman and avid hunter who had fought in France and the Banana Wars. A crack shot, he had been a member of the 1924 U.S. Olympic pistol team. Whaling had faced down the Japanese at China's Suchow Creek and survived the Japanese raid on Pearl Harbor. He later went on to command regiments at New Britain and Okinawa and was an assistant division commander in Korea before he retired as a major general.

Goettge's ad hoc force loaded into Higgins boats and, again against the advice of battle-wise Bill Whaling, departed Kukum at 1800 on the evening of 12 August. The validity of Whaling's warnings came to the fore the following morning when Sgt. Charles C. Arndt returned to the Marine lines at 0530. He informed his superiors that the patrol had been ambushed as it landed and was in serious trouble. Two additional survivors, Cpl. Joseph Spaulding and Plt. Sgt. Frank L. Few, later made their way back and reported that the rest of the patrol had been wiped out.

Captain William P. Kaempfer's Company A, 5th Marines, was dispatched to find and rescue the lost patrol at dawn. Company A was reinforced by two platoons of Company L and a machine-gun section from Company M. This search-and-rescue force landed at Point Cruz and worked its way back to the Marine perimeter along the coast looking for survivors. Company A searched the coastal road while the Love Company detachment provided inland flank security. They encountered some light opposition but discovered no sign of the missing Marines. Company A reentered the Marine lines late on the thirteenth and Detachment L came in the next morning.

The 1st Marine Division operations section formulated an operation to clear the coast. A much larger patrol, actually a battalion-sized reconnaissance in force, was mounted into the same area on 19 August. This action, later dubbed the "First Matanikau," was planned as a three-prong exploitation of the Matanikau and Kokumbona villages. Companies B and L were to make a coordinated pincer attack on Matanikau in the east, and Company I was to conduct an amphibious landing to the west. Both groups would then join forces about halfway down the coast. The Marines expected to engage a disorganized and demoralized foe and this, combined with the desire to quickly avenge the Goettge patrol, led to undue haste in the planning process. A Japanese battalion secretly landed at Kokumbona on the night of the seventeenth, and the Marines unexpectedly encountered this powerful enemy force. The ad hoc nature of the planning, lack of a single tactical commander, use of units from different parent organizations, and poor communications between the widely separated elements were all felt by the Marines during the fighting.

Captain Hawkins's Company B attacked west across the mouth of the Matanikau River while Capt. Lyman D. Spurlock's Company L crossed footbridges farther upstream to conduct a flanking movement. Lieutenant Colonel Whaling joined Capt. Bert W. Hardy Jr.'s Company I as it traveled three miles by boat to the village of Kokumbona to cut off any retreating enemy. There is an interesting side note. Who were reputed by their peers to be the two richest men in the Corps, 2d Lt. George L. Mead (prospective heir to the Mead Paper Company fortune and a world-class polo player) and 1st Lt. Walter S. McIlhenny (of the Louisiana Tabasco pepper sauce family), participated in this action. Mead was Company L's executive officer and McIlhenny was Company B's executive officer.

Company B moved down the coastal government track in the late afternoon on the eighteenth. Hawkins's men captured some stragglers as they moved ahead, then encountered minor enemy resistance after making bivouac that night. Company L was able to cross the river and hack its way to within two thousand yards of the coast. All seemed to be going about as expected when the Marines dug in for the night. The men of Company B were startled to see an enemy warship approaching their positions when they awoke the next morning. Luckily, it turned back to sea without firing a shot. At about 0800 on the nineteenth, Companies B and L began their attacks to take Matanikau. Company B was unable to cross the river because of intense enemy fire and several men were caught in the open. Lieutenant McIlhenny moved to an exposed position and called in mortar fire to cover their withdrawal, an act of heroism that earned him the Navy Cross. Company L caught the enemy by surprise and was able to easily penetrate to the center of the village, but a platoon sergeant and Lieutenant Mead were killed and several enlisted men were wounded in the process. The turning point came when Gunner Edward W. "Bill" Rust, who had been acting as the company guide, led a thirteen-man platoon from Company L in the first bayonet charge by the 1st Marine Division. This bold action ended the Japanese resistance and enabled the two companies to continue their advance.

Company I endured a most unusual journey that day; its Higgins boat convoy left Kukum in good order, but was shelled en route by two Japanese destroyers and the cruiser spotted earlier by Company B. Undeterred, Company I landed at Kokumbona, overcame stiff resistance, and took the village. Some Marines from 1st Platoon, Company M, then used two captured three-inch naval guns to fire twenty rounds at the Japanese ships, but all shots fell short. An American B-17 Flying Fortress bomber finally arrived and drove the enemy flotilla away. Companies I and L made contact at midday and returned to the perimeter by boat after capturing some documents and inflicting an estimated sixty-five enemy casualties. The Marines suffered four killed and eleven wounded. Additionally, Gunner Bill Rust identified the body of a Marine corporal from the Goettge patrol and reported he had located the remains of either Lieutenant Colonel Goettge or Captain Ringer. The remains belonged to a very large man, a factor that limited them to those of either Goettge or Ringer, but they were too decomposed to be certain which of the men had been discovered. The Company I patrol was ordered back before further exploration could be made or Rust's discoveries could be confirmed.

The 1st Battalion mounted a similar operation over the same terrain eight days later. The battalion was ordered to make a shore-to-shore movement from Kukum to Kokumbona, and from there to clear the coastal road as far as Matanikau, then reembark and return to the Marine lines before dark. This mission started well. The battalion moved west by boat and arrived at Kokumbona at about 0730. The landing caught the Japanese by surprise, and they fled without a fight. The Marines searched the village but found only hot food and no sign of the enemy. Difficult terrain, inadequate communications, intense heat, and uncertain enemy strength combined to slow follow-on operations. The main body, consisting of Headquarters, A, B, and D Companies, was able to navigate along the coastal road, but Company C had to hack its way through thick vegetation as it moved along a ridge that paralleled the coast. The ridge was frequently cut by steep ravines and was covered by five-foot-high kunai grass. The movement progressed at a snail's pace. Within an hour, Company C had fallen behind, and its exhausted Marines had to be relieved by a reinforced platoon from Company B. During the movement, the Marines discovered a previously unknown coral ridge that angled toward the coast near the Matanikau River to create a natural funnel. The lead elements of the patrol, following this landmark, stumbled into an enemy ambush, and the Marine main column was forced to deploy at about 1100. Company B quickly formed a firing line, Marine mortars began to hit suspected enemy positions, and Company C tried to make a flanking movement. Unfortunately, jumbled communications—all of the fragile TBY radios were inoperable, and most runners became heat casualties while trying to contact battalion headquarters—doomed this effort. As darkness approached, the battalion commander ordered a fighting withdrawal and informed headquarters that the boats should be sent to Kokumbona rather than Matanikau. Infuriated by the lack of progress and perceived contravention of orders, Colonel Hunt relieved the battalion commander. Major Milton V. O'Connell, the battalion executive officer, took over with orders to continue to press the enemy. Meanwhile, Colonel Hunt soon arrived at the front and took personal command of the operation, but the advance the next morning encountered no resistance because the Japanese had silently slipped into the jungle during the night. The battalion returned to Marine lines on the twenty-eighth. Again, as on the nineteenth, patrol results were inconclusive.

The 1st Battalion commander's relief seems to have been caused by uncertainty about the patrol's primary mission. No written orders were issued, so there is no documentary record, but several witnesses reported the safe return of the patrol before dark was stressed, whereas others asserted that clearing the coastal road was the objective. Regardless, there is no doubt division headquarters pressured Colonel Hunt to take drastic action, and Maj. Donald W. Fuller, the 2d Battalion executive officer, took over the 1st Battalion on the thirtieth.

While the 5th Marines was defending Kukum and probing the Matanikau, the first major attempt to overrun the Marine perimeter was made by the Japanese Ichiki Detachment, which hit the 1st Marines lines along the Tenaru River. The Marines won this battle, but the threat of more action caused General Vandegrift to recall his forces on Tulagi in order to shore up the Guadalcanal perimeter. The 2d Battalion, 5th Marines, came over to the big island the next day, was made the division reserve, and settled into positions near Henderson Field. Marine engineers and navy Seabees had completed initial Japanese airfield construction, and the operational airfield was named for Lofton Henderson—a Marine flier who died during the Battle of Midway.

Lieutenant Colonel Rosecrans and his executive officer, Maj. George T. Skinner, were hit during a Japanese bombing raid on 11 September, so "Wild Bill" Whaling, the regimental executive officer, took over until a permanent commanding officer could be appointed. The battalion executive officer slot went unfilled until 1 October.

On 10 September, a composite battalion of Raiders and paratroopers under Lieutenant Colonel Edson was assigned to a "rest area" located on an undulating finger of kunai-covered land that jutted into the jungle from the airfield. Signal intelligence, captured documents, prisoner-of-war interrogations, enemy bombing activity, and patrol contacts convinced Red Mike that this unnamed ridge was about to become a major attack route for the Japanese Kawaguchi Brigade. He, therefore, ordered his men to dig in and cover their front with barbed wire. These prudent actions, coupled with the good use of preregistered artillery fires, helped the Marines repel a series of Japanese attacks on the night of 12–13 September. The following morning, Edson ordered his men to strengthen their defensive lines and moved Whaling's 2d Battalion, 5th Marines, closer to the action. Bill Whaling used the daylight hours to conduct a reconnaissance of the ridge and ordered his company commanders to familiarize themselves with Edson's plans and positions. It was a case of "preparation meeting opportunity" when the 2d Battalion moved up to reinforce the hard-pressed defenders of the ridge later that night.

The Japanese returned to the ridge in force at 1830. When the Raiders on the right and the Paramarines on the left were driven back into a small, horseshoe-shaped perimeter, Edson called for his reserve. The 2d Battalion was committed to the fight at about 0400. Whaling's companies were sent up piecemeal to shore up sagging portions of the Marine lines. First in was Company G, which was hit by enemy machine-gun fire as it moved forward from its assembly area to assume positions on the Marines' left. The other companies, moving into the line at intervals, filled other gaps in the Raider lines until Maj. Gen. Kiyotake Kawaguchi's final assaults were repulsed. The last attacks were broken just before daylight. The Marines moved down the ridge to eliminate small pockets of survivors after the Japanese main body retreated into the jungle. In a secondary attack, the Oka Detachment hit the 3d Battalion on the night of 13–14 September. The planned attack was disrupted by accurate artillery fire and broken by close combat. This action marked the end of what became known as the Battle of Bloody Ridge for the 5th Marines.

The 1st Marine Division began receiving a steady stream of reinforcements a few days later. This led to changes in Marine leadership and tactics. Many deserving Marines were promoted and changed jobs in the days following the assaults on Bloody Ridge. A few veterans were designated to return home so they could share their experiences and catalog the lessons learned thus far about fighting in the Pacific. Among the officers selected to go back to the United States was Colonel Hunt, who was promoted to brigadier general upon his return. Newly promoted Col. Merritt Edson, the hero of Bloody Ridge, replaced him as the 5th Marines commander on 22 September. Edson then made several key personnel changes. Major Robert O. Bowen replaced Lieutenant Colonel Biebush as commander of the 3d Battalion on the twenty-second; Maj. Walker A. Reaves, executive officer of the 3d Battalion, 1st Marines, became a lieutenant colonel on the twenty-third and was given command of the 2d Battalion; and recently promoted Maj. William H. Barba became the 2d Battalion executive officer on 1 October.

The increased strength of the 1st Marine Division allowed Vandegrift to realign his forces. The 5th Marines moved out of Kukum village and shifted its lines west into the jungle to defend the Kukum Trail. Vandegrift also initiated a series of spoiling attacks to keep the enemy off balance. One such attack, conducted from 24–26 September, developed into a major fight known as the Second Matanikau. Lieutenant Colonel Lewis B. "Chesty" Puller's 1st Battalion, 7th Marines, pushed across the foot of Mount Austen and was headed for the Matanikau River when it ran into an unexpected Japanese camp. After a sharp firefight, Puller was forced to use the bulk of his unit to evacuate casualties and he asked for reinforcements. The 2d Battalion, 5th Marines, joined Puller's headquarters and Company C, 7th Marines, to form the Puller Group. This ad hoc unit moved to the mouth of the Matanikau River, where the attack bogged down. The 2d Battalion incurred many casualties, including twenty-five men killed in action, trying to cross the river. The 1st Raider Battalion joined the fight and ran into the same buzz saw. Colonel Edson, who had been placed in charge of this confused operation in midfight, tried to use Puller's returning companies as an amphibious interdiction force to save the day. Unfortunately, this small group was cut off and had to be evacuated. Walker Reaves's 2d Battalion and the Raiders disengaged under cover of darkness and returned to the Marine lines on the twenty-eighth. The steep price of the Second Matanikau was 160 Marine casualties.

The 5th Marines participated in a third Matanikau operation from 7–9 October. This time the assault force consisted of six rifle battalions: the 2d and 3d Battalions, 5th Marines; 3d Battalion, 2d Marines; the 1st and 2d Battalions, 7th Marines; and a scout-sniper detachment known as the Whaling Group. Red Mike Edson was in charge. Edson's plan was for the 5th Marines to act as a demonstration force operating near the coast while the other units enveloped Japanese positions from the jungle. The 5th Marines would pin enemy defenders along the Matanikau River so Whaling's unit could roll up their flank. Two battalions of the 7th Marines would push father inland to make a deep turning movement to cut off the Japanese by establishing blocking positions in the vicinity of Point Cruz. Unlike the earlier Second Matanikau, this offensive was carefully planned and close air support, naval gunfire, and artillery fires were well coordinated.

The 5th Marines jumped off on 7 October under the cover of a deluge of supporting arms. The 3d Battalion ran into heavy resistance on the west bank of the Matanikau at about 1015. Concurrently, the 2d Battalion sealed off a Japanese salient located about seventy-five yards from the mouth of the river. Company I was on the right, Company L in the middle, and Company K held the left. A deadly stalemate quickly developed. Company I, supported by heavy machine guns from Company M, was able to stop all Japanese movement across the river. The Japanese could not retreat, but the 5th Marines were unable to progress because it had unwittingly bumped into fresh enemy units from the 4th Regiment, 2d "Sendai" Division, and had to be reinforced just to hold on. Company I repeatedly engaged enemy forces in hand-to-hand combat as they tried to slip away in the darkness. This hard-hit unit was relieved by elements of the 1st Raider Battalion at 0500 the next morning. The all-out attack planned for the next morning was postponed by torrential rains that made ground movement difficult and combat support impossible. Plans for the 5th Marines to push across the Matanikau, pass through the Whaling Group, and then move down the coast to capture Kokumbona were overcome by events on the ninth, when General Vandegrift was warned of an impending attack and decided to call off offensive operations at that time.

Major Lewis W. Walt, a burly ex-Raider and former star athlete at the University of Colorado, took over the 2d Battalion on 12 October. This organizational move formalized what had already become reality. Walt, who became the 5th Marines's operations officer when Edson took command, had been given tactical control of the 2d Battalion and its attached Raiders during the just-ended operation.

Months of field living and short rations took their toll—so much so that nonbattle casualties in the regiment overtook the number of wounded by late October. Worn-out Marines began succumbing to battle fatigue, malaria, and dengue fever in alarming numbers. Almost a third of the regiment reported for sick call at one time or another. It was obvious the veterans needed a rest. There was, however, one major fight left before the 5th Marines could retire from Guadalcanal.

The battlefield was once again the familiar stretch of coast between Matanikau and Kokumbona. This time the mission was to clear the area of enemy and push Japanese artillery out of range of the airfield. The 5th Marines were to force a crossing inland from the mouth of the Matanikau and then drive toward Kokumbona while the Whaling Group provided flank security and the 2d Marines followed behind the regiment, ready to exploit any opportunity that presented itself. Once the area was cleared, the 2d Marines would hold jump-off positions for follow-up attacks, and the 5th Marines would return to Kukum. The advance was carefully planned and every hill, ravine, and streambed in the objective area subjected to preregistered artillery and mortar fires. The main avenue of approach was the coastal ridge that angled toward the base of Point Cruz.

The 1st Engineer Battalion threw three floating footbridges across the Matanikau upstream from the river's sandy mouth on the night of 31 October–1 November. A platoon from Company E crossed the river in rubber boats to secure the crossing sites at 0200 on the morning of the first. The Marine main body moved out at first light, just as Japanese artillery began to pepper the 5th Marines assembly area. Major William K. Enright's 1st Battalion and Maj. Lew Walt's 2d Battalion were across the river by 0700 and the regimental reserve, Maj. Bob Bowen's 3d Battalion, was on the far shore by 0800. The crossings were preceded by an intense artillery preparation, air strikes, and naval gunfire. The 5th Marines fanned out with 1st Battalion moving along the coastal road, the 2d Battalion following the crest of the ridgeline, and the 3d Battalion moving behind on the inland downslope. The 2d Battalion encountered no opposition and reached the first objective at 1000 and the second objective at 1440.

The 1st Battalion met stiff opposition immediately after crossing the river and was forced to halt. Company A was only lightly engaged as it moved down the beach. Company C, on the other hand, was pinned in place by heavy enemy fire. Company B rushed up to assist, but was also pinned down. Both units were able to pull back, but they suffered heavy casualties and were rendered combat ineffective thereafter. Corporal Anthony Casamento was badly wounded, and his machine-gun squad was almost wiped out. Casamento had been hit several times but refused to withdraw. Instead, he kept delivering covering fire that allowed his comrades to escape. Thirty-eight years later, Pres. Jimmy Carter presented Casamento the Medal of Honor at a White House ceremony.

The 3d Battalion moved into the line to reinforce the 1st Battalion as the Japanese fell back to the vicinity of Point Cruz. The 2d Battalion moved west to extend the Marine lines and outflank the Japanese defenders the next morning. Company A held the beach, the 2d Battalion was in position on the ridge leading to Point Cruz, and the 3d Battalion held positions in the flat land to the east. Company F shifted right to make contact with the 3d Battalion at about 1400 on the second and the cordon was complete. Point Cruz was then pounded into submission by artillery, mortars, machine guns, and naval gunfire. Companies I and K cautiously probed forward but met heavy resistance. Captain Erskine Wells led Company I forward as the Japanese fell back. Another Japanese pocket was reduced by Weapons Company's 75mm SPM half-tracks operating with the 3d Battalion headquarters and the 1st Battalion, 164th Infantry (a North Dakota National Guard regiment assigned to the army's Americal Division, which had recently arrived on the island). Company I repulsed a major Japanese breakout attempt just before dawn the following morning.

The regiment's last push of the campaign came at 0800 on 3 November. It was a classic hammer-and-anvil attack with the 2d Battalion sweeping down the beach while the 3d Battalion manned ambush positions along likely egress routes. The last Japanese in the area were eliminated, marking the end of operations. The battered 1st Battalion had previously returned to the Marine lines, and the 2d and 3d Battalions were relieved by elements of the 2d Marines and the 164th Infantry. Colonel Edson turned over command of the operation to the commanding officer of the 2d Marines at noon. This final action was a testament to Edson's skill: it was the most successful operation for the 5th Marines on Guadalcanal. More than three hundred enemy were killed, and the regiment's haul of weapons included one field piece, twelve antitank guns, and thirty-four heavy machine guns.

The 5th Marines was placed in reserve and manned beach positions for the rest of the month. From these positions, the tired veterans watched as more and more fresh American units poured in as the 1st Marine Division prepared to pull out in early December. The 5th Marines departed what was by then simply known as "the Island" for Australia on 9 December 1942 after five months of difficult jungle fighting.

The Battle of Guadalcanal was a turning point. It was to World War II in the Pacific what Belleau Wood had been to World War I. Never again would the enemy mount a significant offensive, and from that time on the initiative was in Allied hands. The 1st Marine Division's heroic stand in the face of tremendous adversity earned it a Presidential Unit Citation. In a less official, but no less important, gesture, the word *Guadalcanal* was etched into the red numeral on the division patch to commemorate that epic struggle in perpetuity.

While the 1st Marine Division rested and rehabilitated in Australia, other army and Marine units elbowed their way along the New Guinea coast and island-hopped up the Solomons. They were headed toward the biggest prize in the South Pacific: the Japanese military complex at Rabaul. The fall of Buna and Salamaua on New Guinea, along with landings in the Russells, New Georgia, and Bougainville, cleared the way for Allied forces to finally target New Britain.

New Britain

The 5th Marines was not in good shape when it departed Guadalcanal. The regiment had been depleted by combat losses and illness. Malaria or other jungle diseases plagued most of the survivors. All were tired and suffered from months of uninterrupted service in a combat zone. Australia was the perfect tonic for what ailed the veterans of Guadalcanal. The 5th Marines was originally sent to Camp Cable, a Spartan Australian army facility located in a dismal swampy area forty-five miles from the northern town of Brisbane. Unfortunately, Camp Cable was totally unsuited for rehabilitation and training, and malaria was rampant. General Vandegrift's vehement protests got the location shifted to the cooler climate and urban temptations of southern Australia. This change of venue was quite a culture shock for men used to primitive jungle conditions. The city of Melbourne was a modern one with wide streets, numerous public houses, and comfortable hotels where Marines could take a hot shower, enjoy a pint of beer, meet an Australian lass, and sleep be-

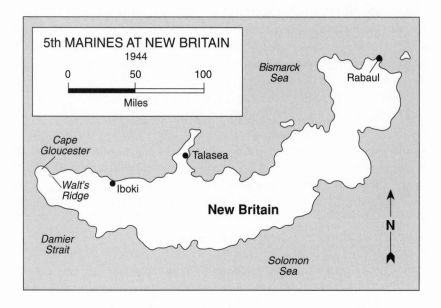

5th MARINES AT NEW BRITAIN
1944

tween the clean sheets of a comfortable bed. This brief period was a most enjoyable time and has gone into the lore of the 1st Marine Division as the "Great Debauch." Memories of Melbourne in January and February 1943 still bring smiles to veterans of the Great Debauch decades later. There can be no doubt this all-too brief interlude was the highlight of the 5th Marines's Pacific sojourn.

Training initially focused on the reorganization and reequipping of units and stressed individual physical conditioning. All hands became familiar with the new M1 Garand semiautomatic rifles, which replaced their trusted Springfields. The Marines were sorry to part with their beloved '03s, but the increased firepower of the new Garands could not be denied. The 5th Marines made practice landings at Port Philip Bay near Melbourne in April and May. The 1st Marine Division was reorganized into regimental-sized "combat teams" and battalion-sized "landing teams" on 25 May. The rest of the summer was devoted to turning these teams into combat-ready units.

The 5th Marines departed Australia for Milne Bay, New Guinea, on 27 September 1943. There, the regiment began advanced training that emphasized shore-to-shore amphibious operations and utilized terrain closely resembling that found on New Britain, the Marines' next target.

New Britain was a huge (more than three hundred miles in length), crescent-shaped island located northwest of the Solomons. Five airfields and ninety thousand defenders sat at volcano-ringed Rabaul Harbor on New Britain's northeast tip. Rabaul was the most potent Japanese air and naval base in the Southwest Pacific theater, so its destruction dictated Allied strategy there. An alternate two-field airdrome was located at Cape Gloucester on the western end of the island. Bisecting northern New Britain's coastline, about equidistant between Rabaul and Cape Gloucester, was the Willaumez Peninsula.

The Guadalcanal veterans, who bragged they had already experienced the world's worst jungle, were in for a shock when they got to New Britain. For three months they would be attacked by jungle insects, bombarded by monsoon rains, mired in sticky mud, immersed in bottomless swamps, and battered by gale-force winds. New Britain's rugged terrain was covered by dense vegetation that grew right to the shoreline. Unceasing rain, intense heat, high humidity, endless swamps, impenetrable jungle, and a determined foe combined to make New Britain a jungle inferno for those who fought there.

The 5th Marines (less the 3d Battalion) was the major component of Combat Team A. Colonel John T. Selden commanded Combat Team A. Selden enlisted as a private in 1915, was commissioned in 1918, served tours in Haiti and China, and saw considerable sea duty between the wars. His executive officer was Lt. Col. William K. Enright. The regiment was composed of Landing Teams 15, 25, and 35 (named for their respective battalion numerical designators without hyphen or slash). Then-current amphibious doctrine described regimental-sized combat teams as "the normal tactical unit" and battalion-sized landing teams as "temporary embarkation units," but at New Britain landing teams often operated independently and doctrine was amended to reflect reality. Each landing team consisted of a rifle battalion and appropriate combat support units to form an independent maneuver unit. Major Barba commanded the 1st Battalion, recently promoted Lt. Col. Lew Walt led the 2d Battalion, and Lt. Col. David S. McDougal commanded the 3d Battalion.

The 1st Marine Division, now commanded by General Rupertus, was part of the army's Alamo Force commanded by Lt. Gen. Walter Kreuger. However, historians note that although Kreuger was the titular commander, General MacArthur, commander of the Southwest Pacific area, allowed his subordinates very little latitude and acted as the de facto

commander. Operation Dexterity was the name given to the campaign
to capture western New Britain. The original plan was to seize the airfields at Cape Gloucester on the northwest coast, and then continue to
attack east to capture Rabaul. To do this, MacArthur invoked an inor-
dinately intricate scheme of maneuver. He split the 1st Marine Division
into three combat teams to conduct separate operations and planned
an airborne landing by army paratroopers. Combat Team A was scheduled to land at Gasmata on New Britain's southern coast. This needlessly
complex plan was suddenly revised and simplified in late October. According to Marine legend, Col. Edwin A. Pollack, the division operations
officer, outspokenly pointed out planning flaws to General MacArthur
during a preoperation briefing. Then—to the surprise of all present—
the egotistical and imperious theater commander recognized the tactical value of this criticism and the plans were immediately changed. The
airdrop was eliminated, the Gasmata operation was canceled, and the
1st Marine Division was reunited. The new operations plan made Combat Team A the 1st Marine Division reserve. As such, the 5th Marines (less
the 3d Battalion) might be called on to reinforce the Cape Gloucester
landings, conduct operations against offshore islands, or be used as an
exploitation force. Landing Team 35 was not assigned to Combat Team
A, but instead constituted an independent landing force scheduled to
scout Long and Rooke Islands, which lay just off Cape Gloucester.

The 1st and 7th Marines went ashore at New Britain without opposition on 26 December 1943. The landing was slowed by unexpectedly difficult jungle and deep swamps. Once off the landing beaches, the
Marines started moving inland, where they ran afoul of Japanese defenses and were unable to push through to Cape Gloucester. The 1st
Marines's drive to the airdrome stalled at Hell's Point. This led General
Rupertus to call for help. Combat Team A was released to him on the
twenty-seventh, but its ships could not make landfall at the staging area
until the next day, which was spent loading Landing Ship, Tank (LST)
vessels and APDs. It turned out that Landing Team 35 was not needed
after the planned island seizures were canceled, so the orphaned 3d Battalion was sent to reinforce the 7th Marines instead.

The 5th Marines got off to an inauspicious start at New Britain. The
fog of war clouded Combat Team A's operations before the landings began and did not dissipate until it was reunited inside the airfield defensive perimeter the next day. Combat Team A was originally scheduled to
land at Yellow Beach, and that was the plan when the Marines boarded

APD fast transports for the ride to Cape Gloucester. In the interim, however, the 1st Marines secured Blue Beach, which was three miles closer to the objective. It was then decided to bring Combat Team A in at Blue Beach. Colonel Selden's command group, two companies of Landing Team 15, and most of Landing Team 25 got ashore in the designated area by 0730. However, due to a combination of poor communications and bad weather, the rest of the 1st and 2d Battalions landed at Yellow Beach between 0700 and 0800 on 29 December. These units then had to make a combined motor and foot march four miles west to the 5th Marines's command post.

It was midafternoon before the assault troops assembled at the 0-0 Line to begin the attack to capture the Cape Gloucester airdrome. The plan to seize the airdrome seemed sound enough. It called for the 1st Marines to bypass Hell's Point and attack along the coastal road that led into the airdrome's eastern sector. The 5th Marines would simultaneously conduct an inland envelopment to strike the enemy from the south. Unfortunately, New Britain's rugged terrain validated the old axiom "no operations plan makes it past the line of departure." Unexpected movement difficulties slowed the advance, which then separated the columns, and eventually turned the envelopment into an uncoordinated one-battalion attack. Luckily, no serious resistance was encountered.

Colonel Selden's plan was to go forward in column with Walt's 2d Battalion in the lead and Barba's 1st Battalion moving in trace. As it turned out, however, the units became hopelessly separated during the fifteen-hundred-yard approach march through a swamp mislabeled as a "damp flat" on operations maps. Instead of only a few inches of water, the mire reached depths of up to five feet. As one wag put it, "the flats were damp up to your neck." This morass slowed movement and caused an accordion effect that spread the battalions farther apart as time passed.

Aware that the attack was faltering, Colonel Selden established a regimental observation post in a former Japanese hillside bivouac overlooking the objective. Lieutenant Colonel Walt, Major Barba, and Colonel Selden assembled there, looked over the terrain, coordinated their final plans, and then returned to their troops. Colonel Selden accompanied Walt and fell in with the 2d Battalion. Captain John B. Doyle Jr.'s Company F led a column of 2d Battalion companies forward at about 1500. Unfortunately, there were problems during the approach march and the 1st Battalion was not yet at the line of departure, but the attack could not be postponed because darkness was fast approaching. The lagging 1st Battalion would just have to catch up after it got out of the swamp. Cross-compartment movement over a series of alternating ridges and streams slowed the pace and created the proverbial accordion effect whereby the rear of the column alternately lagged behind or pushed into the vanguard. Jungle forest and high kunai grass made navigation difficult. Luckily, there was no contact with Japanese defenders, and all enemy fortifications discovered along the way were empty. The 2d Battalion finally reached Airstrip Number Two at about 1925 and promptly dug in to man its share of the defensive perimeter.

Meanwhile, Major Barba's 1st Battalion was unable to make it to the objective. The battalion was slowed by the terrible terrain and did not reach the line of departure until after 1900. Instead of continuing the attack over unfamiliar terrain in pitch darkness and drenched by monsoon rains, Major Barba wisely stopped at a relatively dry piece of ground and established a circular defensive position. Unfortunately, Barba was unable to contact either the 2d Battalion or regimental command posts by radio to notify them where he was.

A patrol sent to find Barba's "lost battalion" the next morning made the first significant enemy contact. First Lieutenant John S. Stankus led his patrol through Marine lines in the vicinity of Airfield Number Two at about 0730. About fifteen minutes later, he and another Marine stumbled into a Japanese bivouac not far from the razorback ridge where the Marines had discovered abandoned fortifications the previous day. A dozen enemy soldiers were just getting up when the two Marines bumped into them. Stankus pulled back after an exchange of gunfire and called for help. Although it first appeared these Japanese were stragglers, this was not the case and a major engagement quickly developed. Company F's 3d Platoon, commanded by 2d Lt. Henry W. Stankus, brother of the patrol leader, rushed forward to help. This movement stirred up a hornet's nest. A sharp fight ensued when the surprised Japanese mounted an impromptu banzai counterattack. The attackers were beaten back, but Japanese mortars and a 75mm gun ranged the Marine positions. Fortuitously, Pt. Sgt. Clark Kaltenbaugh, who came forward on impulse, brought an SCR-636 handheld radio. He quickly called for reinforcements, then directed Marine counterbattery fire using his "Spam can" radio.

Second Lieutenant Bill Rust, promoted for his fine work on Guadalcanal, led the 2d Platoon into the fray while Captain Doyle brought the rest of Company F forward. The 2d Platoon entered the jungle and crossed a stream to protect the 3d Platoon's flank as Company F's mortars and machine guns were used to good effect. Company F was able to hold the enemy at bay, but it was obvious tank support was needed to eject the Japanese from their underground fortifications. While Company F waited for reinforcements, a second banzai charge occurred. It was beaten back but the 3d Platoon was reduced to about half strength. Regardless of these losses, the remaining men fell in behind the first tank to attack the trench line. While the 3d Platoon made its frontal assault, Rust's 2d Platoon swept in from the left, rolled up the Japanese flank, and knocked out two dozen or so bunkers using grenades and automatic-rifle fire. At about 1130 the fighting stopped as quickly as it had started two hours earlier. The fight for No Name Ridge cost the Japanese about a hundred dead. Company F lost thirteen killed and nineteen wounded, including Hank Stankus, and returned to the airdrome by midafternoon.

Unknown at the time, the "lost" 1st Battalion was hitting the same Japanese force with enfilade fire. Major Barba's unit had come under mortar fire as it searched for the airdrome that morning. Companies A and B maneuvered into a firing line and engaged a force of unknown strength. A Japanese sally was broken by fire, and then the Marines launched a counterattack supported by mortar fire. The enemy had slipped away and the positions were empty by the time the Marines arrived. It was later discovered this fight actually took place in the rear of the position Company F had attacked. The 1st Battalion suffered six dead and a dozen wounded before it arrived at the airdrome and entered the Marine lines at about 1800. The new arrivals were inserted into expanded defensive lines that included both airfields before dark.

Landing Team 35 came ashore at Yellow Beach on the night of 30–31 December to support the 7th Marines. There it joined the ADC Group, so called because that unit was commanded by the 1st Marine Division's assistant division commander (ADC), Brig. Gen. Lemuel Shepherd. Shepherd's mission was to protect the beachhead, coordinate beach operations, and clear the enemy from Borgen Bay. The ADC Group included a support element composed of shore party, transportation, and supply units. Shepherd's combat element included Landing Team 35, the 7th Marines, the 11th Marines, and elements of the 1st Tank Battalion.

The new year began with the ADC Group's drive to clear Borgen Bay. The 7th Marines moved along the coast and pushed forward to Suicide

Creek. The terrain was as difficult a foe as the Japanese. Thick ground cover masked terrain features and hid enemy fortifications. The Marines had to slowly probe the unfamiliar ground. Luckily, a captured map depicted Japanese positions; not so luckily, the Marines were unable to accurately locate these areas on the ground. The heart of the Japanese resistance was on Aogiri Ridge, which intelligence officers mistakenly thought was Hill 150. Actually, Aogiri Ridge was hidden by jungle and did not appear on any American maps. This mystery ridge, however, was about to be discovered by the 3d Battalion, 5th Marines.

The drive along the coast bogged down in the muck until Seabees and Marine engineers built a log road through the quagmire so tanks could be brought forward. The 7th Marines overran Hill 150 but the Japanese fire did not let up, and it soon became obvious Hill 150 was not Aogiri Ridge. While the 7th Marines were taking Hill 150, Lieutenant Colonel MacDougal's 3d Battalion crossed Suicide Creek and began searching inland for Aogiri Ridge on 4 January 1944. Three days later, MacDougal was felled by Japanese fire. His place was taken by the executive officer, Maj. Joseph S. Skoczylas. Unfortunately, Skoczylas was hit less than five hours later. Lieutenant Colonel Chesty Puller, temporarily commanding the 3d Battalion, 7th Marines, assumed overnight command of both battalions until Colonel Selden sent up a replacement the next morning.

The new commanding officer of the 3d Battalion was Lew Walt, who had only recently left the 2/5 to become the regimental executive officer. Walt took command just as the 3d Battalion bumped into a steep slope about fifteen hundred yards southwest of Target Hill. The Marines were soon stopped by savage fire, and Walt decided to dig in and protect this foothold on what he correctly assumed was Aogiri Ridge. Walt was well aware of the difficulty of reducing fortified positions without armor support, so he called for tanks and self-propelled guns. But drenching rain, thick mud, and swollen streams held up the armor. The only direct-fire support available was a 37mm antitank gun laboriously dragged up the slope on the afternoon of the ninth. The Marines launched a coordinated attack to capture Aogiri Ridge the next morning. Artillery hammered the crest as the 1st and 3d Battalions, 7th Marines, moved out to protect Walt's flanks. The steep slope and withering Japanese fire slowed the advancing Marines. By nightfall, Walt's men held only a narrow sliver of ground on the ridge top and had reached the limit of their physical endurance. In fact, they were so worn down, it seemed questionable that they could even hold on to their hard-earned gains. It is in such dire circumstances that leadership often determines the outcome of a battle. The 3d Battalion was fortunate Lew Walt was a superb leader.

Walt ordered the 37mm gun into action when the attack began to peter out. It had been a Herculean effort to manhandle the heavy gun up the slippery slope, but the effectiveness of its fire was testimony that the toil was worth it. Gunners would fire a canister round filled with grapeshot to make the enemy take cover then, during the ensuing break in enemy fire, Marine riflemen would scurry forward a few yards. The resulting advance was slow but relentless. The main problem was that the 37mm gun had to keep pace with the front line to be effective. The Japanese quickly began to concentrate their fire on this deadly but vulnerable adversary. Most of the nine-man crew was soon wounded by enemy fire. Calls for volunteers went unheeded, and the attack stalled after the gun fell silent. At that point, Walt took the bull by the horns. He and his runner crawled over to the gun and began inching it forward with the help of the remaining crewmen. The gun cut a swath through the dense undergrowth and silenced an enemy machine gun, but this effort was not without cost. Walt aggravated an old football injury when he dislocated his shoulder pushing the heavy gun up the hill. Buoyed by Walt's selfless bravery, however, other Marines wrestled the weapon forward until the crest was conquered.

The battle for Aogiri Ridge was far from over, though. The enemy was not ready to cede the hill to Walt's men. Instead, the undaunted enemy chanted, "Marines prepare to die!" The tired Marines dug in at the top of the ridge as they exchanged fire with Japanese troops dug in only about ten yards away. The Japanese emerged from their holes an hour after midnight and charged forward under cover of a curtain of rain. This was the first of five banzai attacks that night. Each was repulsed by hand-to-hand fighting. Marine forward observers had to adjust artillery fire by sound instead of sight, but managed to create a wall of steel only fifty yards out. A carrying party delivered clips and ammunition belts with only minutes to spare before the final Japanese onslaught. During one attack, the Japanese closed to within only a few feet of Lew Walt's foxhole command post. Just as Walt drew his pistol and prepared to make his last stand, a providential artillery round exploded in the trees and killed all the attackers, including a sword-wielding Japanese officer. The nightlong fight for Aogiri Ridge was a close-run thing, but when the Marines moved forward at first light they did not encounter a single living Japanese. After his postbattle inspection, General Shepherd reported, "I found [dead] Marines and [Japanese] . . . lying on the ground together." It was Shepherd's opinion that this was the critical battle of the Cape Gloucester campaign because Aogiri Ridge controlled a carefully camouflaged supply route through which all Japanese supplies and reinforcements had to pass. From then on, that piece of key terrain was called "Walt's Ridge" to honor the 3d Battalion commander, who later received the Navy Cross for his inspirational leadership there.

With Cape Gloucester secured, General Rupertus ordered the 1st Marines to defend the airdrome, the 7th Marines to patrol to the south, and the 5th Marines to move east down the coast. The bulk of the 5th Marines moved down to Yellow Beach from the airdrome, and Colonel Selden was given responsibility for the southeast beachhead area on 16 January. The regiment soon began to search down the coast for the next Japanese line of resistance. Major Barba's 1st Battalion, forewarned by captured Japanese documents, ran into a Japanese stronghold on the way to Natamo Point on the twentieth. Expecting to meet only an enemy platoon and one machine gun, Barba was surprised by the volume of fire and the strength of the resistance, which he estimated to include at least one full company supported by 20mm, 37mm, and 75mm crew-served weapons. Rather than press a costly frontal assault, Colonel Selden tried to dislodge the defenders using artillery fire and air strikes. For two days 11th Marines's howitzers pounded suspected Japanese positions, halting their fire only to allow Army Air Forces medium bombers to drop their loads. Major Harold T. A. Richmond, the battalion executive officer, led a small task force composed of Company C reinforced by Company D's heavy weapons and four Sherman tanks across the east bank of Twin Forks River on the afternoon of the twenty-third. This fight was followed by a series of sharp skirmishes as the Marines advanced to the Natamo River. Determined enemy resistance again stopped the advance. Tanks, self-propelled guns, artillery fire, and a rocket-firing amphibious truck were unable to displace the defenders. Major Barba therefore sent patrols upriver to find a suitable ford so he could envelop the position.

Reconnaissance patrols from Company E, 2d Battalion, were also working their way inland at the same time. They followed a trail leading to Magairapua, where they discovered that the Japanese had pulled out of this relatively elaborate former command complex. Farther inland, a patrol from the 7th Marines ran into stiff resistance and required assistance. Major Barba diverted his ford search patrol and sent Companies

A and C to help out on the twenty-eighth. The rescue force encountered occasional mortar and machine-gun fire as it moved swiftly down a corduroyed trail but pushed on. Major Barba's patrol linked up with both Company E and a strong patrol consisting of Company G reinforced with heavy weapons and numerous native bearers under Maj. Charles R. Baker, the 2d Battalion executive officer, at Nakarop village. Nakarop had been the Japanese 65th Brigade headquarters and yielded a treasure trove of information regarding Japanese plans and displacements.

This evidence, combined with other actions such as the one at Natamo Point, convinced headquarters that the Japanese were conducting a planned withdrawal. It was decided to take a calculated risk and push the pursuit more aggressively. Although this decision may seem an obvious choice in hindsight, it was not a simple decision at the time. The Marines had already accomplished their primary mission: the capture of Cape Gloucester. In any future action they would be facing an unknown enemy in unfamiliar terrain. Intelligence was not sure whether the Japanese were actually retreating or were merely pulling Marines away from the Cape Gloucester airdrome to set up a counterattack. Physical evidence, translated documents, and prisoner interrogations eventually confirmed a well-planned withdrawal was under way and that the egress route was along the northern coast. From then on, cutting the Japanese line of retreat became the highest priority. This sudden change of plans came as a surprise to Colonel Selden, who was accompanying an inland patrol when he received orders to attack along the coast.

Iboki Plantation, located on the coast almost sixty miles east of Borgen Bay, was identified as the Japanese rallying point. Colonel Selden elected to leapfrog down the coast in a series of coordinated overland and shore-to-shore movements to capture it. The army's 533d Engineer and Boat Regiment manned the ten Landing Craft, Mechanized (LCMs) that provided the amphibious lift. These "amphibian" soldiers were so helpful that most Leathernecks routinely called them "Marines" by the end of the campaign. Marine spotters flying in L-4 Piper Cub light observation aircraft scouted the track from the air and would occasionally drop supplies or messages to the Marines below. The Piper Cub–mounted Cape Gloucester Air Wing was an ad hoc organization consisting of Marine infantry and artillery volunteers who "wore no wings, carried no flight orders, received no flight pay, and were not designated naval aviators." Nevertheless, their aerial support was deeply appreciated.

The month of February was devoted to exploitation of the coastal route and pursuit of the retreating Matsuda Force. These operations were skillfully carried out, but the Japanese always seemed to be just a step ahead of the Marines. The only enemy troops encountered were demoralized and sick soldiers who put up little resistance. Unfortunately, bad weather interfered with Marine operations. Low-lying clouds often blocked aerial observation and rough surf sometimes canceled landing plans. High seas frustrated a landing attempt at Namuramunga on 4 February, so overland patrols by the 2d Battalion followed the Japanese trail toward Kokopo. The rest of the 2d Battalion landed at Aliado on the fifth and moved down the coastal trail to Gorissi. The 2d Battalion bagged twenty-four enemy killed and took nine prisoners during this drive. The 3d Battalion (less Company I) moved to Gorissi by boat on the twelfth. One patrol moved down the coast until it reached the mouth of the impassible El River. An amphibious patrol leapfrogged this position and came ashore at the Arimega Plantation on the nineteenth, then conducted an overland-waterborne pincer movement to capture the Karai-ai supply depot just west of Iboki. From there, a platoon-sized overland patrol and two LCMs at sea proceeded to Iboki on the twenty-fourth. They found it deserted except for a few stragglers. The remainder of the 5th Marines moved forward and the regimental command post opened at Iboki on the twenty-seventh. The drive down the coast had been mounted on the spur of the moment, but it moved more than five thousand men and their supporting equipment sixty miles through or around dense jungle. Colonel Selden recalled that the march was accomplished "four days prior to the deadline without loss . . . quite a feat." Noteworthy as they were, however, these excursions neither located nor trapped the main enemy force. It was readily apparent the Marines would have to move all the way to the Willaumez Peninsula to corner the elusive Matsuda Force.

The 5th Marines received a weeklong respite while final plans for the upcoming operation were worked out. Orders came down on 1 March to seize and occupy the Willaumez Peninsula, which lay about fifty-five miles east of Iboki. The peninsula jutted about twenty-five miles north of the mainland into the Bismarck Sea. It had four large plantations, a dozen mountains, a German mission, and an airfield. Talasea Airfield on the far side of the peninsula was thought to be the hub of the enemy's withdrawal activity, so its capture was the primary objective. This operation within an operation was code-named "Appease." The assault force

(Combat Team A) consisted of the 5th Marines (Reinforced), which would be carried from Iboki to Volupai Plantation by a joint army-navy flotilla. Upon landing, the regiment would move across the peninsula to capture Talasea and patrol south to Numundo Plantation at the eastern base of the Willaumez Peninsula. An estimated four thousand Japanese were on Willaumez, along Kimbe Bay, and at Cape Hoskins.

The 5th Marines got a new commanding officer on 1 March 1944. Colonel Oliver P. Smith took over after Colonel Selden became the 1st Marine Division chief of staff. Smith was a tall, lean, taciturn intellectual who possessed great tactical acumen. He carefully analyzed and weighed his options before acting, and his plans always seemed to yield good results with minimum casualties. Smith had a distinguished academic career. He had studied at the army's Infantry School, was both a student and instructor at the Marine Corps Schools, and graduated from the prestigious French *Ecole Superieure de Guerre*. His field experience included tours on Guam and Haiti. The new regimental executive officer was Lt. Col. Henry W. Buse Jr. Major Barba retained command of the 1st Battalion, Maj. Gordon Gayle had replaced Lew Walt as 2d Battalion commander just before the battle for Aogiri Ridge, and Lt. Col. Harold O. Deakin became 3d Battalion commander when Walt resumed his duties as regimental executive officer on 12 January.

The assault waves began boarding thirty-eight LCMs, seventeen LCVPs, and five landing craft, tank (LCTs) at 1300 on 5 March. Five PT boats would escort this motley flotilla to the objective. There were no large warships available for fire support, so five Sherman tanks carried in LCMs would provide improvised naval gunfire support with their 75mm guns. An intricate air-support plan relied on the Fifth Air Force since the Marines had no organic air support at hand and no carrier aircraft were available. Intelligence reported the Japanese 1st Battalion, 54th Infantry Regiment, defended Volupai, and at least five strong points had been identified.

Two boats fell out during the overnight run to Volupai. One contained the Air Liaison Party (ALP); the other carried Major Gayle, Lt. Col. Noah P. Wood Jr. (the artillery commander), and the artillery reconnaissance and communications advance parties. Major Gayle's command boat encountered the ALP boat by sheer chance and, although it significantly slowed movement, the ALP boat was taken under tow after Major Gayle correctly assumed the ALP communication assets would be vital to the success of Appease and were too valuable to leave behind. This added burden kept Major Gayle from reaching the line of departure by H-hour, so Major Baker, the executive officer, led the 2d Battalion ashore. The scheduled air support failed to show up because the strike force was weathered in. In fact, the only airplane in the area was a single unarmed Marine Piper Cub. After waiting about forty-five minutes, Colonel Smith ordered the troops ashore without air cover. The tracked landing vehicles (LVTs) carrying Companies A and B ran down the ramps of the LCTs that brought them from Iboki, splashed into the surf, and swam toward shore under the cover of 75mm gunfire from the LCM-mounted tanks. The last part of the ten-minute run to the beach was made through Japanese mortar and artillery fire. The assault companies hit the beach and pushed forward to establish a beachhead. Captain Richard F. Nellson's Company A met little resistance on the right. Company B was stopped by an impassible swamp and had to thread its way inland between the swamp and little Mount Worri to the north. The main pocket of Japanese resistance was inside a coconut grove.

The 2d Battalion had some difficulty getting to the beach. Riding ashore in landing boats rather than amphibious tractors, the second wave had to follow an irregular route and move in single file to avoid reefs and hidden coral heads. Although the landing began at 0930, it was still under way when Major Gayle's boat finally reported to the control boat at 1230. Company E, the first 2d Battalion unit to get ashore, launched its attack up the plantation track at about 1100. It did not get far; a Japanese roadblock about two hundred yards inland stopped the Marine vanguard. A Sherman tank moved up the track and knocked out the offending machine gun, but was itself disabled by a handheld mine during the fight. Company E continued to advance toward Volupai Plantation supported by two tanks and covered by the 1st Battalion's 81mm mortars. The Marines penetrated the enemy lines after a particularly sharp fight during which a map of the area and its defenses was recovered from the body of a Japanese officer. This information bonanza was quickly put to use and greatly speeded the attack. As a result of this information windfall, the Marines were about two thousand yards inland by the time darkness fell.

The 1st Battalion manned a half-moon-shaped linear defense to protect the beachhead while the 2d Battalion set up an all-round defense inside the coconut grove. Resupply was accomplished using amphibian tractors to move back and forth along the muddy tracks. The Japanese tried to infiltrate the Marine lines at about 0200, but the attackers were quickly repulsed. This action convinced Colonel Smith that the Japanese were mounting a delaying action. The stay-behind forces were well fed and well armed, but they did not defend to the death and always broke contact after slowing the Marine advance. This circumstance had an ironic result: The rear echelon at the beach suffered more casualties than the forward assault units. All day long the Japanese lobbed 90mm mortar rounds into the crowded beach area. The heaviest toll was inflicted on the cannoneers of the 11th Marines. Lieutenant Commander Richard M. Forsythe, the 5th Marines's surgeon, died of wounds suffered while he treated casualties at the aid station.

The original plan called for Colonel Deakin's 3d Battalion to load on board the returning boats for the journey to Red Beach and assume responsibility for the beachhead defense. Unfortunately, the last boat to leave for Iboki was not loaded with wounded until about 1830. This late departure from Red Beach meant daylight was waning by the time enough landing craft were at hand to load Deakin's Marines. General Rupertus therefore ordered the flotilla to remain at Iboki until morning rather than risk a dangerous nighttime approach through the uncharted waters. The relief force could not leave until dawn on 7 March, so the 3d Battalion's arrival was delayed until late afternoon. This situation forced a change of plans at Volupai.

Colonel Smith ordered the 2d Battalion to continue its advance across the peninsula toward Bitokara Mission, Talasea airstrip, and Waru village. Meanwhile, the 1st Battalion remained to defend the beachhead. Major Barba could only spare Company C for a patrol to search for Liapo village. As it turned out, this was a futile effort because the trail petered out before Company C reached the objective. There was no resistance at first in front of 2d Battalion, but Company E did discover an abandoned mortar position.

The 2d Battalion thereafter advanced unopposed until it neared Mount Schleuther, a 1,130-foot peak that dominated the Bitokara-Talasea track and all connecting trails. This vital position was defended by elements of the Japanese 54th Infantry Regiment. A brisk firefight broke out at about 1145. Major Gayle built a base of fire at the track and maneuvered Company F through the jungle to stop a Japanese flanking movement. This maneuver resulted in a meeting engagement near the crest of the slope. Gayle promptly sent a platoon from Company H up the slope to help out. Second Lieutenant James M. Newman's men wiped out an enemy position and captured a Japanese machine gun, which they used to mow down enemy reinforcements. This small fight turned the tide. The Japanese fled, leaving behind about forty dead and the captured machine gun. After that, Major Gayle established an all-round perimeter defense and had his men dig in for the night.

The 1st Battalion was involved in a tragic friendly fire incident on 8 March. Companies A and B were moving along parallel trails east of Mount Worri when a firefight broke out. Marines from Company A spotted a figure wearing a Japanese uniform moving through the dense undergrowth and opened fire. Unfortunately, the "enemy" scout was a Company B native guide wearing discarded Japanese clothing. One Marine was killed and a number of others were wounded in the ensuing fusillade. This incident so disrupted the advance that neither company was able to reach Liapo before dark.

Patrols from the 2d Battalion initially reported the Japanese were dug in to defend Bitokara Mission, but the main body found the positions there empty when it closed in. Company F then pushed forward to capture the abandoned airstrip at Talasea. Other patrols ran into resistance as they tried to scale Mount Schleuther. Fire from Japanese small arms, 90mm mortars, and a 75mm gun inflicted eighteen casualties on the 2d Battalion. Major Gayle elected to dig in rather than press a risky night attack. It was a wise decision, because Marine artillery prevailed during the resulting nightlong duel.

The next day, 9 March, the 1st and 2d Battalions mounted a coordinated attack to carry Mount Schleuther. Company G took the crest with surprising ease because the Japanese had pulled out during the night. The Marines found one dead Japanese and captured two stragglers on the summit. The only loss occurred when a booby-trapped 75mm gun wounded one curious Marine. The villages at the base of the mountain were not defended, and Companies B and C cleared them by 1300. With this action, the 5th Marines had successfully opened the route across the Willaumez Peninsula and secured Garua Island located in the bay near Talasea. That afternoon, the 3d Battalion's Company K escorted Colonel Smith to Bitokara, where he established the regimental command post. The 1st Battalion continued clearing operations in the vicinity of Waru, the 2d Battalion held Talasea, and the 3d Battalion maintained the Volupai beachhead. The first phase of Operation Appease cost the regiment seventeen Marines killed and 114 wounded.

The 5th Marines constantly searched for, but never encountered, a sizable enemy force between 10 March and 25 April. Patrols moved north to Woganki and Pangalu; west and south from Waru to Kumeraki-1 and -2, Kambili, and Garu; and south along Kimbe Bay to Bola, Garilli, Patanga, Kilu, Numundo Plantation, Kulingai, San Remo Plantation, Ruange, and Buluma. This forty-seven-day period resulted in 151 Japanese killed and 88 prisoners captured. The 5th Marines lost 3 killed and 8 wounded. The major action was an extended patrol by Capt. Andrew A. Haldane's Company K. The "King" Company Marines left Bitokara on 11 March with orders to reach Numundo Plantation within three days. All went well at first, and Captain Haldane reported Garilli had been abandoned. The Japanese then engaged the Marines in a four-day running gunfight along the trail from Patanga to Kilu. At Kilu, the defenders were holding the Marines at bay with a 75mm field gun when landing craft carrying Lieutenant Colonel Deakin and the 3d Battalion 81mm mortar section suddenly appeared on the horizon. Deakin's small force was able to land despite enemy fire and helped Company K dislodge the defenders. Company K entered Numundo Plantation without further contact two days later. This action secured all of the Willaumez Peninsula. The cost of the patrol was one officer killed and seven Marines wounded.

The 1st Battalion netted some enemy stragglers with an ambush in the vicinity of Garu to the north. Company I replaced Company K and was in turn replaced at Numundo by the rest of the 2d Battalion.

While Company K was chasing the Japanese down the coast, the regimental headquarters was settling down in the pleasant area around Bitokara Mission. The 3d Battalion moved over from Volupai on the twelfth and acted as the honor guard when Colonel Smith and Lieutenant Colonel Buse raised the same flag that had earlier flown over Cape Gloucester. The 2d Battalion moved from Numundo to San Remo Plantation, which Major Gayle described as "a very pleasant place," on 30 March.

One platoon participated in a reconnaissance patrol to Cape Hoskins, an action that marked the farthest Marine penetration to the east. This patrol spurred scuttlebutt that the Marines were going to attack Rabaul. But in far-away Washington, D.C., the Joint Chiefs of Staff had already decided to bypass and isolate that formidable strong hold instead.

The last 5th Marines clash of the campaign occurred on 22 April, when a 2d Battalion patrol ambushed a Japanese platoon, killing twenty. The last Marine killed in action on New Britain died during this fight.

Bitokara-Talasea seemed almost a paradise after the travails of fighting at Cape Gloucester and Borgen Bay. The view from the German mission was spectacular. It occupied a high hill overlooking scenic Garua Harbor and the picturesque Talasea coconut grove. Hot springs abounded and were turned into field-expedient spas where dirty Marines could bathe away the grime of New Britain. These were the first hot baths many of the men had taken since departing Australia. Although technically in a combat zone, the 5th Marines soon adopted a normal garrison routine. Close-order drill, field training, and division schools became the order of the day. Free hours were whiled away sampling the new ten-in-one rations, swimming and fishing, and speculating about how the Marines would spend their well-deserved and long-overdue liberties when the division returned to Australia.

Orders to ship out were not long in coming. The 1st and 3d Battalions moved from Talasea to Borgen Bay at about 1630 on 25 April, and the 2d Battalion departed San Remo at about 2000. The entire regimental movement was complete by 1930 the next day. The men of the 5th Marines could look back with satisfaction at their achievements on New Britain. Operation Appease was one of the best-planned and well-executed operations of World War II. Except for the short interlude at Bitokara, however, the Marines had not enjoyed their time in the "green inferno" and looked forward to a respite. Their glee at leaving New Britain was tempered when the men learned they were not returning to Australia as expected. There would be no repeat of the Great Debauch because the 1st Marine Division was headed for a place far different than the friendly streets of Melbourne.

Peleliu

Instead of parading down the streets of Melbourne, the 1st Marine Division was unceremoniously dumped on a rain-soaked, rat-infested, odoriferous island purgatory known as Pavuvu. This palm-studded swamp in the Russell Islands near Guadalcanal turned out to be a most unsatisfactory base. Chosen in haste without a suitable survey, Pavuvu provided neither rest, relaxation, nor adequate training space. Most Marine veterans, in contrast to their fond remembrances of Melbourne, recalled their time on Pavuvu with disgust. In fact, veterans described the island as being nothing more than a gigantic garbage dump. The unharvested coconut plantation left the ground littered with rotting debris, and "the monsoon season died a slow death in the Russells," so the low-lying land was cov-

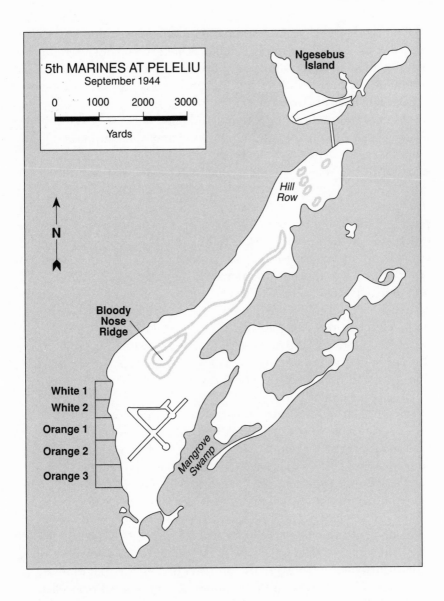

5th MARINES AT PELELIU
September 1944

0   1000   2000   3000

Yards

Ngesebus Island

Hill Row

N

Bloody Nose Ridge

White 1
White 2
Orange 1
Orange 2
Orange 3

Mangrove Swamp

ered by knee-deep muck. To make matters worse, mangy rats and blue-black land crabs crawled all over the landscape, and both species relentlessly attacked the men without mercy each night. Any poor soul who failed to tuck in his mosquito netting was likely to find a rat gnawing on his feet, and loose clothing quickly became a crab tenement.

There had been virtually no preparation when the gaunt, sick Marines landed. Upon arrival, therefore, combat training could not be conducted because all hands had to turn to in order to construct roads and build rudimentary camp facilities. This unexpected tasking was an ironic twist of fate. The major reason Pavuvu had been selected was so the Marines would not have to furnish the daily work parties that were required on Guadalcanal. Adding insult to injury, food and water supplies were totally inadequate. The diet quickly became a monotonous blend of Spam and dehydrated vegetables, meals that were neither tasty nor filling and did not meet the men's daily caloric needs. Local wells belched up a putrid liquid that had to be mixed with lemonade powder to make a barely potable, foul-tasting beverage the Marines contemptuously called "battery acid." Needless to say, there was little in the way of recreation. Beer was in short supply and evening movies were "grade Z" flicks rejected by other units. Only through the personal intervention of legendary entertainer Bob Hope were the Pavuvu Marines able to enjoy a single live variety show. "Nothing is too bad for the 1st Marine Division" was a common refrain to describe this time at Pavuvu. Historian Frank Hough noted that morale in the division plummeted to its lowest point during this period. It was not until rumors of a new operation were confirmed that spirits began to rise. In retrospect, it would be hard to imagine a worse staging area.

The 5th Marines underwent a major reorganization at Pavuvu. The new F-series table of organization changed personnel and equipment authorizations. More importantly, it embodied a radical new tactical concept as well. Rifle squads increased in size to thirteen men and were subdivided into four-man fire teams. Fire teams consisted of a team leader, an automatic rifleman, an assistant automatic rifleman, and a scout. These changes tripled squad firepower and eased small-unit command and control. Each rifle squad had three BARs instead of only one, and squad leaders were now responsible for the control of three units instead of nine individuals. A further benefit was that when squad leaders moved up the chain of command, experienced troop leaders would replace them. This minimized the disruption of cohesion in small units.

There were other changes as well. The regimental supply section was redesignated a "service section." Two SPM half-tracks were added to the regimental Weapons Company, bringing the total to four 75mm self-propelled guns. Battalion weapons companies (D, H, and M) were dissolved.

Their 81mm mortars were placed in battalion headquarters companies, and their machine-gun platoons were reassigned to individual rifle companies. Machine-gun platoons were armed with six air-cooled and six water-cooled machine guns. These changes made the 5th Marines a more compact and more efficient fighting force.

The next stepping stone to Japan was the high-reef island of Peleliu in the Palaus, whose capture was deemed necessary to protect General MacArthur's flank for the American return to the Philippines. Lobster-claw-shaped Peleliu was six miles long and about two miles wide. Its terrain was mostly coral and limestone covered by thick vegetation. The coastal areas were generally low and flat, but three-hundred-foot-high Umurbrogol Ridge formed a jagged spine that dominated the airfield that was the primary reason Peleliu had been selected as a target. The east coast consisted of a thin strip of land that joined a series of small islands ringing an extensive mangrove swamp. Two small islands, Ngesebus and Kongauru, were attached to Peleliu's northern tip by a causeway. Equatorial Peleliu was infamous for its furnace like heat and debilitating humidity, but it almost never rained at Peleliu, placing a premium on potable water. Intelligence reported about ten thousand Japanese, a mix of army and navy troops, defended the island.

The battle for Peleliu is often referred to as the forgotten campaign, but those who had to endure its horrors will never forget it. This ill-fated debacle was destined to become a repeat of bloody Tarawa. It was a scandalously costly fight whose high casualties shocked the high command. As at Tarawa, high-level decisions had devastating consequences for the rank and file who had to do the fighting. Peleliu is now considered to have been a battle that should not have been fought. There was no compelling strategic reason, intelligence about the target was sketchy at best, the troops were inadequately trained, and the preliminary bombardment was totally inadequate. Yet the single most important factor in this fight was what was arguably the poorest performance by a Marine division commander in the Pacific. He is a man historians have characterized as callous for sentencing his men to the "hell of Pavuvu" while spending his time in Australia and making little effort to improve their lot after being alerted to the dismal conditions on that wretched island. They also accuse him of being tactically inept because he did not participate in the planning, steadfastly refused to grant his subordinates a free hand, and stubbornly fought a battle of attrition even after it became obvious his division was being bled dry. Fortunately, the blunders of the high command were offset, albeit at a terrible cost, by the courage and determination of the fighting Marines of the "Old Breed."

The Palau invasion force was III Amphibious Corps (III AC) commanded by Marine Maj. Gen. Roy S. Geiger. Expeditionary troops for Operation Stalemate included the 1st Marine Division and the army's 81st "Wildcat" Infantry Division. The Marines were to take Peleliu while the Wildcats made an amphibious demonstration at Babelthuap in the north and seized Angaur Island to the south. The high command wanted to take Peleliu quickly, so all three infantry regiments were going in abreast; an unusual tactical concept that left the division commander no ready reserve. The 1st Marines on the left flank would land on the north and capture Umurbrogol Ridge, the 5th Marines would move straight inland in the center to take the airfield, and the 7th Marines would secure the southern flank on the right then become the division reserve. General Rupertus, in what was one of the most inaccurate forecasts of the Pacific War, predicted the operation would be "short but tough," and he brashly told the press that Peleliu would fall in only a few days.

Despite the division commander's assurances of quick success, two factors stood in the way of the promised quick seizure of Peleliu: an ineffective preliminary bombardment and a radical change in Japanese tactics. Only three days were allotted for the prelanding softening up, and naval gunfire targeting procedures left much to be desired. The resulting bombardment was termed "the least adequate of the Pacific War," by historian Edwin Simmons. Concurrently, the Japanese changed tactics at Peleliu. Instead of defending the beach and then trying to eject the attackers with a fanatical, all-out counterattack, the Japanese decided instead to fight a drawn-out battle of attrition. No futile banzai attacks were planned at Peleliu. Instead, Col. Kunio Nakagawa's defense forces were dug into caves on the high ground. Nakagawa's goal was to inflict maximum casualties on the exposed attackers. Victory was not an option, so his sole intent was to make the Americans pay dearly for every inch of ground they gained. These tactics proved so successful that they were later repeated at Iwo Jima and Okinawa.

Colonel Harold D. "Bucky" Harris commanded the 5th Marines. Harris was a brilliant scholar who graduated from the Naval Academy and attended the *Ecole Superieure de Guerre*. He had served in the 1st Marine Division intelligence section on Guadalcanal, where he favorably impressed General Vandegrift, and he was Bill Whaling's executive officer in the 1st Marines on New Britain. Harris had been suddenly pulled from the division intelligence section when Col. William S. Fellers, of the 5th Marines, had to be evacuated stateside due to severe malaria in August. Although primarily a staff officer rather than a field commander thus far in his career, Bucky Harris would soon prove under fire that he was both an astute tactician and a compassionate commander. In fact, some historians opine that he was actually running the division during the later stages of the operation. The regimental executive officer was Lt. Col. Lew Walt, the adjutant was Capt. Alan F. Dill, the intelligence officer was Capt. Levi T. Burcham, the operations officer was Maj. Walt McIlhenny, and the logistics officer was Maj. Joe Skoczylas.

Combat Team 5 (code-named Lonewolf, after its introspective commander) included Landing Teams 1/5 (Lt. Col. Robert W. Boyd), 2/5 (Maj. Gordon Gayle), and 3/5 (Lt. Col. Austin C. Shofner). Gayle was a very promising young officer. A 1938 Naval Academy graduate who had served as the 1st Battalion operations officer on Guadalcanal, Gayle was typical of the "new breed" of officers—intellectuals who were well schooled in modern war-fighting theory rather than battle-tested veterans who had pulled a hitch or two in China or chased banditos during the Banana Wars. Austin Shofner, commander of the 3d Battalion, was a living Marine legend. He had been captured on Corregidor early in the war, escaped to fight with local guerrillas, returned to Australia in 1943, and was now out to avenge his lost shipmates.

Colonel Harris could call on direct support from 75mm howitzers, M4 Sherman medium tanks, and a wide variety of skilled specialists. Combat support detachments assigned to Combat Team 5 included the 2d Battalion, 11th Marines; Company B, 1st Tank Battalion; Company B, 1st Engineer Battalion; Company B, 1st Pioneer Battalion; 2d Platoon, 1st Military Police Company; Company B, 1st Medical Battalion; 2d Platoon, Ordnance Company, 1st Service Battalion; and a fire support team from the 1st Joint Assault Support Company.

Combat Team 5 was slated to come across Peleliu's Orange Beaches One and Two with two battalions in assault and one in reserve. The plan was for the assault battalions to drive straight across the island to a mangrove swamp on the eastern shore, a zone that included the southern portion of the airfield. The reserve battalion was to come ashore and then pivot north to take the rest of the airfield support complex. After the airfield was secured, the 5th Marines would continue the attack to seize the flatlands to the northeast, then occupy the eastern coastal strip

(Purple Beach) and outlying islands. Four days were allotted to accomplish these missions.

Preassault training culminated when the 5th Marines boarded the ships that would carry it to Peleliu. The regiment moved to the Tassafaronga area of Guadalcanal to conduct final landing exercises on 27 and 29 August 1944. The rehearsal went well. The Marines then waited aboard ship while the 81st Infantry Division conducted its rehearsal. The slow-moving LSTs carrying the assault companies departed for Peleliu on 4 September and the faster transports followed four days later. The journey was an uneventful but uncomfortable one for the Marines, who were stuck in cramped, hot, humid, and poorly ventilated troop compartments as the convoy sailed along the equator.

The 5th Marines had been fortunate at Guadalcanal and New Britain, where there was little opposition during the initial ship-to-shore movements. This was not the case at Peleliu. In fact, that landing turned out to be the toughest in the regiment's history. The LVTs left the line of departure at about 0800 on 15 September and encountered a deluge of Japanese steel on the way in. The rain of shells increased in scope and intensity as the amtracs lurched toward the beach. The fire was so intense that the reef was soon littered with burning vehicles. The leading waves made it ashore at about 0830 and the surviving amtracs gingerly picked their way through a minefield. Luckily, most of the mines had been exposed by erosion or were buried too deep by the shifting sands to be effective. But antitank ditches, coral ridges, and thick jungle stopped the inland advance.

The 5th Marines, landing in the division center, was not subjected to the enfilading fires that devastated the flank units. In fact, Bucky Harris's unit suffered the least amount of disruption of the three assault regiments on D day. The 1st Marines on the left was immediately pinned down, suffered heavy casualties, and could not get off the beach. The 7th Marines on the right was so severely mauled by intense enemy fire that it veered off course as it came ashore. On the other hand, the 5th Marines landed in a coconut grove whose evenly spaced trees fortuitously masked movement but did not obstruct maneuver.

Landing Team 1/5 crossed Orange Beach One and quickly gained its initial objective, the O-1 Line, and tied in with the 1st Marines. The 1st Battalion dug in for protection against murderous mortar and artillery fires that covered the open airfield and were ranging Marine positions. Landing Team 3/5 came in over Orange Two and immediately pushed forward into the jungle. The 2d Battalion patiently waited at the transfer line offshore until its amphibian tractors could arrive.

Bucky Harris was aware that the Japanese possessed armor and realized the flat airfield was an ideal avenue of approach, so he ordered 37mm antitank guns and heavy machine guns placed along the forward edge of the 1st Battalion lines. Three of the five Sherman tanks assigned to the 1st Battalion finally got ashore with the fourth wave. Lieutenant Colonel Boyd ordered them to assume hull-down positions with a good view of the airfield. The 2d Battalion, 11th Marines, placed its 75mm pack howitzers to the rear of the 1st Battalion. Battery E was in action just after noon.

Two Marines from the 1st Battalion were awarded Medals of Honor for their actions on D day. Corporal Lewis K. Bausell led a squad assault on a pillbox near the beach. He was the first to reach the target and was firing his automatic rifle into the aperture when one of the Japanese inside flung a grenade out. Bausell unhesitatingly threw himself on the deadly missile to protect the rest of his squad at the cost of his own life. First Lieutenant Carlton R. Rouh, a twenty-five-year-old former enlisted man who already had been awarded the Silver Star for his valor at Guadalcanal, was searching an enemy dugout that was to be used as an 81mm mortar observation post when he was shot. Two men dragged the wounded officer away from the bunker entrance and were busy rendering first aid when a grenade landed nearby. Rouh, despite his weakened condition, placed his own body between the grenade and his benefactors. He took the full brunt of the explosion, but survived the war to receive his Medal of Honor from Pres. Harry S. Truman. This incident had a romantic aspect to it as well. While recuperating in Australia, Rouh discovered that Phyllis Rowland, his former sweetheart, was an army nurse stationed there. They rekindled their friendship while he was in the hospital and were later married.

The landings at first went about as planned despite fierce resistance, but by midafternoon the 3d Battalion was thoroughly engulfed by the fog of war because the situation at Orange Beach Two was far more confused than at Orange One. Many LVTs were knocked out and the survivors had to wade through enemy fire to get to the beach. Major Robert M. Ash, the Landing Team 3/5 executive officer, was killed within moments of landing. The LVT carrying most of the battalion communications personnel and signal equipment was destroyed on the reef. Concurrently, amtracs carrying the 7th Marines swerved north to avoid the intense fire and landed at Orange Two instead of Orange Three. Lieutenant Colonel Shofner's Landing Team 3/5 soon mixed with elements of the 3d Battalion, 7th Marines. This was most unfortunate because similarly named units (i.e., there were two I, K, and L Companies) mingled in the dense vegetation, a circumstance that caused much confusion.

Captain John A. Crown's Company I landed on the left and Capt. Andrew A. Haldane's Company K came in on the right. Company L, the battalion reserve, followed them in. Company I was at the O-1 Line and had tied in with Landing Team 1/5 by 0930. Company K encountered heavy resistance, ran into elements of the 7th Marines, and slowly made its way inland through dense scrub brush that limited visibility and movement. Captain Haldane lost contact with the rest of Landing Team 3/5 and Company K inadvertently moved well forward of the 7th Marines. Although not according to the landing plan, Company K temporarily formed the division flank because the 7th Marines had been so disoriented by the Japanese firestorm. Colonel Harris realized his units were being fragmented by the heavy fire and thick vegetation and that a huge gap had developed. Company L was committed to close the line, but it was unable locate Company K amid the turmoil. Instead of rushing blindly into the bush, Company L stayed in close contact with the Marines on its left flank.

Major Gayle's 2d Battalion came in at about 0930, consolidated on the beach, and then moved to the O-1 Line, where it relieved Company I of responsibility for the 5th Marines's center about a half hour later. Company I was then sent to fill the gap between Companies L and K. The 2d Battalion conducted a turning movement to secure the southern portion of the airfield not long thereafter. The battalion's right flank moved forward like a swinging gate while the left remained anchored on the 1st Battalion. Company L of the 3d Battalion kept abreast until it reached the mangrove swamp on the far right flank. Unfortunately, this maneuver separated Company L from its parent unit. While Company L participated in the 2d Battalion's turning movement, Companies I and K were held up in the scrub while they eliminated enemy strong points with the aid of tanks earmarked for Landing Team 3/7.

Just after midday, division headquarters discovered that physical contact between the 5th and 7th Marines had been lost, and Colonel Harris was told to close the gap. Lieutenant Colonel Shofner made radio contact with the neighboring unit but was incorrectly informed as to the exact location of the front lines. Unaware of this error, Shofner ordered his Marines forward to the reported spot. This move inadvertently opened—rather than closed—the distance between the units, and the 3d Battalion was actually a quarter mile ahead of the 7th Marines by 1600. When Shofner realized the true situation, he ordered "Ack-Ack" Haldane to bend Company K's lines back until contact was established. The reserve platoon and headquarters personnel were sent forward, but the gap still could not be closed. Shofner repeatedly tried to move Company I, but was unable to contact Captain Crown because that unit's radio batteries were depleted and the spares had been destroyed during the landing. Thus, Landing Team 3/5 was separated into three groups, none of which were in direct contact with the other, as darkness approached. Shofner was working to straighten this mess out when disaster struck. A well-placed enemy mortar barrage hit the battalion command post, seriously wounding Lieutenant Colonel Shofner, killing the communications officer, and destroying most of the battalion's communications equipment.

Landing Team 3/5 was hopelessly scattered, out of radio contact, and leaderless. Just when things looked darkest, a familiar figure from the 5th Marines's past once again rose to the fore and brought order from chaos: Lt. Col. Lew Walt came down to take temporary command. Walt and his runner unhesitatingly plunged into the dark jungle determined to straighten out the situation. Walt first located Company L and ordered that unit to move to the edge of the airfield to bolster the thinly held 2d Battalion line. He eventually found Company I in defensive positions in front of the 7th Marines about two hours later. Captain Crown was told to move his company north to the airfield. This was done, but Company I was unable to establish contact with other friendly units in the darkness. Crown's company therefore manned an isolated perimeter just south of the airfield. Walt next found Company K and ordered it to bridge the gap between the 7th Marines and the airfield. Walt's three companies were each facing a different direction and communications were shaky at best, but the 3d Battalion stood firm throughout its first night ashore.

The 1st and 2d Battalions were establishing the beachhead and the 3d Battalion was struggling through the dense vegetation when the Japanese mounted their most vigorous effort to oust the Americans from Peleliu. The battle for the beachhead began in the late afternoon on D day. The Japanese attack was first announced by a noticeable increase in the focus and amount of enemy shelling of Marine positions at the edge of the airfield. This barrage covered the deliberate movement of an enemy infantry company toward the Marine lines. Suddenly, about a dozen Japanese Type 95 light tanks burst from behind the built-up area north of the airfield and raced across the eastern landing strip toward the juncture of the 1st and 5th Marines. Lieutenant Colonel Boyd's 1st Battalion opened up with all its organic firepower, as did the rest of the Marine line. A navy dive-bomber swooped in and hit the center of the Japanese attack with a five-hundred-pound bomb. The cannoneers of the 11th Marines used direct fire against the oncoming tanks and indirect fire to pin down the advancing infantry. The 75mm main guns of the Sherman tanks took on their Japanese counterparts in a wild shoot-out. Major Gayle of the 2d Battalion immediately released his attached Shermans from 2d Platoon, Company B, 1st Tank Battalion. These four American medium tanks sped out of the Marine lines and crashed into the exposed Japanese flank. The enemy infantry began to pull back, but the Japanese tanks continued to bear down on the 1st Battalion at full speed.

Six Japanese tanks hit Company B and penetrated the Marine lines. This futile armored attack failed to dislodge the American defenders and a trail of burning enemy tanks littered the field of battle. The riflemen let the tanks through, and then quickly closed ranks to repel a follow-up infantry assault. The unsupported enemy tanks rampaged through the rear area without apparent coordination or direction. All six were knocked out by 37mm guns and 2.36-inch bazooka rockets before they reached the beach. The enemy infantry attack melted away long before it reached the Marine lines. Two Company B Marines were killed during this action, both crushed by tank treads. The exact number of enemy tanks used in this attack has never been conclusively established. Japanese figures and American eyewitness accounts vary from ten to seventeen, but the most commonly cited figures indicate there were about a dozen. The attacking tanks were so thoroughly destroyed that battlefield survey teams were unable to make an accurate count.

Major Gayle used the lull after the action to move the 2d Battalion forward. This hard-charging unit reached the center of the airfield as darkness closed in. The 2d Battalion thus registered the greatest gain of any assault battalion on D day. American artillery harassment fires and illumination rounds kept the Japanese at bay throughout the first night ashore. The Japanese probed the lines near the juncture of the 1st and

2d Battalions but were easily repulsed. A second probe hit the 1st Battalion just before dawn. It failed and cost the Japanese their last two tanks.

One major problem on D day was the supply situation. The navy beach master and his replacement were both killed by artillery fire. Many of the LVTs scheduled to haul supplies were knocked out during the assault or were shanghaied at the beach for use as evacuation vehicles. The intense heat and high humidity led to ever increasing demands for potable water. Unfortunately, most of the drinking water had been contaminated when fuel drums were inadequately cleaned before being filled with water. This created a Hobson's choice: Marines who drank the water became ill, and those who did not rapidly dehydrated or succumbed to heat prostration. Additionally, units that ran short of ammunition had difficulty replenishing it. Heavy enemy fire and the fact that many units were temporarily out of contact with the rear echelon or were lost in the scrub brush caused a supply crisis as the day wore on. Unfortunately, effective resupply of assault units remained a problem throughout Operation Stalemate.

The second day at Peleliu was a costly one for the 5th Marines. It began with a near catastrophe. More than a dozen Japanese shells hit a zigzag communications trench that housed the regimental command post. One wiped out the field telephone switchboard, and a number of veteran communicators in the wire section were killed or wounded. Another shell landed on the parapet and buried the command group. The regimental adjutant, operations officer, and the naval gunfire liaison officer were all seriously wounded and had to be evacuated. Colonel Harris was not hit, but he wrenched his knee badly enough that he was partially incapacitated and was in great pain for some time afterward. Luckily, Lieutenant Colonel Walt was away from the command post leading the 3d Battalion. Silent Lew was quickly recalled to act as de facto regimental commander for the morning attack. Major John H. "Gus" Gustafson, the former 2d Battalion executive officer, took command of the 3d Battalion and Maj. Hierome L. Opie, the battalion's operations officer, became its executive officer in midafternoon. Major McIlhenny, the former 3d Battalion commander and obvious choice to take over, was not available. He was wounded when the regimental command post was hit and had to be evacuated.

The replacement regimental adjutant was Capt. Paul H. Douglas. Douglas had been a respected economics professor at the University of

Chicago for more than ten years before the Japanese bombed Pearl Harbor. He entered the Marine Corps as a private in 1942 and went through boot camp at age fifty, before being commissioned and sent to the Pacific, where he became a staff officer with the 1st Marine Division on New Britain.

The morning's mission was to seize the O-2 Line, which included the rest of the airfield and the area adjacent to the mangrove swamp. This would be no easy task because the open area was under direct observation and had been zeroed in by Japanese artillery. This situation called for a closely coordinated combined-arms attack. Fortunately, such operations were Bucky Harris's forte. Old Breed historian George MacMillan noted that "Harris . . . used supporting fires more fully and more wisely than [any other] regimental commander [at Peleliu.]" The 5th Marines launched a determined tank-infantry attack supported by air strikes, naval gunfire, artillery, mortars, and heavy machine guns. Companies A and B, with Company C trailing, crossed the airfield and cleared the ruined hangars and administrative buildings. The 1st Battalion reached the O-2 Line but pulled back to more defensible positions before dark. The 2d Battalion kept pace on the right flank as it fought its way through thick scrub jungle. Major Gayle was unable to use tanks in the heavy vegetation, but the overhead cover provided the 2d Battalion some relief from enemy artillery. The 3d Battalion, still reeling from its losses of the previous day, played only a minor role on D-plus-1. Company L stayed with the 2d Battalion, Company K worked with the 7th Marines, and Company I was ordered to reinforce the battered 1st Battalion.

The next morning, 17 September, the 1st Battalion moved out under cover of well-placed supporting fires and retook the O-2 Line before being relieved in place by the 3d Battalion. This was accomplished with great difficulty because the area was under heavy enemy fire and both units suffered numerous cases of heat exhaustion along the way. The 1st Battalion became the regimental reserve upon completion of the passage of lines, and the 2d Battalion continued its attack through the jungle. This movement was relatively safe from enemy observation and Gayle's men encountered only scattered sniper fire. However, movement was painfully slow because the Marines had to hack their way through the dense jungle, suffering many heat casualties in the process. When the day ended, the 2d Battalion was seven hundred yards past the O-2 Line with Company E on the left, Company F on the right, and Company G in reserve. The 3d Battalion had been unable to advance because of the combination of reorganization delays and intense enemy fire.

The 5th Marines jumped off at 0700 on the eighteenth. The 3d Battalion moved forward to East Road at the foot of Umurbrogol Ridge. It was slow going because of difficult terrain and stiff enemy resistance. Things went much faster on the right where the 2d Battalion was still concealed from enemy observation. At first, the advance was slowed by flanking fires from the mangrove swamp on the right, so Major Gayle called for artillery covering fire. High-explosive shells burrowed into the muck and exploded with little effect, but a switch to airbursts soon smothered all resistance from that direction. Company E reached a causeway through the swamp that led to an island like spit of land called Ngardolok after about two hours. Things then began to sour for the hard-luck 2d Battalion.

The narrow causeway road was a dangerous bottleneck, but intelligence reported that Ngardolok, more commonly called the "RDF area" because it contained a Japanese radio direction finding station, might be unoccupied. A patrol from Company F crossed the causeway at 1120 without drawing enemy fire. To be safe, however, an air strike was requested to prepare the way for a crossing in force. The strike was way off target, so Major Gayle called for an artillery preparation. When this fire lifted at 1335, he sent Companies F and G across the causeway. Unbeknownst to Major Gayle, higher headquarters had ordered a second air strike to make up for the failed first one. The new wave of planes arrived on station just as the 2d Battalion moved out and mistakenly strafed the advancing Marines. This tragedy was the result of a series of mishaps that began when the air liaison officer was wounded, his radio was destroyed, and most air panels were shredded by enemy fire. To compound the problem, Major Gayle was temporarily out of contact with regimental headquarters because the 2d Battalion command post was concurrently displacing forward. Not long after that incident, Company E and battalion headquarters were bracketed by misdirected Marine artillery and mortar fires. Sadly, almost all of the 2d Battalion's thirty-four battle casualties that day were the result of friendly fire.

The 3d Battalion, less Company L, which remained at East Road to guard the northern flank, rushed across the causeway to reinforce the 2d Battalion. Companies I and K were integrated into the south side of the 2d Battalion's defensive lines by 1700. The next morning, the 1st Battalion moved into the RDF area. Clearing operations there went well. The 2d Battalion encountered only scattered resistance from the shell-shocked remnants of the defense force who appeared more eager to hide than to fight. The 3d Battalion moved to Purple Beach on the east coast and cleared that area, encountering only light resistance. Mines, tank traps, barricades, and swampy ground held up operations far more than did the Japanese. As those obstacles were gradually overcome, Company G secured the rest of the northeastern peninsula.

On the twentieth, a patrol discovered that Island Able was unoccupied. The same day, Company I moved southwest where, alerted by war dogs, it uncovered a Japanese ambush. The resulting firefight ended at nightfall, and the position was secured without great difficulty the next morning. From that time until the end of this phase of Operation Stalemate the 5th Marines rapidly pushed up and down Peleliu's eastern coast. Company G occupied Island Able and seized Ngabad Island on the twenty-first. The unnamed northernmost island was taken on 23 September. Meanwhile, the 3d Battalion organized defenses on Purple Beach, and the 1st Battalion did the same on Ngardolok. Company L, orphaned when its parent unit crossed the causeway on D-plus-3, continued to work along East Road, joining the 1st Marines as that regiment slugged its way along rugged Umurbrogol Ridge. Of course, no good deed goes unpunished, so Company L missed out on the few days' rest afforded the 5th Marines's other companies during the consolidation of Purple Beach and the islets.

The 5th Marines entered the third phase of operations on 25 September. The purpose of this phase was to complete the capture of northern Peleliu. This would isolate the remaining Japanese inside a constricted pocket atop Umurbrogol Ridge and would virtually end the threat to U.S. airfield operations. The first objective was the junction of the East and West Roads, which met about fifteen hundred yards south of Peleliu's northern tip. Follow-up objectives were the capture of a radio station and a ruined phosphate refinery, whose seizure would secure jump-off positions for a shore-to-shore assault to take Ngesebus and Kongauru Islands. To reach the jump-off line, the 5th Marines would have to seize Amiangal Mountain and "Hill Row," which formed an inverted T. Although unknown at the time, this area was the site of the largest and most elaborate cave complex on the island. Four heights collectively known as Hill Row stretched across Peleliu's narrow northern tip. The palm-covered flatland there was ideal tank country, but taking it would be no easy task because Hill Row stood in the way and enemy positions on Amiangal Mountain and Ngesebus formed a dangerous gauntlet once Hill Row had been penetrated, and northern Peleliu was stoutly defended by Japanese Imperial Marines of the 45th Naval Guard Force.

The 5th Marines moved from eastern to western Peleliu by motor march on the 25th and was ready to attack within a few hours. This was no small feat because units of the 5th Marines were scattered all along the east coast when Colonel Harris received the order to move out at about 1130 on D-plus-10. The 1st Battalion, located at the Ngardolok RDF area, was the first to load. The 3d Battalion came over from Purple Beach and was next to mount out. The 2d Battalion had to wade across several hundred yards of reef to make its rendezvous. "The prompt assembly and displacement of the [5th Marines] was a remarkable and noteworthy accomplishment," wrote official historian Frank Hough.

The 5th Marines debarked in a rear area held by the 81st Infantry Division's 321st Regimental Combat Team (RCT), which had recently arrived to replace the badly battered 1st Marines. The Marines then advanced to the road junction, where elements of the 1/5 took the radio station before dusk. The 3d Battalion pushed to East Road against minor resistance and occupied the center of an elongated perimeter. The 2d Battalion brought up the rear and dug in about six hundred yards north of the 321st RCT's lines. Although the Marines were isolated, the night was uneventful except in the 1/5 sector. The battalion's defensive lines lay in the shadow of Hill Row, well within the range of Japanese mortars there and guns dug into caves on Ngesebus Island. The 1st Battalion repelled three counterattacks that night. Captain John McLaughlin's Company C later staged a night raid to destroy a pair of troublesome enemy machine guns before dawn.

The main attack resumed the next morning. Major Gayle's 2d Battalion held firm while Major Gustafson's 3d Battalion secured Hill 80 to its immediate front and continued east until it reached the swamp that abutted Peleliu's northeastern shore. The 1st Battalion had the toughest row to hoe on D-plus-11. Lieutenant Colonel Boyd's Marines came under heavy fire from Hill 1, the northernmost elevation in Hill Row. Despite excellent support by tanks and flame-throwing LVTs, the Japanese continued to pour fire down from their cave positions and the Marine attack stalled. Captain John W. Holland's Company B was able to mount Hill 2 at 1400, but Company C had to be pulled back off Hill 1 before dark.

As the 1st Battalion bogged down in front of Hill Row, the 2d Battalion made a flanking movement on the left. It was not an easy maneuver because the Marines were subjected to plunging fires from Hill Row on the right, came under direct fire from Ngesebus Island, and were held up by strong emplacements and an antitank ditch that blocked the way to the refinery. By dark, the 2d Battalion manned an isolated perimeter north of Hill Row near the antitank ditch, the 1st Battalion was partially atop and partially at the foot of Hill Row, and the 3d Battalion securely held the far right flank.

Reducing Hill Row was a slow and frustrating process because the enemy time and time again popped out of supposedly secured cave mouths to open fire. Holding the top of a hill did not mean the enemy below had been neutralized. Each suspected position was blasted individually with a variety of weapons, but often even this did not work because the Japanese emplacements constituted a unique defense in depth that was vertical as well as horizontal and lateral. Frustrated Marines on the summit could smell enemy cooking fires and hear Japanese conversations coming from below, but they could do nothing about it because the elaborate tunnel complex was almost invulnerable. The 5th Marines was able to neutralize the area by 30 September, but it was not until months after the Marines departed Peleliu that all the caves were finally sealed. Still, the die-hard survivors of one Japanese platoon did not surrender until 1947.

Just as the 2d Battalion got ready to move out on the morning of the twenty-seventh the command post was raked by mortar fire. Major Gayle was the only one to escape unhurt. The 2d Battalion attack went forward as scheduled despite this setback. The solitary remaining tank-dozer, a Sherman tank mounting a bulldozer blade, filled in an antitank ditch that enabled the 2d Battalion to approach the refinery and finally take the ridge at Peleliu's northern tip. The 2d Battalion made it there after Company E secured the ridgeline to the right and an LVT flamethrower hosed down the refinery building, cremating that makeshift bunker and its sixty or so defenders. Company F seized the north ridge and established observation posts on the crest, but the Japanese still held the cliff face that dominated the road.

These enemy positions had to be wiped out before Ngesebus could be taken. It promised to be extremely slow going and very costly to reduce them using infantry demolition teams. Unfortunately, time was of the essence. This challenge proved how well Colonel Harris could orchestrate combined-arms support. He had the artillery lay a continuous barrage on Ngesebus while naval gunfire pummeled Kongauru. The defenders were blinded by tank and artillery smoke shells. Five LVT(A)s floated into the channel concealed by that smoke and fired their 75mm howitzers directly into the cliff face. Company G and nine tanks then by-passed these positions, moving inland while the defenders remained under cover deep inside the caves. An LVT flamethrower later worked over the honeycomb of cave entrances. After successfully side stepping the enemy, the 2d Battalion dug in on top of the ridge to support the capture of Ngesebus and Kongauru.

The 1st Battalion spent most of the day securing Hill 1. Foot patrols found a covered approach, then provided security while engineers cleared the route of mines. After that, the tank-dozer returned from the refinery and laboriously cleared a passage for other tanks and flame-throwing LVTs. Companies B and C made slow but steady progress. They eliminated four 75mm guns and four 37mm guns as they moved ahead. Demolition teams then began systematically sealing all openings of by-passed positions.

By the end of the day on 27 September, the 2d Battalion was firmly atop the northern ridge and the 1st Battalion held most of Hill Row. The 3d Battalion played no role in the day's actions because Major Gustafson's battalion would make the shore-to-shore landing to seize Ngesebus at 0900 the next day.

For the assault on Ngesebus, the 3d Battalion was the assault force and the 1st Battalion, 7th Marines, was in reserve. Assault support consisted of one battleship, one cruiser, two destroyers, division and corps artillery, a Marine fighter squadron, and one company each of tanks, LVT(A)s, and LVTs. H-Hour was set to coincide with low tide so the tanks could easily across the reef. The plan called for the 3d Battalion to attack across the shallow reef mounted in LVTs as thirteen Sherman tanks led the charge and a like number of LVT(A)s moved up on each flank.

This attack once again demonstrated Colonel Harris's mastery of supporting arms. Carefully planned fire support and low-level strafing by VMF-114 kept the Japanese from effectively manning their beach defenses as the 3d Battalion launched its shore-to-shore assault. The only glitch occurred when three tanks were swamped during the assault, but LVT(A)s quickly filled in for them. Companies I and K jumped off at 0905 and crossed the reef in less than six minutes. All tanks, LVT(A)s, and the LVTs carrying Company L were ashore by 0930. So effective were supporting arms that the 3d Battalion suffered no casualties during that phase of the attack. The scattered defenders were then eliminated one position at a time. Concurrently, Company L, mounted in three LVTs and supported by two tanks, secured Kongauru and the unnamed islet beyond it. All except for a few hundred yards of Ngesebus were in Marine hands by nightfall. The rest of the island was secured at about 1500 on 29 September. The 3d Battalion then returned to an assembly area at Ngardolok. Marine losses were fifteen killed and thirty-three wounded.

This assault was an object lesson in the advantages of proper use of fire support. High-level after-action reports, written at headquarters, claimed there had been only light resistance, but the Marines who conducted the assault had a much different opinion. Their ground-eye view revealed that more than 450 well-armed Japanese defended the islands from more than a hundred well-positioned bunkers and fighting holes. A more accurate assessment came from Lieutenant Colonel Walt, who attributed the effective use of supporting arms and the skillful adaptation of weapons and tactics, not the lack of Japanese manpower or fortifications, for the swift conquest and low Marine casualty count.

Back on Peleliu itself, the 1st and 2d Battalions continued the attack on Hill Row simultaneously with the Ngesebus assault. The 2d Battalion attacked south along the coastal ridge with three Sherman tanks in support to envelop Hill Row from the rear. Company G assaulted through a coconut grove at 0700, eliminated 150 enemy troops by midmorning, and then dug into positions from which it could support the 1/5's attacks to seize Hill 3 and Radar Hill. At one point, LVT-mounted elements of Company E pursued an estimated seventy Japanese who broke and ran for cover on outlying islets. Those who did not surrender were killed in this action. The 1st Battalion took the final objective, Hill 3, at about 1600.

The 1st Battalion spent the following day reducing Japanese positions on Radar Hill using demolitions, flamethrowers, and bazookas. Patrols from Company B moved north to contact Company G, which was busy clearing its sector in the wooded flatland. Unfortunately, contact was not established and the patrols returned empty-handed. Company G was harassed by fire from caves dug into the slopes on the ridge and tried, without effect, to silence them using 75mm tank guns. Additionally, bypassed enemy began firing on Company G from the rear. Company E searched the area and drove the survivors out of their holes onto the reef, where LVT patrols dispatched or captured them. Company F worked the ridge top, where the Japanese often reopened sealed caves from the inside.

The 5th Marines was relieved of responsibility for the northern tip of Peleliu by the 321st RCT on the thirtieth. During the final action, the 1st Battalion pushed through the coconut groves and scrub brush to join Company G, then moved to the radio station for transportation to the reserve area. The 2d Battalion pulled off the northern ridge and the enemy tunnel complex located there was then hit with heavy artillery, including the direct fire of a 155mm howitzer dragged by hand to within a hundred yards of one cave entrance. Fleeing Japanese were gunned down by ambushes set up by Company E. Combat engineers moved into the resulting vacuum to permanently seal many of the cave openings. The final enemy casualty count on northern Peleliu was more than eleven hundred. This was an interesting figure, because the division intelligence officer had stubbornly assured Colonel Harris that less than four hundred Japanese were located there. The 1st and 2d Battalions mounted trucks, LVTs, and DUKWs that afternoon as the 5th Marines began to move to the rest area at Ngardolok.

While the 5th Marines was clearing out Peleliu's northern tip, the rest of the Japanese on the island had been compressed into what was called the Umurbrogol Pocket. This area was a nondescript jumble of rugged coral ridges and narrow defiles located roughly in the center of Umurbrogol Ridge. The major terrain features were a pair of ridges later known as Baldy and Wattie Ridges and Hill 140 at the north end; the Walt, Boyd, and Number Three Ridges were on the east side; the Five Brothers hills were in the center; an escarpment known as the China Wall lined the west; and the Five Sisters and Hill 300 dominated the southern entrance. A freshwater pond was located in a U-shaped depression called the Horseshoe that bent around the Five Brothers.

It was tough going in the Umurbrogol Pocket because the Japanese had strengthened the natural defenses in the area by hollowing out its limestone ridges. Colonel Nakagawa's command post and most of the troop quarters were located in this remote area, where they could not be hit by flat-trajectory fire. Indirect fire was difficult to adjust because of the broken nature of the terrain, so the most effective supporting arms tactic was to use air-delivered napalm gel to saturate the target area, then ignite it using white phosphorous mortar shells. This novel approach assured no friendly troops would be inadvertently immolated by a misplaced air strike.

The 7th Marines had been investing the area throughout the second phase of the campaign, but that depleted unit was worn out and overdue for relief. The 3d Battalion, 5th Marines, was attached to the 7th Marines on 2 October, then vainly tried to capture the Five Sisters twice before reverting to Colonel Harris's operational control on the sixth. Back at the division command post, General Rupertus repeatedly rejected offers of army reinforcements, so the weary 5th Marines, which had been in almost uninterrupted action for nearly a month, was called on to finish the job. Rupertus had earlier told Colonel Harris that the 5th Marines would be one of the first units to leave Peleliu, but his promise was overcome by events. The worn-out and badly depleted 1st Marines was already on its way and the 7th Marines was preparing to leave, thus, the 5th was the only Marine regiment left to clear the Umurbrogol Pocket.

All assaults on the Pocket up to that time had come from the south, but Colonel Harris wisely decided to change the direction of the main attack after careful study of the tactical situation. He correctly noted that movement from the north would allow methodical reduction of enemy positions with the least risk to the attackers. His new approach was slow but steady and conserved Marine lives. Unfortunately, it also put Colonel Harris in the line of fire from higher headquarters, which continually pressed him to speed the assault. General Rupertus insisted that speeding the attack would save lives, but subsequent analysis clearly showed that frontal assaults resulted in only minor gains at excessive cost. To his credit, Harris refused to buckle to unrelenting pressure from above and continued to use this lifesaving method. He also repeatedly ignored questionable tactical directions from officers who had not visited the front. Colonel Harris later complained about constant meddling by various staff officers who based their uninformed tactical assessments on inaccurate maps and out-of-date situation reports, neither of which adequately portrayed the true situation at the front. A fact almost totally lost in the dustbin of history is that Bucky Harris showed his moral courage was as great as his physical bravery under fire during the reduction of the Umurbrogol Pocket, where he demonstrated that the lives of his men were more important to him than his career. Actually, Harris's career was saved by the unexpected arrival of the III AC commander. Harris and Rupertus were arguing over tactics at the division command post. Harris refused to rush into action until the target had been thoroughly worked over by air and artillery. Threatened with relief, Harris was telling his division commander, "I am lavish with supporting arms, but I am stingy with the lives of my Marines," just as Roy Geiger entered the room and added, "That sounds like a good idea to me!"

The final phase of the campaign for the 5th Marines began on 6 October. The 1st Battalion took over positions on Walt and Boyd Ridges to the east, the 2d Battalion faced Baldy Ridge in the north, and the 3d Battalion was allowed a respite after its costly assault on Five Sisters. Major Harold Richmond, the 1st Battalion executive officer, commanded a provisional rifle unit composed of combat support detachments pressed into service as infantrymen. This group and several other volunteer outfits composed of support troops held the western ridgeline against enemy infiltrators while the remaining infantrymen made a futile stab.

Company E led the 5th Marines into the Umurbrogol Pocket at 0900 when it attacked an area nicknamed "the Badlands." This attack was another of Bucky Harris's combined-arms specialties. The Marines took two knobs but were then stopped by heavy enemy fire. Company G made a blind frontal attack only to discover the objective was an untenable position used as an observation post by the Japanese. The assault platoon pulled back then covered the exposed crest with fire. The 2d Battalion thereafter remained in place while it prepared for the next major attack. Company E's 60mm mortars fired on suspected enemy positions, while machine-gun and antitank-gun fire was directed at caves and embrasures as Company G scouted likely avenues of approach. Company F patrolled the gap between Companies E and G. Bulldozers cleared the way for tanks and flame-throwing LVTs as close air support hit the Horseshoe and artillery peppered likely cave entrances with direct fire from 75mm pack howitzers dragged into hillside positions.

The 3d Battalion escorted six Sherman tanks into the Horseshoe at 0900 on the seventh. Army tanks, protected by Marine infantry, fired on all enemy positions that could be located. Several tanks were hit but none were seriously damaged before they pulled back to refuel and rearm at about 1045. The tanks returned at 1215, this time accompanied by two LVT flamethrowers and an engineer platoon. Company I moved up behind the tanks and flamethrowers. Company L simultaneously tried to enter the valley by a different route, but was repulsed by heavy fire from the China Wall. All known enemy positions inside the Horseshoe were eliminated before the tanks ran out of ammunition and pulled back for good. The mission was successful because these sorties had been made to eliminate specific enemy heavy weapons positions, and no more enemy fire came from the targeted areas. The Japanese inside the Pocket were thereafter effectively penned in; they could no longer interfere with American activities elsewhere on the island. It thus seemed logical to Colonel Harris for his regiment to simply isolate the Pocket and mop it up over time using fresh troops instead of continuing costly offensive operations there. However, General Rupertus overruled this course of action.

Once the division commander made his decision, there was nothing for the 5th Marines but to go back at Bloody Nose Ridge one more time. The depleted 1st and 2d Battalions stayed in place while artillery and air pounded the Pocket. The battered 3d Battalion returned to its bivouac and became the regimental reserve. The push to clear the Pocket was renewed when 2d Lt. Robert T. Wattie of Company G led his platoon up a narrow ridge on 9 October. This action denied the Japanese clear fields of fire on the West Road and provided direct access to the next objective, Baldy Ridge. Wattie's platoon cleared the enemy and then pulled back to less exposed positions until the following morning. That afternoon, LVT flamethrowers moved up on newly created trails and burned vegetation off of both Baldy and the razorback ridges east of it. A lucky artillery shot induced a landslide that sealed off a large cave entrance and reduced a major source of resistance. The 2d Battalion, already supported by tanks and LVTs, was additionally reinforced by a 105mm howitzer battery and an army M10 self-propelled 76mm gun for the next day's attack. All was ready for the final Marine push.

Lieutenant Wattie led his platoon back up the ridge that later bore his name and then moved on to Baldy on the morning of 10 October. This small unit proceeded to blast and burn its way across Baldy's crest, established itself atop some dominating heights, and took about fifty prisoners by noon. Spurred on by Wattie's success, Company E moved out to take Hill 120 at 1215. This was done with comparative ease. Company G then secured Ridge 120, one of the razorbacks that branched off Baldy Ridge.

Satisfied with his progress and not wanting to bite off more than he could chew, Major Gayle ordered his men to stop and consolidate. He moved one platoon from reserve Company F up to reinforce Company G. By dark, the 2d Battalion was not physically tied together, but its weapons covered the entire area by fire.

On the morning of 11 October, Major Gayle ordered that Hill 140, the final objective, be taken. Seizure of this ground would allow American artillery to fire directly into the Horseshoe and guaranteed a covered route into the Umurbrogol Pocket from the East Road. Companies E and G moved forward along parallel routes. Company G used a ravine to mask enemy fires, and Company E did likewise using Number Three Ridge to shield its movement. Both units were eventually stopped by frontal fires. After that, Company F passed through and completed the assault, securing Hill 140 at about 1500. The cost of the last attack was two Marines killed and ten wounded. Company F consolidated its gains then cleared the hill. An LVT flamethrower set off ammunition stored in a cave, which caused a tremendous explosion that blew part of the hill into the air and severely wounded one Marine. The 2d Battalion firmly held Baldy, Number Three Ridge, and Hill 140 when darkness fell. The desperate enemy made a final counterattack that night, but it was easily repulsed.

While Major Gayle's 2d Battalion had been chipping away at the ridges lining the Umurbrogol Pocket, Colonel Boyd's 1st Battalion tightened its grip on the Pocket's southern entrance. The 1st Battalion was relieved in place on the morning of the tenth and thereafter occupied reserve positions in the south. Company K of the 3d Battalion scoured the hills looking for some elusive snipers. The Marines never spotted a live Japanese during the next two days, but they sealed up every opening they could find. This did the trick and the sniping stopped.

The weary 2d Battalion was relieved in the northern end of the Umurbrogol Pocket by the 3d Battalion on 12 October. Company L assumed positions on Hill 140, and Companies K and I took up positions on Number Three Ridge. It was a difficult relief conducted under heavy enemy fire, and the Marines suffered twenty-two casualties. Unfortunately, most of the 2d Battalion positions were zeroed in by enemy artillery, so the Marines there were pinned down. A platoon from Company I was ambushed as it moved into position and had to call for smoke shells to cover its withdrawal. Captain "Ack-Ack" Haldane, the much-respected Company K commander, was killed as he scouted the line of advance. This is a sorrowful loss. After the war, his fellow officers purchased a trophy known as the Haldane Cup, which his alma mater, Bowdoin College, annually bestows on a senior student who has demonstrated outstanding qualities of leadership and character in honor of Haldane's memory.

The 1st Battalion remained in the rear area until 1900 on the twelfth, when 1st Lt. Roy O. Larsen, the assistant regimental intelligence officer, led a combat patrol from Company C to infiltrate and occupy the top of the Five Sisters under cover of darkness. The movement was masked by heavy artillery fires, but the patrol encountered a group of Japanese and was forced to withdraw after a brief firefight.

The 3d Battalion was the only 5th Marines unit in contact with the enemy on 13 October. Its mission was to attack westward to further constrict the Umurbrogol Pocket. Patrols from Company I and 1st Lt. Thomas J. Stanley's Company K moved forward under cover of mortar and artillery fires. Each was able to penetrate about seventy-five yards without meeting any enemy resistance. The success of these probes resulted in plans for a new attack the following morning. The Marines moved forward after napalm strikes and heavy preparatory fires on the fourteenth. Company I encountered intense sniper fire but gained more than 250 yards before stopping for the night. Companies L and K conducted clearing operations in the wake of Company I's movement. The 1st Battalion, 7th Marines, which was attached to the 5th Marines at that time, conducted a supporting attack that gained about 125 yards. The Umurbrogol Pocket had been significantly reduced by the time dusk closed in. The Japanese tried to infiltrate Company L that night but were repulsed.

The regiment's fighting days on Peleliu were finally over. The next day, III AC Order 13-44 placed the 321st RCT under General Rupertus's operational control and 1st Marine Division Field Order 9-44 called for this unit to relieve the 5th Marines. This was done by 1100 on 15 October. The 5th Marines then moved into defensive positions on the northern tip of Peleliu. The regimental command post was established at a radio station previously captured. The 1st Battalion defended the northern coast; the 2d Battalion occupied Ngesebus, Kongauru, and Garakayo Islands; and the 3d Battalion set up along East Road facing the sea. The 5th Marines did not see any further combat on that hellish island, but the casualty toll was not yet final. The assertion that Operation Stalemate was jinxed from start to finish was given credence when the last member of the 5th Marines to die at Peleliu was killed by an accidental weapon discharge while boarding ship for the return to a rest area.

Most of the 1st Marine Division had already sailed by 26 October, but the 5th Marines was stuck on Peleliu because of a ship shortage. The 5th Marines thus became part of a provisional Marine unit commanded by Brig. Gen. O. P. Smith under the operational command of the army's 81st Infantry Division during the remainder of its stay. This unit, an emergency reserve, was never committed into active combat but it did man some coastal defensive positions until the SS *Sea Runner* finally arrived at Purple Beach on the twenty-seventh. The 5th Marines quickly embarked and left "Nothing Atoll" three days later. The cost of the fierce battle was evident when a regiment that required three APA transports and six LSTs to get to Peleliu five weeks before was able to sail away on board a single ship. Morale sunk when it was learned the 5th Marines's destination was not the hoped for Australia. Instead the regiment was once again headed for the Russell Islands. When asked how he felt about returning to Pavuvu, one anonymous Marine remarked, "At least it isn't Peleliu."

Operation Stalemate had been the 5th Marines single toughest fight since Blanc Mont Ridge in 1918. The regiment suffered 1,378 casualties (40 percent of its strength) in only one month. When called on to assess the campaign, Major Gayle stated: "Every Marine [that fought at Peleliu] is an expert. If he wasn't, he wouldn't be alive."

The bloody seizure of Peleliu has, unfortunately, become a relatively forgotten event in the annals of World War II. It turned out the Japanese never actually had sufficient resources in the Palaus to threaten MacArthur's conquest of the Philippines. The Peleliu airfield had been used only for routine operations, and the island primarily served as a transient stopover for those headed to or from the combat zone. In retrospect, Peleliu played no important strategic role and the campaign took place in a relative backwater area that received little contemporary press coverage. As a result, this hard-fought battle receives only scant mention in most history books. Peleliu will, however, never be forgotten by those who were there.

Okinawa

After the fall of the Philippines and the capture of Iwo Jima, General MacArthur's and Adm. Chester W. Nimitz's twin drives toward Japan intersected. There were several potential targets: Formosa off the southern China coast, China itself, or the island of Okinawa lying in the western Pacific only slightly more than three hundred miles from mainland Japan. After careful study and much discussion, Okinawa was selected because its proximity to Japan and large size made it an almost ideal staging base for the invasion of the Japan homeland.

Pavuvu's habitability had been vastly improved with time, but it was still not an adequate training base. Basic infantry training, small-unit field

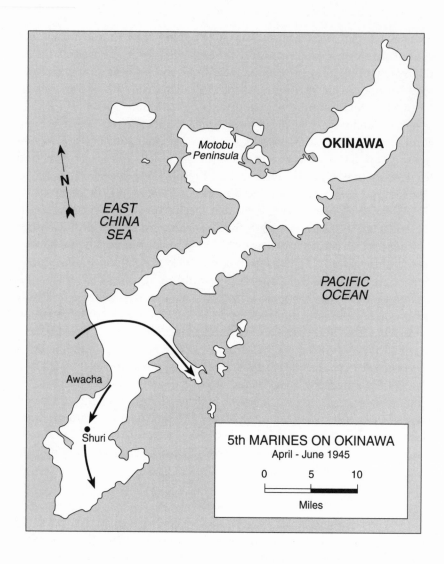

problems, and special schools could be conducted there, but it was necessary to send the whole regiment to Guadalcanal for two weeks of combat training. This was because the terrain of the upcoming target placed a premium on combined-arms operations that required close cooperation between tanks, infantry, artillery, and air support. These areas thus received the most attention during training.

A major problem affecting the regiment's combat readiness was a lack of experienced officers and staff NCOs. Most Marines in the 1st Marine Division with thirty months overseas, a number that included almost every Guadalcanal veteran, were sent home. This rotation policy drained the regiment of many majors and almost all of its experienced captains. Thus, the 5th Marines had a new commanding officer, virtually all regimental staff officers had been replaced, and only one battalion commander at Peleliu was still on the muster roles. About a third of the enlisted men were brand-new, about a third had served at Peleliu, and about a third were combat veterans of two operations or had been with the regiment for more than a year.

There were equipment and organizational changes within the regiment as well when the 1st Marine Division adopted the G-series tables of equipment and organization. The number of man-portable flamethrowers in the regiment was reduced, but nine flame tanks were added to the 1st Tank Battalion. Four M7 "Priest" self-propelled 105mm howitzers replaced the 75mm SPMs in Weapons Company. Each rifle battalion headquarters company added an assault platoon to deal with enemy fortifications. The rifle companies added two more light machine guns. Finally, men formerly armed with carbines now carried .45-caliber pistols for personal protection.

The 1st Marine Division's assault units—including Combat Team 5 consisting of the reinforced 5th Marines—embarked for Tassafaronga, Guadalcanal, to conduct advanced training on 1 March 1945. The next day, debarkation and ship-to-shore drills were held. Simulated air and naval gunfire support were added on the third, and the assault units actually landed. However, maneuvers ashore had to be curtailed so more amphibious practice could be conducted. The assault units made a final full dress rehearsal on the sixth and then returned to Pavuvu for the last time.

The focus of this attention was the island of Okinawa in the Ryukyu chain. "The Rock" was a slender, nondescript land mass roughly 50 miles long that varied in width from less than 2 to more than 18 miles. Located less than 350 miles from Japan, it was the site of excellent potential air and naval facilities and was an ideal staging base for an invasion of the home islands. The northern half of the island was a rugged mass of jungle-covered hills and deep, narrow, stream-filled valleys. The south featured rolling terrain covered by terraced rice paddies dotted with towns and villages. Okinawa did not have Peleliu's torrid heat and, except in the northern wilds, its foliage was far less challenging than the jungles of Guadalcanal or New Britain. There were, however, some hauntingly familiar companions—torrential rains, grotesque terrain, and a determined foe—awaiting the Operation Iceberg landing force.

Okinawa was defended by the sixty-five-thousand-man Japanese Thirty-second Army commanded by Lt. Gen. Mitsuru Ushijima, who plotted an extended campaign of attrition designed to inflict maximum casualties on the American attackers. As at Peleliu, the plan was not to win but instead to extract a high cost from the invasion force by relying on defense in depth. Most Japanese lurked in well-prepared defensive positions on the southern half of the island. There, resolute defenders were holed up in caves and concrete tombs that formed a series of mutually supporting defensive lines that stretched across the island to protect Shuri Castle.

On the other side of the coin, the most formidable American force thus far assembled in the Pacific was ready to storm the island. The Tenth Army, commanded by Lt. Gen. Simon B. Buckner Jr., included the army's XXIV Corps and the Marine III AC, a total of 182,112 men—81,165 of whom were Marines. The XXIV Corps consisted of three army infantry divisions with a fourth in reserve. Major General Roy Geiger commanded III AC, which included the 1st and 6th Marine Divisions. The 1st Marine Division was commanded by Maj. Gen. Pedro del Valle. Major General Lem Shepherd, promoted since he commanded the ADC Group at New Britain, commanded the brand-new 6th Marine Division. The 2d Marine Division was the theater reserve. This unit was commanded by Maj. Gen. LeRoy Hunt, who had been twice promoted since Guadalcanal and was once again in the Pacific.

Combat Team 5, commanded by Col. John H. Griebel, consisted of the 5th Marines; Company B, 1st Engineer Battalion; Company B, 1st Pioneer Battalion; Company B, 1st Medical Battalion; Company B, 1st Motor Transport Battalion; the 1st Amphibian Tractor Battalion (less detachments); detachments from the 1st Service Battalion; 2d Platoon, 1st Military Police Company; and an army DUKW detachment from the 454th Amphibious Truck Company. Lieutenant Colonel Charles W. Shelburne commanded the 1st Battalion, Lt. Col. William E. Benedict the 2d Battalion, and Major Gustafson continued in command of the 3d Battalion.

The Tenth Army was scheduled to land near Hagushi village located about a third of the way up Okinawa's west coast. The XXIV Corps was to land on the right flank, capture Kadena airfield, cut across the island, and then turn south toward Shuri Castle. The Marines were to land on the left, push directly inland, and seize and occupy the northern half of the island. The 6th Marine Division was given the northern (left) sector abutting the Ishikawa Peninsula. The 1st Marine Division was assigned the III AC's right (southern) flank. The 5th Marines was to move inland maintaining contact with XXIV Corps on the right. Colonel Griebel placed the 1st and 2d Battalions in the assault waves and held the 3d Battalion in reserve.

The LSTs of the Northern Tractor Flotilla sailed on 12 March. Transport Squadron 18, carrying the bulk of the 5th Marines, departed for Ulithi Atoll in the western Carolines three days later. Task Force 53 of the Fifth Fleet remained at Ulithi from 21–28 March. The Marines got a chance to get ashore for conditioning and recreation, final planning conferences were held, and the assault units transshipped to the LSTs that would carry them to the objective. Okinawa was worked over by carrier air strikes and naval gunfire while the transport groups were assembling at Ulithi. The assault units moved into the transport area off the Okinawa coast in the early hours of Easter Sunday, which was also April Fool's Day.

The landings on 1 April 1945 went much better than expected. The invasion fleet slipped into the attack area just west of Okinawa under the cover of darkness, and Transport Squadron 18 took its positions at 0510 on L day. A three-hour shore bombardment began at 0530. The order "Land the landing force" sent the amtracs of the first waves churning toward shore. The offshore reef caused no delays, but a few vehicles were lost to unexpected potholes. The first Marines on the beach made an amazing discovery at 0839: there was almost no resistance. It turned out that Love Day was the beginning of a monthlong Easter holiday before the Marines were sent south into the meat grinder known as the Shuri Line.

The nearly unopposed assault forces moved rapidly forward. The 6th Marine Division took the Yontan airfield before noon, and the 1st Marine Division encountered similar success in its zone. The first three waves carrying the 5th Marines came ashore at Yellow Beach right on schedule. There was so little resistance that the 1st and 2d Battalions were able to move inland standing up. The 5th Marines captured the first day's objective, the O-1 Line, in about an hour. In an ironic April Fool's Day turn of events, the 2d Marine Division demonstration force suffered more casualties than did the assault waves.

While things were going much better than expected, it was not a perfect day for the regiment. One unit landed on the wrong beach, and a battalion commander was lost to enemy fire. Similarly colored beach markers confused the 4th wave, carrying Company B and the 1st Battalion's backup command group. The 5th Marines was assigned Yellow Beach and the adjoining 7th Infantry Division had Purple Beach, but there was no purple bunting so the army unit used a combination of yellow and blue markers that were misread by the incoming Marine fourth wave. In the confusion, the Marines inadvertently crossed the XXIV Corps boundary and landed in the army zone. This navigation error was discovered by alert troop leaders in the following waves who redirected their craft to the correct beaches, so the mistake was not repeated. Colonel Griebel quickly dispatched amtracs to Purple Beach to pick up his stray units. These LVTs recovered all but about two dozen men by 0930. The remaining two Marine squads and their platoon leader remained in the army zone until L-plus-3.

The reserve 3d Battalion was quickly picked up by LVTs at the transfer line and was ashore by noon. It then assumed positions along the division southern boundary about four hundred yards behind the 1st Battalion by midafternoon. About an hour later, Major Gustafson was cut down by fire from a bypassed pocket of Japanese and evacuated. Major Martin C. Roth, the executive officer, took temporary command of the 3d Battalion until Lt. Col. John C. Miller Jr. arrived on 4 April.

The main operational difficulty for the 5th Marines on L day was maintaining contact with army units on the right. The fast advance, difficult terrain, and tendency of the adjoining units to bear to the right toward the main objective made maintaining contact a tough chore. Forward units became so spread out during the advance that Capt. Robert P. Smith's Company L had to be placed in a blocking position on the division's right flank to cover the wide-open corps boundary.

The 5th Marines spent a relatively quiet first night ashore, and then kicked off a new attack at 0730 on L-plus-1. For most Marines, the next few days were a pleasant walk in the sun. The weather was almost perfect, and a cool breeze offset the heat of the bright sun. So little resistance was encountered that the 5th Marines secured its entire sector to

the O-13 Line within only four days. The close of the second day found
the 5th Marines just short of the O-5 Line. The regiment had covered
so much ground that the 1st Marines had to be inserted in echelon to
protect the III AC's flank. Only four enemy soldiers were encountered
across the entire regimental front on the third. The 1st Battalion reached
Agina, the 2d Battalion occupied Tengan, and the 3d Battalion maintained contact with the 1st Marines that day. Lieutenant Colonel Benedict's 2d Battalion, which had been moving over rough terrain since leaving Ishimine village at 0800 on the second, reached the east coast at
about 1700 on the fourth. The 5th Marines dispatched saturation patrols
to reconnoiter the east coast, the Katchin Peninsula, and four nearby islands: Ike, Taka Banare, Heanza, and Hamahiki. From 10–28 April the
5th Marines occupied the narrow central sector south of Ishikawa and
north of the southern III AC boundary.

Although the battle for Okinawa was going well for the Marines in
north and central parts of the island, this was not true for army units in
the south, where the XXIV Corps advance came to a standstill. General
Buckner therefore ordered the 1st Marine Division south. The 1st and
5th Marines were ordered into the line on the left and right respectively.
The 5th Marines departed Inubi village in central Okinawa and moved
south to replace the 27th Infantry Division's 105th and 106th Infantry
Regiments near Machinato airfield on 1 May. The relief was effected at
about 1700 that day with few casualties. This move was the turning point
in the battle for the 5th Marines. The Easter holiday was over and the
regiment was about to engage in some of the most bitter fighting in its
history.

Colonel Griebel's first missions at Machinato were to support the 77th
Infantry Division by fire and to reduce the Awacha Pocket, a labyrinth
of enemy positions dug into steep, clifflike ridges and tangled gorges defended by the Japanese 62d Division. Fanatical Japanese defenders
would not surrender when surrounded, instead, they fought to the
death. The only way to take such positions was to use combined arms to
neutralize them and close combat to destroy them. Air strikes, naval gunfire, and artillery pounded suspected positions while the ground troops
closed in. The Americans used "corkscrew and blowtorch" tactics perfected at Peleliu to eliminate the enemy on Okinawa. Small infantry combat teams working with gun and flame-throwing tanks would concentrate
their fires on a single position. Man-packed flamethrowers would drive
defenders away from their guns so demolition teams could approach and

toss satchel charges into any available opening. While the defenders reeled in shock, the caves were sealed or the defenders were immolated. Obviously, quarter was neither asked nor given by either side. These attrition tactics were effective, but it was very slow going and the assault teams suffered many casualties as they closed with the enemy.

The attack toward the Asa River began on 2 May in a driving rainstorm that limited visibility and rendered close air support impossible. The 5th Marines jumped off when artillery and naval gunfire shifted to isolate the objective at about 0900. Japanese machine-gun, mortar, and artillery fires quickly pinned down the 2d Battalion. First Lieutenant Michael D. Benda's Company E was taken under fire immediately. First Lieutenant William A. Taylor's Company F and 1st Lt. Richard R. Breen's Company G advanced about two hundred yards against moderate resistance, but were eventually hit by the same withering fire that halted Company E. Within two hours, the 2d Battalion was forced to pull back to the jump-off line under the cover of a smoke screen. Hospital Apprentice Robert E. Bush, a navy corpsman attached to the 2d Battalion, was administering first aid to a wounded officer when he was attacked. He used a pistol and a carbine to kill six attackers, then calmly returned to his medical duties. Despite his own serious wounds, which included the loss of an eye, Bush refused to leave until the patient he was attending had been evacuated. Bush was later awarded the Medal of Honor for his heroism.

The 3d Battalion was stopped by the same fire not long after it crossed the line of departure. In the words of Major Roth, "the advance was untenable and [we] had to be withdrawn to [our] initial positions." The first attack on the Awacha Pocket failed and casualties were heavy. The remainder of the day was spent conducting limited patrols and extensive clearing operations in the assembly area.

The next morning, Capt. Julian D. Dusenbury's Company A and 1st Lt. Walter E. Lange's Company C of the 1st Battalion passed through the 2d Battalion's lines. They gained more than five hundred yards, but Lieutenant Colonel Shelburne had to stop the attack because the adjoining 3d Battalion slowed its advance in order to seize a vital hill. Meanwhile, the 2d Battalion shifted left to take over the outskirts of Awacha village from the 77th Infantry Division's 307th Infantry. Lieutenant Taylor was wounded during this action, and 1st Lt. Joseph H. Bowling took over Company F. Unfortunately, furious machine-gun and mortar fire drove the 3d Battalion off the crest of the hill in the late afternoon.

The 1st Marine Division's attack on 4 May was postponed so its units could reorganize and be resupplied. The 5th Marines, working on the division's left flank, made encouraging progress and pushed forward six hundred yards. The 1st Battalion pivoted on the 2d Battalion and swung its right wing through four hundred yards of hotly contested ground. The 2d Battalion supported attacks by the 307th Infantry on the left and Lieutenant Colonel Shelburne's 1st Battalion to its front from its positions on the high ground. The 3d Battalion maneuvered to cut off the enemy entrenched in a gorge in front of Awacha village. Captain Smith's Company L tied in with the 1st Battalion, and Capt. James P. O'Laughlin's Company I moved forward 250 yards as it kept pace with the 1st Marines. The 3d Battalion was soon stretched so thin that a large gap between Companies L and I developed by early afternoon. To relieve this situation, General del Valle attached the 3d Battalion, 7th Marines, to the 5th Marines at 1500. Colonel Griebel placed this unit in reserve behind Lieutenant Colonel Miller's 3d Battalion, although Company K of the 7th Marines moved up to plug the aforementioned gap.

The 5th Marines gained three hundred yards on the fifth. The 1st Battalion, supported by fifteen Shermans and a pair of "Zippo" flame tanks, took the high ground west of Awacha before being stopped by enfilading fire from both flanks. The 2d Battalion covered 250 yards moving through a deluge of enemy artillery fire. The reserve 3d Battalion spent the day cleaning out bypassed enemy and destroying a bunker complex in the vicinity of its night defensive positions. The 5th Marines was solidly tied in by dusk. The 2d Battalion beat back a heavy enemy counterattack at dawn on 6 May, then resumed its advance down the division boundary to link up with the 307th Infantry behind a four-battalion artillery barrage. The 2d Battalion held an L-shaped line by noon. Companies F and G were arrayed along the division boundary and Company E tied in with the 1st Battalion. The 1st and 3d Battalions, supported by tanks and self-propelled guns, blasted and burned out caves in the assembly area from which the Japanese had so fiercely resisted the previous day's advance.

General del Valle and Colonel Griebel met with Lieutenant Colonels Shelburne, Benedict, and Miller to discuss the upcoming effort to clear out the Awacha Pocket. They decided extensive air, naval gunfire, and artillery bombardments would precede the attack, which would kick off at noon with an entire tank company in support. The attack went off on schedule but the results were disappointing. The 1st Battalion gained about four hundred yards in the center, but the flanking battalions were unable to do much more than straighten their lines. Captain O'Laughlin of Company I was wounded, but he refused evacuation and remained in action. Private First Class Albert E. Schwab, a flamethrower operator in the 1st Battalion, destroyed two enemy positions before receiving a mortal wound. He was awarded the Medal of Honor for his actions on 7 May. The following day marked the end of the war in Europe, but the event went almost unnoticed on Okinawa, where the Marines were too busy fighting their own war to celebrate victory in another theater.

The 5th Marines attacked the mouth of Awacha Draw at noon on 9 May. The 3d Battalions of both the 5th and 7th Marines conducted the assault while the 1st and 2d Battalions of the 5th Marines provided fire support. The two assault battalions moved rapidly at first and the initial objective fell, but intense fire from the left flank held up the attack after that. Captain Paul Douglas, the regimental adjutant, was seriously wounded while acting as a volunteer stretcher bearer. Considering his age and his position as a staff officer, Douglas did not have to be at the forward edge of the battlefield. But such was not his way. He had proved his courage many times over and this was not his first Purple Heart, he had also been wounded at Peleliu. This time, however, his wounds were so serious that he was hospitalized for more than a year.

General del Valle issued a new operations order on the afternoon of the ninth. The 5th Marines (less the 3d Battalion, which was attached to the 7th Marines) was assigned a narrow zone of action and was ordered to clear out that portion of the Awacha Pocket the next day. The enemy made numerous attempts to infiltrate the 5th Marines's lines during the night of 9–10 May. The 1st Battalion fought off two counterattacks between 0200 and 0300, driving the enemy back each time only after extended hand-to-hand fighting. Lieutenant Colonel Shelburne issued an attack order at 0600 on 10 May despite the previous night's assaults, and the 1st Battalion crossed the line of departure at 0800. Company A led the column of companies forward for four hundred yards, then Company C was committed on the left to extend the battalion front. At about 0845, heavy enemy fire surrounded the 1st Battalion and made it impossible to advance, withdraw, or evacuate casualties. Captain Dusenbury, commanding Company A, was wounded but refused evacuation. With the Marine advance stymied, Colonel Shelburne had to order a smoke screen to mask an afternoon pullback. The 1st Battalion was back at its start line at 1945 that evening. There was nothing to show for the day's effort except a slew of casualties.

The 2d Battalion had more success. Lieutenant Colonel Benedict's men were able to overrun all Japanese positions within the assigned sector. Company G moved into the Pocket accompanied by a dozen gun tanks and three flamethrower tanks. The Marines cut down many fleeing enemy as they advanced. Companies E and F moved in trace and cleared out all bypassed positions. Lieutenant Bowling, the Company F commander, was wounded and evacuated. His place was taken by 1st Lt. Robert F. Fry. The Marines cut the Japanese main line of resistance by nightfall, but numerous individual positions remained intact. The 2d Battalion cleared out the last remnants inside the Awacha Pocket and the 1st Battalion wiped out bypassed strong points with the assistance of the 7th Marines the next day.

What has been termed "the second most famous Marine combat photograph of World War II" was taken by Pfc. Robert Bailey on the morning of 10 May. He snapped a dramatic action shot of Pvt. Paul E. Ison, a twenty-eight-year-old demolitions man known to his squad mates as "Pop" because of his four children, as he raced across Death Valley to support Company L, 3d Battalion, 5th Marines. This dramatic photo that so vividly portrays the Marines' determination to move forward under enemy fire has graced the covers of several books (including this one), and a monument depicting this action is used to inspire Marines attending the Camp Pendleton combat leadership school.

Final organized resistance in the Awacha Pocket ended on 11 May. The 1st Battalion manned lines between the 7th Marines and the 305th Infantry along the division boundary at dusk, and 2/5 was in contact with the 307th Infantry and 1/5. The 3d Battalion returned to Colonel Griebel's control at 1800. The 5th Marines then remained in place as the division reserve for the next three days.

The regiment moved south on 14 May and relieved the 1st Marines in front of Wana Draw in the early morning hours on the fifteenth. The relief was complete by 0400, and at 0630 Colonel Griebel officially assumed responsibility for zone west of Wana village.

The 5th Marines's first day in the new sector was devoted to scouting and clearing the mouth of Wana Draw, a flat area dominated by the fortified cliffs that lined Wana Ridge. General del Valle, acting on the recommendations of both regimental commanders, decided to neutralize the high ground on both sides of the draw using naval gunfire, artillery, air strikes, and the direct fires of tanks and assault guns. Colonel Griebel reported that "Wana Draw was another gorge like the one at Awacha [that] would have to be pounded before it could be taken." Virtually all of the supporting arms available to the Marines were employed before the regiment tried to carry the draw by storm.

Colonel Griebel elected to use Colonel Benedict's 2/5 in the assault, Colonel Miller's 3/5 in support, and Colonel Shelburne's 1/5 in reserve. Twelve gun tanks and three flame tanks were placed in direct support, each escorted by a Marine fire team. These tank-infantry teams were used in platoon relays to allow the tankers to rest, rearm, conduct minor maintenance, and coordinate their next attack. Individual tanks often had to be used as resupply or medical evacuation vehicles. Tanks had to be used because the open-top, lightly armored 105mm self-propelled howitzers originally earmarked for infantry support were too vulnerable to be used at the front and usually remained behind the lines to provide indirect fire support.

Nine Sherman tanks protected by fire teams from Company F scouted the mouth of the draw on the fifteenth. They discovered that battered Wana Ridge was still well defended. The enemy fire was so intense that the riflemen had to cover the tanks from long range because they dared not expose themselves. Three different tanks took at least five hits each during this scouting foray. At 0900 on the sixteenth, a force of thirty gun tanks and four flame tanks moved into the draw blasting and burning positions identified the day before. The Japanese again responded with intense antitank, artillery, and mortar fire. Two tanks were quickly knocked out and two more were temporarily disabled. This was a problem because enemy demolition teams invariably destroyed disabled tanks left overnight. Infiltrators then converted the remaining hulks into armored sniper nests. Marine recovery teams had to brave enemy fire to retrieve the immobilized tanks. Luckily, during the fighting two enemy antitank gun positions were clearly identified and destroyed by naval gunfire.

After two more days of tank, artillery, mortar, air, and naval gunfire preparation the 5th and 7th Marines once again began their methodic advance toward Shuri Castle. The 2d Battalion led the 5th Marines's main effort. Colonel Benedict sent tank-infantry teams into the north end of Wana Draw. The tanks worked over the ridge while riflemen scurried forward and destroyed enemy strongholds one at a time. It was slow, hard, costly work. Lieutenant Fry was wounded and had to be replaced by 1st Lt. William H. Brougher, who became Company F's fourth commander since the landing. Company E was able to capture a foothold at the base of Hill 55. By noon, however, the enemy fire was so fierce that the 2d Battalion had to pull back, leaving an isolated platoon to its own devices. Fortunately, tanks could resupply this isolated unit and evacuate its casualties.

The advance was renewed on the eighteenth. The tanks and assault guns poured more than seventy thousand 75mm and 105mm rounds into the cliffs. Engineers and flame tanks cleared the lower slopes around the mouth of the draw. Still the fighting was fierce. Pharmacist Mate 2d Class William O. Halyburton used his body to shield wounded Marines, an act that cost him his life on 19 May. He was awarded the Medal of Honor for his selfless bravery. The Marines finally took the crest of Wana Ridge on the twentieth after intense hand-to-hand fighting. Lieutenant Breen's Company G held its positions at Half Moon Hill, and Lieutenant Benda's Company E secured a low ridge between Hill 55 and the Naha-Shuri Road. This allowed tanks to support clearing operations on the reverse slope of Hill 55. Wana Draw was finally taken. The Marines were now ready to enter what was thought to be the final ring of General Ushijima's stronghold. The 5th Marines now held positions overlooking daunting Shuri Ridge, the last barrier in front of the Japanese headquarters.

The 1st Battalion moved into the front lines replacing the 2d Battalion as the assault unit on the night of 20–21 May. First Lieutenant Walter Lange's Company C relieved Company E shortly before dawn on the twenty-first. Companies B and C briefly scouted Shuri Ridge, then retired amid a deluge of fire when it became obvious the enemy held the place in strength and would have to be rooted out position by position. This was going to be no easy task because the incessant rain significantly curtailed close air support and turned the low ground in front of the 5th Marines into a bottomless morass that prohibited tank support. The mire was so deep that the Marines stopped offensive operations and devoted the next few days to resupply, reorganization, and clearing out bypassed positions.

This brief interlude also allowed time for some organizational changes as well. The 3d Battalion, now commanded by former regimental executive officer Maj. Frank W. Poland Jr., moved to the front to replace the 1st Battalion on the twenty-third. The next day, 1st Lt. George B. Loveday replaced 1st Lt. Thomas J. Stanley as commander of Company K, and Captain O'Laughlin of Company I was wounded and replaced by 1st Lt. John A. Fredenberger.

The 5th Marines's brief respite ended when the weather cleared and the offensive resumed. The 3d Battalion led the 5th Marines toward Asato Gawa at 1015 on 28 May. Resistance was generally weak, mostly long-range mortar and machine-gun fire. The Marines took their objective by noon. Despite this progress, the operation continued to take a heavy toll of officers and men. One of the casualties was Lieutenant Fredenberger, who was replaced by 1st Lt. Carroll R. Wilson after just four days as Company I commander. Lieutenant Benda of Company E was hit and evacuated the next day. Captain Franklin D. Sills succeeded him.

The 5th Marines advanced with the 1st and 3d Battalions in the assault on 29 May. The 3d Battalion soon bogged down. Company L made good progress until it was held up about a mile from Kokuba village. Companies I and K rushed up to help, but they too were soon pinned down. Things went much better in the 1st Battalion area where Companies B and C gained the top of Shuri Ridge much quicker than expected. These new positions revealed an interesting sight: famous Shuri Castle, a major Corps objective, lay exposed and seemed almost undefended.

Lieutenant Colonel Shelburne requested permission to overrun the castle, but had to be temporarily held back because that position was in the army zone of action. After a review of the situation, General del Valle determined that the 77th Infantry Division was not in position to immediately seize Shuri so he gave Shelburne the go-ahead signal. Company A drove east along the muddy ridge, overcame light resistance, and secured the castle at 1015. As luck would have it, Captain Dusenbury of South Carolina did not have an American flag, so he hoisted a Confederate battle flag to signal that the castle had been secured. Unknown to the Marines slogging forward, alert air liaison personnel spotted the stars and bars banner and averted a planned air strike by only the slimmest of margins. Sensing victory was at hand, General del Valle quickly sent the 1st Marines through the 5th Marines's lines to reinforce Company A. The encirclement of Shuri was completed when patrols from the 838th Infantry made contact with Walt Lange's Company C on the thirtieth. The Japanese logjam at Shuri was broken. Ushijima's defenses were finally beginning to crack.

The 5th Marines received a much-needed airdrop, which delivered water and ammunition, then began searching for the next Japanese line of resistance on the thirty-first. The 3d Battalion moved out in the lead at 1445 and encountered only scattered resistance until it bumped into some hills just north of Shichina village. There, intense rifle and machine-gun fire forced Major Poland to order his Marines to dig in for the night. Company F moved up to bridge a gap along the boundary between 1st and 3d Battalions. The 5th Marines gained eighteen hundred yards the next day, highlighted by the capture of a railroad bridge over the Kokuar River before the Japanese could blow it up. The attack was then halted for the night.

It was obvious the final American push was about to begin, so Ushijima launched a series of spoiling attacks to cover a massive Japanese withdrawal. The 5th Marines repulsed numerous Japanese attempts to penetrate its defensive lines on the night of 2–3 June. Lieutenant Wilson, commanding Company I, was killed. He was replaced by 1st Lt. Richard A. Singewald. Platoon patrols began to probe forward from the Shuri Line at dawn the next morning, but most were soon pinned down by heavy fire coming from Tsukasan and Gisushi. The Americans now held the upper hand, but the final battle was not yet over.

When the 1st and 3d Battalions could move no farther forward, the 2d Battalion was alerted to move up. Colonel Benedict was ordered to outflank the Japanese position by making a wide arc through the XXIV Corps zone of action. The 2d Battalion moved light, taking only weapons and equipment the Marines could easily carry. It was a difficult two-and a-half-hour trek over muddy ground, but it placed the 2d Battalion on the ridge overlooking Gisushi. Companies E and G jumped off at 1820 and carried the positions after encountering only slight enemy resistance. The 1st and 3d Battalions covered the 2d Battalion's assault by fire. Enemy resistance faded as the day wore on. All three battalions resumed the attack late in the afternoon and halted just before dark after gaining about fifteen hundred yards.

Colonel Benedict's men atop the ridge discovered it was honeycombed with underground living bunkers and fighting positions. They immediately started sealing entrances and blowing up tunnels. During one of these actions someone threw a white phosphorous grenade into a tunnel mouth. The grenade landed in an ammunition storage area and the resulting explosion blew up the entire side of the hill in Company E's sector. Three Marines were killed and seventeen wounded Marines were evacuated with what official reports noted as "invaluable assistance" from the army's 2d Battalion, 382d Infantry. Company F seized Hill 107 without opposition at dawn the next morning. The 1st

Marines passed through the 2d Battalion lines at noon and the 5th Marines became the III AC reserve at that time. Lieutenant Colonel Robert E. Hill took over 3/5, and 1st Lt. Robert D. Metzger, who went on to become a lieutenant general, replaced Captain Smith as commander of Company L on 8 June.

The 5th Marines moved forward again beginning on 14 June. Lieutenant Colonel Benedict, Captain Sills (Company E), and Lieutenants Brougher (Company F) and Breen (Company G) were able to make a personal reconnaissance of their new zone of action by riding forward in tanks. Benedict decided the tactical situation precluded daylight operations and sent only a small force to man the seventy-five-yard front line. The general relief was completed under the cover of darkness that night. The 3d Battalion assumed forward positions on Yuza Hill the next morning. Colonel Griebel became responsible for the new zone of action, which extended southeast of Shuri toward Kunishi Ridge and Makabe village at 0800 on 15 June.

The 2d Battalion attacked at 0730 on the sixteenth to take an area between Kunishi Ridge and Hill 69. Close-quarters battle was the order of the day as 2/5 made slow but steady progress. Enemy infiltrators unsuccessfully tried to breach Marine lines at several locations that night. The 2d Battalion resumed its attack to clear Kunishi Ridge on the seventeenth. This effort was assisted by a very effective rocket barrage and tanks, which were able to scale the ridge on a road built by Marine engineers using an armored bulldozer. Unfortunately, a murderous cross fire inflicted numerous casualties at the crest of the hill. Enemy fire remained undiminished despite pounding by Marine tanks, artillery, mortars, and rockets. Every Marine tank in the area was pressed into service as an armored ambulance at some time during this fight. The situation became so desperate that Lieutenant Colonel Benedict committed his battered reserve company and reinforced it with 133 Marines from a replacement draft that had only recently joined the battalion. This last-ditch effort worked, and the 2d Battalion was able to secure most of the twelve-hundred-yard ridge top by nightfall. Colonel Griebel sent Company K up to reinforce the decimated 2d Battalion. This was a sound tactical move because a Japanese counterattack hit the Marines on top of the ridge but was repelled in hand-to-hand fighting.

The Tenth Army commander, General Buckner, was killed the next day, and Maj. Gen. Roy Geiger, the senior officer present, took command of Tenth Army and was hurriedly promoted to lieutenant general.

Geiger thus became the first Marine officer to command a field army. However, this had little direct impact on the 5th Marines, which continued scheduled operations. The 1st Battalion took part of Hill 79 northwest of Makabe that day. It passed through the 8th Marines's zone to outflank the Japanese, but the 0730 infantry attack bogged down until tanks arrived at about 1100. This armor support allowed 1/5 to carry its part of the hill by noon. The reserve 3d Battalion, less Company K, then rushed up to consolidate the hard-won position. Flag-raising Captain Dusenbury of Company A was wounded during the attack but refused to be evacuated.

The battle for the lower slopes of Hill 79 was still raging as night fell. An attack on the nineteenth to take the rest of the hill failed despite tank and assault gun support, so the day ended with the 5th Marines back at its jump-off positions of the day before. Colonel Griebel, frustrated by the strong enemy resistance and the lack of progress by frontal assaults, decided to use 2/5 to attack Hill 81 from the rear. The 2d Battalion moved out in the midafternoon and was in the assembly area just before dusk. Lieutenant Colonel Benedict launched an attack about fifteen minutes later. The 2d Battalion was caught by heavy fire as it crossed a half-mile of open ground and was forced to double-time to reach cover. This action resulted in only a few Marines wounded, but there were almost two dozen heat exhaustion cases. Benedict personally led Company G's attack at 1950, but the lead platoon was soon pinned down by enemy fire. The condition of his men, the lateness of the hour, and the intensity of enemy resistance caused Benedict to call off the attack and order the 2d Battalion to dig in for the night.

Meanwhile, the 3d Battalion, moving apace with the 8th Marines, made a twenty-five-hundred-yard advance to the coast and reached its objective late that afternoon. Colonel Hill's men added fifty Japanese prisoners and more than two thousand civilians to the III AC detainee total in the process. These Marines conducted some clearing operations and then supported the 7th Infantry Division's attack by fire from Komesu Ridge. Marine patrols finally linked up with elements of the 1st Battalion, 184th Infantry, on 20 June.

The inland fighting for Hills 79 and 81 continued unabated despite the successful march to the coast. These positions were the center of enemy resistance and great pressure was being exerted to finish the job quickly. The 1st Battalion continued its attack to clear Hill 79 at 0730. Lieutenant Colonel Shelburne used all three of his companies abreast.

Company C got to within seventy-five yards of the crest as Companies A and B destroyed sniper and machine-gun nests with the support of flame and gun tanks. Company A briefly held the top of the hill, but was forced back by intense fire. Shelburne ordered his Marines to dig in at dusk. He reported to Colonel Griebel that his men would take the rest of the hill the next day. That task was accomplished by midafternoon.

A brief soaking downpour on the morning of the twentieth turned the roads into quagmires, so the tanks and assault guns did not reach 2/5's line of departure until around noon. Companies E and F jumped off about three and a-half hours later. Company F was pinned down by fire within a half hour, and enemy fire was so intense that a smoke screen was required to evacuate casualties. Company E was likewise pinned down only about a hundred yards farther ahead. Companies F and G were then ordered to pass through and continue the attack. Enemy machine-gun and mortar fire soon caught both. When the supporting tanks ran out of ammunition, a reluctant Lieutenant Colonel Benedict was ordered to continue the attack without tank support or infantry reinforcements. Sadly, as Benedict had warned, this unsupported assault stalled and the Marines were forced back after taking heavy casualties. Company E was able to crest the hill almost unopposed the following morning. Companies F and G, however, had to slug it out all the way up, burning and blasting cave after cave as they made a torturous ascent. Colonel Griebel, falsely informed that all other resistance on Okinawa had been overcome, ordered the 2d Battalion to press the attack without reinforcements or further support. Lieutenant Colonel Benedict reported to the regimental command post after vehemently protesting these orders, and Maj. Richard T. Washburn temporarily took command of 2/5. Lieutenant Colonel Hill arrived at the 2d Battalion command post in midafternoon to form a composite unit made up of the 2d and 3d Battalions. This unit carried the position at 1700. The last organized enemy opposition in the III AC zone finally ended as darkness fell. The 5th Marines consolidated and then began a final sweep of its zone as it moved north toward the Mobotu Peninsula to prepare for embarkation.

The bloody battle for Okinawa had cost the 5th Marines 2,130 casualties, roughly two-thirds of the regiment's strength. The actual figures were 373 killed and 1,757 nonfatal casualties, including wounded and those suffering from combat fatigue. Particularly hard hit were company-grade officers—2/5 had nine different company commanders for three slots, and 3/5 had eight, for a nearly 300 percent casualty rate among rifle company commanders.

The anxious Marines were sure they would not be sent to a Pavuvu-like rat hole this time. Scuttlebutt had it their destination was Hawaii, the next best place to stateside. Surprisingly, this belief was based on fact, not idle gossip. General del Valle had promised such a trip, and most hands knew the 5th Marines's rear party was already en route to Hawaii from the Russell Islands. The tired Marines licked their lips in anticipation of beer-soaked luaus and dreamed of a chance to meet American women as they sunned themselves on Oahu's sandy beaches. At last, a fitting reward for three years service in the Pacific without visiting a liberty port was close at hand. This optimistic view of future events was, alas, too good to be true.

The official word came down on 30 June 1945. The 1st Marine Division was not going to Hawaii after all, but would remain on Okinawa. There were no existing facilities, so the Marines would have to build their own rest camps and training areas in the Okinawa mud. The familiar refrain coined at hated Pavuvu—"Nothing is too bad for the 1st Marine Division!"—was repeatedly heard, and morale plummeted after the shock of recent combat wore off. The only bright spot for a few veterans was that they might finally have accumulated enough rotation points to be sent home. Thus, the end on Okinawa was anticlimactic. All hands knew the next operation would carry them to Japan, and they forlornly hoped they would live to "see the Golden Gate in Forty-eight" as they readied themselves for one more campaign.

Occupation Duty

Everyone in the regiment, from the commander to the lowest-ranking private, was disappointed at not going to Hawaii and dismayed at having to re-create the first Pavuvu experience on Okinawa. Unfortunately, the press of time and a lack of transport ships conspired to keep the 5th Marines from enjoying the pleasures of civilization.

Operation Downfall, the long-awaited invasion of the Japanese home islands, was subdivided into two major operations: Olympic, the invasion of Kyushu; and Coronet, the invasion of Honshu. The V Amphibious Corps was scheduled to land the 2d, 3d, and 5th Marine Divisions across Kyushu's western shore as part of a four-pronged assault on or about 1 November 1945 during Operation Olympic. The 5th Marines, as part of the 1st Marine Division, was assigned to III AC, which included the 1st, 4th, and 6th Marine Divisions. For Operation Coronet, the U.S. First Army, which included III AC, was to land on the Honshu coast between Choshi and Ichinomaya, cross the Kanto Plain, and seize Tokyo and Yokohama sometime after 1 March 1946. The Coronet plan was still in its early stages when President Truman announced that Japan had accepted Allied surrender terms after atomic bombs destroyed the Japanese cities of Hiroshima and Nagasaki. Representatives of the Japanese government signed the formal surrender on board the battleship USS *Missouri* in Tokyo Bay on 2 September 1945. World War II was finally over.

The 5th Marines did not, however, participate in the long-awaited victory parade through Tokyo. Instead, the 5th Marines, much like the 5th Regiment after World War I, remained in the field to occupy former enemy territory and to ensure final peace negotiations went smoothly. Accordingly, V AC was immediately sent to Japan and III AC was ordered to occupy northern China. Long-serving veterans had earned enough rotation points to return home, so every unit in the Pacific, including the 5th Marines, underwent a great deal of personnel turbulence. Soon, all of the Guadalcanal and New Britain veterans were gone, although many midwar replacements who had served at Peleliu and Okinawa still remained in the ranks at the end of September 1945.

The new III AC commanding general was Maj. Gen. Keller E. Rockey, who had been awarded the Navy Cross while serving with 1/5 in France during World War I. Major General DeWitt Peck, who commanded the 55th Company during World War I, took over the 1st Marine Division. Colonel Julian N. Frisbie assumed command of the 5th Marines on 25 June 1945. The battalion commanders were: 1st Battalion, Lt. Col. John H. Masters; 2d Battalion, Lt. Col. John B. Baker; and 3d Battalion, Lt. Col. Joseph L. Winecoff. The regiment was reorganized under peacetime tables of and equipment organization, which theoretically increased regimental personnel and equipment authorizations. In reality, however, the new organization was manned at only about 80 percent strength, so the number of men actually serving declined.

Orders to China meant a homecoming of sorts for some senior officers and NCOs who had served there during the interwar period, when being a China Hand was a prestigious status symbol. For most Marines, however, this would be their first extended stay in the exotic and enchanting orient. Unfortunately, chances of a peaceful stay seemed slim because China was a country in turmoil. A Chinese civil war was brew-

ing, and the Marines had been warned to look out for Japanese treach-
ery. The U.S.-backed Nationalist forces of Generalissimo Chiang Kai-shek
and Mao Tse-tung's Soviet-backed Communists both wanted to fill the
vacuum left when Japanese occupation forces pulled out. Both the Nationalists and Communists had fought the Japanese for the last decade,
but they were now fighting each other. In fact, the most populous country in the world was entering a civil war that would have long-range consequences for the United States. The occupation forces sent to China
had to enter the dragon's lair with caution and carefully step through
the mysterious labyrinth that was Chinese politics if the U.S. mission was
to be a success.

The Americans were officially being sent to China to accept the surrender of Japanese forces in northern China's Hopeh Province and to
assist with the repatriation of the thousands of Japanese soldiers and civilians. Unofficially, the Americans were to occupy the area to prevent it
from falling into Communist hands. Hopeh Province included the ports
of Taku, Tientsin, and Chinwangtao. The crown jewel of this area, however, was the great walled city of Peiping, as the modern city of Beijing
was then known. Peiping had been China's capital for seven hundred
years, and legendary Marine Dan Daly earned his first Medal of Honor
defending the Legation Quarter there during the Boxer Rebellion in
1901. This time around the Marines were charged with occupying the
major cities and protecting lines of communication and supply depots.

The plan was for III AC to move to China in late September. The 7th
Marines would protect the Taku-Chinwangtao railway, the 11th Marines
would hold Taku port and Tangku city. The 1st Marines sector included
Tientsin and the Taku-Peiping railway as far as Langfang. The 1st Marine Aircraft Wing would provide aviation support and the 7th Service
Regiment would control logistics. The 5th Marines sector included
Peiping and the Taku-Peiping railway north of Langfang. Of particular
importance in this area were Peiping's Lantienchang and Nan Yaun airports. Regimental headquarters was established in the old Marine barracks inside the Legation Quarter.

The occupation of northern China began on 30 September. The initial landings were conducted as tactical, not administrative, movements
because the situation was so uncertain. The 7th Marines landed at Taku
Bar on the Gulf of Chihli then sent advance forces to Tientsin and Chinwangtao. The 5th Marines arrived at Taku Bar on 2 October, unloaded
supplies and equipment on the fifth, and the troops moved ashore on

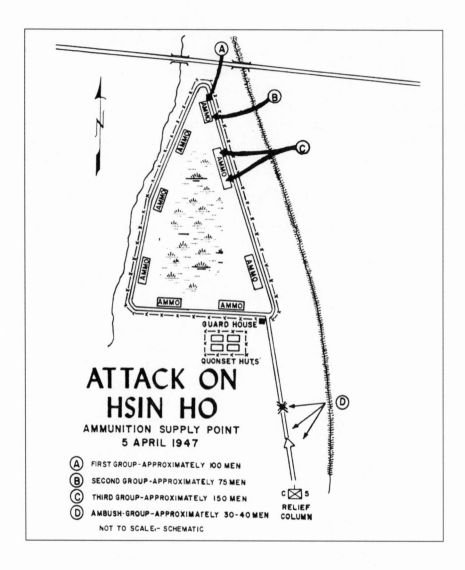

ATTACK ON
HSIN HO

AMMUNITION SUPPLY POINT
5 APRIL 1947

(A) FIRST GROUP-APPROXIMATELY 100 MEN
(B) SECOND GROUP-APPROXIMATELY 75 MEN
(C) THIRD GROUP-APPROXIMATELY 150 MEN
(D) AMBUSH-GROUP-APPROXIMATELY 30-40 MEN

NOT TO SCALE.- SCHEMATIC

C ⊠ 5
RELIEF
COLUMN

the sixth. The 2d and 3d Battalions were assigned to Brig. Gen. Louis R. Jones's Peiping Marine Group, and the 1st Battalion was attached to the 11th Marines at Tangku.

During a stormy prelanding meeting, Communist general Chou En-lai had warned Brig. Gen. William A. Worton that his forces would violently oppose any Marine move toward Peiping. The Marines remained undaunted and continued to plan for the occupation of the capital city.

The first shooting incident between the Marines and Communist forces occurred when an engineer party tried to clear the road for the 5th Marines's move to Peiping on the sixth. About fifty Communists opened fire on the Marines from a roadblock located twenty-two miles northwest of Tientsin. The Marines pulled back, but returned the next day in force covered by carrier aircraft. The roadblocks were thereafter removed without trouble, and the 5th Marines convoy reached Peiping before nightfall on 7 October without further incident.

Colonel Frisbie set up shop in the old Marine barracks, which had been manned by a crack detachment from 1905 to 1941. The traditional spit-and-polish sentry post at the main gate of the American compound was immediately restored to the satisfaction of the old China Hands. One rifle company was sent to each of the two major airports, patrols roamed as far south as Ho-Hsi-Wu, and a reinforced platoon manned the railway station at Langfang.

There were several incidents during October. Six Communist soldiers were killed after firing at the Langfang-Peiping train on the eighteenth, and three Marines were wounded in separate incidents while patrolling in jeeps. Most incidents stopped after General Peck, an old China Hand who spoke fluent Chinese and was intimately familiar with the ways of the people, declared that any ditches dug in the road would be filled from the nearest cultivated field. This warning did the trick, and the rest of the year passed nearly incident free, allowing the men of the 5th Marines to enjoy the fruits of occupation duty.

Colonel Frisbie was reassigned on 11 October. He was temporarily replaced by Lt. Col. Robert Hill until Col. Theodore A. Holdhahl took over on 9 November. Lieutenant Colonel August Larson assumed command on 15 March 1946 and held that post until 15 July, when Colonel Frisbie returned. Frisbie remained in command until 31 May 1947 when regimental headquarters was dissolved.

At higher headquarters, Maj. Gen. Samuel L. Howard replaced General Rockey as commander of the occupation forces on 18 September 1946, and presidential envoy General of the Army George C. Marshall negotiated terms between the Nationalists and Communists that relieved the Marines of responsibility for Chinese railways and other economic interests. Marine Forces China (formerly III AC) was thereafter responsible to protect U.S. property, personnel, and installations; to maintain port areas and communications security; and to provide support to other U.S. forces in China. The American occupation forces were reduced by about one-third in April 1946, and this led to a change of stations for the 5th Marines. Headquarters was established at Tangshan, 1/5 remained at Tangku, 2/5 moved to Linsi, and 3/5 was disbanded. The 1st Battalion continued protecting lines of communication and guarded several ammunition and supply depots. The 2d Battalion used its companies to protect nearby mines, bridges, and power plants. The regiment was relieved of guard duties at Linsi in August, and regimental headquarters and the 2d Battalion returned to Peiping.

By early 1947, American efforts to bring about peace in China had been continually frustrated by both the Nationalists and Communists. General Marshall was recalled to the states, and the U.S. role in China and the Far East was critically reappraised. As a result of this strategic reassessment, plans were made for the complete withdrawal of U.S. forces from Hopeh Province, but the Marines departure was tied to the safe evacuation of American families and property from Peiping. The regiment provided train guards, standby rescue parties, and motor transportation as needed, in addition to its normal security duties. Upon the withdrawal of the Americans from China, the 5th Marines was slated to move to Guam as part of the 1st Provisional Marine Brigade.

The 5th Marines had only two really significant encounters with Communist forces in nineteen months of occupation duty in northern China. Both occurred after the Communists renewed their belligerent activities in late 1946. The first incident occurred that fall. One Marine from the 1st Battalion was wounded when a Communist company unexpectedly attacked the Hsin-Ho ammunition dump on the night of 2 October. The Communist raiders escaped with some ammunition, but most of it was subsequently recovered.

The second encounter was the most serious attack of the entire Marine occupation. The Hsin-Ho depot was reorganized after the October attack. Its oval shape was reconfigured into a triangle, and supplies were moved into eight canvas-covered warehouses. Jeeps regularly patrolled the one-by-two-mile perimeter, and one- and two-man outposts dotted the fence line at regular intervals. The guardhouse was located at the main gate. Compound security was designed to reduce thievery and to hold off minor raids until a reaction force from Tangku could arrive—not to repel a major assault.

A 350-man Communist battalion made just such an attack on the morning of 5 April 1947. The raid started with a bugle call at about 0115. The two Marines guarding the north outpost held the enemy off with rifle fire for about ten minutes, but both defenders were killed during the firefight. At least two enemy groups penetrated the compound. One of them ambushed a jeep patrol, killing all three Marines. The rest of the intruders carried off mortar and artillery munitions while the Marine guards were pinned by fire. Eight Marines were wounded during this fight. A reaction force built around Company C, 5th Marines, at Tangku was immediately dispatched to Hsin-Ho. A self-propelled 105mm howitzer leading the relief column was knocked out by a mine at about 0200. The jeep and two trucks accompanying it then received small-arms fire from a nearby drainage ditch. About fifty Communist soldiers rushed the disabled convoy, but they were driven back by well-placed Marine fire. This force did, however, keep the Americans in place for about fifteen minutes to cover the withdrawal of the raiding party. Eight more Marines were wounded during this engagement. The raiders made off with six or eight carts loaded with artillery and mortar rounds and fuses. The rest of the 1st Battalion and Marine aircraft were on the way at dawn, but the Communists were long gone by that time. They had crossed on the Chin Chung ferry and melted into the population on the far side of the river before the sun crept over the mountains.

This incident marked the beginning of the end of the American occupation of China. The last convoy carrying 5th Marines personnel and gear left Peiping on 12 May 1947. Headquarters and 2d Battalion sailed from Taku Bar for Guam that evening. The 1st Battalion followed on 24 May. Interestingly, U.S. Marines finally returned to China when BLT 1/5 of the 31st MEU, landed at Qindao (formerly Tsingtao) in 1997, fifty years after the Marines departed in 1947.

The United States lost much face in the international community when the Communists defeated the Nationalists in 1949. Chiang Kai-shek's followers took refuge on the island of Formosa (today known as Taiwan) while Mao Tse-tung's Communists ruthlessly consolidated their hold over mainland China. From that point on, the People's Republic of China continued to gain stature while Nationalist China lost prestige. Today, the two Chinas still remain separate, and the Formosa Strait continues to be a potential international flashpoint.

The first elements of the 5th Marines reached Guam in the southern Mariana Islands on 31 May 1947. This movement coincided with broad reforms throughout the Marine Corps. Personnel shortages, limited funds, and a new tactical concept that called for small, flexible, mobile combat teams led the Marine Corps to adopt the J-series tables of equipment and organization. This radical reorganization did away with regiments and replaced them with independent battalion landing teams controlled directly by brigade or division headquarters. Accordingly, Lt. Col. Theodore M. Sheffield's 1st and Lt. Col. Ralph A. Collins Jr.'s 2d Battalions became the maneuver units of the 1st Provisional Marine Brigade on 1 June. Regimental headquarters personnel were reassigned to the brigade command element. Infantry units throughout the Marine Corps transitioned into one-battalion regiments on 1 October. The 1st Battalion became the 5th Marines while the 2d Battalion was redesignated the 9th Marines on that date.

The 1st Brigade was the U.S. strategic reserve force for the western Pacific, and its units were the most combat ready in the Marine Corps at that time. The brigade was on call to reinforce American forces in the Far East if there was war with Communist China, or to spearhead a Persian Gulf invasion force if war broke out with the Soviet Union. In reality, Lieutenant Colonel Sheffield's primary task was combat training because the bulk of his Marines were on their first enlistments. The highlight of training at Guam was a major fleet landing exercise in the spring of 1949.

The J-series tables of equipment and organization faded and the Fleet Marine Force reorganized after only two years without regiments. The 1st Battalion remained on Guam while elements of the 1st, 6th, and 7th Marines formed the 2d and 3d Battalions of the 5th Marines at Camp Pendleton, a coastal strip of land between Los Angeles and San Diego at Oceanside, California. The new regimental commander was a diminutive, energetic, intellectual who was determined to whip the 5th Marines into fighting shape in spite of formidable obstacles. He was Col. Victor H. Krulak, a tough Marine who proudly bore the nickname "Brute." Brute Krulak's 5th Marines was the only infantry regiment assigned to the 1st Marine Division under peacetime manning levels, and even this unit was shorthanded because it mustered only two companies per battalion. Brigadier General Frederick P. Henderson recalled that under Krulak's firm hand the 5th Marines spent more time in the field than in the barracks. Field exercises were held in October and November, the regiment conducted an amphibious demonstration for the army's Command and General Staff College, and then it conducted extensive field exercises that lasted until Christmas.

It was more of the same in the spring of 1950. The 1st Battalion arrived from Guam in February. After that, the full—albeit understrength with only two rifle companies of two platoons each—regiment spent most of February and March in Camp Pendleton's hilly, grass-covered boondocks. Amphibious Exercise Demon III in May was used to again showcase Marine abilities for students from the army's Command and General Staff College. Lesser field exercises continued after that.

Colonel Krulak departed on 9 June 1950, suddenly ordered away for a special covert mission. Lanky Lt. Col. Raymond L. Murray, a much-decorated and highly respected Marine officer who had served with the 2d Marine Division in the Pacific, replaced him as regimental commander. Concurrently, Maj. Gen. O. P. Smith, who commanded the 5th Marines on New Britain, became the 1st Marine Division's commanding general.

Postscript

Many members of the 5th Marines during World War II enjoyed brilliant careers. Among those who achieved four-star rank were Lew Walt, LeRoy Hunt, and O. P. Smith. Walt commanded the 5th Marines in Korea and subsequently became the first officer not to serve as commandant to wear four stars on active duty. LeRoy Hunt, who served with the 5th Regiment during the Great War and was regimental Commander on Guadalcanal, received his fourth star upon retirement—an honorific upgrade known as a "tombstone" promotion. Lieutenant General O. P. Smith's fourth star was also the result of a tombstone promotion. Brute Krulak eventually rose to lieutenant general. Much like General Shepherd in Korea, Krulak was a hands-on FMFPac commander during the Vietnam War. He was very involved in the day-to-day activities of his Marines, as well as an unofficial architect of U.S. policy in Vietnam. In addition to his Marine Corps duties, he was also a highly respected ex-officio adviser to Pres. Lyndon B. Johnson. After retirement, Krulak penned a well-received book, *First To Fight*, which touted the Marine Corps's traditional tough training, constant readiness, and its ability to fight as a combined-arms combat team—all traits that his former 5th Marines had demonstrated in Korea. His son, Charles C. Krulak, later became Commandant. In retrospect, most historians feel a large measure of credit for the 5th Regiment's outstanding performance early in Korea was due to Krulak's brilliant and tough-minded leadership during the difficult times after World War II.

John Selden and Henry Buse both became lieutenant generals. Selden commanded the 1st Marine Division in Korea, and Buse commanded FMFPac during the Vietnam era.

Paul Douglas, the economics professor and former regimental adjutant who was twice wounded while rescuing injured men, required more than a year of hospitalization before he was released from active duty and subsequently elected to Congress. He served in the U.S. Senate from 1948–67. During his first term, Douglas cosponsored a 1952 bill that virtually ended the bitter interservice unification controversy by setting a statutory floor on Marine Corps strength and allowing the Commandant to meet with the Joint Chiefs of Staff when Marine Corps matters were on the agenda. Douglas had time and again proved his bravery on the battlefield, but his courageous stand against the probable dissolution of the Marine Corps, a measure supported by both Presidents Truman and Eisenhower, made him even more of a hero in the eyes of many Marines. The hard-working Douglas was also an early proponent of the civil rights movement, and he could always be counted on to improve working conditions and push for higher wages for American workers. While a college professor, Douglas wrote two widely acclaimed books: *Real Wages in the United States* and *The Worker in Modern Economic Society*. Then, after leaving the Senate, he penned his autobiography, *In the Fullness of Time*.

The most bittersweet postwar story is that of "Red Mike" Edson. Throughout World War II Edson had proved his mettle in a variety of military milieus. He received the Medal of Honor for his courage under fire on Guadalcanal's Bloody Ridge, was considered a combat leader without peer by his contemporaries, performed outstanding staff work during his nearly four years in the Pacific, and many of his behind-the-scenes organizational suggestions were adopted. Probably the most courageous decision of his career, however, did not take place on a traditional field of battle. The new arena was the halls of Congress. His objective this time around was not a heavily defended enemy bastion, but gaining the approval of the American public. After the war, Red Mike sacrificed his career (and some say his life) to save the Marine Corps. General Edson forsook certain promotion when he voluntarily placed himself on the retired list so he could publicly speak out against a move to unify the services that would certainly have led to the loss of Marine Corps aviation and threatened either the transfer of Marine ground forces to the army or the reduction of the Corps to only a couple of battalion landing teams. His effort was successful, but at great personal cost: Red Mike died soon afterward under ambiguous circumstances, probably suicide.

Colorful Lou Diamond, the legendary Guadalcanal mortarman, had to be evacuated when he became ill. Cantankerous as ever, he managed to slip out of the hospital in New Zealand and make his way more than two thousand miles across the South Pacific to rejoin his old outfit. The old salt was not physically fit for combat and was sent home to train new Marines, a position for which he was perfectly suited. General Vandegrift commended him with the words: "To every man in your company you were a counselor, an arbiter of disputes, an ideal Marine. Your matchless loyalty and love of the Marine Corps [has been] an inspiration [to all who have served with you]." Lou Diamond, "Mr. Marine," was finally "surveyed" out of his beloved Corps in November 1945.

5: Korea

While headquarters was fighting in the halls of Congress to save the Marine Corps and the 5th Marines was moving from northern China to Guam to California, the Far East remained a boiling cauldron filled with trouble. Buoyed by the Communist victory in China, other Soviet client forces in the Far East, notably those in Indochina and North Korea, decided to test the waters. Both eventually pulled the United States back into armed conflicts in the Far East during the upcoming years.

The Korean Peninsula, long under Japanese hegemony, was temporarily divided at the 38th Parallel, which bisected that land after Japan's surrender in 1945. The semi-industrialized northern sector was under the repressive thumb of Communist dictator Kim Il Sung, while the agricultural south was controlled by octogenarian president Syngman Rhee. The postwar plan was to eventually hold elections to unify Korea, but relations between the north and south were so contentious that it was unlikely fair elections could be held anytime soon. Instead, both leaders solidified their internal control while consistently rattling their sabers at each other. Kim Il Sung, with significant support from Soviet strongman Joseph Stalin and China's Mao Tse-tung, quickly built the North Korean People's Army (NKPA) into a well-equipped regional power. In the south, however, the Republic of Korea (ROK) Army was little more than a lightly armed counterguerrilla constabulary because South Korea was still under the American defense umbrella. Unfortunately, the American occupation army in Japan was a hollow force—ill trained, poorly equipped, and utterly unprepared to fight a major land war in Asia.

Ironically, the U.S. Marine Corps had no combat units in the Far East by the summer of 1950. The Corps, in fact, had shrunk to only two weak

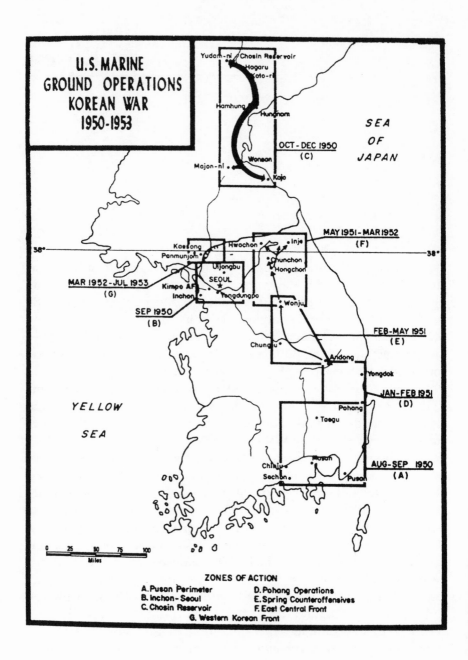

U.S. MARINE GROUND OPERATIONS KOREAN WAR 1950-1953

ZONES OF ACTION

A. Pusan Perimeter
B. Inchon-Seoul
C. Chosin Reservoir
D. Pohang Operations
E. Spring Counteroffensives
F. East Central Front
G. Western Korean Front

one-regiment divisions and a pair of similarly truncated air wings. Harkening back to the days of the famous 4th Marine Brigade in World War I, the ground units were the 5th and 6th Marines respectively. There was one division and one wing on each coast of the United States, with no Marine units permanently stationed overseas. The Fleet Marine Force (FMF) was actually hard-pressed to furnish one war-strength battalion landing team for the Mediterranean. Such was the state of affairs when Joseph Stalin secretly gave Kim Il Sung the green light to reunify Korea by force.

Eight NKPA divisions burst across the border into South Korea on 25 June 1950 without warning or provocation while the free world watched in horror. The United Nations quickly condemned this action and asked its member nations for military forces to stop North Korea's naked aggression. General of the Army Douglas MacArthur, the commander in chief of the U.S. Far East Command (FECOM), was authorized to commit American troops, and by 4 July Task Force Smith was in contact with the enemy near Osan. Unfortunately, the first Americans sent to Korea from Japan were poorly equipped and vastly outnumbered. They could not stand up to the enemy assault, and the NKPA quickly pushed United Nations Command (UNC) forces back toward the southeast corner of the Korean Peninsula, an area soon to become famous as the Pusan Perimeter.

The Marine Corps Commandant, Gen. Clifton B. Cates Jr., immediately offered FMF units to bolster the U.S. presence in Korea. His proposal was accepted and the 1st Provisional Marine Brigade, composed of Regimental Combat Team (RCT) 5 and Marine Air Group (MAG) 33 under the command of Brig. Gen. Edward A. Craig, was formed in California on 7 July. The 5th Marines was the nucleus around which the 1st Brigade ground combat element was formed. At the time, the regiment was only a skeleton unit composed of six understrength rifle companies and a few small combat support units. Lieutenant General Lem Shepherd, an old 5th Marines hand who had just become commanding general of the Fleet Marine Force Pacific, recommended that Marine units be brought to full strength before shipping out to the combat zone. Accordingly, a third platoon was added to each rifle company by stripping all the other infantry units at Camp Pendleton. However, the third rifle companies for each battalion could not be formed in time to sail. Personnel shortages meant new units were made up of Marines from widely scattered posts and stations, ship detachments, and activated Reservists.

Sadly, not enough of them could be gathered in the short time available before the 5th Marines embarked.

The bobtailed regiment that sailed for the Far East included regimental headquarters, a 4.2-inch mortar platoon, an antitank company, three heavy weapons companies, and three two-company rifle battalions. Added to these organic 5th Marines units were the 1st Battalion, 11th Marines; Company A, 1st Motor Transport Battalion; Company C, 1st Medical Battalion; Company A, 1st Shore Party Battalion; Company A, 1st Tank Battalion; 1st Amphibian Tractor Company; and service, ordnance, signals, military police, and reconnaissance detachments that combined to form Marine RCT 5.

The 5th Marines commander, Raymond L. Murray, was a tall, highly respected combat veteran. He graduated from Texas A&M, served in China and Iceland before World War II, and held the Navy Cross and two Silver Stars for gallantry at Saipan, Guadalcanal, and Tarawa. Although only a lieutenant colonel, Murray was held in such high esteem that he was allowed to command the regiment. Lieutenant Colonel George R. Newton's 1st Battalion was composed of Capt. John R. Stevens's A and Capt. John L. Tobin's B Companies and Maj. John W. Russell's Weapons Company. Lieutenant Colonel Harold S. Roise's 2d Battalion had Capt. John Finn Jr.'s D and Capt. George E. Kittredge's E Companies and Maj. Theodore F. Spiker's Weapons Company. Lieutenant Colonel Robert D. Taplett's 3d Battalion included 1st Lt. Robert D. Bohn's G and Capt. Joseph C. Fegan Jr.'s H Companies and Capt. Patrick E. Wildman's Weapons Company.

The 5th Marines spent four days packing, boxing, and preparing supplies and equipment for embarkation at Camp Pendleton. A few men were hurriedly sent to the range to familiarize themselves with new weapons like M20 3.5-inch rocket launchers and M26 Pershing tanks. Concurrently, streams of men from Camp Pendleton and trainloads of refurbished World War II–era equipment from the desert supply center at nearby Barstow flooded the port of embarkation at San Diego. There, beginning on 11 July 1950, the 2,643 riflemen and combat support specialists assigned to the 5th Marines boarded the transport ships USS *Henrico, George Clymer, Pickaway,* and the dock landing ships *Gunston Hall* and *Fort Marion.* The last of these vessels departed the West Coast on 14 July. A further 1,135 men earmarked for the as yet unformed rifle companies (Companies C, F, and I) would later sail from San Diego in August with the rest of the 1st Marine Division.

It was not a smooth sail for the Marine Brigade. En route the *Henrico*, carrying the 1st Battalion, developed engine trouble and had to steam from San Clemente Island to San Francisco for repairs. The hard-luck "Happy Hank" (as the ship was known in the fleet) finally caught up to the convoy just as it closed on the Korean coast in early August. The convoy's original destination had been Japan, where the Marines were to debark, organize for combat, conduct last-minute training, combat load, and then proceed to Korea. However, this plan was overtaken by events in Korea—due to the serious combat situation there, the landing site was hastily changed to Pusan Harbor.

Pusan

The embarked Marine air-ground task force became the first American unit to reach Korea directly from the United States. The 1st Marine Brigade arrived there on 2 August. The UNC was barely holding on when the 5th Marines came ashore. The ROK Army held a short northern line that ran inland from Pohang-dong on the east coast to Andong about forty miles away, and the U.S. Army had four divisions dug in along the Naktong River to form the longer western edge of the Pusan Perimeter. The situation was desperate. Before the Pusan Perimeter had been formed, many UNC troops bolted in the face of the enemy during unauthorized movements derisively called "bug outs" by the press. General Craig addressed this issue when he told his officers "Troops now fighting in Korea [have often] pull[ed] back. . . . You will never receive an order to retreat from me."

When the 1st Marine Brigade emerged from the bedlam at the Pusan waterfront it was assigned to Lt. Gen. Walton H. "Bulldog" Walker's Eighth Army. The 5th Marines was immediately ordered to move into reserve positions at Changwon. Lieutenant Colonel Newton's 1st Battalion led a forty-mile motor march northwest out of Pusan over dust-choked, bumpy roads. The last Marines were in position by about 1600. The 1st and 3d Battalions formed a defensive arc, while the 2d Battalion protected a centrally located hill where headquarters and the artillery positions were located.

On 6 August, the 5th Marines received orders to move about thirteen miles southwest to Chindong-ni to participate in the first Eighth Army offensive in Korea. The first Marine unit out was Taplett's 3/5, which was attached to the 25th Infantry Division. On 7 August, the eighth anniversary of the 5th Marines's landing on Guadalcanal, 2d Lt. John M. Cahill's 1st Platoon, Company G, 3/5, was ordered to reinforce a hard-pressed army rifle company atop Hill 342 near Sangyong-ni about four miles away. The Marines were harassed by friendly fire, suffered terribly in the hundred-degree heat, and were taken under long-range fire by the enemy as they crossed open rice paddies before climbing the steep slope. Only thirty-seven of the fifty-two men who started out reached the crest. This action was the first direct-fire engagement by Marine ground troops in Korea.

The 2d Battalion left Changwon at about 0200 on the seventh and arrived at Chindong-ni three hours later. Not long after that, Captain Kittredge was wounded by mortar fire and was evacuated. First Lieutenant William E. Sweeney took his place as Company E commander. That evening both 2d Battalion rifle companies moved across the open valley to Hill 342, where they helped repulse a dawn attack by the NKPA. Captain Finn was wounded and turned command of Company D over to 1st Lt. Robert T. Hannifen Jr., who commanded Dog Company until the arrival of Capt. Andrew M. Zimmer. Eleven Marines were killed or seriously wounded, but the hill was held and more than three hundred attackers from the NKPA 6th Division were left on the battlefield when the enemy pulled back.

With Hill 342 safely in American hands, Task Force Kean (a joint task force composed of elements of the army's 5th and 27th RCTs and the 5th Marines) directed its attack toward Kosong. The 5th Marines fought alongside army units for the next two days to clear the enemy from a key road junction at Tosan. Captain Fegan of Company H led an attack across open ground to force the enemy off dominant terrain. The 1st Battalion mounted a successful assault to capture Hill 308 on 9 August. The 2d Battalion then launched a night attack to secure Paedun-ni. This unrelenting pressure was too much for the NKPA. The In Min Gun units pulled back eight miles with the 2d and 3d Battalions, 5th Marines, in hot pursuit on the tenth. This was an important milestone, the first significant retreat by the enemy thus far in the Korean War.

On 11 August Marine air and artillery caught an enemy motorized column in the open and wiped it out in what became known as the Kosong Turkey Shoot. The following day, Capt. Kenneth J. Houghton's reconnaissance platoon led the 1st Brigade more than ten miles down the road toward Sachon without encountering any enemy opposition until the advance guard prematurely triggered an ambush at Changchon. The

Marines on the road were able to fight their way out only after elements of the 1st Battalion secured the heights on both sides of the road and Lieutenant Colonel Newton directed air strikes on the enemy. A patrol from Company B annihilated the enemy atop Hill 202 during the fighting. As the sun disappeared from the summer sky, the Marines were holding the high ground and had dug in for the night.

At about midnight, higher headquarters abruptly canceled the next day's attack. Lieutenant Colonel Newton was ordered to have his men waiting on the road for truck transport to a new sector at dawn. These plans, however, ran into some glitches. At about 0400 on 13 August, the NKPA began probing the Company B positions on Hill 202 then launched a surprise attack that overran one platoon. The fighting was so desperate that the Marines were forced to knock out two of their own machine guns when the enemy began using them. Company B had to conduct a fighting withdrawal in order to reach its assigned position on the road. That hilltop was engulfed by air strikes and artillery fire when the last Marines left the slope at about 0900. Company B lost 15 men killed, 33 wounded, and 8 (presumed dead) missing in action during the fight for Hill 202. Many men had a bitter taste in their mouths when ordered not to retrieve the bodies of their fallen comrades. No warrior wants to leave behind the dead, but sometimes there is no other choice. This was one of those times. Unknown to the men of Company B was that the situation elsewhere had taken a turn for the worst and required immediate action by all available forces.

Lieutenant Colonel Murray faced an unusual tactical situation. The 5th Marines had to attack in two opposite directions at the same time. While the front of the Marine Brigade was fighting at Changchon, the rear element had to reverse its order of march to recapture the high ground at Chindong-ni. This latter task fell to the 3d Battalion. Luckily, the objectives were lightly held, and only one Marine was wounded when Lieutenant Colonel Taplett's men retook the familiar ridges. The Marines then searched for survivors of an overrun army artillery battalion before calling for air strikes to destroy the abandoned self-propelled howitzers.

Although most Marines were unaware of it at the time, the reason they were called back from Chindong-ni and Changchon was that the enemy had penetrated the Naktong River Line and threatened the key road junction and communications center at Masan. It was imperative that the resulting "Naktong Bulge" be eliminated or the entire Pusan Perimeter would be at risk. The Marines were considered the most reliable of the UNC forces, so they were used as a "fire brigade" to be moved around to shore up the most threatened sectors of the UNC perimeter.

The 5th Marines enjoyed a day's well-earned rest at Miryang on 15 August. After eating their first hot meal since arriving in Korea almost two weeks before, the Marines were ordered into action at the Naktong Bulge. They captured all of their objectives and pushed the NKPA back across the river. These actions became a showcase of the effectiveness of the Marine air-ground team concept. Ground assaults were closely coordinated with air strikes and were preceded and continually supported by accurate artillery fire. Prompt evacuation of casualties, some by helicopter, kept the number of deaths from wounds to a minimum. Unfortunately, numerous laudatory media reports about this action—not unlike the publicity at Belleau Wood in 1918—occasionally drew the ire of other service commanders, most notably over the effectiveness of Marine close air support when compared to that provided to the army by the air force. This later fostered interservice jealousy.

A shortage of trucks meant the Marines had to shuttle to the battle area battalion by battalion throughout the evening of the sixteenth and during the following morning. The 3d Battalion departed Miryang at 1900 and made the two-hour trip to Yongsan. Taplett's men were then followed in turn by the 2d and 1st Battalions, but the last Marines were not in place until 0730 on the seventeenth. The overall scheme of maneuver called for the Marines to push forward to the Naktong River in order to support by fire an army attack to push the enemy farther north. Lieutenant Colonel Murray's plan was to attack in a column of battalions. The 3d Battalion would hold Observation Hill and support the other attacks with fire. The 2d Battalion would seize the first objective, Obong-ni Ridge, by taking the northern slope and then pushing uphill to successively seize Hills 102, 109, 117, 143, 147, and 153. The 1st Battalion would jump off to take Hill 207 located about halfway to the Naktong River after Obong-ni was in friendly hands. Hopefully, this ambitious plan could be completed by midafternoon. The last objective, Hill 311, would be taken by the 3d Battalion, which would move forward from Observation Hill on order.

The attack began at 0800 on 17 August with Roise's 2d Battalion pushing toward Obong-ni. Captain Zimmer led Company D across the silent rice paddies and up some scrub-covered slopes reminiscent of Camp Pendleton's rolling hills. About halfway to the top of the first slope, enemy machine guns found the range and forced most of the attackers to seek cover. However, ten men were able to seize the crest of Hill 109. On the left, Lieutenant Sweeney's hard-luck Easy Company was first hit by short rounds from American artillery and then suffered more hits from an American air strike. This attack finally stalled when enemy machine gunners ranged the Marine lines. Casualties were heavy: by noon 2/5 had lost 23 dead and 119 wounded of the 240 men in the assault waves.

About an hour later, Lieutenant Colonel Newton's 1st Battalion passed through and resumed the Marine assault. Not long after that, Captain Tobin was seriously wounded and Capt. Francis I. "Ike" Fenton Jr. assumed command of Company B. Captain Stevens's Company A moved through Company E at about 1500 and immediately came under heavy machine-gun fire. This attack stalled in the saddle between Hills 117 and 109 when small arms, machine guns, and grenades pinned down Company A.

As the tired Marines prepared night defensive positions, word filtered back that the NKPA was mounting an armored attack spearheaded by T-34s, the Soviet-supplied tanks that had thus far been nearly invulnerable to UN fire. This warning gave the Marine air-ground team another chance to show its stuff. Chance-Vought F4U-4 Corsairs from MAG 33 were called in. They located the column, destroyed one tank, and dispersed the accompanying infantry. When the remaining enemy approached the Marine positions, a 75mm recoilless rifle knocked out the lead T-34 and the other two fell victim to bazooka rocket launchers and fire from 90mm tank guns. The supposed invincibility of the T-34 was thus proved to be no more than a sea story in less than five minutes by the skillful use of combined arms. Numerous reporters located on Observation Hill admiringly described this victorious fight for "Red-Slash Hill" in the national media. This hopeful news dramatically reversed the bleak outlook for the Pusan Perimeter, and MacArthur's headquarters in Tokyo could begin to once again think seriously about offensive action instead of planning a Dunkirk-like amphibious withdrawal from the Korean Peninsula.

That night, 1/5 on Obong-ni was hit by well-placed mortar fire that was followed by two counterattacks. The hard-pressed Marines held, although they were pushed back in some spots. The next morning Company A, aided by effective air strikes and well supported by 81mm mortars and 90mm fire from M26 tanks, slowly gained the momentum and took the northernmost hills atop Obong-ni Ridge after engaging in fierce hand-to-hand fighting. The Marines held all of Obong-ni Ridge by midafternoon.

The difficult struggle for Obong-ni forced a change of plans. Lieutenant Colonel Taplett's 3d Battalion was charged with taking Hill 207 on 18 August. Companies G and H moved up the slopes against light opposition and reached the crest at about 1230, but Captain Fegan was wounded and evacuated as Company H fought its way to the top of Hill 311. Captain Wildman of Weapons Company replaced him, and Capt. Murray Ehrlich took over Weapons Company. Lieutenant "Dewey" Bohn's Company G maneuvered to envelop the enemy and overran about half the hilltop before being thrown back. The 3d Battalion then spent a relatively quiet night on the slope before grabbing the summit of Hill 311 the next morning.

The actions of the 5th Marines were noteworthy. The vaunted In Min Gun got its first real taste of defeat at the Naktong Bulge. This time it was the Communists who were bugging out as they scurried back across the Naktong River on 18 August. Their retreat became a rout that turned into a slaughter when Marine supporting arms caught the disorganized enemy in the open. Air strikes, artillery, and mortars pummeled the hapless North Koreans as they raced for safety. The next day was devoted to clearing out bypassed pockets of the enemy and combing the hills for NKPA wounded. The First Battle of the Naktong cost the Marines 66 dead, 278 wounded, and 1 missing, but the NKPA 4th Division had been decisively defeated and was no longer combat effective.

The 5th Marines was detached from the 24th Division's operational control on the twentieth. The Marine Brigade then returned to a reserve position in the agricultural flatland near Masan known as the "Bean Patch." Accolades soon came pouring in from the 24th Division commander and Eighth Army headquarters. South Korean president Syngman Rhee visited the 1st Brigade on 29 August. Eighty-seven Marines were decorated in what was commonly called the "Purple Heart Parade." In a moving speech, Rhee promised that each member of the 1st Provisional Marine Brigade would receive a special decoration, then declared: "You have brought us victory when all we had known was defeat." But the official proclamations were not nearly as important to the morale of most of the assembled Marines as the hot chow, refreshing cold baths, and the opportunity to catch up on much-needed sleep that they enjoyed during this break from frontline duty. Replacements, most of them volunteers from units already in the Far East, filled spaces left by the casualties. Unfortunately, plans to release the regiment to its parent 1st Marine Division, which had just arrived in Japan, had to be shelved when the NKPA once again crossed the Naktong.

The 5th Marines returned to Miryang on 1 September and, scarcely thirty-two hours after the Purple Heart Parade ended, was attached to the U.S. 2d Infantry Division, the same division in which the regiment had served during World War I, to fight the Second Battle of the Naktong. This time Lieutenant Colonel Murray's plan was for the 1st and 2d Battalions to advance up the Yongsan road with the 3d Battalion in support. The 2d Battalion reached the road junction at about 0430 on 3 September, where it off-loaded and began an administrative move to the line of departure. This road junction and the nearby heights were supposedly in American hands. Unfortunately, such was not actually the case. Much like in the Champagne offensive during World War I, Companies D and E had to clear enemy from the main supply route in order to reach the jump-off point north of Myong-ni by 0800.

Fifty-five minutes later, Companies A and B launched the 1st Battalion's assault from Chukchon-ni to capture Hill 91 East. The riflemen waded across knee-deep rice paddies covered by superb supporting fires delivered by air, artillery, mortars, and army tank destroyers. Just as the Marines started their attack, many stragglers from U.S. units began to emerge from hiding places in the foothills. This unexpected turn of events briefly interfered with the Marines's advance. Enemy artillery fire also temporarily delayed the attackers, but the intermediate objective, a small ridge, was secured by noon and Hill 91 East was in Marine hands by 1630.

First Lieutenant H. J. "Hawg Jowl" Smith, the Company D commander, reported that he was taking fire from Hill 117 west of Myong-ni. Lieutenant Colonel Roise ordered Smith to assault the troublesome hill and told Capt. Samuel Jaskilka, the new Company E commander, to support Company D's attack by fire from Myong-ni. Company D was able to gain only a small foothold on the lower slope before being pinned down by enemy artillery and small-arms fire. The 2d Battalion lost eighteen killed and seventy-seven wounded, mostly from Company D, that day. As darkness fell on the night of 3–4 September, the 1st and 2d Battalions were widely separated. Each spent a miserable, wet night isolated from the other. Luckily, Korea's unpredictable weather interceded and chilly rain and strong winds prevented the enemy from mounting a coordinated counterattack.

On the fourth, Lieutenant Colonel Murray ordered the 3d Battalion to pass through the hard-hit 2d Battalion. Company H made a wide arc north of Hill 117 as Company G attacked straight on. This envelopment worked, and Hill 117 quickly fell. Thereafter, the 3d Battalion conducted a daylong attack that carried the Marines beyond Kang-ni. Simultaneously, the 1st Battalion moved with Companies A and B abreast from Hill 91 East past Yu-ri village, crossed a barren valley, and secured Cloverleaf Hill. There was little resistance during most of the day in the 1st Battalion zone of action south of the road. The Marines advanced three thousand yards over broken ground that day and took all of their objectives before nightfall. That night, however, the 3d Battalion was shelled by enemy artillery and the 1st Battalion command post suffered a direct hit.

The 1st Battalion supported the 9th Infantry Regiment on 5 September as that army unit carried Hill 165. The Marines then focused their attention on Observation Hill, which had been held by the 1st Marine Brigade during the first Naktong battle less than two weeks before. Company B took Hill 125 and held it against two NKPA attacks. During this fight the Marines destroyed two more T-34 tanks and an enemy armored personnel carrier at about 1420. Company A took the northern half of Observation Hill and then moved over to reinforce Company B in midafternoon. The 3d Battalion crossed the familiar ground between Cloverleaf and Observation Hills to clear the southern ridge facing Obong-ni Ridge.

Regimental plans were being formulated to continue the attack to clear the rest of the Naktong Bulge when Lieutenant Colonel Murray learned the 5th Marines was going to be pulled out of the line. The regiment was to begin moving to a staging area near Pusan by road the next morning. Ironically, the 3d Battalion was hard hit by enemy artillery and suffered twenty-four casualties as it left Observation Hill. The 1st Battalion was the last Marine unit out, moving to Yongsan at about 0600 on the sixth. The Second Battle of the Naktong was the last combat action in this area for the regiment. The Pusan Perimeter had been saved, and the 5th Marines were now needed elsewhere.

In thirty-five days at Pusan the 5th Marines had traveled more than 380 miles, inflicted more than nineteen hundred casualties on three different NKPA divisions, and won three major engagements that helped to turn the tide in Korea. For its superior performance, the regiment was awarded U.S. and Korean Presidential Unit Citations for combat actions from 7 August–7 September 1950.

The Marine Brigade could finally be withdrawn because the situation in the Pusan Perimeter was no longer critical, and highly skilled amphibious experts were desperately needed elsewhere. General MacArthur had been planning an amphibious turning movement since the very beginning of the war. His original concept, Operation Bluehearts, would use the army's 1st Cavalry Division to spearhead a landing at Inchon and then cut off the NKPA's supply lines by capturing Seoul deep in the enemy rear. The timetable called for the landing to occur on 22 July, but this ambitious plan had to be canceled due to the press of events on the battlefield. Indeed, by mid-July every American soldier and Marine available was needed in the front lines. It was, in fact, with only great reluctance that Bulldog Walker let "his" Marines go. But, MacArthur had dusted off his amphibious concept and now had the perfect instrument to make a successful landing: The 1st Marine Division was on its way to Korea.

Inchon and Seoul

The 5th Marines rejoined the 1st Marine Division for Operation Chromite, the new code name for the plan to conduct a strategic turning movement at Inchon to isolate the NKPA south of the 38th Parallel. While the regiment had been fighting in Korea, its parent division was building up at Camp Pendleton, using newly activated reservists and active-duty Marines hastily recalled from around the world. Division headquarters, the 1st Marines, appropriate combat support and service support elements, and units slated to join the 5th Marines sailed from San Diego in late August. The last transport group carrying this truncated (it was still short one infantry regiment and miscellaneous support units) division arrived at Kobe, Japan, during the first days of September.

The two-regiment 1st Marine Division was to be the amphibious assault force that would land at Inchon and then spearhead the X Corps's inland advance to recapture Seoul. General MacArthur had overall control of Operation Chromite as the FECOM commander, VAdm. Arthur D. Struble was commander of Joint Task Force Seven, Maj. Gen. Edward M. "Ned" Almond commanded the X Corps, and Maj. Gen. Oliver P. Smith led the 1st Marine Division.

Operation Chromite called for the 1st Marine Division to land at Inchon, seize Kimpo airfield, cross the Han River, take Seoul, and establish blocking positions to protect the city. Hydrographic conditions dictated the landing must be made on 15 September, a circumstance that left the 5th Marines less than one week to reorganize, refit, and combat load its assigned ships. The late release of the 5th Marines from the Pusan Perimeter, finally ordered by General MacArthur at the last minute over strenuous objections by the Eighth Army commander, caused Lieutenant Colonel Murray problems preparing for the upcoming amphibious operation at Inchon. The 5th Marines played virtually no part in the planning and had no chance to conduct even a cursory amphibious rehearsal. Murray would have to execute plans created by others, and the 5th Marines would join the 1st Marine Division at sea only hours before going into combat.

Inchon is a port city located about halfway up Korea's west coast at the mouth of the Han River. It serves the capital city of Seoul, located about twenty miles inland. The Inchon-Seoul area was a lightly defended vital communications hub that provided the only suitable land corridor between North Korea and the Pusan Perimeter to support large-scale logistics movements. If the UNC could take this area, the Communist forces in the south would have to stop their attacks on Pusan and redirect their effort against the forces operating in the north. It was estimated that only a couple of thousand second-string NKPA troops were located at the port. Inchon was a very valuable strategic target, but landing there was fraught with practical problems. Inchon was, alas, one of the least desirable spots for an amphibious operation in Korea. As navy and Marine planners wryly noted, "If you made a list of 'amphibious don'ts,' Inchon seemed to have all of them." The only approach, Flying Fish Channel, was a meandering waterway subject to swift currents and difficult tides. Low tide made Inchon Harbor a gigantic mud flat from just after dawn until just before dusk. The harbor entrance, dominated by a hilly outcrop known as Wolmi Do, would have to be taken and held for more than nine hours before the main landings could be made or any help could be sent. There was no true landing beach in the 5th Marines's zone, only a built-up urban area lined by a seawall that blocked landing vehicle passage across the beach.

Chromite was an ambitious plan that allowed little wiggle room if things went wrong. General MacArthur dismissed navy and Marine Corps warnings about the formidable natural barriers. He stubbornly refused to relent, asserting that Inchon's amphibious unsuitability guaranteed that surprise would make for an easy victory. The die was cast.

Chromite planners divided Inchon into three landing areas: Green Beach on Wolmi Do in the center, Red Beach to the north, and Blue Beach south of the city. Lieutenant Colonel Taplett's BLT 3/5 was assigned to land at Green Beach on the morning of 15 September and hold Wolmi Do until evening. No reinforcements could be sent in, and there was no way to pull the embattled assault wave off the beach if things went bad. The isolated 3d Battalion would be on its own most of the day. The rest of the 5th Marines would land at Red Beach and the 1st Marines would hit Blue Beach about two hours before dark.

Lieutenant Colonel Murray was concerned because there would be no opportunity for the 5th Marines to conduct an amphibious rehearsal even though more than a third of his regiment had just arrived from the United States. After being released from Eighth Army control, the regiment was finally brought up to full strength when 1st Lt. Poul F. Pederson's C, Capt. Udel D. Peters's F, and Capt. Robert A. McMullen's I Companies and their attached combat support detachments were welcomed on board at Pusan. As soon as those handshakes were over, however, the 5th Marines instituted a round-the-clock loading schedule. Training was limited to some small-arms familiarization firing and a couple of conditioning hikes for the recent arrivals. Also, a few veterans were pulled out of the 5th Marines to help train the newly activated 1st Regiment, Korean Marine Corps (KMC), which was later attached to the 1st Marine Division and served with distinction during the remainder of the war.

The Wolmi Do assault force, Lieutenant Colonel Taplett's BLT 3/5, was the first unit to embark. Its units were assigned to three high-speed transports and one dock landing ship. Headquarters and the combat support elements were on board the USS *Fort Marion,* Company G was on the USS *Diachenko,* Company H was on the USS *Horace A. Bass,* and Company I was on the USS *Wantuck.* The 1st Battalion was assigned to the familiar transport *Henrico,* the 2d Battalion to the USS *Cavalier,* and the rest of the 5th Marines was split between the attack transport *Pickaway* and the cargo ship *Seminole.* Most Marines boarded ship on 10 and 11 September and were under way on the twelfth—a day early because a typhoon was rapidly approaching.

All hands were informed about the 1st Marine Division's overall mission and received detailed briefings as to their specific roles while the convoy sailed to the target area. The specific missions were for BLT 3/5 to land over Green Beach at L-hour on D day to seize and defend Wolmi Do; RCT 5 was to land across Red Beach at H-hour on D day, seize the

O-A Line—which roughly bisected Inchon City—effect a juncture with RCT 1 moving north from Blue Beach, and then jointly seize Objective O-1, which comprised the force beachhead line (FBHL).

The eight-ship task group carrying the 5th Marines joined the rest of the invasion fleet on 14 September. Almost all training took place while the regiment was at sea. Each man was issued one day's rations and ammunition. All Marines were assigned to boat teams and conducted onboard debarkation drills moving from their bunks to assigned deck stations. Men in the assault waves were instructed how to use the scaling ladders needed to get over the sea wall. The amphibious task force neared the entrance to Flying Fish Channel in darkness, and the ships quietly slipped into their assigned positions as the unsuspecting enemy slept in the early morning hours on the fifteenth.

The naval bombardment opened at 0540, rocket boats delivered their deadly missiles at 0615, and Marine Corsairs strafed Wolmi Do just as the first landing wave neared Green Beach. The boats carrying Lieutenant Bohn's Company G hit the beach on the northern tip of Wolmi Do at 0633, and Captain Wildman's Company H landed moments later. Company G waded ashore, quickly claimed Radio Hill, and secured the causeway to Lighthouse Point on So Wolmi Do. Twenty minutes later, Sgt. Alvin E. Smith, Company G's 3d Platoon guide, secured an American flag to a shell-torn tree to signify Radio Hill was in Marine hands. Upon landing, Captain Wildman sent a detachment to Wolmi Do's northern tip and led the rest of Company H forward to secure the causeway from the mainland. The Marines painstakingly cleared the shattered ruins of an industrial complex along the east shore. Captain McMullen's Company I hit stiff resistance as it cleared North Point and had to call for tank assistance to eliminate dug-in defenders. Still, just after 0800, Lieutenant Colonel Taplett reported Wolmi Do was secure. General MacArthur replied, "The Navy and Marine Corps have never shone more brightly than this morning." The 3d Battalion then consolidated its gains, interned 136 prisoners, and made ready to take Lighthouse Point. A small combined-arms task force led by 2d Lt. John D. Counselman of Company G accomplished this last task at 1115. All objectives on Wolmi Do had been seized by noon, with no Marines killed and only seventeen wounded. The 3d Battalion then had to wait all alone until the rising evening tide brought the rest of the Marines ashore.

Not long after Wolmi Do fell, the ships carrying the rest of the regiment sailed into the transport area off Red Beach. Navy and Marine aircraft and naval gunfire pounded Inchon throughout the day. In midafternoon, the assault waves climbed into the bobbing LCVPs and were pelted by stinging rain as the open boats circled, awaiting the move to the line of departure scheduled for 1700. Newton's 1/5 and Roise's 2/5 were going in with columns abreast. Captain Stevens's Company A and Captain Jaskilka's Company E were in the fore of their respective battalion formations. The dominant terrain feature ashore was Observatory Hill south of Causeway Road. The intermediate objectives were Cemetery Hill near the beach, a flour mill where the causeway met the mainland, and a brewery at the base of Observatory Hill.

Eight landing craft gunned forward across the line of departure at 1724 under covering fire from eight- and five-inch naval guns as well as Marine mortars, machine guns, tanks, and even an enemy 76mm gun captured on Wolmi Do. Marine Corsairs and navy Skyraiders roared low over the beach and peppered the objective with bombs and gunfire as the LCVPs approached the sea wall. Fortuitously, smoke from the burning city billowed over the harbor to form an unplanned screen that providentially concealed the landing force.

The first boats bumped into the dominating sea wall just after 1730 and the Marines inside scrambled up the scaling ladders onto the rocky shore. Most enemy resistance came from the left, where the 1st and 3d Platoons of Company A became mixed. First Lieutenant Baldomero Lopez, a former navy enlisted man and postwar Naval Academy graduate who voluntarily gave up advance schooling to join Company A at the last minute, scaled the sea wall and led his men forward in the face of this fire. Just as he primed a grenade, Lopez was struck in shoulder and dropped the deadly missile. The brave young officer quickly covered the live grenade with his body to shield the other members of his platoon. Lieutenant Lopez thus became the first Latino Marine awarded a posthumous Medal of Honor. Company A lost a total of eight dead and twenty-eight wounded taking Cemetery Hill.

Captain Jaskilka's Company E landed on the right flank and moved parallel to the beach to take the flour mill and the British consulate against only light opposition. The 2d Battalion held all its intermediate objectives by 1845. However, the push to take the final objective was temporarily delayed by an unplanned naval gunfire barrage that engulfed the top of Observatory Hill. Company C was already there and was in the beaten zone, but Lieutenant Pederson was unable to signal this due to defective star cluster flares. Unaware of Pederson's plight, Lieutenant

Colonel Newton ordered Capt. Ike Fenton to take Company B up the hill. Fenton's men encountered brief resistance along the way before they made contact with Company A and reported the true situation.

In the 2d Battalion zone to the south, Hawg Jowl Smith's Company D came under unexpectedly heavy fire and was temporarily pinned down until the enemy position was overrun by a flanking attack just as darkness closed in. Captain Peters's Company F searched the city west of Observatory Hill without encountering any enemy.

Lieutenant Colonel Murray came ashore and opened the regimental command post at the flour mill at about 1830. The 5th Marines occupied all three thousand yards of the O-A Line before dark. The 1st Battalion stretched from Cemetery Hill to Observatory Hill, the 2d Battalion's lines wrapped around Observatory Hill south through an urban maze to the tidal basin sea wall, and the 3d Battalion crossed the causeway at about 2000 and became the regimental reserve. The night of 15–16 September was a quiet one except for one incident that cost two Marines their lives when they wandered into an enemy field of fire. It had been a very good day, and General MacArthur's prediction of success had been accurate beyond even the most optimistic expectations.

Lieutenant Colonel Roise's 2d Battalion led the 5th Marines's attack to seize the O-2 Line and seal off the Inchon peninsula the next morning. Company E moved out with Companies F and D in trail against no opposition. The 1st and 3d Battalions followed close behind as the column snaked through the eerily quiet town on the way to Ascom City about seventy-five hundred yards down the road. The first objectives, two hills north of the Inchon-Seoul road, fell without opposition. The 2d Battalion made contact with the 1st Marines at Hill 117, then pushed on through Sogam-ni to the O-3 Line. The 2d Battalion continued to move toward Kansong-ni along the highway, but the 3d Battalion veered north to seize the high ground west of Ascom City that formed the northern edge of the FBHL. The 2d Battalion encountered only sporadic resistance, although its supporting tanks knocked out three T-34 tanks en route to Ascom City. Roise's 2/5 Marines dug in on the commanding ground about three thousand yards short of the FBHL. The 3d Battalion took its objective in the late afternoon. In doing so it suffered no casualties and garnered a dozen enemy prisoners.

The NKPA finally mounted a counterattack at dawn on 17 September. Six tanks and a supporting company of infantry from the NKPA 18th

Division sortied out of Seoul headed for Ascom City. This force blundered into a Marine ambush and then tried to run a gauntlet formed by Company D. The enemy first became aware of the Marines's presence when they came under fire from a reinforced platoon outpost on a hill abutting the road. Marine small arms cut down the infantry, and Cpl. Okey J. Douglas knocked out one tank and damaged a second with his "obsolete" 2.36-inch rocket launcher. The remaining tanks raced forward until they were taken under fire by the rest of Company D, tanks, recoilless rifles, and the 1st Marines. All five T-34s were destroyed and more than two hundred NKPA soldiers were killed at the cost of one Marine wounded. General MacArthur soon visited the battle site to personally congratulate the Marines on their stunning victory. Not long after MacArthur left, seven NKPA were discovered hiding inside the culvert on which the general's jeep had been parked.

The regiment's 17 September attack was delayed by this abortive counterattack and it was 0930 before the advance resumed. This movement once again split the 5th Marines. The 2d Battalion headed north through Ascom City for Kimpo airfield, the 1st Battalion continued due east protecting the regimental right by maintaining contact with the 1st Marines, and the 3d Battalion, in regimental reserve, backed up the 3d KMC Battalion on the left. The move through Ascom City was nerve wracking because the shantytown was a veritable warren of bypassed NKPA stragglers and deserters who occasionally offered spirited but disorganized resistance. The 2d Battalion did not reach Kimpo until dusk and was unable to take the entire airdrome before dark. Rather than conduct a risky night attack, Lieutenant Colonel Roise ordered Companies D, E, and F to button up in three separate perimeters that collectively covered the southern half of the main airfield. The 1st Battalion encountered only fleeting resistance throughout the day as it kept pace with Chesty Puller's 1st Marines and seized commanding terrain south of Kimpo airfield. The 3d Battalion assisted the KMCs' clearing operations in the western section of Ascom City and was occupying a vital road junction when night fell.

Most NKPA fled across the Han River in panic when they learned of the American advance. Despite the almost total collapse of organized resistance, some North Korean diehards managed to launch a series of counterattacks in the predawn hours on the eighteenth. A company-sized Communist force attacked a reinforced platoon from Company E at a blocking position north of Soryu-li at about 0300. It took three assaults and tank support to dislodge the Americans, who then made their way back to Marine lines at about 0500. Farther south, Company F repelled a five-man NKPA sapper team intent on blowing up a vital overpass. A second probe was beaten back at about the same time Company E's outpost was being overrun. The final attack on Company F was ruined before it began when the 1st Battalion's Lieutenant Colonel Newton directed fire from supporting arms onto the enemy assembly area. Second Lieutenant James E. Harrell's Company F platoon and Marine engineers defending the overpass easily turned the few remaining NKPA back. Elements of Companies E, F, and C pursued the fleeing enemy and combed the battleground for stragglers in the early morning daylight. All of Kimpo was in Marine hands by 1000. The last action occurred when Company D took Hill 131 on the banks of the Han River unopposed at 1145. The Marines lost four killed and nineteen wounded while capturing ten prisoners and inflicting well more than a hundred casualties on the enemy. After the successful seizure of Kimpo, the first two phases of Operation Chromite were complete. Moreover, the NKPA had been routed with only light Marine casualties.

Two old hands with strong ties to the regiment, Lt. Gen. Lem Shepherd and Col. Brute Krulak, hopped off an HO3S-1 helicopter, the first U.S. aircraft to land at Kimpo, and congratulated the Marines on a job well done.

Despite being prodded by his Corps commander to speed the advance by launching a straight-ahead attack, General Smith wisely decided to take Seoul using a double envelopment with the 5th Marines as the northern pincer and the 1st Marines as the southern one. Liberation of the city itself would be left to the Koreans. General Smith told Lieutenant Colonel Murray to cross the Han River at Haengju, seize Hill 125, and attack southeast along the highway leading to Seoul to secure the heights that dominated that city's northwestern approaches. Murray issued his orders on the night of 18 September. The 1st Battalion was to advance directly east to take Hills 80 and 85, which dominated Yongdung-po, a suburb of Seoul on the far side of the Kalchon River. From there, Lieutenant Colonel Newton's Marines could support the 1st Marines attack by fire and simultaneously act as the regimental reserve. The bulk of the 5th Marines would cross the Han River farther north.

Lieutenant Colonel Newton realized that to take Hills 80 and 85 his 1st Battalion would first have to seize the heights of Hill 118, the ridge upon which these twin gateways to Yongdung-po were located. He opted to use Lieutenant Pederson's Company C to maneuver on the north and

Captain Fenton's Company B on the south. Captain Stevens's Company A would remain in place and support these attacks with fire. Things did not, however, go exactly according to plan. Company C came under heavy mortar fire before it could jump off, and Pederson reported an enemy battalion was moving toward Kimpo airfield. Company C immediately took the attackers under fire, as did supporting arms. Marine artillery and close air support was so effective that the attack was crushed before it got started. Company B was able to use this covering fire to surge to the top of Hill 118 without suffering a single casualty. Company C suffered two killed and six wounded in its action, but the NKPA lost an estimated four hundred men. While Company B consolidated, Captain Fenton called for air strikes to clear Hill 80 and directed artillery fire on retreating enemy trying to cross the Yongdung-po bridge. Company C took Hill 80 at 1500 and Hill 85 at 1650, and then dug in on the reverse slopes, where the Marines were shielded from Communist direct fires coming out of Yongdung-po.

The 2d and 3d Battalions encountered no opposition as they moved to jump-off positions at Haengju. Unsure of the enemy situation on the far side of the Han River, Lieutenant Colonel Murray decided to feel his way across by sending a small reconnaissance team over first. The rest of Captain Houghton's Reconnaissance Company would scurry across the river under cover of darkness in LVTs to seize Hills 95, 125, and 51 and hold them until the main attack was launched at 0400 on the twentieth. The 3d Battalion would lead the assault, followed by the 2d Battalion two hours later. The 1st Battalion would move out of reserve and cross on order, and the 3d KMC Battalion would protect the left flank as tanks and vehicles ferried across the Han River on fifty-ton floating bridge sections later in the day.

The plan was to feel out the enemy defenses and if, as expected, they were not strongly manned, use the division reconnaissance company to hold dominating Hill 125 while the rest of the regiment crossed the river in amphibian tractors. A dozen recon Marines swam across the Han unobserved at about 2040. They quickly overpowered two North Korean sentries, but found no evidence of other enemy activity in the area. Things began to change when Captain Houghton called back and ordered the rest of his company across the river. The noisy LVT engines alerted enemy gunners atop Hill 125, who quickly zeroed in on the crossing area. Captain Houghton was wounded by this fire and had to be evacuated. To make matters worse, four LVTs became mired in sticky mud.

Only two were extracted before dawn. Thus, the first try to cross the Han River was unsuccessful. As the first rays of daylight cracked over the horizon, there was no choice but to pull the lightly armed reconnaissance party back.

Lieutenant Colonel Murray quickly formulated a new plan. This time he approached the river crossing as he would an amphibious operation, albeit a small one. The 3d Battalion would make a daylight crossing of the Han covered by a tightly controlled supporting arms preparation beginning at 0630. The rest of the regiment would then ferry across, gradually expanding the beachhead as each successive assault wave reached the far shore.

Captain McMullen's Company I debarked under covering fire from its amphibian tractors at 0650 despite heavy enemy fire. It was a tough fight for Hill 125. Captain McMullen suffered his sixth combat wound since Guadalcanal but remained in action and led what X Corps commander Ned Almond called "one of the finest small unit actions I have ever witnessed." Companies H and G soon followed across the river and proceeded to their assigned objectives. Luckily, Hills 95 and 51 were far less well defended than Hill 125. The 3d Battalion suffered forty-three casualties, mostly in Company I, but inflicted more than two hundred NKPA casualties. With the bridgehead secure, the 2d Battalion began crossing the Han at 1000.

The rest of the day's operations went as planned. Lieutenant Colonel Roise's 2d Battalion took the high ground dominating the highway and railroad tracks leading to Seoul. General MacArthur was on hand to personally congratulate Lieutenant Colonel Murray for a job well done that afternoon. With the 5th Marines safely across the Han before nightfall, Murray moved his command post to the town of Sojong only about four miles from the Korean capital. The 5th Marines advance continued the next day and by the evening of the twenty-first the regiment occupied high ground near Sachon Creek with the 1st Battalion on Hill 68 in the south, the KMC battalion on Hill 104 in the center, the 3d Battalion in the north, and the 2d Battalion in reserve. At that point, what had thus far been an almost festive advance from the Han reached the NKPA main line of resistance. The battle situation was about to change, and it would take the 5th Marines a full week of desperate fighting to cover the last four miles to Seoul.

Three hills on the far side of Sachon Creek, each labeled "105" on the maps, blocked the way to Seoul. These ominous triplets were defended by the well-prepared NKPA 25th Brigade, which also occupied an undulating ridgeline that branched out from Hill 296 (alternately called An-san Heights). Lieutenant Colonel Murray hoped to use the quick seizure of Hill 296 as a pivot upon which the regiment's attack toward Seoul could hinge. The plan of attack for 22 September called for Lieutenant Colonel Newton's 1/5 to seize Hill 105 South; the KMC battalion would press forward to take Hills 56, 88, and 105 Center; and Lieutenant Colonel Taplett's 3/5 was to cross the creek, clear Hill 296, and then take Hill 105 North. Of course, the NKPA commander had other plans—and this time he had the firepower to back them up.

The battle commenced at 0700 on the twenty-second when Company H moved out to take Hill 296. The attack went well despite enfilading fire from Hill 338 north of the highway. Company H was able to take the crest, repel a counterattack, and dig in for protection from Communist harassing fires. Company I had an all-day fight to take and hold the town of Nokpon-ni on the far left flank. The 1st Battalion encountered heavy fire as it assaulted Hill 105 South. Captain Stevens led Company A forward, but was soon pinned down. Lieutenant Pederson then swung Company C to the right (south) but was soon stopped by enemy machine guns. Finally, Ike Fenton's Company B was able to carry the hill from the far south after a well-placed artillery preparation. However, holding the hill turned out to be a very costly chore because that exposed position was under constant enemy mortar and artillery fire. The Korean Marines in the center were unable to advance and had to pull back. Marine aircraft then pounded the center of the ridge with bombs and napalm. The regimental command post took a direct hit that day. Lieutenant Colonel Murray was wounded and stayed on, but the regimental executive officer, Lt. Col. Lawrence C. Hays Jr., had to be evacuated. When night fell, the 5th Marines's perimeter formed a large U with the 1st and 3d Battalions forward on both flanks and the KMC battalion back where it had started the attack twelve hours earlier.

The regiment renewed the attack to take the central ridge at 0700 on the twenty-third. The U.S. Marines on each flank supported the Korean Marines by fire as the latter attempted once again to seize Hill 56. Enemy artillery, mortar, and machine-gun fire punished the attackers as they pushed forward. Unfortunately, the Korean Marines were hitting the strongest point in the NKPA line. When they failed to carry the hill, Murray decided to commit Roise's 2d Battalion. Roise's Marines passed through the KMC line at about 1500 with Lieutenant Smith's Company

D and Captain Peters's Company F leading the assault. Company F seized a razorback ridge that formed the southern spur of Hill 56 while Company D moved ahead unobserved along a sunken road. However, the supporting tanks became bogged down in the muck and could only support the Marine attack with intermittent fire from their main guns. Communications problems kept Company F's mortars silent. Company D at first encountered little resistance as it emerged from its covered approach and advanced north along the ridge to link up with the 3d Battalion. This maneuver was easily drawn on a sketch map, but it was much harder to do in reality. The lead platoon was virtually wiped out, and Lieutenant Smith was wounded as he led the survivors to safety. Smith wisely called off the attack and ordered Company D into a tight all-round defense.

The situation on the night of 23 September had the 1st Battalion pinned down on Hill 105 South with such ferocity it had been unable to conduct daylight resupply. According to Capt. Ike Fenton, "Their mortar fire was very accurate . . . they could really drop it right into your lap [my men] were hit in their foxholes [because] there was no way to keep the enemy from delivering plunging fire right on top of us." At the same time, the 3d Battalion was parrying repeated NKPA thrusts from the northwest. The 2d Battalion had two companies holding isolated perimeters by relying on the 11th Marines's artillery fires to keep the enemy at bay. This was the toughest fighting in Korea since the regiment had left the Pusan Perimeter.

Meanwhile, back at headquarters, Generals Smith and Almond were disagreeing about the best way to finish the capture of Seoul. Almond wanted to launch a freewheeling flank attack that left the 5th Marines holding the bag northwest of the city. Smith, on the other hand, felt it was imperative that the 1st Marine Division not be fragmented. He wanted it to remain a cohesive tactical entity and advance as a single unit. To this end, O. P. Smith argued for more time until Almond relented and finally allowed him one more day to take the ridge. This tactical disagreement, indeed this very issue, was only one of many arguments the two generals had, and they became increasingly argumentative over the next few months. Luckily, nothing like the infamous clash involving Marine Maj. Gen. Holland M. Smith and the army's Maj. Gen. Ralph Smith during World War II occurred in Korea to poison army-Marine relations.

On the morning of 24 September, Lieutenant Colonel Roise faced a difficult row to hoe. His two companies on the ridge had been badly battered and neither mustered even half its original strength. He therefore decided to send Captain Jaskilka's relatively untouched Company E straight ahead to take Hill 105 North and use the rest of the 2d Battalion to clear Hill 56. The arrival of the 1st Marines allowed Lieutenant Colonel Murray to shift Newton's 1st Battalion north so Taplett's entire 3d Battalion could attack south along the An-san Heights. It was hoped this Marine vise could squeeze out the remaining NKPA and break the enemy's main line of resistance.

The 11th Marines pounded the ridge and suspected NKPA positions with intense artillery support, then checked fire at first light to let Marine Corsairs plaster the hills with bombs. Lieutenant Smith's Company D advanced into the wooded area that had previously been the center of enemy resistance. These Marines stumbled into a haze-shrouded hornet's nest. By midmorning, each of Smith's platoons had been whittled down to squad size and his mortars had fired their last 60mm round. The enemy fire became more effective as the morning fog lifted, so Smith had no choice but to round up his last forty-four men for a final try to clear the ridge. Aircraft strafed and bombed the enemy and then made a pair of dry runs that signaled it was time for the ground attack. The last remnants of Company D rose from their foxholes and made a World War I–style bayonet charge. It worked. The NKPA fled, leaving more than fifteen hundred dead behind. Unfortunately, Hawg Jowl Smith was killed leading the final assault. This bloody battleground was thereafter dubbed "Smith's Ridge" in his honor. First Lieutenant George C. McNaughton, who had been wounded in earlier fighting but was still on the job, became the acting company commander. Company D could muster only twenty-six effectives when it began digging in at 1300. An enemy counterattack was smashed by supporting arms and well-placed rifle and machine-gun fire before it could get under way or the precarious Marine grip on Hill 56 might have been lost.

Captain Peters's Company F, reduced to two jury-rigged assault platoons and an ad hoc support force, cleared the lower ridge and forced the NKPA to move back to Hills 72 and 105 Center. Company E encountered numerous bypassed enemy troops on Hill 56 and was held up while the Marines cleaned them out. Thus delayed, Captain Jaskilka's men were unable to take Hill 72 before dark, so they dug in for the night. Lieutenant Colonel Roise was one of the Marines wounded that day, the victim of one of the incessant NKPA 120mm rounds that ranged the 2d Battalion's command post. By nightfall, the 1st and 3d Battalions were both on Hill 296, but 24 September had been a very difficult day for the 2d Battalion.

The 5th Marines entered the final stage of the drive for Seoul when Lieutenant Colonel Murray received orders from General Smith later that night. The regiment, with the division reconnaissance company and the 1st KMC Battalion attached, was to seize, clear, and defend a one-and-one-half-mile-wide zone in the northwest portion of the city. The final objective, the high ground overlooking the Seoul-Uijongbu road, was six miles from the line of departure. This area included a very prestigious target: Duksoo Palace, the seat of South Korea's government. Murray opted to use a rather complex plan. The 2d and 3d Battalions would conduct the initial assault. The 2d Battalion's objective was Hill 105 North and the 3d Battalion was to clear the An-san Heights. The 1st Battalion would remain on the left flank to support these attacks by fire. The 3d Battalion would pinch out the 2d Battalion when both units had secured their objectives. Roise's battalion would then become the regimental reserve and the 1st Battalion would attack Hill 338. The Korean Marines were to clear bypassed areas and handle prisoners of war.

Air strikes and artillery fires preceded the attacks. Company E began 2/5's main attack when it jumped off at 0700. Badly battered Company D, now commanded by 1st Lt. Karle Seydel, moved in echelon on the left flank, and Company F was in reserve. A tank platoon and fires from Company F and the 3d Battalion supported Captain Jaskilka's Company E men as they moved toward the far ridgeline. Company E was temporarily pinned down by accurate fire from Hill 72. This objective was finally taken at 1335, but the assault platoon suffered heavy casualties. Company D took Hill 88 at about the same time. Finally, Company E seized Hill 105 North at 1545 after encountering only moderate resistance. The worst fighting of the day occurred in the 3/5 zone, where Companies G and H made slow but steady progress moving down the two spurs leading from Hill 296 to Hill 105 North. Company H was particularly hard hit, so Company I passed through at about 1700. Not long thereafter, the NKPA mounted a company-sized counterattack. Close-quarters fighting raged into the night with the enemy suffering about half their number killed before withdrawing. The 1st Battalion manned blocking positions in the north.

That evening, General Smith received word from X Corps that the enemy was in full retreat and that he should launch a night attack to keep the pressure on. Stunned by such an ill-advised order, Smith called X

Corps to explain that the NKPA were not on the run in the 1st Marine Division sector but were defending in force and the proposed advance was irresponsible folly. This discussion bore no fruit, and O. P. Smith was bluntly told to carry out his orders. The X Corps pronouncement that the NKPA was on the run had an ironic turn with regard to the 5th Marines. Colonel Murray was told of the X Corps attack order at about 2215, not long after Company I became embroiled in its wild melee to repel the NKPA. Regimental executive officer Lt. Col. Joseph L. Stewart sarcastically remarked to Colonel Murray, "I'm afraid we'll have to delay our pursuit of the 'fleeing enemy' until we see if Tap[lett] can beat off this counterattack." The X Corps attack was scheduled to begin at 0145 on 26 September, but it had to be canceled due to events in the 1st Marines's zone of action. There can be little doubt this auspicious postponement saved many Marine lives.

The 3d Battalion carried the regiment's load on the twenty-sixth. Companies I and G once again pushed down the slopes of the An-san Heights. It was tough going for both units. Private First Class Eugene A. Obregon of 1st Lt. Charles D. Mize's Company G rushed across open ground to rescue a wounded man, dragged him to safety, treated his wounds, and then shielded him from an incoming grenade. Obregon suffered fatal wounds in the process and was later awarded the Medal of Honor. The casualty toll was high: virtually every small-unit leader in Company I became a casualty. Captain McMullen was evacuated after suffering his seventh wound, and Lieutenant Counselman and Sgt. Jack Macy were each hit again. It marked the fifth wound for each since landing at Pusan just fifty-three days before.

By nightfall an enemy counterattack had been foiled, and the 3d Battalion resumed its clearing operations on the lower slopes of Hill 296 at 0645 on the twenty-seventh. Within an hour the last NKPA had been eliminated, and all of the An-san Heights was safely in Marine hands. At long last, the high ground west of Seoul had been conquered in the stiffest fighting since the Pusan Perimeter.

Lieutenant Colonel Taplett's men made contact with the 1st Marines at about 0930 and wheeled north to seize a nearby school and the high ground overlooking Duksoo Palace about a half-mile farther on. The 3d Battalion moved ahead through the streets of Seoul guided by an enemy flag that was clearly visible whipping in the wind. The way was eased after Communist resistance melted away when a much-feared flame tank led 3/5 up Kwangwhamun Boulevard. Company G soon burst through the palace gates and into the Court of Lions, where GySgt. Harold Beaver tore down the enemy flag and replaced it with the U.S. national colors at 1508.

The 1st Battalion moved out behind the 3d Battalion and peeled off to take Hill 338 on the left. Company A encountered only moderate resistance as it took that hill and an intermediate objective. The 3d Platoon, led by TSgt. George W. Bolkow, was at the summit of Hill 338 by 1850. With this action, the regiment had secured its final objective in the battle for Seoul.

The next day was one of rest for the tired 5th Marines. The regiment prepared defensive positions and ran patrols, but encountered virtually no resistance. General Smith's consolidation plan called for all three regiments to form a protective fan with the 5th Marines northwest of Seoul, the newly arrived 7th Marines to the north, and the 1st Marines to the northeast. At the divisional commanders' meeting on the twenty-eighth, Lieutenant Colonel Murray was ordered to occupy blocking positions, conduct a battalion reconnaissance in force to the town of Suyuhyon in the north, and have a company-sized reaction force standing by. The 5th Marines was reinforced by the 1st Battalion, 11th Marines; Company A, 1st Tank Battalion; Company A, 1st Engineer Battalion; a truck detachment from the 1st Motor Transport Battalion; and a detachment from the army's 50th Antiaircraft Artillery Battalion for the operation.

The regiment had two more meeting engagements with the enemy before being relieved at Seoul. At about 0600 on 1 October, the 3d Battalion, reinforced by Company C from the 1st Battalion, moved out toward Suyuhyon. The trip was slow but uneventful, and the column halted at dark just short of its objective. Earlier in the day, at about 1030, a 2d Battalion patrol discovered an enemy force of about 150 men and called for air strikes. Close air support and mortar fire killed about thirty of the enemy, and the rest took to their heels. In the north, Taplett's reconnaissance force came under enemy attack at about 0230 on the second. Sixty-seven NKPA soldiers were killed in this predawn battle, and Suyuhyon was occupied without incident later in the day. This skirmish was the regiment's last battle action of the Inchon-Seoul campaign. The regiment was ordered to return to a staging area at Inchon on 5 October, and on the sixth General Smith solemnly performed his last official act of the Inchon-Seoul campaign when he laid a wreath on the grave of Cpl. Richard C. Matheny, a squad leader in the 5th Marines who had earned the Bronze Star, Silver Star, and Navy Cross during the drive inland.

The Frozen Chosin

The Inchon landing and the campaign to liberate Seoul were successes of the first magnitude. MacArthur's brilliant counterstroke was an achievement practically unparalleled in the annals of military history. Never before had a U.S. military force gone from the brink of defeat to the pinnacle of victory in so short a time. As the X Corps invested Seoul, the Eighth Army broke out of the Pusan Perimeter and the rout of the NKPA was soon under way. At about the same time Gunnery Sergeant Beaver was running up the U.S. colors at Duksoo Palace, the Joint Chiefs of Staff in Washington, D.C., authorized General MacArthur to pursue the NKPA north of the 38th Parallel. This formidable decision to ignore the boundary delineating North and South Korea was reached only after lengthy debate between political and military authorities, but the bottom line was that the Korean War irrevocably entered a new phase once that border was crossed.

With the NKPA crumbling, and having been given permission to enter North Korea, General MacArthur formulated a new campaign plan. He decided to split his command: the Eighth Army would continue land operations by driving north up the western half of the peninsula while X Corps conducted amphibious operation along the east coast. His scheme of maneuver called for Eighth Army to take Pyongyang, the capital of the Democratic People's Republic of Korea. Simultaneously, X Corps would trap fleeing elements of the NKPA in the east. To do this, X Corps would make an amphibious landing at Wonsan on Korea's northeast coast and sweep across the peninsula toward Pyongyang. Supposedly, American forces were restricted from moving too close to the Yalu River by the Joint Chiefs because they feared Red China might feel threatened and intervene in Korea. Unfortunately, MacArthur rashly dismissed this warning.

The 1st Marine Division remained part of X Corps for the upcoming offensive. General Smith was going to use the 1st and 7th Marines in the assault with the tired (after almost three months in combat without relief) 5th Marines in reserve. Lieutenant Colonel Murray led the regiment back over the Han River to Inchon on 5 October. There, it absorbed replacements and reorganized as an amphibious landing team for the new operation. The 5th Marines embarked on board its assigned ships—the 1st Battalion and regimental headquarters on the *Bayfield*, the 2d Battalion on the *George Clymer*, and the 3d Battalion on the *Bexar*—from 8–11

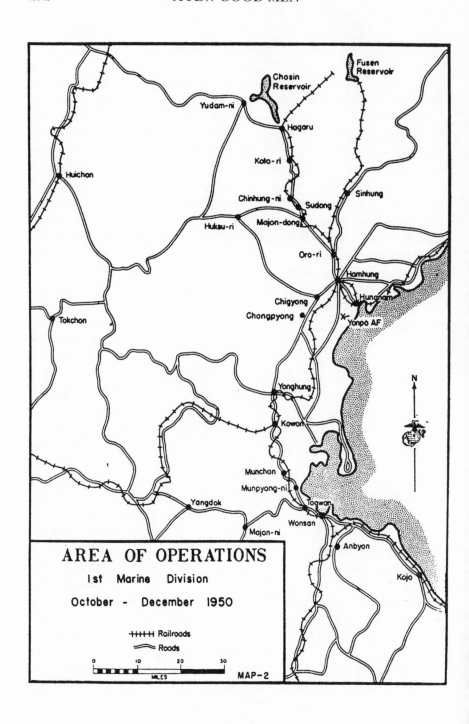

AREA OF OPERATIONS

1st Marine Division

October - December 1950

+++++ Railroads

Roads

0   10   20   30

MILES

MAP-2

October. The *George Clymer* and the *Bexar* left Inchon Harbor on the night of the sixteenth, and the *Bayfield* sailed the next morning.

The Eighth Army began its northward push as the Marines were embarking at Inchon. The ROK Army started its offensive in the east on 11 October and reached the Hamhung-Hungnam-Yonpo area six days later. The unexpectedly easy advance by UNC forces on all fronts led General MacArthur to amend his plan. Instead of an assault landing followed by a cross-country drive to Pyongyang, X Corps would make an administrative landing at Wonsan and push north into eastern Korea. Unfortunately, the Wonsan landing was delayed for almost two weeks by the presence of a large number of underwater mines. While the waters near Wonsan were being painstakingly swept, Task Force 90 sailed up and down the coast, changing course about every twelve hours. This monotonous steaming was promptly dubbed "Operation Yo-Yo."

The 5th Marines's advance party finally landed on 25 October. Cargo was unloaded first and the troops remained aboard ship overnight before moving to an assembly area about three miles northwest of Wonsan, where Lieutenant Colonel Murray established his command post on the twenty-sixth. The veterans were not disappointed they did not have to make an amphibious assault, but they were chagrined to find that Bob Hope's USO troupe and the 1st Marine Air Wing (MAW) had beaten them to Wonsan.

General Smith issued his operations order on the twenty-eighth. The 1st Marine Division would support the ROK Army movement to the Manchurian border. The 7th Marines was to lead the advance north toward Changjin above the Chosin Reservoir. The 5th Marines, less the 1st Battalion, was to move in trail of the 7th Marines and relieve I ROK Corps elements in the vicinity of the Fusen Reservoir, then establish roadblocks and patrols to prevent enemy movement within the area. Specifically, the 5th Marines, reinforced by the 1st KMC Battalion, was assigned security duties at Munchon and Yonghung, located about fifteen and thirty miles from Wonsan respectively. Lieutenant Colonel Newton's 1st Battalion was ordered to be ready to stand up BLT 1/5 on order to conduct an amphibious landing at Chongjin on the far northeast coast.

From 28–31 October the 5th Marines—except for the 2d Battalion, which was under the operational control of the 1st Marines as a Wonsan security force—made a motor march north from its assembly area to the assigned objectives. There was no contact with enemy forces during this move. The situation was so peaceful in the entire X Crops zone that General Almond moved his timetable ahead. He canceled the proposed landing at Chongjin, the 2d Battalion rejoined the regiment, and Lieutenant Colonel Murray was ordered to move north to Hamhung with all possible speed. The 1st Battalion remained under division control at Majondong, the 3d Battalion held the key road junction at Oro-ri, and the 2d Battalion was sent to relieve ROK units in the Sinhung Valley on 4 November.

Lieutenant Colonel Roise's mission was twofold. The 2d Battalion was to block the Sinhung corridor and explore overland routes between the Fusen and Chosin Reservoirs. Numerous patrols made no contact with enemy forces and discovered no suitable routes to either objective other than one already designated the main supply route. Major Merlin R. Olson, the 1st Battalion executive officer, led a reconnaissance in force that included Captain Stevens's A and 1st Lt. John R. Hancock's B Companies west toward Huksu-ri on 8 November. Along the way the Marines encountered an enemy force of unknown size and became involved in a running firefight that lasted until Major Olson was ordered to return to Oro-ri. That same day, Capt. Samuel S. Smith's Company D captured a soldier from the Chinese 126th Division, the first confirmed Chinese Communist Forces (CCF) prisoner of war taken by the 5th Marines.

The next day, Lieutenant Colonel Murray ordered Newton and Taplett to pull in their patrols and concentrate forces along the MSR prior to mounting out for Changjin and the Chosin Reservoir. The 1st Battalion was at Majon-dong and the 3d Battalion occupied Chinhung-ni. There was a minor delay when the entire 1st Battalion had to be used to extricate Capt. Jack R. Jones's Company C, which had become heavily engaged while on patrol. The 2d Battalion relieved the 7th Marines at Koto-ri just south of the Chosin Reservoir on the thirteenth. Although contact was light, twelve NKPA and one Chinese People's Volunteer had surrendered to the 2d Battalion by the fourteenth. While things were generally quiet in the X Corps zone, the same was not true for the Eighth Army, which was being probed by newly arrived CCF patrols prior to an all-out offensive that would catch the UNC off guard.

There were several command changes within the 5th Marines. Lieutenant Colonel John W. Stevens II, the former 2d Battalion executive officer, took over the 1st Battalion on 17 November. Major Glen E. Martin replaced Stevens as executive officer, and Maj. James W. Bateman replaced Martin as 2d Battalion's Weapons Company commander. Captain

Harold B. Williamson took over Company H, Capt. James B. Heater became the commanding officer of Company A, Capt. Chester R. Hermanson took over Company G, and Maj. Harold W. Swain became the 3d Battalion Weapons Company commander.

Lieutenant Colonel Murray was ordered to push up the east side of the Chosin Reservoir—a narrow, thirteen-mile-long man-made lake on a north-south axis serviced by only one overland road that ran seventy-eight miles from the port of Hungnam through Hamhung, Oro-ri, Majon-dong, Sudong, Chinhung-ni, the Funchilin Pass, Koto-ri, and Hagaru-ri. Murray's final objective was the town of Kyomul-li located about five miles past the reservoir's northern tip. His orders were to pass at least one battalion through Hagaru-ri to seize Sinhung-ni about seven miles north, then be prepared to continue the advance on order after the rest of the regiment was in place east of Chosin.

Unwritten, but well understood by all Marine commanders, was the dictum to move deliberately and not to race for the Yalu as X Corps headquarters was urging. Cautious O. P. Smith was well aware that the Chosin Reservoir was a potential trap. He carefully hoarded and prudently stashed supplies as his division moved north. There were no alternate supply routes, so if the main route was cut, the Marines would have to fight their way free without outside support. Smith's combat wise veterans refused to be lulled into a false euphoria just because of a recent lack of resistance. To each man they felt it was too quiet out there, and all were sure something sinister was afoot. Of further concern was the changing weather. The late fall chill was giving way to bitter cold as the Marines moved ever higher into the rugged, snow-topped mountains where Siberian winds whipped across the Taebek Plateau. The temperature fell well below freezing at night and soon would hit only single digit highs during the days as well.

The 3d Battalion, the northernmost 5th Marines unit, led the way to the Chosin. Lieutenant Colonel Taplett advanced to Sinhung-ni, where it dug in four miles north of Pungnyuri-gang inlet. The 3d Battalion ate Thanksgiving dinner in the field at this position on 23 November. Two days later, the entire regiment had assembled on the east side of the reservoir and was ready to move north. The farthest penetration was by a 3/5 motorized patrol accompanied by two tanks that reached the north end of the reservoir on the twenty-fifth. This reinforced platoon captured a 75mm recoilless rifle, killed five Chinese, and took one prisoner.

The regiment was poised to attack in strength when Lieutenant Colonel Murray was informed that General Almond had received new marching orders changing the X Corps direction of advance from north to west. The 1st Marine Division, which was originally supposed to move northwest to Changjin above the Chosin Reservoir, was now ordered to link up with the Eighth Army in central Korea instead. This sudden change required the 5th Marines to pull back to Hagaru-ri and advance through Yudam-ni to Mupyong-ni about forty miles farther west. The Marines east of Chosin were relieved by elements of the army's 7th Infantry Division on 25 and 26 November. This organization, dubbed Task Force Faith, was later cut off and annihilated by vastly superior CCF forces.

Lieutenant Colonel Murray was ordered to pass the 5th Marines through the 7th Marines in order to lead the 1st Marine Division advance. The 2d Battalion moved west out of Yudam-ni at 0800 on the twenty-seventh. Hal Roise's men gained about fifteen hundred yards against scattered opposition and then assumed fishhook-shaped defensive positions before nightfall. Bob Taplett's 3d Battalion moved to Yudam-ni from Hagaru-ri that afternoon and occupied a flat area in the lee of North Ridge. Lieutenant Colonel Jack Stevens's 1st Battalion entered the valley east of Yudam-ni in the late afternoon and set in just after dark. Regimental headquarters and some support units were stuck at Hagaru-ri because there were not enough trucks to transport the entire regiment at one time. That night, the Marines endured the second abrupt temperature drop in two days. This one brought the mercury to twenty degrees below zero. Such bitter cold mercilessly froze men, machines, and weapons and ruthlessly exposed inadequacies in Marine cold-weather gear.

As the miserable Marines huddled for warmth that dark night, equally miserable elements of the Chinese 9th Army Group, consisting of nine CCF divisions sent south specifically to destroy the 1st Marine Division, silently crept into positions on the ridges around Yudam-ni. The enemy probed a Company D roadblock protecting the MSR at about 2100. This action was followed by bugle calls, scattered shots, and grenades meant to expose Marine positions in the hills. After a mortar barrage walked its way across the ridge, the Chinese launched an all-out assault at 2125. This massive attack hit Companies E and F full force. The attackers breached Company F's lines at about 2215, but were eventually pushed back by timely employment of the battalion reserve and accurate 81mm mortar fire. This first attack was over by midnight, and numerous enemy soldiers lay dead after the CCF units pulled back. Another attack hit the 2d Battalion and adjoining units at about 0300. This time Captain Jaskilka's Company E wiped out several hundred attackers moving up a defile between Northwest Ridge on the left and Hill 1403 on the right known as Easy Alley. The only major setback of the night occurred when a CCF battalion pushed part of Company F off an exposed spur and two machine guns were lost in the predawn darkness. Of even greater concern to Lieutenant Colonel Roise, however, was the loss of neighboring Hill 1403, which meant the 2d Battalion was outflanked. He called for assistance, but there was no help available because the main force at Yudam-ni was also under attack.

Lieutenant Colonel Taplett's 3d Battalion had encountered some harassing sniper fire as it moved forward during the day, but this ineffective and scattered opposition was no real threat. The battalion command post was located inside a notch in North Ridge just north of Yudam-ni. Headquarters and Service (H&S) Company and Weapons Company protected the command compound. There appeared to be no one guarding the heights above, but Taplett had few men to spare. Unbeknownst to him, a rifle company from 2/7 was on top of the hill, but the rugged terrain masked its positions. The best he could do was send a Company I platoon up the hill to man a combat outpost while the "Wharrangs," a forty-man ROK police unit attached to the regiment, occupied a spur just above the 3d Battalion. Companies H and I protected either side of the MSR and Company G faced Southwest Ridge across the road. At about 2045, the outpost on North Ridge manned by Company I reported taking enemy fire. About thirty-five minutes later the first survivors from Hill 1403 entered Marine lines. At 0115 on 28 November, the 3d Battalion went on full alert. An hour after that, two CCF companies overran the Company I outpost, pushed back the outnumbered Wharrangs, and poured plunging fire on the 3d Battalion command post. Major John J. Canney, the battalion executive officer, was killed while he directed H&S Company's defense. Canney, a World War II dive-bomber pilot, was awarded a posthumous Navy Cross for his heroism that night. Company G sent a two-platoon counterattack force over to help out at about 0300. These Marines quickly retook the lost ground, rescued seven men from the overrun outpost, and by daylight were scaling the slopes of Hill 1282 when they were recalled. This swift and effective action saved the day for the 3d Battalion. Additionally, more survivors were able to use this fighting as cover to safely reach Marine lines.

Lieutenant Colonel Stevens's 1st Battalion was first alerted for action by the sounds of small-arms fire. Elements of Captain Heater's Company A were sent forward to reinforce Company E, 7th Marines, located on Hill 1282, a terrain feature that dominated North Ridge. Both units suffered heavy casualties while attempting to stem the Red tide that threatened to swamp Yudam-ni. Captain Jack Jones's Company C was next into the breach. He and his executive officer, 1st Lt. Loren R. Smith, led Charlie Company on a two-hour trek up Hill 1282. At 0430, Company C, assisted by splendid mortar fire, mounted an attack that cleared the crest of enemy in hand-to-hand combat. It was a tough fight. The Marines lost fifteen killed and sixty-seven wounded that night, but Yudam-ni was still in Marine hands when the sun finally peeked over the horizon. The arrival of Marine aircraft overhead ensured Yudam-ni was safe for at least one more day.

The next two days were devoted to defending Yudam-ni, consolidating and reorganizing units, and preparing to break out of the Chinese encirclement. Lieutenant Colonel Murray and the commanding officer of the 7th Marines, Col. Homer L. Litzenberg, held a dawn meeting on the twenty-eighth to decide what to do. They agreed to closely coordinate plans. To do this, Murray often worked out of the 7th Marines command post while Lt. Col. Joe Stewart, a former award-winning scholar and three-letter athlete at Auburn University who later became a general officer, ran the 5th Marines headquarters in Murray's absence. The regimental commanders made a momentous decision to switch from offense to defense on their own initiative. A planned advance was canceled at 0545, although higher headquarters did not give this decision a formal blessing for another ten hours, and units of the 5th and 7th Marines were told to dig in.

Company E mounted a counterattack at about 0600 on the twenty-eighth to retake the positions on Northwest Ridge lost during the night. This was done by 0800. Three hours later, Lieutenant Colonel Roise was told to move the 2d Battalion back to Southwest Ridge and join the Yudam-ni defensive perimeter. Lieutenant Colonel Stevens's 1st Battalion remained scattered. Elements of Company A and all of Company C were defending North Ridge along with the survivors of Company E, 7th Marines. Company B was in reserve at Yudam-ni. The old adage "every Marine is a rifleman" proved its value at Yudam-ni that day. Members of H&S Company, 1/5, moved more than a hundred wounded down the hill in the morning, then most volunteered to serve in provisional rifle platoons or go into the line as infantry replacements. Like-minded drivers, clerks, cooks, antitank gunners, and cannoneers from combat support units soon joined these volunteer riflemen. Company I of the 3d Battalion replaced Jack Jones's hodgepodge unit defending North Ridge at midday. Companies H and G remained in blocking positions on either side of the road at the northwest tip of the perimeter. That afternoon, elements of Company A and its volunteer riflemen were assigned to the Provisional Battalion, 7th Marines, a composite force intended as an emergency reserve that might lead the breakout, relieve a hard-pressed unit, or fill breaks in the line.

While the Marines and army units of X Corps were holding out in the east, the Eighth Army was being shattered in the west. Many outnumbered Eighth Army units broke under Chinese pressure, and it was obvious a major setback was in the making. General Almond consulted with General Smith on the thirtieth and then ordered the Marines to leave Yudam-ni. The corps commander authorized the Marines to abandon or destroy any equipment that might slow them down and suggested an aerial evacuation from Hagaru-ri. An annoyed General Smith icily replied that the Marines were coming out as a cohesive unit and would bring all of their wounded, dead, and serviceable equipment with them as they moved to Hungnam via Hagaru-ri, Koto-ri, and Chinhung-ni. Unspoken was the not-so-subtle message that the Marine march out of the Chosin trap would be a disciplined military movement and not a helter-skelter "bug out."

The Marines at Yudam-ni began to disengage on 1 December. Taplett's 3d Battalion was the vanguard of the long convoy. Roise's 2d Battalion and Stevens's 1st Battalion were assigned to the screening force. The plan was for the 2d Battalion to move down the road as the convoy rear guard as the 1st Battalion covered the east flank moving cross-country. The move to Hagaru-ri began in midafternoon. The difficult fourteen-mile journey took seventy-nine hours, and the last of the Yudam-ni Marines did not enter Hagaru-ri until the afternoon of the fourth. The main body was primarily composed of service and support units. Vehicle space was reserved for the dead and severely wounded, everyone else walked. The lead element, consisting of a tank and an engineer detachment, removed or destroyed many roadblocks along the way, flankers moved from hilltop to hilltop as the column snaked its way slowly through Toktong Pass, and the rear guard kept the trailing enemy beyond striking range. Navy and Marine close air support was a vital component during this subfreezing trek across Korea's barren mountains. Skyraiders and Corsairs scouted the flanks from the air and delayed the pursuing enemy with bombs and aerial cannon fire.

After the Marines had moved only about three-quarters of a mile down the road, the 3d Battalion came under heavy enemy fire. Captain Williamson and Capt. Harold G. Schrier, a former enlisted Raider who led the Marine patrol that raised the first flag at Iwo Jima, maneuvered Companies H and I to outflank the enemy, but the Chinese were not neutralized until well after dark. The Chinese recoiled, but later attacked Company I. As Schrier's Marines grudgingly gave ground, SSgt. William G. Windrich organized a small reaction force to cover the withdrawal. Seven of Windrich's dozen men were wounded, and he was hit in the head by grenade shards. Despite his wounds, Windrich returned to his platoon and gathered volunteers to rescue the wounded. He was hit again but ignored his wounds in the heat of battle until he eventually succumbed to loss of blood. Windrich was subsequently awarded a posthumous Medal of Honor. By the end of this fight, Company I could muster only twenty effectives, and Company H had only two understrength platoons left. There was no time to reorganize, so Companies G and H immediately moved out as flank guards while the Provisional Battalion, 7th Marines, led the convoy down the road toward Hagaru-ri.

The delaying force at Yudam-ni was hard-pressed to hold on, and indeed might not have, without excellent night bombing support from VMF(N)-542. The rear screen consisted of a three-battalion arc located just outside Yudam-ni. The 3d Battalion, 7th Marines, held a hilltop line on the right flank, 2/5 protected the road, and 1/5 was on the left near the south end of the reservoir. The plan was for these units to move back by echelon. They would displace under the cover of artillery concentrations, air strikes, and supporting infantry fires from overwatch positions. Of course, not all went according to plan. Captain Peters's Company F was forced off Hill 1542 early on the second, and two night counterattacks to retake that ground failed. At dawn, Corsair fighter-bombers blasted the stubborn Chinese defenders, and Company F was able to return to the top of the hill. The Marines then came under heavy machine-gun fire and had to fall back. By midmorning it was time to move out, so Lieutenant Colonel Roise prudently dropped plans for a fourth counterattack.

Back on the road, the column crawled forward at a snail's pace because 3/5 had to fight its way down the road. There was a very real sense of urgency because a beleaguered company was barely holding on to Fox Hill to keep the Toktong Pass open. Company G took Hill 1520 at noon, and Company H overran an enemy strong point on the afternoon of the second. Captain Hermanson was wounded in that action and Lieutenant Mize jumped at the chance to leave the S-3 shop to take over a rifle company once again. Unfortunately, when he arrived there were only thirty-four men available. He reorganized them into two elements—a single rifle platoon and a composite assault and machine-gun section.

What came next was one of the epic combat actions of all time. A blown bridge held up the column about a thousand yards short of Fox Hill. Six inches of snow fell that night, and the temperature hovered around minus twenty degrees as a 7th Marines relief force battled its way overland toward Fox Hill. The Chinese besiegers, surprised by the Marine flank attack, fled directly into 3/5's line of fire. Several hundred of them were gunned down at 1030. Thereafter, the 7th Marines took the point and 3/5 joined the 4th Battalion, 11th Marines, in the main body. The 1st and 2d Battalions echeloned their rifle-depleted companies for flank security, and the march to Hagaru-ri resumed before noon.

The tail end of the column ground to an unexpected halt in the early hours of 4 December. All three 5th Marines battalion commanders moved to the stall point, where they held an impromptu conference to decide what to do about eight howitzers whose prime movers had run out of fuel. While the stalled Marine cavalcade waited in the snow, the Chinese hurriedly erected a roadblock. A 105mm howitzer, a heavy machine-gun from 1/5, and some men from 3/5's H&S Company provided supporting fires while a platoon from Company E overran this obstacle. This action was the last fight before entering Hagaru-ri. The first step on the road to the sea had been taken, but the cost was high. The 3d Battalion's rifle companies were so reduced by battle and weather-related losses they could collectively muster only 194 men on 5 December. The 1st and 2d Battalions suffered only slightly fewer casualties.

The 5th Marines manned most of the division perimeter at Hagaru-ri. The 1st and 3d Battalions held the west side, and the 2d Battalion was dug in on the northeast in the shadow of East Hill. Luckily, Hagaru-ri was largely untouched during the next two days. The main tasks were to regroup, warm up, and evacuate the most seriously wounded by air. Navy,

Marine, and air force aircraft evacuated 4,312 wounded in five days. The regiment's chief surgeon, Lt. Comdr. Chester M. Lessendon, remained on the job despite suffering from painful frostbite in both feet. The battalion surgeons—Lts. (j.g.) John P. Luhr and Daniel M. O'Toole in 1/5, Henry Litvin and James E. Sparks in 2/5, John H. Moon and John E. Murphy in 3/5, and Alan A. Basinger and Howard P. Creaves in regimental headquarters—and corpsmen did yeoman work under the most trying conditions to treat the wounded and speed them on their way to recovery. About half the men passing through the medical facilities were treated for severe frostbite. Men suffering from combat fatigue were placed in warming tents where they were given hot coffee and a chance to rest. Such efforts boosted morale, especially when the Marines realized how poor enemy medical treatment was after interrogating Chinese prisoners of war.

General Smith planned to move down the road to Koto-ri with the 7th Marines in the lead and the 5th Marines in trail. Lieutenant Colonel Murray's orders were to cover the movement out of Hagaru-ri, protect the 1st Marine Division rear until it reached Koto-ri, and then become the division reserve for the move from Koto-ri to Hungnam. During the layover at Hagaru-ri, a reporter asked General Smith which term best described the planned movement: retreat or retirement. "Neither," Smith curtly replied. He then patiently explained that there were so many Chinese (intelligence reports said up to seven divisions) between Hagaru-ri and Hungnam that the 1st Marine Division's march to the sea was neither a retreat nor a retirement, but an attack and would be conducted as such. The press, harkening back to Lloyd Williams's colorful reply in 1918, summarized O. P. Smith's remarks as "Retreat Hell, we're just attacking in a different direction!" General Smith, a reserved and devout individual who neither drank nor swore, denied making this statement, but *Retreat Hell* has been used in the title of both a movie and a book about the Chosin campaign.

At 0700 on the sixth, the Marines began moving out for embattled Koto-ri, where Chesty Puller's reinforced 1st Marines were fighting to keep the Chinese at bay. Before the march started, however, enemy positions on top of East Hill had to be neutralized. This difficult task fell to Hal Roise's 2d Battalion. The battle for East Hill turned out to be the most hotly contested 5th Marines action of the entire breakout, a twenty-two-hour slugfest in which 2/5 carried the hill but suffered heavy casualties. The hill mass was too large to be taken in its entirety, so Lieutenant

Colonel Roise decided to use two companies to cut out a semicircular swath that would eliminate all direct fire on the road to Koto-ri. Captain Smith's Company D opened the fight by moving up a horseshoe-shaped ridge at 0900. Objective A was taken with one Marine killed and three wounded. Captain Peters's Company F then moved up to occupy the key terrain already taken, and Company D went after Objective B at 1100. These two companies slaughtered a pending Chinese assault when the attackers were caught in a saddle that served as their assembly area late in the day. Provisional rifle platoons from Capt. Rex O. Dillow's Antitank Company and an army signal detachment rushed up to fill the gap between Companies D and F at dusk. From then until 0200, the Marines were in a constant battle to hold on to the ridge. Much of the fighting was hand-to-hand combat. Two heroes of Company D's earlier fight at Smith's Ridge once again rose to the fore. First Lieutenant George McNaughton's platoon captured more than two hundred Chinese, and 1st Lt. Karle Seydel killed seven enemy soldiers in close combat before he fell mortally wounded.

The Marine defenders were finally forced back in the early morning hours on the seventh. The Chinese moved through the cracks and pressed ahead to attack the main perimeter in a spectacular three-hour firefight. Companies A and E, with excellent support from an army tank platoon, inflicted tremendous losses on the advancing human waves. Lieutenant Hancock's Company B moved up from its reserve positions to reinforce the main line and restored all lost territory by dawn. As it always seemed to do in Korea, American firepower ruled the battlefield that day. More than eight hundred Chinese were killed in this futile attack at the cost of ten Marines killed and forty-three wounded.

The 5th Marines played only a minor role thereafter during the move to Koto-ri. The Chinese scattered at daybreak when aircraft began prowling the sky in search of targets. Lieutenant Colonel Taplett's 3d Battalion, which had not participated in the fight for East Hill, was sent forward to assist a portion of the division trains that had stalled. The 1st Battalion was joined by elements of the British Royal Marines's 41st Commando and moved out before 1000. The 2d Battalion covered a demolition stay-behind force and then became rear guard at noon. The last Marines departed East Hill as Hagaru-ri burned in the background. Ironically, the convoy's vanguard was actually entering Koto-ri before 2/5 hit the road. It took a total of thirty-six hours to move more than ten thousand men the eleven miles to Koto-ri.

For the march to Hungnam, the 5th Marines was assigned the mission of protecting the east (left) flank of the MSR from Koto-ri to Chinhung-ni. To do this, Lieutenant Colonel Murray ordered 1/5 to seize dominating terrain in the vicinity of Hill 1457 about two and one-half miles southeast of Koto-ri and hold it until relieved by elements of the 1st Marines. The rest of the regiment would march with the main body. Lieutenant Colonel Stevens led 1/5 out of Koto-ri at about noon on the eighth. Company B left the road after traveling about a mile to take some intermediate high ground. Captain Jack Jones's Company C, reinforced by a provisional army platoon, drove the enemy from Hill 1457 in the midafternoon. A weak CCF counterattack was easily repulsed just as darkness closed in. Company A set up for the night along the road as the British Marines occupied a reserve position on some high ground between the road and Hill 1457. The 1st Battalion held these positions throughout the next day while the bulk of the 5th Marines remained at Koto-ri.

The main body of the convoy moved out of Koto-ri for Chinhung-ni on the tenth. The only interruption was a single firefight to overrun an enemy machine-gun position. The rest of the move was uneventful. The main body arrived at its destination around dusk. The 1st Battalion was relieved of its duties that evening, and the last elements of the security force entered Chinhung-ni early on the eleventh. The embarkation process was hampered by the absence of loading plans and limited dock space, but the regiment was still ready to sail within two days. The navy task group carrying the regiment departed Hungnam for Pusan on 15 December.

The subzero two-week ordeal at the "Frozen Chosin" was over. Although the UNC suffered a strategic reversal, the Marines's performance in the Chosin campaign was undoubtedly a tactical and moral victory. In this epic battle the outnumbered 1st Marine Division had re-created the classic retreat of Xenophon's 10,000 using modern weapons but relying on similar tactics to soundly defeat the enemy forces sent to destroy it. The Chinese 9th Army Group was so badly battered (intelligence estimated less than 10,000 of the more than 60,000 besiegers survived) that it was no longer combat effective and could not link up with its counterparts in western Korea to pursue the Eighth Army as ordered. Additionally, bleak news reaching the U.S. home front was significantly brightened by reports of the Marines's successful march to the sea. General MacArthur once again lauded the Marine efforts, and the 1st Marine Division was awarded a Presidential Unit Citation for the period 27

November–11 December 1950. True to General Smith's prediction, the "Chosin Few's" move from Yudam-ni to Hungnam was not a retreat in the normal sense; it instead became what historian Robert Leckie called "a march to glory."

The East-Central Front

After the Chosin campaign, the 5th Marines moved back to the Masan Bean Patch rest area, where its men had earlier recovered between the Naktong fights while defending the Pusan Perimeter six months before. The regiment was assigned a security sector and provided daily platoon-sized motor patrols, but the main activities were rest and recuperation. Physical exercise, athletics, hot food, and sleep were the order of the day. Within a few days, a constant hacking cough seemed to be the only ill effect left from the rugged Chosin operation. New uniforms were issued and most of the equipment damaged at Chosin was replaced, although there were some shortages that could not be filled. Replacement drafts reported to division headquarters, and new arrivals to the 5th Marines soon made up about a third of the regiment. Christmas trees and holiday decorations sprouted up in the Bean Patch as the holiday season approached. Entertainers, including Bob Hope, stopped by to put on USO shows, and the regimental choir sang carols for General Smith and his guests on Christmas Eve.

The 1st Marine Division passed from X Corps to Eighth Army control at 2400 on 18 December. Lieutenant General Matthew B. Ridgway, USA, was named Eighth Army commander after General Walker was killed in a jeep accident. General Ridgway inspected the Marines at Masan and observed field training. He was satisfied with what he saw and complimented the 1st Marine Division for its quick recovery. There were many other high-level visitors during the lull at Masan. Among them was Capt. John Ford, USNR, the famous movie director, who had been called to active duty. He gathered background material for a documentary he was filming, and some film clips shot at Masan were later used in the feature movie *Retreat Hell*. Also on hand was noted military historian Col. Samuel L. A. Marshall, USAR, who interviewed numerous Marines for a classified report about infantry combat in Korea, excerpts of which were later published in his anthology *Battle At Best*.

After four restive weeks at the Bean Patch, the 1st Marine Division moved from Masan to Pohang—the only port on Korea's east coast and

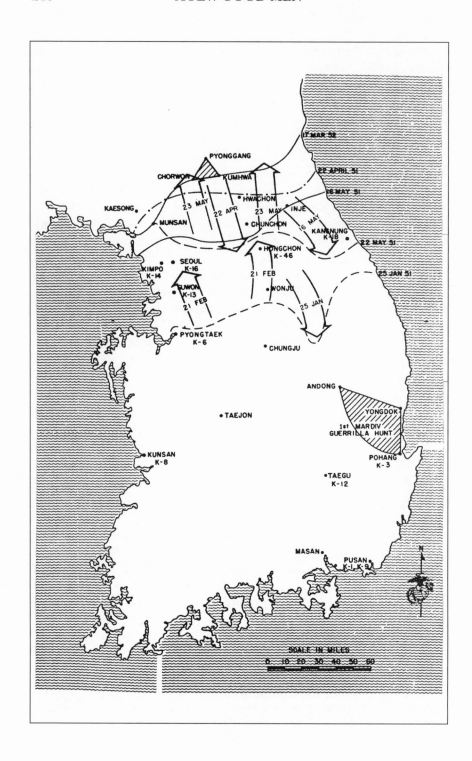

the site of the only jet-capable airfield in the area—about sixty-five miles away. There, the 5th Marines participated in what became known as the "Pohang Guerrilla Hunt." Regimental Combat Team 5 was responsible for Zone B, a fifty-by-twenty-mile arc that covered the inland supply route from just west of Pohang to past Uihung. Lieutenant Colonel Murray established regimental headquarters at Yangchon in the center of the zone. The road was monitored by constant motorized patrols and the interior was covered by foot-mobile "rice paddy patrols" made up of fire teams and squads. It was not uncommon to mount more than two dozen such patrols each day. Although few enemy troops were encountered, these patrols provided excellent training. The physical exercise toughened the Marines and units soon developed into cohesive combat teams. Captain Jack Jones's Company C conducted the regiment's largest counterguerrilla operation. It surrounded the village of Chachon-dong using a dozen small patrols that converged during the night. They established a cordon intended to ambush an enemy food-carrying party that was expected about dawn. Unfortunately, the operation turned up a dry hole when no enemy appeared.

The 1st Marine Division was assigned to IX Corps for Operation Killer, a limited offensive intended to inflict maximum casualties on the CCF, on 19 February 1951. Elements of the 5th Marines were trucked to Wonju in the central-front area about 115 miles northwest of Pohang. The plan was for the 1st and 5th Marines, moving abreast with the 5th on the right, to seize a key ridgeline south of Hoengsong. The narrow front allowed Lieutenant Colonel Murray to use 1/5 in the assault with 3/5 in support. The 2d Battalion was the division reserve. Unfortunately, heavy use and heavy rains made the MSR a sea of mud, so the trucks carrying the regiment arrived late. Just as their forebears had done at Soissons in World War I, the men of Lt. Col. John L. Hopkins's 1/5 had to double-time to get to the line of departure at the appointed hour and immediately moved into the attack without taking time to rest or organize. Luckily, there was little enemy resistance and the Marines suffered only three lightly wounded. The 1st Battalion encountered only sporadic long-range fire as it moved forward in a bone-chilling mix of thawing snow, sticky mud, and ankle-deep slush. The Marines reached their objective and then dug in for a miserable night spent in foxholes half filled with water. Each man was, in the words of Lt. Col. Joe Stewart, who now commanded 3/5, "wet to the bones—including his clothes, parka, weapon, and ammo." The attack continued without opposition for two more days.

"All we did was walk, walk, walk—I don't think I've been so tired or foot-sore in my life," recalled Capt. Franklin B. Mayer of Company E.

Operation Killer ended for the 5th Marines on 24 February when the regiment became the 1st Marine Division reserve. All objectives had been taken on schedule with few casualties incurred. The only serious hitches were resupply and insufficient air support. Korea's muddy roads and steep hills severely limited the effectiveness of motor transport. The solution was to assign about a hundred local laborers to each battalion in order to carry supplies forward on A-frame backpacks. These laborers were officially called *cargodores,* but were affectionately known as "Chiggy Bears" by the Marines. Although their labors have been often ignored by history, the hard-working Chiggy Bears repeatedly exhibited stamina and fortitude as they carried much-needed rations and supplies to hard-pressed Marine units. Air support was a different matter. The 1st MAW was no longer in direct support of the 1st Marine Division but was instead tasked to provide general support for all UNC forces under the overall control of the U.S. Air Force. On no less than three occasions during the 5th Marines's advance, air support was either hours late or badly missed the target. Fortunately, the limited enemy resistance during Operation Killer kept air support from becoming a major problem. This was, however, a harbinger of future trouble and the quality of close air support became a source of increasing interservice discontent as the Korean War dragged on.

The second phase of General Ridgway's offensive was dubbed Operation Ripper. When the attack resumed on 7 March, the 5th Marines was the 1st Marine Division reserve. By that time, most of the Pusan Perimeter veterans had departed and the regiment underwent numerous command changes. Lieutenant Colonel Glen E. Martin had taken over the 2d Battalion on 20 February. On 14 March 1951, Colonel Murray left the regiment and Col. Richard W. Hayward became the new commanding officer. Hayward, a Paramarine during World War II, enlisted in the Marine Corps in 1926 and was promoted to second lieutenant while serving with the 5th Marines in Nicaragua in 1932. Lieutenant Colonel Stewart, who was due for rotation home soon, once again became regimental executive officer. Lieutenant Colonel Donald R. Kennedy replaced him as 3/5's commander.

The regiment resumed its march forward from Phase Line Buffalo on 17 March. The advance to Phase Line Cairo was made against light opposition. The 5th Marines was pinched out at that point and thereafter supported the 1st Marines and 1st KMC Regiment by fire. On 1 April,

Colonel Hayward learned the 5th Marines would be one of the assault units when the 1st Marine Division pushed across the 38th Parallel to take Line Kansas. For his last assignment, Lieutenant Colonel Stewart worked out a plan to get the regiment across the swiftly flowing Soyang-gang. The 1st and 2d Battalions crossed the river at a narrow ford and the 3d Battalion came over mounted in DUKW amphibious trucks. Upon reporting back to regimental headquarters, Lieutenant Colonel Stewart began his homeward journey. His departure marked the end of a cycle: He was the last 5th Marines member of the 1st Provisional Marine Brigade to leave Korea.

The regiment moved forward and quickly took its assigned objective, then became division reserve on 5 April. As such, it conducted security patrols for ten days. The 5th Marines was at Hwachon on the Quantico Line when the CCF launched an unexpected counterattack at the end of April. A ROK Marine battalion on the right suddenly came under attack. First Lieutenant James T. Cronin's Company B rushed forward to defend Hill 313, but the enemy was already there and a stalemate short of the military crest developed in the early morning hours of 23 April. First Lieutenant James H. Honeycutt Jr.'s Company F then moved to Hill 313. The Korean Marines finally rallied and swept the enemy from Hill 509 at dawn. This action made Hill 313 untenable and the CCF units quickly withdrew.

Enemy pressure elsewhere along the front forced the UNC forces to fall back to an unmarked boundary quickly dubbed the "No Name Line." The 5th Marines conducted an orderly, carefully controlled retrograde to the Pendleton Line and then moved back to Line Kansas on 24 and 25 April respectively. They reached Soyang-gang on the twenty-sixth and dug in on the left flank of the 1st Marine Division sector on the No Name Line on the thirtieth. There, the regiment improved defensive positions and conducted aggressive patrols while biding its time until the next CCF blow struck.

The regiment's largest engagement of the CCF Fifth Phase Offensive occurred at 0445 on 20 May when Maj. Morse L. Holladay's 3d Battalion caught elements of the CCF 44th Division in the midst of an administrative move, unaware the Marines were nearby. Holladay's Marines opened up with every weapon at their disposal and called in air and artillery. When the Chinese withdrew later that morning, several hundred enemy bodies and more than a dozen badly wounded men were left behind.

As soon as the CCF offensive died, UNC forces launched a backhand blow to keep the enemy off balance and punish him further. The 1st Marine Division, now commanded by Maj. Gen. Gerald C. Thomas, was re-assigned to X Corps with orders to drive forward from the No Name Line to capture Yanggu, a vital road junction at the eastern tip of the Hwachon Reservoir. The 5th Marines was assigned to the right flank during most of this drive. The regiment moved forward against mostly sporadic resistance as the enemy retreated north toward the protection of mountains north of Hwachon. The 2d and 3d Battalions ran into the first stiff resistance as they approached some hills northeast of Hangye on 24 May, but Capt. John A. Pearson's Company I and Capt. Sam Smith's Company D were able to seize Hills 1051 and 883, and Colonel Hayward reported that all his objectives were in Marine hands by midnight.

The next stumbling block was Hill 566 near Kwagchi-dong. On the evening of the twenty-seventh, Company C moved into position to relieve pinned-down elements of the 7th Marines. The next day, 1st Lt. Richard J. "Spike" Schening was severely wounded by 120mm mortar fire, so 1st Lt. Richard E. Wagner assumed command of Company C. It took three assaults by Companies B and C and more than fifteen hours to capture Hill 566 on the twenty-ninth. Private Whitt L. Moreland, a scout from 1/5's intelligence section, volunteered to join Company C. First, Moreland delivered accurate rifle fire that enabled his unit to maneuver to seize the objective. Then, while defending the captured ground, a barrage of enemy grenades landed in the position occupied by Moreland and several other Marines. Unable to throw all of the grenades out, Moreland fell on the remaining ones and absorbed the full blast with his own body. He was later awarded a posthumous Medal of Honor. Enemy resistance faded after that, and the regiment was six thousand yards northeast of Yanggu by the end of the month.

After the so-called Battle of Soyang, the UNC attack continued unabated toward Line Kansas, which was located at the southern edge of a natural amphitheater formed by an ancient volcanic crater known as the Punchbowl. This time the enemy chose to defend rather than run. Lieutenant Colonel Martin's 2d Battalion encountered fierce resistance from an estimated two hundred enemy atop Hill 651 not long after it jumped off. The ground assault had bogged down by noon, so Marine air pounded the hilltop until the defenders from the NKPA 12th Division broke and ran.

The next morning, 2 June, the 1st Battalion took over the attack to secure the southwest tip of a long ridge that dominated the corridor leading north toward Line Kansas and the Punchbowl. The first step was to seize a sharp ridge known as Hill 610, but the objective was actually a series of three hills. The Marines moved across the valley under the cover of air strikes and rocket and artillery fires. Lieutenant Cronin's Company B was on the right, Lieutenant Wagner's Company C on the left, and Capt. John L. Kelly's Company A was the reserve. Company C, 1st Tank Battalion, was in support. The plan was for each of Company C's three platoons to take one of the hills by leapfrogging from one objective to the next. Direct 90mm tank gun fire enabled the Company C riflemen to scramble up the forward slope of Hill 610 until the lead platoon, commanded by 2d Lt. Paul N. McCloskey Jr., was ordered to stop within range of enemy mortars while Marine air pounded the hilltop. Unfortunately, enemy mortar fire hit the 1st Platoon, and the attack quickly became disjointed. McCloskey and his radioman wound up taking the first hill alone. Not long after the rest of the hard-luck platoon arrived and established a hasty defense, it was hit by misdirected Marine artillery. Second Lieutenant Charles U. Daly's 2d Platoon advanced up the next height, but it required several more platoons to secure the final hill after the initial assaults failed. Despite stiff resistance, the last enemy position had been cleared by 1945. That night, Companies A and C beat back an enemy counterattack. Meanwhile, the 2d Battalion was able to successfully press its attack on a neighboring ridge despite long-range enemy interdiction fire and being mistakenly attacked from the air by U.S. F-80 Shooting Star jet fighter-bombers.

The next objective was Hill 680, located about a thousand yards farther along the ridge. Company A led 1/5's assault after the objective had been napalmed and bombed. The attackers closed to within hand grenade range following close upon the heels of a rolling barrage. Hill 680 was in Marine hands by midafternoon, and Company A tried to push on to the next knob, Hill 692. The advance was stopped there by enemy small-arms and mortar fire. An air strike was requested, but was delayed two hours by poor weather. Company A began moving forward again a couple of hours later and gained the summit, only to be driven back by another misdirected air strike. Several more casualties were incurred from mortar fire of undetermined origin that fell among the retreating Marines. Hard-hit Company A had to be replaced by Korean Marines who eventually eliminated the remaining NKPA and took Hill 692.

The 5th Marines spent a few days in reserve and absorbed a new replacement draft to make up for the veterans who rotated home on 5 June. For the next two weeks the 5th Marines advanced over washboard-like terrain formed by a series of five steep ridges. The first of these was Hill 729, which 2d and 3d Battalions took by attacking abreast of each other on 6 June. The attack began in the afternoon and was not completed until after dark. The regiment then proceeded to capture the remaining four ridges, advancing step-by-step and taking heavy casualties despite support from air, artillery, mortars, and recoilless rifles. The enemy probed for weaknesses at night and conducted a skillful, resolute defense by day all during this advance to the Punchbowl. The fighting was so bloody that some rifle companies lost more men than they had at the Chosin Reservoir. The regiment's final objective, Hill 907, fell on 17 June.

The Communists, having taken a tremendous beating since launching their ill-fated spring offensive, requested truce talks to negotiate an end to the war in Korea. Skeptical field commanders characterized this as a blatantly insincere effort by the enemy to gain time to reorganize and reequip, but their warnings were ignored by national command authorities far from the battlefield. This development led to a period of relative calm during which the fighting continued, but at a much-diminished level. The 5th Marines patrolled the Badger Line until 15 July, when the 1st Marine Division was pulled out of the line to become X Corps's ready reserve. The regiment moved back to Inje, a village five miles north of the 38th Parallel but more than fifteen miles south of the Eighth Army main line of resistance. The days, and some nights, were devoted to intense combat training and rigorous physical conditioning. Some members of the regiment tested prototypes of armored vests that later become standard issue in Korea and Vietnam. The unexpected lull lasted until the Communists, by then well rested and resupplied, walked out of the peace negotiations on 22 August.

The 5th Marines patrolled Line Kansas and protected its defensive installations until the end of August. Colonel Richard G. Weede, who had replaced Colonel Hayward on 7 August, received a warning order on the twenty-seventh. The regiment was to move up the narrow Soyang Valley behind the 7th Marines as the latter unit advanced toward the Hays Line. On 1 September, Lieutenant Colonel Kennedy's 3d Battalion slipped into the MLR to free the 2d KMC Battalion to join the attack. The next night, NKPA infiltrators probed the regiment's positions along Line Kansas, but they were easily repelled. The regiment continued its reserve role with one company at Line Kansas while the rest backed up the 7th Marines south of the Hays Line until mid-September.

At that time, the UNC launched a series of limited offensive actions designed to force the Communists back to the peace table. The 5th

Marines moved into an assembly area on the night of 15 September, then launched an assault on Hill 812 the next morning. The barren mass offered little cover or concealment to those on its slopes. Like so many other hills in Korea, it was crossed by a low ridge that formed a T that exposed attackers to a vicious cross fire from the surrounding heights. Lieutenant Colonel Houston Stiff's 2d Battalion made the main effort with Kennedy's 3d Battalion in support and Lt. Col. William P. Alston's 1st Battalion in reserve. Captain William E. Melby's Company F spearheaded the attack in the early afternoon on 16 September. Progress was slow and the attack was halted before dusk to evacuate casualties and regroup. Unfortunately, aircraft operating in support of 3/5 mistook the 1/5 Marines for enemy and strafed the harried 1st Battalion. Luckily, the pilots spotted air recognition panels and broke off the attack before causing any casualties. Bright moonlight that night kept the enemy at bay and Companies F and D passed a relatively quiet night.

Captain Melby directed artillery fire onto a group of unsuspecting NKPA who were spotted just as Company F prepared to move out at dawn on the seventeenth. Melby's men exploited this opening and quickly pushed up the slopes leading to Hill 812 until they were taken under heavy machine-gun fire. Captain William L. Wallace's Company E then picked up the assault covered by artillery, 81mm mortars, 75mm recoilless rifles, and 4.2-inch mortars. The hill fell after a little more than half an hour of close-quarters combat. The momentum of the assault carried the Marines well past the assigned limit of advance, but Colonel Weede had to refuse permission to continue the attack to seize Hill 980 because that position was deemed untenable due to its exposure to direct enemy fire from Hill 1052. Colonel Weede instead ordered 2/5 and 3/5 to consolidate their positions on the best ground available and prepare for a night defense. Company E had to pull back about six hundred yards to do this. The 2d Battalion position atop Hill 812 left Companies E and F exposed to enemy 76mm guns dug in on Hills 980 and 1052, so Lieutenant Colonel Stiff restricted daylight movement to Hill 812's reverse slope to reduce casualties after several Marines were wounded. Fox Company's SSgt. Stanley J. Wawrzyniak, one of the regiment's most decorated enlisted Marines of all time, was awarded the Navy Cross for his actions at Hill 812, and less than six months later received a second Navy Cross while serving as Company E's gunnery sergeant.

The 2d Battalion was hit by two successive counterattacks and subjected to enemy artillery fire throughout the day on the eighteenth. One of the western outposts was lost, and 2/5 had to give some ground in the early morning hours before repelling an enemy daylight follow-up attack. The battalion suffered most of the 1st Marine Division casualties reported that day: sixteen killed and ninety-eight wounded. With the forward edge of the Marine lines under observation and plentiful enemy gunners on the neighboring ridges, there was a critical need for field fortification materials. Delivery of these bulky and heavy supplies was accomplished using an innovative method. Operation Windmill II, as the mission was dubbed, used sixteen flights of ten HRS-1 helicopters each to deliver sandbags, barbed wire, land mines, food, ammunition, and water to 2/5.

The 2d Battalion was ordered to outpost a huge outcrop called the Rock, but it turned out the Marines controlled only the southern half of this granite slab. This terrain became the focal point of operations for the next few days. The 2d Battalion suffered heavy casualties trying to protect its portion of the Rock on 19 September, so 1/5 moved up that evening to relieve Lieutenant Colonel Stiff's hard-pressed Marines. The next day, an NKPA company rushed forward out of the early morning darkness behind mortar and artillery fire to push Captain Wallace's recently arrived Company E back. The fighting seesawed until Captain Melby's Company F launched a pincer movement to retake the lost positions. This counterattack forced the enemy back to their own side of the Rock. Corporal Jack A. Davenport, a squad leader with Company G, 3/5, earned the Medal of Honor when he smothered a grenade with his body to shield his companions during an enemy attack in the vicinity of Songnae-dong on the twenty-first.

This four-day action to seize the Minnesota Line was the last major offensive for the 5th Marines in Korea. From then until the armistice was declared almost two years later, the UNC eschewed offensive operations for positional warfare. Only attacks to take or retake ground in the immediate vicinity of the MLR were mounted. After September 1951, the war in Korea became a deadly stalemate along the 38th Parallel using tactics that would have been very familiar to the Marines of the 5th Regiment manning trenches near Verdun during World War I. Both sides settled into combat operations that featured long-range sniping, occasional small but bitter fights over individual pieces of key terrain, and nightly forays into no-man's-land by squad- and platoon-sized raiding parties.

The 5th Marines was assigned the center of the 1st Marine Division sector, a seven-thousand-yard-long V-shaped line with Hill 812 at its apex.

Colonel Weede was ordered to organize, construct, and defend defensive positions as well as to patrol forward of the MLR and in the rear areas. The familiar pattern of constant vigilance, nightly patrols, and occasional company-sized raids continued throughout the rest of the year, but there were very few lengthy firefights. This lull in the action was a result of renewed peace talks being held at Panmunjom.

The regiment was pulled off the line in October 1951 and returned to the Minnesota Line just in time to celebrate the Marine Corps's birthday during Operation Switch, the largest helicopter troop movement up to that time. The move began at dawn on 11 November. Lieutenant Colonel Kirt W. Norton's 1/5 was lifted to Hill 884, thereafter known as "Mount Helicopter," from Airfield X-83 by relays of a dozen HRS-1 helicopters. About 950 Marines were delivered in slightly less than ninety-seven hours of flight time. Timely naval gunfire from the battleship USS *New Jersey* kept the enemy's heads down while this time-consuming operation was under way.

Colonel Frank P. Hager Jr. assumed command of the regiment on 19 November 1951. At that time the Marines were spending most of their off-duty time "winterizing" living bunkers. Much-improved, cold-weather clothing, including insulated black-rubber "Mickey Mouse" boots that replaced the inadequate shoepacs of the previous winter, was available for this second Korean winter.

A New Year's Eve patrol from Capt. Charles W. McDonald's Company B, 1st Battalion, conducted the first Marine combat action of 1952 when it ambushed six NKPA soldiers at about 0400 on 1 January, killing one and wounding four. There were no Marine casualties. Ten days later, the 5th Marines was relieved at the MLR and moved into reserve at Camp Tripoli located about seventeen miles from the front. Major General John T. Selden, who had commanded the regiment on New Britain during World War II, took over the 1st Marine Division on 11 January. Selden's staff included former 5th Marines commanding officers Brig. Gen. Bill Whaling and Col. Dick Weede. Concurrently, in far-away Washington, D.C., another old 5th Marines hand, Gen. Lem Shepherd, became Commandant of the Marine Corps.

The 5th Marines returned to the line on 17 February after participating in Operation Clam-Up, a sophisticated ruse to draw the enemy out into the open. All Marine units, including the 5th Marines in division reserve, pretended to withdraw from the MLR. A few enemy units probed forward and were destroyed by air and artillery, but the bulk of the Communist forces did not take the bait and instead stayed put. The 5th Marines's relief of the 1st Marines in the wake of Operation Clam-Up was the first one conducted at night. Almost all of the enemy's activity for the next month was directed at the sector held by 2/5. No positions changed hands and there were few casualties during this period.

West Korea

In March, Eighth Army launched Operation Mixmaster. This was a complicated rearrangement of UNC units that required the 1st Marine Division to move about 180 miles from the east-central sector of the MLR to the extreme left flank on the west side of the Korean Peninsula. There the regiment would man the Jamestown Line, which guarded the northern approaches that have been the traditional overland invasion route to Seoul. The 5th Marines was at first slated to go to the Kimpo peninsula, where it would conduct amphibious training and act as the Eighth Army reserve. These plans, however, had to be changed en route. General Selden alerted the new regimental commander, Col. Thomas A. Culhane Jr., that the regiment would move directly into the line instead of going to Kimpo.

The 5th Marines mounted a five-day trek through mud, sleet, snow, and rain to reach the Jamestown Line on 29 March. The Jamestown MLR roughly paralleled the Imjin River from its mouth near Kimpo to a point about twenty miles—later expanded to more than thirty miles—inland. In addition to guarding the MLR, the 5th Marines had to man an outpost line. This was a series of unconnected squad and platoon strong points atop key terrain located about twenty-five hundred yards forward of the MLR. The close proximity of Panmunjom to the regiment's sector resulted in a specially designated "no fire" corridor that ran from Kaesong to Munsan-ni, and Colonel Culhane considered this the weak point in his defensive bulwark. The first task upon arrival at the Jamestown Line was improvement of defensive positions. This was done while conducting an active defense that used reconnaissance and combat patrols to search the entire defensive zone. Infantry positions were backed up with dug-in tanks, snipers constantly sought out long-range targets of opportunity, and artillery kept up a drumbeat of harassment and interdiction fires.

The combat lull abruptly ended after Communist negotiators once again skulked out of Panmunjom, bringing the peace talks to a sudden

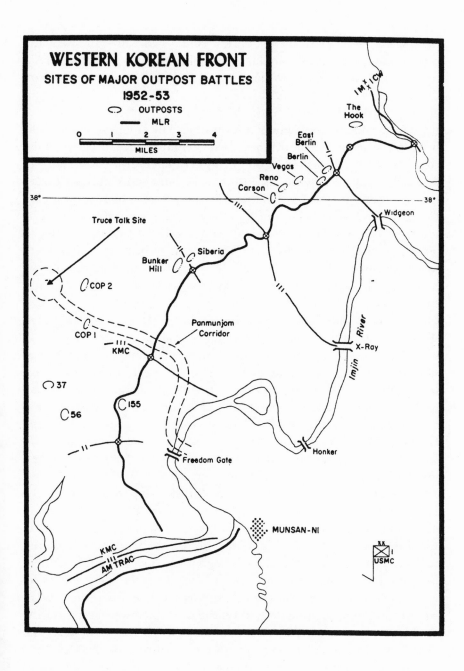

WESTERN KOREAN FRONT
SITES OF MAJOR OUTPOST BATTLES
1952-53

halt. At that time, Lt. Col. William H. Cushing's 2d Battalion was on the regimental left, Lt. Col. Franklin B. "Brooke" Nihart's 1st Battalion was in the center, and Lt. Col. William S. McLaughlin's 3d Battalion was on the right. Patrols from the 5th Marines apprehended thirty-four civilians and captured a Chinese soldier in the netherworld between the MLR and the outpost line on the night of 5 April 1952. The enemy stepped up activity in the second week of April. Two Communist patrols probed the regiment's line for weak spots on the night of 12–13 April. Each was easily beaten back. Two nights later, the enemy launched a more serious attack against Capt. Charles C. Matthews's Company E, which was manning Combat Outpost No. 3 just north of the Panmunjom corridor with a reinforced platoon. The position had been briefly shelled twice on the fifteenth, once in the afternoon and then again at dusk. One Marine was wounded during the second attack. The enemy pounded Outpost No. 3 with 76mm guns and 120mm mortars starting at about 2330. This fire shifted to another outpost just after midnight. A ground assault to take Outpost No. 3 soon followed. During the attack, the enemy was able to surround and cut off the outpost but was unable to carry the position despite getting close enough to engage in hand-to-hand combat. The assault was finally called off at about 0315. This unsuccessful attack cost the enemy more than 50 dead, a like number of wounded, and 3 captured. Marine casualties were 6 killed, 25 wounded, and 5 missing. During the fighting for Outpost No. 3, twice-wounded machine gunner Cpl. Duane E. Dewey covered an enemy grenade to shield his comrades. He survived the explosion and later received the Medal of Honor from President Eisenhower at a White House ceremony.

The next major action occurred in May when a patrol from Brooke Nihart's 1st Battalion was scheduled to temporarily occupy high ground overlooking Outpost No. 3. The plan was for the support element to use this area as a base of fire to cover the rest of the patrol as it moved around. First Lieutenant Ernest C. Lee's Company A was instructed to find out if CCF forces occupied the old outpost and to determine how well developed their defenses were. Lee's patrol departed the MLR at sunup. Company A was setting in on the first objective when a Marine aerial observer spotted a CCF company preparing to attack. The alerted Marines took an enemy platoon under fire and killed fourteen Communists with well-placed small-arms fire. One Marine was killed and four were wounded in the exchange. This action was followed by several air strikes that successfully covered the Marines's withdrawal. Lee and his men avoided two ambushes on their way back, but stumbled into an uncleared and unmarked minefield. Two more Marines were killed and an additional three were wounded before an engineer mine-clearing party arrived.

Colonel Culhane eventually decided to oust the Chinese from Outpost No. 3 and ordered the 1st Battalion to do so on 8 May. Lieutenant Colonel Nihart established three intermediate objectives (labeled S, V, and X respectively) en route to Outpost No. 3 (Objective Y). A battalion-strength combat patrol, consisting of the 1st Battalion less Company B but reinforced by regimental combat support assets, was assigned this task with orders also to take Objective Z (an emeny outpost) if necessary. Lieutenant Lee's Company A was the assault force, Capt. Leland Graham's Company C was the diversionary force, and 1st Lt. Ross L. Tipps's Weapons Company was in support. On-call artillery and air strikes were scheduled, and a tank platoon was standing by. Nihart's men moved into position under the cover of darkness and crossed the line of departure at 0430. Within three hours, Company A had moved fifteen hundred yards and captured Objective V, but five men were wounded. The next phase was more costly. As the Marines moved toward Objectives X and Y, they were subjected to heavy enemy artillery fire. They took both objectives but were hit by a fierce counterattack. Outpost No. 3 proved untenable, and Company A had to pull back. The entire raid force was back behind American lines at dusk. This largest Eighth Army offensive action since the previous September cost the 5th Marines seven dead and sixty-six wounded. The regiment was replaced along the MLR by the 7th Marines and reverted to division reserve soon thereafter.

Newly appointed Eighth Army commander Lt. Gen. Mark W. Clark inspected the Marine lines in early June. A veteran of the static mountain warfare in Italy during World War II, Clark quickly changed Eighth Army's operational methods. The 5th Marines, like all other 1st Marine Division units, was ordered to be prepared to launch large-scale raids and limited-objective attacks. The 1st Marine Division's assigned frontage was extended almost ten more miles as part of a divisional realignment. The 5th Marines once again occupied the Jamestown Line on 15–16 June. This time, Lt. Col. Thomas J. Cross's 2d Battalion was on the left, Maj. Paul H. Bratten's 1st Battalion was on the right, and Lieutenant Colonel McLaughlin's 3d Battalion was in reserve. The 3d Battalion participated in amphibious training and conducted a landing exercise at Tokchok Island while in reserve.

The war again heated up when the Communists picked up the pace. A sixteen-man patrol from Company G came under heavy small-arms fire and was forced to pull back on 22 June. Ten men made it safely back to the MLR, and five took refuge at a nearby combat outpost. A follow-up patrol later discovered the body of the missing man, who had been killed by Chinese artillery. Concurrently, a patrol from Company E was taken under fire after successfully recovering the body of another Marine. It lost one man killed and another wounded during the return to friendly lines.

The Chinese attacked positions held by the 2d Battalion two days later as part of what became known as the "Anniversary Attacks" because it was second anniversary of the NKPA invasion of South Korea. The Marines came under sporadic but sometimes intense mortar and artillery fire throughout the afternoon and early evening of the twenty-fourth. Late in the evening the enemy mounted an attack against elements of Capt. Harold C. Fuson's Company F occupying position Yoke on Hill 159. The Chinese quickly surrounded Yoke and forced its thirty-four defenders underground. Although the Chinese overran the position, they were unable to evict the Marines, who were holed up in various bunkers. While attempting to reduce the American positions, the attackers were exposed to deadly artillery air bursts. The Reds finally had enough and pulled back at about 0300, but they renewed the attack when Marine reinforcements moved forward and the deadly artillery fires had to be lifted. This second action became a repeat of the first. Once again the Marines took to the bunkers while the enemy was plastered by artillery fire. Nine Marines were killed and 23 wounded defending Yoke. One man was killed and 13 others were wounded in other attacks in the 2d Battalion zone that night. Enemy losses were a dozen killed and possibly three times that number wounded.

On the night of 2–3 July, Company A was directed to take three outposts near Samichon. This force met no enemy before it was ordered to return to friendly lines. A patrol from the 2d Battalion had a tougher time the next day. It became embroiled in an hour-long firefight and had to withdraw under the cover of artillery-delivered smoke shells. One man was killed and eleven were wounded in this action. A second patrol from the same battalion was able to pick off six enemy soldiers and wounded an additional eight without suffering a single loss. It safely returned before the artillery launched a deluge of time-on-target attacks to celebrate the Fourth of July during Operation Firecracker.

The enemy became even bolder in August. The Chinese secretly occupied Marine Outpost Elmer in front of the 2d Battalion on the night of 6 August. It had become standard U.S. practice to man such outposts only during the day, so the Chinese had little trouble infiltrating no-man's-land. The Marine patrol moving up the next morning was surprised by fire and was unable to occupy Elmer that day. Five days later, the Chinese repeated this tactic at Outpost Hilda. A Marine squad moving to occupy Hilda as part of a diversionary attack was forced to withdraw in the face of overwhelming enemy fire just before midnight. On the night of 17 August, another Marine patrol was pinned down by enemy fire from Outpost Irene. Reinforcements were likewise pinned by heavy and accurate Chinese artillery fire. During this engagement Pfc. Robert Simanek of Company E unhesitatingly threw himself on an enemy grenade to save the other members of his squad. This courageous act prevented further casualties. Simanek survived and was later presented the Medal of Honor by President Eisenhower, who praised the Marine's daring initiative and personal valor during a White House ceremony. Despite Company E's efforts, Outpost Irene remained in Chinese hands. Company F was involved in two separate squad actions on the night of the twenty-second. Both sides suffered heavy casualties on each occasion. Activity for the rest of the month was curtailed by heavy rainfall and the resulting flash floods, which washed out vital bridges and collapsed defensive fortifications.

The 5th Marines, commanded by Col. Eustace R. Smoak since 15 August, encountered increasing enemy activity in its sector during September. The front was screened by a series of outposts. From south to north they were: Allen, Bruce, Clarence, Donald, Elmer, Felix, Gary, Hilda, Irene, and Jill. Three of these—Elmer, Hilda, and Irene—had been ceded to the enemy in late August because their tactical value was not deemed worth the casualties it would cost to hold them. Emboldened by these successes, the CCF mounted a series of attacks against five of the remaining outposts on 5 September. Outpost Gary was shelled and the other four came under both artillery and infantry attack. An ambush set up by Company C of Lt. Col. Alexander W. Gentleman's 1st Battalion delayed the assault on Felix. Outposts Allen and Clarence were attacked for almost two hours before the Communists withdrew.

The fight for Outpost Bruce was one of the most intense small-unit actions of the entire Korean Conflict, and three of its defenders were awarded Medals of Honor for their bravery during the fifty-one-hour siege. Captain Edward Y. Holt Jr.'s Company I held the position. Private First Class Alford L. McGloghlin fired a pair of machine guns, alternating them when his hands blistered from the searing heat, into an onrushing CCF company and stopped the enemy attack. Private First Class Fernando L. Garcia covered a grenade with his body and died saving the lives of several other wounded men. Navy Hospitalman 3d Class Edward C. Benfold was ministering aid to wounded Marines when two enemy grenades landed in the shell crater he was using for cover. Benfold picked up one deadly missile in each hand and hurled himself at approaching CCF soldiers. The resulting explosion killed two of the enemy and Benfold. By the next morning, all of the Marine bunkers on the forward slope of Bruce had been obliterated and only two on the reverse slope had escaped destruction. Thirty-two of the thirty-four Marine defenders were dead or wounded. 3rd Battalion commander Lt. Col. Oscar T. Jensen Jr. quickly sent reinforcements and supplies to shore up Bruce's defenses, and the survivors were on their way back to the MLR by midmorning.

Ten air strikes hit suspected enemy positions north of the 5th Marines's sector on the Jamestown Line during the day while the Marines at Outpost Bruce struggled to shore up fortifications despite a thunderstorm of enemy mortars and artillery. Just after midnight on 6 September, a thirty-five-minute barrage hit Bruce's defenders. Three hours later the enemy fire picked up once again and the Marines braced for an expected assault. Luckily, the box fires delivered by the 11th Marines dispersed the massing Chinese before a ground assault could by launched. That evening, the CCF made three unsuccessful attempts to capture Bruce and used long-range fires against Outpost Allen. At about 0245, the Chinese once again attacked Bruce after an hour of preparatory fires. This time they almost succeeded. Nearly every Marine was killed or wounded as the enemy tried frontal and enveloping attacks before pulling back. Nineteen Marines died and 38 were wounded during the fight for Outpost Bruce. An additional 5 Marines died and 32 more were wounded at adjacent outposts between 5 and 7 September. An estimated four enemy infantry companies were destroyed during two nights of almost unrelenting attacks to seize Outpost Bruce.

The regiment thereafter moved off the MLR and became the division reserve before moving back into the line on 12 October. From then until the spring of 1953 there was little activity in the 5th Marines's sector. The major emphasis that winter was revamping and strengthening the Jamestown Line and its ancillary positions, and the 5th Marines strung 3,780 miles of barbed wire during Operation Tanglewire.

Colonel Lew Walt became regimental commander on 10 December 1952. Walt was still the aggressive commander he had been at Guadalcanal, New Britain, and Peleliu, and he received permission to take the initiative in his sector on 25 January 1953. Walt proposed to retake troublesome Hills 31 and 31A in the Ungok Hills. He named this regimental raid Operation Clambake. It was a complex plan that used a carefully coordinated tank and artillery feint against Hill 104, Kumgok village, and Red Hill to divert attention away while Lt. Col. Jonas M. Platt's 1st Battalion made the main effort. The objective was for the Marines to capture some enemy and destroy enemy positions and equipment. Five days of rehearsal preceded the operation, with the culminating exercise held on 1 February.

Three tanks rumbled across the line of departure shortly after first light on 3 February. They conducted their feint toward the Ungok Hills, which were being bombarded by the 11th Marines. Two assault forces from Capt. Don H. Blanchard's Company A moved out under the cover of this distraction. The enemy made three counterattacks after the Marines's main effort was correctly identified. Supporting arms blunted each of them, and the withdrawing raiders linked up with the tanks, which had swung left across the frozen rice paddies when their feint was over. Second Lieutenant Raymond G. Murphy, a former three-sport college athlete leading a platoon in Company A, ignored his own wounds and repeatedly carried others to safety despite enemy fire. He led a counterattack, searched for wounded Marines without regard for his own well being, and covered the Marine withdrawal with a borrowed BAR. Lieutenant Murphy was later awarded the Medal of Honor. Almost four hundred Communists became casualties at the cost of fourteen Marine dead, ninety-one wounded, and one flame tank knocked out. No prisoners were taken, but the raid was still considered a success because of the casualties inflicted upon the enemy and the reestablishment of American offensive spirit.

The Chinese stepped up the pace in February by increasing the number of artillery attacks and using a series of hit-and-run probes of Marine outposts. A patrol from Company H, 3/5, used flamethrowers to clear the enemy from positions on Hill 35 about a half-mile south of the Ungok Hills on 22 February.

Colonel Walt followed up Clambake's success by launching Operation Charlie on 25 February. He ordered Lt. Col. Oscar F. Peatross's 2d Battalion to conduct a daylight kill-capture-and-destroy raid on Hill 15. The same formula used during Clambake was once again employed. Supporting arms were carefully coordinated and the attack was patiently rehearsed. Captain Harold D. Kurth Jr.'s Company F moved out in the darkness just before dawn when visibility was reduced to only about three hundred yards. Box fires by Marine and British artillery isolated the battle area and tanks stood by to lend their support if necessary. Captain Theodore J. Mildner's Company B conducted a predawn raid on Hill 31A. After successive air and artillery preparation, two platoons totaling 111 Marines jumped off at 0518. The Chinese had already pulled back off the exposed front slope and were hiding in protective bunkers and the far side of the hill when the Marines reached the crest. Heavy machine-gun fire from the reverse slope caused the Marines to disengage at 0700, but they destroyed the forward enemy positions using flamethrowers before they withdrew.

The general lull in enemy offensive action in the regiment's sector came to an end when the CCF mounted a limited offensive to seize three platoon combat outposts: Carson, Vegas, and Reno. These exposed positions had been jocularly named for Nevada gaming towns because holding on to them was considered such a gamble. The Chinese commander called the Marines's bluff on the night of 26 March. The 5th Marines's sector of the Jamestown Line, prophetically code-named The Wild Zone, had Lieutenant Colonel Platt's 1st Battalion on the left to the west, Lt. Col. Robert J. Oddy's 3d Battalion on the right, and Lt. Col. James H. Finch's 2d Battalion in reserve. The three outposts were in front of 1/5's lines. Personnel from Company C defended Reno and Carson, and Company H, under Platt's operational control, occupied Vegas. From west to east, the 1st Battalion used Companies A, B, and C in the line and the 3d Battalion had Companies H, G, and I abreast.

The last Thursday in March was unseasonably mild. Previous patrols forward of the MLR had revealed no enemy presence, and there had been no contact whatsoever for three days running. If anything, it was too quiet. The serenity came to a sudden halt just after dark on 26 March. Heavy mortar and artillery fires from Hills 44, 40, 35, and 33 hit the 1st Battalion. Enemy small arms and machine guns from Hill 140 joined the fray after about fifteen minutes. Reno and Carson were hit by 76mm guns and 120mm mortars at the rate of about one per second, and a patrol from Company D was pinned down by mortars for almost two hours. The regiment's entire line received some type of fire and, although most communications lines were destroyed, it was obvious to all hands the Chinese were up to something big.

At precisely 1910, the CCF 358th Regiment swarmed down from the hills in a massive assault. Enemy infantry companies assaulted Reno and Vegas while a smaller force took on Carson as part of a well-coordinated three-pronged attack. Marine artillery and tank guns went into action to stem the Chinese onslaught, which threatened the Marine outposts with a twenty-to-one ratio of attackers to defenders. The attackers penetrated the lines on Reno and Carson and fierce hand-to-hand fighting ensued. Within an hour, the Marines at Carson had thrown most of the attackers off the hill and relief squads from Companies C and D were on the way. Over at Outpost Reno, the defenders were forced back into a protective cave as Marine variable time and white phosphorus shells cleared CCF attackers from the hilltop. However, a radio message indicated only seven of the forty Marines defending Reno were still able to fight. Illumination rounds and a flare plane kept the position well lit so supporting American machine guns and tanks could identify targets. The situation was similar at Outpost Vegas, where the Marines also took cover inside a cave and called for artillery fire on top of their own positions. All ground communications lines were knocked out, so radio communications had to be used.

A relief force from Company F was ambushed on its way to reinforce Reno and had to call for help. A platoon from Company C was also ambushed near Hill 47 and suffered ten casualties. The situation was serious, so Company F was attached to the 1st Battalion and ordered to reinforce the depleted ranks of the Company C relief force at a battle position known as the Block. This composite force established a base of fire, but could not move forward due to the intense enemy artillery fire. It held on, though, and eventually cleared Chinese infiltrators from the trench lines and approaches leading to Reno. Three enemy counterattacks were thrown back in desperate hand-to-hand fighting. Navy Hospitalman Francis C. Hammond was struck in the leg early in the evening, but for four hours he continued to deliver lifesaving medical aid while ignoring his own wounds. When his unit was ordered to withdraw to a safer position, Hammond remained in the beaten zone and skillfully directed the evacuation of the wounded before being cut down by a mortar blast. For his heroism that night, Hammond was awarded a posthumous Medal of Honor. Tank and artillery fire wiped out an enemy force massing near Chogum-ni before it could go into action, but the Reno defenders remained under heavy pressure. A situation report indicated the enemy was trying to evict the last Marines holding out inside the cave, and another message about an hour later was so weak it could not be understood. That was the last contact from Reno.

The relief forces sent to Vegas were also soon pinned down and could not effect a proper relief. A counterattack force from Company D met the enemy in hand-to-hand combat on its way to reinforce Vegas, so a platoon from Company E was sent forward. When the enemy renewed the attack on Vegas, Capt. Ralph F. Estey's Company F, 7th Marines, was placed under Lieutenant Colonel Oddy's operational control and sent in to support Vegas. At about 0300, Company D closed to within two hundred yards of Vegas only to discover the outpost was in enemy hands.

It had been a grim night for the regiment. Two of three outposts had been lost, and two relief forces were desperately fighting to survive. More than 150 Marines had been lost on the three outposts, and the ill-fated rescue forces suffered at least that many casualties. Colonel Walt reluctantly ordered the relief forces back to the MLR before dawn. He wisely decided it would be better to regroup and launch a coordinated daylight attack to retake the lost positions. All Marine relief units were back by 0530.

A Herculean effort was needed to help the relief forces disengage and evacuate the wounded. A platoon from the reserve 2d Battalion and a provisional evacuation unit formed from H&S Company, 1/5, worked to help the wounded arriving at the Company C supply point. The 3d Battalion moved its wounded back through the Company H supply point and a nearby Korean Service Corps camp. The most seriously wounded were flown by helicopter to the hospital ships *Haven* and *Consolation.* Medical Companies A, E, and C provided forward aid station support.

While this was going on, the enemy also made diversionary attacks at Outposts Berlin and East Berlin on 3/5's far right flank. Company G successfully held these positions assisted by artillery box fires using variable-time fuses. Reinforcements were quickly dispatched, but neither of the Berlin positions was seriously threatened.

As the 5th Marines prepared to launch its counterattacks to retake the lost positions the next morning, American tanks, artillery, rockets, and mortars pounded Reno and Vegas. The 1st MAW provided spotter aircraft and made several night bombing runs to disrupt enemy assembly areas and isolate the two outposts. From nightfall on 26 March until dawn the next morning, the cannoneers of the 11th Marines fired more than ten thousand rounds. Colonel Walt was given operational control of the

2d Battalion, 7th Marines, the division reserve, for the counterattack. Smoke shells began to blind enemy gunners on Hills 57A and 190 about an hour before noon on the twenty-seventh. Preparatory fires massed on the two objectives and counterbattery fires blasted all suspected enemy artillery positions that could range Reno and Vegas.

Captain John B. Melvin led Company D across the line of departure at 1120. This force immediately came under heavy enemy fire and was stopped twice by heavy shelling. The Marines crawled forward through rain-swollen rice paddies and up the muddy slopes leading to the objective. Within half an hour the lead platoon had been reduced to only nine men. Chinese reinforcements made their way to Vegas from Hill 153 despite heavy Marine fire. Just as the riflemen from Company D reached Vegas, a provisional company from 2d Battalion commanded by Capt. Floyd G. Hudson and Capt. Herbert M. Lorence's Company E moved out to support the attack. Captain Estey's Company F, 7th Marines, soon followed them. Companies D and E were pinned down by intense enemy mortar fire as they reached the crest of Vegas. When help arrived, Captain Melvin led his Marines back to the regimental command post after four harrowing hours in the meat grinder. Companies E and F joined forces to push the enemy back, and by 1930 were approaching the summit after an hour and a half of hand-to-hand fighting. That night the Chinese hit the Marines with several fierce counterattacks that pushed the Americans back to the base of the hill. Thus, after ten hours of savage fighting and suffering more than three hundred casualties, the Marines held only a small part of Vegas.

Attempts to retake the summit on the morning of the twenty-eighth initially failed. This was no surprise because by then Company F had been reduced to only about forty effectives. Company E resumed the attack that afternoon, captured the summit, and then began digging the Chinese out of their holes. Almost immediately, the CCF replied by pounding the heights with artillery and mortar fire to cover a counterattack. The Marine defenders, led by Plt. Sgt. John L. Williams, took cover and repelled the enemy advance with the assistance of well-placed supporting arms. Vegas was declared secured at 1407 when Maj. Benjamin G. Lee, the 2d Battalion operations officer, took charge and directed resupply and consolidation efforts. By that time only sixty-six Marines were left on Vegas—fifty-eight from Company E and eight from Company F, 7th Marines—but they were determined to stay until the arrival of two platoons from Capt. Ralph L. Walz's Company F, 5th Marines, later that afternoon. Vegas was once again back in Marine hands, but the question was, for how long?

Two Chinese battalions mounted three separate attacks against Vegas on the night of 28–29 March. The first came at about 2215, and by 2230 Lee's Marines had been pushed from the top of the hill, but were holding on in close-quarters combat. The Marines were able to clear the summit with a determined counterattack. However, more than two hundred Communists attacked just before midnight and Vegas was soon surrounded. The enemy was finally forced to retreat by a thirty-seven-minute artillery concentration in which more than six thousand rounds were fired. Company E, 7th Marines, broke through the encirclement and joined the Marine defenders just as the bulk of the enemy began to withdraw. Marine artillery continued to pound Reno over the next two hours and fired some "danger-close" missions to eject the remaining enemy on Vegas. By dawn the Marines had recaptured the critical northern segment of outposts the enemy had taken earlier. It was, unfortunately, a costly attack: Major Lee and Captain Walz were both killed.

The last enemy soldiers were dispatched in the growing morning light, and the Marines set about consolidating their positions. Smoke shells screened them as they dug in. Major Joseph S. Buntin, the 2d Battalion executive officer, brought up reinforcements and took command of Vegas. He placed two platoons in the main defenses and ordered a third to set up on nearby high ground. Bunkers, fighting positions, and weapons pits were repaired. The shell-pocked trench line was at least waist deep everywhere by noon, and most areas were up to shoulder height. After the sound and fury of the previous hours, the rest of the day was quiet.

The Chinese tried to repeat success with a carbon copy of the earlier 26 March three-prong assault that evening. This time, however, the Marines were primed and ready. American artillery boxed in Vegas and counterbattery fire disrupted enemy supporting arms. The Chinese that made it through the Marine curtain of steel were repulsed in a short, brisk fight. A small enemy probe, possibly by a casualty recovery team, was turned back around midnight. The Chinese were, however, not yet through. A final two-company attack was made from Reno and Hill 153 at about 0215, but was broken up by Marine supporting arms. Vegas was still in American hands at dawn, and the enemy had suffered more than three hundred casualties.

The Marines once again turned to rebuilding Vegas's battered defenses on 30 March. The day was clear and Marine aircraft were able to deliver bombs with pinpoint accuracy, destroying enemy positions at Reno and Hill 153. Company F came up from its reserve positions and replaced Company G on the MLR and at Outpost Berlin. Company G then relieved the battered defenders on Outpost Vegas. The last act in the "Battle for the Nevada Cities" occurred when five Chinese approached the Marine lines apparently to surrender, then suddenly opened up with hidden burp guns and tossed some grenades. The Marines cut three down, and the remaining two were wounded and captured. That night, Vegas was unmolested for the first time in five days. The Marines had suffered 1,015 casualties defending the trio of outposts, the heaviest losses suffered by the 1st Marine Division since the drive to the Punchbowl the previous year. Five Medals of Honor and ten Navy Crosses were awarded for deeds of heroism related to this action. The 5th Marines also received a Korean Presidential Unit Citation for this period.

The regiment was ordered to the rear eight days after the Nevada Cities battles. Not long after that, more than eight hundred replacements arrived and several new commanders took over. Colonel Harvey C. Tschirgi became the regimental commander on 14 April. Lieutenant Colonel John T. Hill took over the 3d Battalion on the eleventh, and Lt. Col. Jackson B. Butterfield took over the 1st Battalion on the twenty-ninth.

The 3d Battalion moved to the rear on 10 April for two days of training. However, plans to institute a regiment-wide training program had to be shelved as a result of the Korean weather. The spring thaws and heavy rains eroded the rear-area trenches and bunker fortifications, so the regiment spent most of its time as the division reserve rebuilding them. One exception was amphibious training. Lieutenant Colonel Finch's 2d Battalion conducted five days of shore-based training from 7–11 April in preparation for Marine Landing Exercise (MarLEX) xx. Battalion Landing Team 2/5 boarded its assigned ships on the thirteenth and stormed across Tokchok-to's southern beaches on the morning of the fifteenth despite uncooperative weather and high seas that subsequently modified exercise plans.

The 5th Marines, as part of the 1st Marine Division, became I Corps reserve and moved from Kimpo to Camp Casey in May. The regiment remained the Corps reserve from 6 May until 5 July. After a brief period of camp construction and facilities improvement, the regiment embarked on an ambitious training program. Emphasis was on improving individual skills and progressive unit training to include offensive, defensive, and amphibious warfare. Much of the training was done at night and company-level helicopter operations were included for the first time. The regiment conducted intensive amphibious training from 2–9 May before boarding ships at Inchon on the tenth and sailing for the Yongjong-ni landing area where it conducted MarLEX 1 beginning on the thirteenth. Lieutenant Colonel Andrew C. Geer became the 2d Battalion commander the next day.

The well-rested and well-trained 5th Marines returned to the center of the 1st Marine Division MLR on 7 July. The 3d Battalion moved up on the night of 6–7 July to relieve the army's 35th Infantry Regiment on the eastern half of its new sector at about 0300. The 2d Battalion and antitank support arrived in the late afternoon. Lieutenant Colonel Geer assumed responsibility for the western half of the MLR at 1716. Lieutenant Colonel Butterfield's 1st Battalion was in reserve. Artillery from the 3d Battalion, 11th Marines, was in direct support of the regiment, as was Company B, 1st Tank Battalion. By that time, three of the six outposts the 5th Marines fought so hard to protect in March—Carson, Elko, and Vegas—were no longer in UNC hands, and Outposts Berlin and East Berlin in the adjacent 7th Marines's sector were under constant attack.

There was little change in UNC activity during this last month of the Korean War. The Marines listened to popular music played by the North Korean "Dragon Lady," whose propaganda broadcasts beseeched the Americans to quit fighting and surrender. Routine patrols were conducted and occasional firefights broke out even though a cease-fire announcement was expected at any moment. All hands realized there would likely be one final enemy push before the fighting stopped. A squad patrol from the 5th Marines engaged a similar-sized Chinese force near Outpost Esther on the night of 12 July. Four nights later, another Marine squad engaged in an eight-minute firefight, inflicting three casualties without suffering a loss. That same night, a fifteen-man reconnaissance patrol from 2/5 stumbled into a V-shaped ambush near Hill 90. Close-quarters fighting resulted, and Marine reinforcements rushed forward only to be pinned down as well. Six Marines were dead and one was missing after the two-hour melee ended. The next night, Outposts Ingrid and Dagmar were probed, but the attackers were sent packing by American artillery fire.

The long-awaited final Chinese attack burst out on the night of 24 July. Intelligence reports that heavy attacks on Outposts Hedy and Dagmar were imminent failed to materialize on the night of the twenty-first as only a handful of enemy soldiers probed Hedy at the cost of three killed. Three nights later, the Chinese jabbed at Hedy and Dagmar. Then a battalion of the CCF 408th Regiment tried to overrun Outpost Esther, which was held by 2d Lt. William H. Bates's reinforced rifle platoon from Company H. Overwhelming supporting fires from the 11th Marines, tank guns, and recoilless rifles repelled the attackers. After several harrowing hours, Lieutenant Bates reported all was secure at Esther. The Marines lost twelve killed and ninety-eight wounded, including thirty-five who had to be evacuated. The Chinese were estimated to have suffered almost five hundred casualties. This action was the most intense encounter by the 5th Marines since March, and it was the regiment's last major engagement in Korea.

Post-Korea

A cease-fire agreement took effect at 2200 on 27 July 1953. What followed was neither a hot war nor a true peace. United Nations and Communist forces pulled back from an agreed-upon line of demarcation that ran roughly along the 38th Parallel. They dismantled the front lines inside the designated demilitarized zone (DMZ) and pulled back. There was not, however, an immediate halt to hostilities. Both sides sent out patrols, and occasional clashes resulted during the uneasy armistice. The border between North and South Korea remains a tense area to this day, and there is still a large U.S. military presence there.

The 5th Marines moved off the MLR and was assigned to the division's general outpost line north of the Imjin River. There, the regiment continued to maintain a high state of readiness in case the enemy chose to reengage without notice. The regiment was assigned the mission of defending the forward general outpost line across the 1st Marine Division sector and attended to police and security duties in the UNC portion of the DMZ beginning on 30 July. The 2d Battalion was assigned the left sector formerly held by the KMC regiment, the 1st Battalion stayed in the regiment's old central sector, and the 3d Battalion manned positions on the far right. The regiment dug about 1,650 individual fighting positions, created 400 crew-served weapons sites, 8 fortified infantry observation posts, 30 command bunkers, and manned 15,400 yards of trench lines by October.

Upon completing redeployment and setting up hasty defensive positions, the 5th Marines launched a major effort to tear down fortifications and salvage all removable materials from the DMZ. This was dangerous and difficult work that required both hard labor and great vigilance. The Marines were sleeping only a few hours each day and had to remain constantly wary about enemy infiltration while working through the nights. The regiment recovered more than 2,000 short tons of material, including 2,000 miles of communications wire, 2,850 rolls of barbed wire, 340 rolls of concertina, almost 20,000 picket stakes, 339,000 sandbags, and 150,000 linear feet of timber. For the most part, these assets were incorporated into newly constructed permanent defensive positions.

Colonels Tschirgi, Rathvon McC. Tompkins, Elby D. Martin, Hamilton M. Hoyler, and Robert H. Ruud successively commanded the regiment during the rest of its time in Korea. The 5th Marines conducted strenuous individual and unit training and individual Marines participated in a wide variety of athletic programs. These activities maintained military proficiency, instilled discipline, and kept morale high. In September, the regiment provided personnel to the 1st Provisional Demilitarized Zone Police Company. This unit manned trenches and lived in bunkers while keeping a sharp eye out for Communist infiltrators and line crossers. Small patrols ventured out on a daily basis to repair wire, check minefields, and set up listening posts along likely avenues of approach. The 5th Marines was relieved of responsibility for the Imjin Line on 1 June 1954 and became the 1st Marine Division reserve thereafter.

The regiment conducted two weeks of intense training ashore, moved to Inchon, embarked on board amphibious shipping, and conducted a regimental landing exercise. Thereafter, each battalion conducted its own training schedule, including landing or field exercises. During this time the battalions took turns manning outposts in front of the MLR. On 21 August the 5th Marines received the additional duty of providing security for all United Nations installations in the rear area. In September, the regiment was additionally tasked to maintain a mobile force to assist with riot control in Seoul. The regiment was finally relieved of all tactical missions on 25 January 1955, and moved to Ascom City to prepare to return to the United States. The 1st Marine Division, including the 5th Marines, embarked at Inchon and sailed for San Diego in February 1955.

The Old Breed received a joyous welcome upon its return to California on 17 March. The division paraded through San Diego and then mounted trucks for the fifty-mile ride up the coast to Camp Pendleton. The 5th Marines moved into newly erected concrete buildings at Camp Margarita (Area 33) and settled down in what would be the regiment's home for the next decade. Expansive Camp Pendleton was well suited as a training base. The weather was good almost all year round, the rugged hills and dusty roads were ideal for conditioning hikes, excellent beaches and San Clemente Island were used for amphibious training, nearby bases at Pickle Meadows and Twenty-nine Palms provided cold weather and desert training grounds, and San Diego and Los Angeles offered excellent nearby weekend liberty.

Although they did not directly involve the 5th Marines, several important events affected the Marine Corps after the Korean War cooled down. The Mansfield-Douglas Bill, also known as the Marine Corps Act, became Public Law 416 in 1952. This statute, cosponsored by former 5th Marines adjutant Paul Douglas, specified that the Marine Corps would thereafter consist of at least three active Marine divisions and three air wings, and the Commandant was given a voice on the Joint Chiefs of Staff, albeit only with respect to Marine Corps matters. As a result of this statutory mandate, the Marine Corps became America's premier strategic all-purpose force. The 3d Marine Division and 1st MAW were forward deployed in the western Pacific, the 2d Marine Division and 2d MAW on the East Coast were given contingency missions in the Mediterranean and Caribbean, and the 1st Marine Division and 3d MAW stood by on the West Coast, ready to reinforce either the 2d or 3d Marine Divisions in times of crisis.

Using the lessons of Korea and prodded by the specter of tactical nuclear weapons, the Marine Corps underwent a revolutionary change in organization, tactics, equipment, and doctrine, and the decade before the beginning of the Vietnam War has been compared with the interwar years of the 1920s and 1930s with respect to Marine Corps innovation. This time, however, the focus was not amphibious operations as it had been before World War II. The new method of warfare was "vertical envelopment," which used helicopters to rapidly move troops and extensive logistics support over land or from the sea. Marine ground, aviation, combat support, and service support units were merged into combined-arms teams that could deploy and fight together under a single commander. The largest of these was the Marine Expeditionary Force

(MEF), a division-wing team; the midsize unit was the Marine Expeditionary Brigade (MEB), composed of a regimental combat team and an aircraft group; and the smallest permanent combat team was the Marine Expeditionary Unit (MEU), consisting of a reinforced rifle battalion and a task-organized composite aircraft squadron. Units smaller than MEUs were sometimes formed for specific missions and were called special-purpose forces.

The Fleet Marine Forces were reorganized and equipped to become much more mobile in 1957. The ultimate goal of this reorganization was to be able to transport all Marine divisional units and equipment by helicopter. Heavy equipment (tanks, amtracs, self-propelled artillery, etc.) was taken from Marine divisions and became Force Troops assets. Under the M-series tables of equipment and organization the 5th Marines lost its 4.2-inch mortars, which were transferred to the 11th Marines. Regimental antitank and battalion weapons companies were dissolved, and each infantry battalion added a fourth rifle company. Flamethrowers, 81mm mortars, and 106mm recoilless rifles were transferred into expanded battalion headquarters and service companies. Reliable and familiar infantry small arms (M1 Garands, M1 carbines, BARs, and Browning machine guns) were dropped when the Marines were rearmed with NATO-standard 7.62mm M14 rifles and M60 medium machine guns. Rifle squads were expanded to fourteen men by adding grenadiers armed with M79 40mm grenade launchers. Field uniforms were changed to conform to new standards of universal military equipment. Gone were the distinctive Marine leggings and herringbone dungarees. Green sateen all-service utility uniforms replaced them. Mindful of the World War I experience with common-issue clothing, this time the Marines ironed decals bearing the Marine Corps emblem over the letters "USMC" on the left-breast pocket of their utility uniforms to leave no doubt about which service the bearer belonged to. Boondocker field shoes were replaced with common-issue, all-service, black leather boots. Not every change marked a radical departure from the past, however. The traditional ranks of gunner (warrant officer), gunnery sergeant, and lance corporal were restored.

The 5th Marines participated in the first regimental peacetime field exercise in June 1955, a weeklong training exercise that culminated with an amphibious landing. From that time until 1962, the regiment conducted more than fifty major exercises covering a wide range of military operations. Most of these were designed to perfect amphibious and helicopter-borne landing skills, but the 5th Marines also conducted field tests of experimental equipment and proposed tactics. The most ambitious training exercise conducted by the regiment during this period was Operation Flatfoot in June 1956, which featured a one-hundred-mile forced march. The regiment also provided support for annual reserve training and hosted U.S. Naval Academy midshipmen on their summer cruises. The major real-world contingency of this time occurred when elements of the regiment were assigned to the 5th MEB and sortied through the Panama Canal into the Caribbean during the Cuban Missile Crisis in October 1962. However, the regimental colors remained at Camp Pendleton, where the bulk of the 5th Marines stayed as part of the West Coast rapid reaction reserve.

During this ten-year Cold War stint at Camp Pendleton, the regiment was successively commanded by Colonel Ruud, Lt. Col. Crawford B. Lawton (26 June–31 July 1955), Cols. James S. Blais (1 August 1955–31 August 1956) and Richard Rothwell (1 September 1956–14 June 1957), Lt. Col. David A. Van Evera (15 June–9 July 1957), and Cols. Bruce T. Hemphill (10 July–10 December 1957), Donald Schmuck (11 December 1957–5 March 1958), Tolson A. Smoak (6–8 March 1958), Webb D. Sawyer (9 April 1960–12 July 1961), Charles E. Warren (13 July1961–15 February 1962), James T. Kisgen (16 February–8 August 1962), Homer E. Hire (9 August 1962–17 July 1963), Walter E. Reynolds (18 July 1963–28 July 1964), and Victor J. Croizat (29 July 1964–15 August 1965).

One of the lessons of the Korean War was that there was a need for forward-deployed rapid reaction forces in the western Pacific. The Marine contribution to such a strategic reserve was the 3d Marine Division, which was stationed at Okinawa, and the 1st MAW headquartered in Japan. To keep these forces fully manned and combat ready at all times, the Marine Corps instituted a "transplacement" rotation system whereby entire infantry battalions were sent overseas as part of a thirty-month deployment schedule that consisted of fifteen months training at Camp Pendleton, a thirteen-month overseas tour on Okinawa, one month in transit, and a one-month postdeployment stand-down. The 5th Marines began supplying transplacement battalions in 1959.

There was also a demonstrated need for seaborne reaction forces afloat modeled on Marine battalion landing teams sailing in the Mediterranean and Caribbean. Accordingly, Lt. Col. Warren A. Butcher's 2/5, then stationed at Camp Schwab on Okinawa, was designated the 1st Provisional Battalion Landing Team Afloat. Butcher's battalion was assigned duties as the Seventh Fleet Landing Force and thus became the fore-runner of the Special Landing Force (SLF). The SLF mission was to be prepared to conduct amphibious operations to protect American lives and property at the request of the State Department or to deploy in support of U.S. national interests in Japan, Korea, the Ryukyu Islands, Vietnam, Laos, Cambodia, Hong Kong, Macao, Taiwan, Thailand, Burma, Malaya, Singapore, the Philippines, British Borneo, Indonesia, Netherlands New Guinea, Portuguese Timor, Australia, New Zealand, and Oceania.

Battalion Landing Team 2/5 acted as a test unit to implement this amphibious concept in the Pacific. The unit could not be tailored for a single mission as specified in existing doctrine, so the landing force had to be configured to meet a number of contingencies. A general logistic support package was established and loaded on board ships of the Seventh Fleet. The Marines of BLT 2/5 underwent a special training period and passed numerous inspections prior to sailing on 4 August 1960. Unlike later deployments, this first landing force and its aviation support sailed in different naval task groups. Battalion Landing Team 2/5 traveled to the Philippines, Japan, Taiwan, and Hong Kong during two and one-half months at sea. The cruise was a continuous round of inspections, training exercises, ceremonial reviews, and port calls to show the flag. Although BLT 2/5 made no combat landings, it took a major step in the journey that led to development of modern, special-operations-capable Marine expeditionary units.

Postscript

Several members of the Korean War–era 5th Marines later became general officers and went on to distinguished careers. Two of them, Lew Walt and Sam Jaskilka, became Assistant Commandants of the Marine Corps and achieved four-star rank while on active duty. Lanky Texan Ray Murray eventually became deputy commander of all Marines in Vietnam and rose to the grade of lieutenant general. The highly decorated (two Navy Crosses, an army Distinguished Service Medal, and a pair of Silver Stars) Murray was an old China Hand who had fought at Guadalcanal, Tarawa, and Saipan during World War II then ably led his regiment through every engagement in 1950. A real-life hero, he also received literary notoriety for being the role model for the fictional "High Pockets" Huxley in Leon Uris's best-selling novel *Battle Cry*. Likewise, Dick Weede—the former artilleryman who commanded an infantry regiment with distinction—retired as a lieutenant general after commanding the 1st Marine Brigade in Hawaii and serving as Gen. William C. Westmoreland's chief of staff during the early years of the Vietnam War. Jonas Platt, Oscar Peatross, and Dewey Bohn all retired as major generals. Bohn and Ralph Estey both commanded the 5th Marines as colonels in Vietnam.

Two members of the 5th Marines left the Corps but went on to serve in the U.S. Congress. Pete McCloskey had been a day laborer and semipro baseball player to support himself while attending Stanford University in the late 1940s after service as a navy enlisted man during World War II. Upon graduation he joined the Marines, attended OCS, and became one of the most decorated junior officers in the Marine Corps (Navy Cross, Silver Star, and two Purple Hearts). After leaving active duty, McCloskey became a lawyer but maintained his ties with the Marine Corps Reserve, eventually rising to the rank of lieutenant colonel. He made his initial mark in politics by defeating incumbent Rep. Shirley Temple Black in 1967, then served seven terms in the House of Representatives. During that time he was best known for his outspoken criticism of America's role in Vietnam, and his challenge of Pres. Richard M. Nixon's bid for reelection. In 1992 McCloskey wrote a vivid memoir, *The Taking of Hill 610*, about his experiences in Korea. Enlisted man Andrew Jacobs Jr. was seriously wounded in the fighting around the Punchbowl in 1951. After a ten-year career in law enforcement, he was elected to the House of Representatives from Indiana's Tenth District. Famous for his frugality and rejection of special interest money, Jacobs served on the powerful Ways and Means Committee and was one of the most respected members of that body.

Col. Charles A. Doyen was the first regimental commander. He commanded the 5th Regiment on two occasions, once in 1914 when it was a temporary Caribbean landing force then again in 1917 when he took the regiment to France during the First World War.

The first 5th Regiment of Marines spent most of its initial tour of duty sailing the Carribean on board the armed transport USS *Hancock*. Interestingly, the modern 5th Marines furnishes the ground units that make up the Okinawa-based special landing forces in the Western Pacific.

Brig. Gen. Charles A. Doyen, and Lt. Col. Frederic M. Wise meet during an inspection of the regimental lines near Verdun in the spring of 1918. Doyen was the first regimental commander, and Wise's memoir *A Marine Tells It To You* is still in print more than fifty years after it was written.

The 5th Regiment marching into Germany after the Armistice. When German representatives balked at the Versailles Peace Conference, the Marines marched to Hartenfels stopping only after terms of surrender were accepted.

This drum was jokingly referred to as "the regiment's first combat casualty" after it was holed by German artillery fire on Saint Patrick's Day in 1918. The inverted chevron on the left is a wound stripe, the four chevrons on the right represent campaign participation, and a French *Croix de Guerre* Medal is painted next to the Marine Corps emblem.

Wendell C. ("Buck") Neville was the first former regimental commander to become Commandant of the Marine Corps. Neville's most notable military achievement was commanding the 5th Regiment at Belleau Wood in 1918.

Members of the 5th Marines participate in a reenactment of the battle of Antietam in 1924 to demonstrate how that Civil War battle would have been fought with modern weapons. The popular Civil War Summer Maneuvers of the 1920s effectively combined combat training and showmanship, and they drew more fans than sporting events or concerts.

A 5th Regiment landing force comes ashore at Culebra Island during fleet exercises in 1924. As the infantry component of East Coast Expeditionary Force in the 1920s and '30s the 5th Marines regularly conducted such exercises to test amphibious equipment and doctrine.

A heavily armed Marine mail guard detachment. Members of the 5th Marines were called out to perform such duties twice in the 1920s, and each time the robberies stopped immediately.

The 5th Regiment lines the docks of Norfolk prepared to board the armed transport USS *Henderson* for transport to Nicaragua in order to perform limited peace keeping duty, but the Marines instead became embroiled in five years of fierce antiguerrilla warfare.

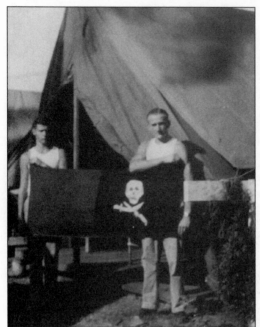

Marines display a "San-danista" flag captured during the epic siege of Ocotal. The 5th Marines carried the brunt of the fighting in Nicaragua from 1927–1933.

Marines hop over the side of a whaleboat during fleet maneuvers in the late 1930s. Quantico was the home of the 5th Marines between the world wars, and while there the regiment was the major test unit for new tactics and equipment associated with amphibious warfare.

A tired column of the 5th Marines moves through the Umurbrogol Pocket after Peleliu was declared secure in 1944. The fight for Peleliu was one of the bloodiest in the regiment's history, yet, that campaign remains almost forgotten by modern historians.

Time consuming but effective "blowtorch and corkscrew" tactics overcame enemy fortified positions, particularly the caves and concrete graves that dotted the southern half of the island of Okinawa in 1945. The enemy was blinded by smoke or hit by supporting fires that allowed flame tanks or flamethrower assault teams to saturate the target before demolitions charges finished the job.

Marine "Minute Men of 1950" board ship at San Diego bound for Korea in July. The 5th Marines was the ground combat element of the hastily assembled 1st Provisional Marine Brigade, the first ground combat unit to arrive in Korea directly from the United States.

Medal of Honor winner 1st. Lt. Baldamero Lopez leads an assault wave of the 5th Marines over a seawall at Inchon in September 1950. The Inchon landing was a classic turning movement that trapped the bulk of the NKPA below the 38th Parallel and dramatically changed the course of the Korean Conflict.

A wounded Chinese prisoner is treated by medical corpsmen immediately after his capture in May 1952. (NARA)

Two Chinese soldiers surrender to U.S. Marines near Koto Ri, 9 December 1950. (NARA)

Members of the 5th Marines escort two Chinese POWs captured during the UN counteroffensive in late May 1951. (NARA)

Men of the 5th Marines pass a knocked out NKPA T-34 tank. The Marines were dubbed the "fire brigade" by the U.S. press during the defense of the Pusan Perimeter in Ausust 1950.

Marines move from the Hwachon reservoir to the No Name Line in April 1951. Within a month the 5th Marines helped to stop the final Chinese offensive of the Korean War then led the drive back to the 38th parallel.

Men of 1/5 enter the ancient Mang Ca gate of the Hue Citadel in January 1968. In what was some of the toughest fighting in the regiment's history, 2/5 cleared southern Hue City while 1/5 cleared the Citadel.

Marines of the 2d Platoon, Company L, 3/5, return VC fire during Operation Meade River while clearing the "Dodge City" area about fifteen miles southwest of Da Nang in 1968. This was one of many combat actions in Vietnam. (Marine Corps History and Museums Division)

The author in the infamous "Arizona Territory," an often fought over agricultural flatland located between the Thu Bon and Vu Gia Rivers north of An Hoa Combat Base in the Republic of Vietnam. It was on this blood-soaked ground that the 5th Marines and the 2d NVA Division fought many fearsome battles between 1967 and 1970. (author's collection)

Task Force Ripper advances through the desert toward Kuwait City during Operation Desert Storm. Elements of the 5th Marines were among the first American units to arrive in Southwest Asia in August 1990, and RLT-5 fought the last Marine battle in the Persian Gulf in March 1991. (Marine Corps History and Museums Division)

Regimental Landing Team 5 (BLTs 2/5 and 3/5) participated in the massive international humanitarian relief effort popularly called "Operation Sea Angel" while in transit from the Persian Gulf to the United States in 1991.

Members of the current 5th Marines wear the French *Fouragerre* over their left shoulder to commemorate the regiment's heroic performance during World War I. This red-and-green braid decoration, often called a "Pogey Rope," was awarded in perpetuity when the gallant 5th Regiment was cited for outstanding performance three different times on the battlefields of France in 1918. (courtesy J. Doug Taylor)

Lemuel C. Shepherd, Jr., a junior officer with the 5th Regiment during World War I, was the Commandant of the Marine Corps from 1952 to 1956. A French *Fouragerre* honor braid adorns his left shoulder.

6: Vietnam

In the early 1960s trouble again began brewing the Far East as a result of the French withdrawal from Indochina. Under the 1954 Geneva accords, Indochina was broken into the independent states of Laos, Cambodia, and Vietnam. Vietnam was temporarily partitioned at the 17th Parallel until elections to decide whether Vietnam would be under Communist rule or not could be arranged. In the interim, however, a civil war broke out. A U.S.-led, free-world coalition backed the Republic of Vietnam against indigenous Communist Viet Cong (VC) guerrillas and their North Vietnamese Army (NVA) allies. For the most part, American military and economic assistance to South Vietnam remained at a relatively low but ominously increasing level under Presidents Eisenhower and Kennedy. The Marine Corps's presence was limited to a handful of advisers, a transport helicopter squadron, some small rotating security detachments, and a few staff personnel assigned to the U.S. Military Assistance Command–Vietnam (MACV).

An irrevocable step into what eventually became America's longest war occurred when the 9th MEB became the first major U.S. ground combat unit sent to South Vietnam. The 9th MEB landed at Da Nang to defend the vital air base located there on 8 March 1965. Not long thereafter, the III Marine Amphibious Force (III MAF)—consisting of the 3d Marine Division, the 1st MAW, and assorted service and support units—became the senior Marine headquarters in Vietnam. Elements of the 1st Marine Division began moving from Camp Pendleton to fill the vacuum left in the western Pacific when the 3d Marine Division deployed to Vietnam in 1965.

Major General Lew Walt, who served so well with the 5th Marines during World War II and in Korea, became III MAF's commanding general.

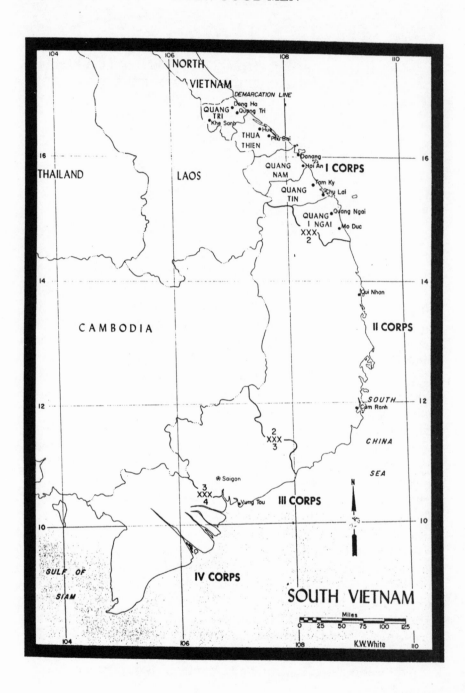

His command was charged with five essential tasks: (1) to defend and develop secure base camps in northern South Vietnam, (2) to support Army of the Republic of Vietnam (ARVN) operations, (3) to conduct offensive operations against the Viet Cong, (4) to be prepared to provide emergency forces throughout South Vietnam, and (5) to conduct "rural construction" (pacification) operations.

General William C. Westmoreland, USA, the MACV commander, ordered the Marines to conduct large-unit search-and-destroy operations to ferret out Viet Cong guerrillas and defeat the NVA in set-piece battles. The Marines followed these orders but, recalling counterinsurgency lessons learned during the Banana Wars, added their own tactical touches. Golden Fleece operations used U.S. Marines to protect Vietnamese farmers as they reaped their harvests, sophisticated cordon-and-search operations were called County Fairs, hand-picked Marine squads were assigned to live and work with local military units in Combined Action Platoons (CAPs), and Marines escorted navy doctors and corpsmen as they visited villages and hamlets as part of the medical civic action program.

The III MAF area of responsibility encompassed the I Corps Tactical Zone, which included Quang Tri, Thua Thien, Quang Nam, Quang Tin, and Quang Ngai Provinces. The terrain in I Corps included rugged, jungle-covered mountains along the Laotian border to the west; fertile, densely populated coastal plains that bordered the South China Sea to the east; and Vietnam's second and third largest cities, Da Nang and Hue. The Marines worked out of three major enclaves: Da Nang, with its excellent airfield and deepwater port; Chu Lai, a military complex and expeditionary airfield built from scratch on a sandy beach about fifty miles south of Da Nang; and Phu Bai, a military complex and airfield located about forty miles north of Da Nang, not far from the old Vietnamese imperial capital at Hue.

The Communists turned out to be very resilient and were far more difficult to subdue than had been anticipated, and MACV required more men and resources as time passed. Increased manpower requirements in Vietnam meant that infantry battalion transplacement rotations had to be dropped in October 1965. Marines thereafter served thirteen-month tours on an individual basis rather than deploying as members of a cohesive unit. Additionally, it was decided to commit the 1st Marine Division to Vietnam at that time. Movement orders were cut in January 1966. The 7th Marines and two battalions of the 1st Marines were already

in country and would stay there. The remaining 1st Marine Division battalions would deploy overseas at the rate of about one per month. Most
units moved from California to Okinawa for final training before they
went on to Vietnam. The 5th Marines, the last infantry regiment slated
to go, was not scheduled to be fully in country until the summer of 1966.

Special Landing Forces

The 5th Marines participated in Operation Silver Lance at Camp Pendleton from 12 February–9 March 1965. This combination amphibious and
counter-insurgency exercise involved the 1st Marine Division, the Hawaii-
based 1st Marine Brigade, the 3d MAW, and navy amphibious forces.
More than 20,000 Marines came over the beach then maneuvered inland to repel a simulated invasion before conducting follow-on anti-guer-
rilla operations. This exercise, the largest war game inside the continental United States since World War II, was the brainchild of former
5th Marines commander Brute Krulak, who was by then a lieutenant general commanding the Fleet Marine Force Pacific. The Silver Lance scenario closely mirrored the existing situation in Southeast Asia. In fact,
as the West Coast Marines were fighting imaginary battles in the hills of
Camp Pendleton, their brothers-in-arms in the western Pacific were
preparing to go ashore to fight real battles in the embattled country of
South Vietnam where a low-intensity Communist insurgency was about
to escalate into a full-scale war that would eventually become the longest
armed conflict in American history.

Major General Lewis J. Fields's 1st Marine Division headquarters was
established at Chu Lai in March 1966. The 1st Marine Division's tactical area of responsibility (TAOR) included the three southernmost
provinces in I Corps: Quang Nam, Quang Tin, and Quang Ngai. The
fighting there was less intense than that near the DMZ that separated
North and South Vietnam at the 17th Parallel, but the southern region
was no less important. The area south of Da Nang was home to a large
population, its rich rice fields and abundant agricultural output made
it the breadbasket of that part of Vietnam, many remote jungle areas
near the Laotian border served as enemy staging areas, and the east-
west river valleys were important avenues of approach into the rice-rich
coastal region.

The 5th Marines left Camp Pendleton in increments. Upon arrival in
the western Pacific, each battalion served for a short time with the Spe-

cial Landing Force (SLF). The SLF was the U.S. Pacific Command's seaborne strategic reserve and usually consisted of a command element, a battalion landing team, a helicopter squadron, and appropriate combat service support detachments embarked upon several ships called an Amphibious Ready Group (ARG). The 9th Marine Amphibious Brigade (MAB) on Okinawa was the SLF's parent unit. Marine air-ground task force designations changed from *expeditionary* to *amphibious* in 1965 for diplomatic reasons: The State Department did not want to remind the Vietnamese of the French expeditionary forces that occupied their country after World War II. The 5th Marines constituted the ground combat element of the 9th MAB while the regiment was stationed on Okinawa, and Col. Charles F. Widdecke served as both Regimental Landing Team (RLT) 5 and Task Group 79.2 commander from 30 March until 26 May 1966. Lieutenant Colonel Harold L. Coffman's BLT 1/5 was the ground combat element of the landing force from 28 February until 7 May 1966, Lt. Col. Robert H. Uskurait's BLT 2/5 served in that capacity from 30 March to 4 May, and Lt. Col. Edward J. Bronars's BLT 3/5 did likewise from 7 May to 1 August.

The 5th Marines departed the U. S. West Coast for the Far East over a period of three months. The 1st Battalion and its support units were sent to Hawaii on 30 June 1965. Upon arrival at Pearl Harbor, BLT 1/5 became the ground combat element of the 1st Marine Brigade and moved into quarters at Marine Corps Air Station Kaneohe. The Marines conducted progressive individual and small-unit training on Oahu and at the Pohakaloa Training Area on Hawaii. This cycle culminated with a landing exercise on nearby Molokai. A final counterguerrilla exercise was held at Oahu's Kahuku Training Area, after which BLT 1/5 moved to Pearl Harbor and sailed for the western Pacific on 19 February 1966. Instead of proceeding to Okinawa as planned, however, the 1st Battalion was diverted to the Philippines to become the SLF. The 2d Battalion embarked at Long Beach and sailed west on 10 January 1966. After a short layover in Hawaii, BLT 2/5 continued on to Okinawa and arrived at White Beach in early February. The battalion underwent an intensive training cycle at Okinawa's rugged Northern Training Area jungle warfare combat center in preparation for its new mission. The 3d Battalion followed about two months later and debarked at White Beach on 26 March after a two-week voyage from Southern California.

The 1st Battalion became the SLF at Subic Bay when it arrived there on 28 February on board the amphibious assault ship USS *Princeton*, the attack transport USS *Pickaway* (one of the ships the regiment used during the Korean War), and the dock landing ship USS *Alamo*. These ships became the SLF's ARG when they arrived at Subic. The 1st Battalion, as part of the SLF, was the first 5th Marines unit to engage the enemy in Vietnam. It participated in Operation Jackstay to clear a vital channel that linked the South China Sea to Saigon from 26 March–6 April 1966. The Rung Sat Special Zone was composed of a series of waterways interlacing waist-deep mangrove swamps. The only sizable piece of land in the zone was the Long Thanh peninsula. This unusual terrain prohibited classic ship-to-shore assaults, so Operation Jackstay was actually a riverine operation rather than a traditional amphibious assault. The Marines made a six-mile transit to shore and landed unopposed at Long Thanh on the morning of the twenty-sixth. There were no large firefights so the only casualties were those resulting from the enemy mines that permeated the area. The Marines thereafter searched the Rung Sat Special Zone from this base using landing craft and helicopters. They came ashore only when they found Viet Cong workshops, supply dumps, food stocks, or fighting bunkers. The Marines were hampered because their equipment and landing craft were not designed for such operations, but they adapted to the situation. Harkening back to the Talasea landings on New Britain, the Marines experimented by placing an Ontos antitank vehicle in an LCM and used its six 106mm recoilless rifles for direct-fire support. Operation Jackstay lasted thirteen days and enjoyed moderate but fleeting success. The channel was temporarily opened, and more than 60 enemy were reported killed. Marine losses were 5 killed, 25 wounded, and 2 missing. Jackstay, however, was most notable in the annals of the 5th Marines because it was the regiment's first combat action since Korea.

Three weeks later, BLT 1/5 participated in SLF Operation Osage in Thua Thien Province from 27 April–2 May. The mission was to destroy a main force Viet Cong battalion and its NVA reinforcements. Alas, this did not happen because the enemy chose not to stand and fight. The landing force encountered only scattered resistance, but the Marines suffered eight killed and nine wounded, many of them lost to "surprise firing devices" (Marine jargon for booby traps). The 1st Battalion reembarked on 6 May, and two days later landed at Chu Lai, where it was released from SLF duties to rejoin its parent regiment.

Concurrent with Operation Kansas (described in detail in the next section) to the south, BLT 3/5 participated in SLF Operation Deckhouse

I. Deckhouse I was the first in a series of SLF landings in support of ongoing operations by allied units ashore. In this case, the army's 1st Cavalry Division was conducting Operation Nathan Hale near Qui Nhon in the II Corps Tactical Zone. The Marines came ashore, but the 2d Battalion encountered only scattered resistance before it was pulled out. The SLF then returned to Subic Bay for replenishment and further training before heading back to Vietnamese waters.

Operation Deckhouse II was next. This time BLT 3/5 supported the 3d Marine Division in Quang Tri Province. There, Operation Hastings—the largest Marine operation in Vietnam to that time—was under way. The Marine mission was to halt North Vietnamese movement across the DMZ and to root out enemy units already inside South Vietnam. Plans called for BLT 3/5 to assume blocking positions about eight miles north of Dong Ha after landing via a combination of surface and helicopter-borne lifts. In accord with amphibious doctrine, once the entire landing force was firmly established on shore, Deckhouse II would be terminated and Task Force Delta would absorb BLT 3/5 as it conducted operations farther inland.

Lieutenant Colonel Bronars's BLT 3/5 landed in moderate seas under clear skies on the morning of 16 July. Companies I and K came in across Blue Beach, located about two miles north of the mouth of the Cua Viet River, at 0630. Company L used a helicopter landing zone about three thousand meters inland of Blue Beach. All elements of BLT 3/5 were ashore by evening. Colonel Bronars established a defensive perimeter and sent out ambush teams to interdict NVA supply routes. Although still under the operational control of the Seventh Fleet, BLT 3/5 was prepared to reinforce Task Force Delta on order.

The amphibious phase was terminated on the morning of the eighteenth and BLT 3/5 was "chopped" to Task Force Delta's control at 0800. The 3d Battalion was then inserted into a suspected NVA marshaling area that had been hit by an Arc Light bomb strike. Only Capt. Harold D. Pettengill's Company M encountered serious resistance. Air strikes allowed Company M to overrun enemy positions that contained twenty-one enemy dead, two machine guns, and eleven assault rifles.

The next day, 1/1 linked up with BLT 3/5 in the Song Ngan Valley. The two units met scattered but steady resistance as they searched the area. Most firefights during the next three days resulted from meeting engagements with enemy stragglers who stumbled into Marine positions, or when the Marines ran into platoon-sized delaying forces. A major action occurred on the twenty-fourth when Capt. Samuel S. Glaize's Company I moved up Hill 362 to establish a radio relay site. The Marines took the top of the hill without trouble, but came under heavy enemy fire as they moved down the far slope. The 2d Platoon took the brunt of the fire and was quickly pinned down. Lance Corporal Richard A. Pittman of the 1st Platoon rushed forward with a borrowed machine gun and covered the Marines as they pulled back. He single-handedly destroyed several enemy positions and repelled an enemy attack. Pittman became the first member of the 5th Marines to be awarded the Medal of Honor in Vietnam. Despite Pittman's heroic one-man charge, the Marines were forced to leave some wounded men behind. These helpless Marines were ruthlessly killed by the NVA, who—once their grisly task was accomplished—turned their attention toward the crest of Hill 362. Deadly enemy mortar fire took a heavy toll of Marines until a UH-1E helicopter gunship strafed positions identified by Capt. James J. Kirche, the 81mm mortar platoon leader, who deduced the enemy positions by doing a quick map study. This aerial attack yielded two secondary explosions and stopped the enemy fire.

When he learned of Glaize's troubles, Lieutenant Colonel Bronars ordered Capt. Richard E. Maresco's Company K up Hill 362. Unfortunately, Maresco's men ran into stiff resistance and were halted by enemy fire at the foot of the objective. Bronars skillfully used artillery and naval gunfire to isolate the Marine positions, but Company M still spent a long, fretful night alone atop Hill 362. At one point, the NVA closed to within thirty feet of the Marine lines before being driven back. Driving rain and thick jungle canopy hindered medical evacuation efforts so not many badly wounded men could be taken out that night. The next morning, Company K resumed its advance and linked up with Company M before noon, but by that time the enemy had fled. Total Marine casualties during this brutal fight with the NVA 6th Battalion, 812th Regiment, were eighteen killed and eighty-two wounded. A few days later, BLT 3/5 reboarded its assigned ships then sailed south to join the rest of the regiment at Chu Lai on 2 August.

Chu Lai

The bulk of the 5th Marines was ashore in Vietnam by the end of May, and the regiment was ready to conduct independent operations by June 1966. The 2d Battalion had been the first 5th Marines unit to permanently deploy to Vietnam. It arrived at Chu Lai on 12 April and was placed under the operational control of the 1st Marines. The 1st Battalion, 5th Marines, followed on 8 May. Regimental headquarters arrived on 27 May. Colonel Widdecke became responsible for Chu Lai and assumed operational control of the 1st and 2d Battalions and some elements of the 1st Marines on the twenty-eighth. Future plans called for the 3d Battalion and the Republic of Korea's 2d Marine "Blue Dragon" Brigade to join the 5th Marines at Chu Lai later that summer.

Marine leaders recognized Vietnam was a unique environment that would require innovative tactics and flexible organization. General Walt wanted to retain maximum operational flexibility, yet realized that stability and constant American presence were also necessary. Accordingly, Marine regiments were assigned a permanent TAOR in which the regimental headquarters and most combat and service support elements remained in the same place. However, the regiment's organic maneuver battalions might be moved anywhere the tactical situation dictated. Thus, a single regiment might have as few as one or as many as five rifle battalions under its operation control at any given time, and none of these would necessarily be the regiment's normally assigned organic units.

The first major contact between the 5th Marines and enemy forces while the regiment was at Chu Lai occurred about two weeks later. It was triggered when a reconnaissance team led by SSgt. Jimmie C. Howard made a heroic stand atop Nui Vu Mountain. These eighteen Marines, supported by artillery and air strikes, held off an enemy battalion from the NVA 3d Regiment throughout the night of 15–16 June. At first light the next morning, Company C, 1/5, commanded by 1st Lt. Marshall B. "Buck" Darling, was lifted in to assist Howard's beleaguered Marines. Buck Darling's men fought their way to the top of the hill to rescue the survivors and then held the enemy at bay while more than a dozen wounded Marines were evacuated. Company C suffered two dead and two seriously wounded in the process. This successful action at "Howard's Hill" is considered to be one of the epic battles of the Vietnam War, and Staff Sergeant Howard was awarded the Medal of Honor for his actions there.

The 5th Marines was scheduled to participate in Operation Kansas, a multibattalion combined-force operation to sweep the Que Son Valley (also known as the Nui Loc Son Basin) north of Chu Lai, in mid-June. However, plans for this first 5th Marines–run ground offensive were

scaled back when ARVN units had to move north to quell civil distur-
bances at Da Nang and Hue City. Instead of the regiment making the
assault, teams from the 1st Reconnaissance Battalion combed the area.
The 5th Marines remained at Chu Lai to provide helicopter-borne
emergency reaction forces, but only Company E was committed to the
fight. It was lifted into the battle area to survey the results of an Arc Light
strike by U.S. Air Force B-52 bombers. The company encountered no
resistance, discovered no evidence of enemy activity, and was airborne
within ninety minutes.

Acting on intelligence reports that the NVA 2d Division had reentered
the Que Son Valley, General Fields ordered Colonel Widdecke to mount
an operation to clear the Hiep Duc–Ly-Ly River area. Not unlike plans
for the earlier Operation Kansas, the 5th Marines and the ARVN 2d Division would work in concert to conduct a classic search-and-destroy
operation. These activities were known to the Americans as Operation
Colorado and to the Vietnamese as Lien Ket 52. A combined U.S. Vietnamese headquarters was located at Tam Ky, just north of Chu Lai on
Highway 1. The ARVN were assigned the area north of Route 534, which
ran from Highway 1 at Thang Binh inland to Hiep Duc. The Americans
had the area south of Route 534. The 1st and 2d Battalions, less one security company each at Chu Lai, were the 5th Marines maneuver elements; the 3d Battalion was held in reserve. The 2d Battalion, 11th
Marines, provided artillery support. Marine Air Groups 16 and 36 provided helicopter lift, MAG-11 and MAG-12 furnished fixed-wing close air
support, and air force B-52s supplied Arc Light strikes.

D day was set for 6 August. Lieutenant Colonel Walter Moore's 2/5
was lifted to Hiep Duc, searched the area for two days, and returned to
Tam Ky without meeting a sizable enemy force. Moore's battalion was
next lifted into blocking positions in the Ly-Ly River Valley on 9 August,
but encountered no enemy.

At about the same time, Lieutenant Colonel Coffman's 1st Battalion
scoured the area east of Que Son and west of Highway 1 for four days
without success. This dry hole evaporated when the 1st Battalion moved
toward Thong Hai hamlet about six miles west of the railroad on the
morning of the tenth. The lead elements of Coffman's column came under long-range enemy fire starting at about 0830. Coffman halted his
men about an hour before noon to hold a commanders' conference to
discuss the situation with Colonel Widdecke before 1/5 resumed the advance. The Marines were in the midst of a heavy downpour as they ap-

proached Ky Phu hamlet in the afternoon. Company A opened fire when some surprised Viet Cong guerrillas were spotted fleeing across an open rice paddy. The Marines cut most of the enemy down before they could escape. However, other nearby VC responded immediately, and all three Marine companies were soon pinned down by heavy fire. The sheeting rain broke at about 1730, allowing Marine air to strike enemy positions from above. Buck Darling's Company C then mounted an assault to clear the enemy trench line. This done, Lieutenant Colonel Coffman pulled his men into a tight perimeter in the gathering darkness. He also ringed the position with air strikes, artillery, and naval gunfire. The next morning, the Marines learned they had solidly beaten the NVA 3d Regiment at a cost of fourteen dead and sixty-five wounded. The NVA lost more than a hundred men. Commandant Wallace M. Greene Jr. flew in to visit the battlefield. During his inspection, Greene asked Buck Darling what happened during the fight. Darling's terse reply was "General, we killed them."

Although the ARVN units engaged in Operation Lien Ket 52 fought several more major battles, the remainder of Operation Colorado was anticlimactic for the U.S. Marines. The 1st Battalion moved into Pineapple Forest against fleeting resistance on 12 August. Most of the civilian population residing there was then escorted to safer areas, and a large rice cache was discovered. The 2d Battalion sent out numerous patrols but encountered no enemy before it returned to Tam Ky on the fifteenth. The rest of the regiment returned to Chu Lai three days later. Colonel Widdecke desperately wanted to continue to pressure the reeling enemy, but heavy fighting near the DMZ preempted his plans. It turned out that the 5th Marines would not be able return to the Que Son Valley in strength until the monsoons ended in April 1967.

In September 1966, the 2d Battalion, commanded by Lt. Col. William C. Airheart after 3 October, moved north to join the 3d Marine Division for Operation Prairie. The battalion encountered only light resistance, but remained in the Dong Ha area until 7 December before returning to Chu Lai. However, instead of rejoining the regiment at that time, 2/5 was placed under the direct operational control of the 1st Marine Division on 30 December. The battalion then moved north into the An Hoa Basin at the head of the Thong Duc Corridor in order to provide security for the proposed construction of an industrial complex. Although the planned industrial complex never came to fruition, An Hoa Combat Base later became the home of the 5th Marines, and much of the regiment's time in Vietnam was spent fighting the NVA 2d Division in and around An Hoa.

Major General Herman Nickerson Jr. moved the 1st Marine Division's headquarters north from Chu Lai to Hill 327, later known as "Division Ridge," near Da Nang. This left only four infantry battalions, including the 1st and 3d Battalions, 5th Marines, at Chu Lai under the tactical control of Task Force X-Ray commanded by Brig. Gen. William A. Stiles. The 7th Marines was given operational control of the maneuver battalions while the 5th Marines's headquarters served as the Task Force X-Ray staff until 25 April 1967. Colonel Widdecke and his successor, Col. Fred E. Haynes Jr., served as successive Task Force X-Ray chiefs of staff during that time. The 1st and 3d Battalions mounted an uncounted number of local security patrols, assisted with Golden Fleece and County Fair pacification efforts, and conducted spoiling operations code-named Napa, Monterey, Mustang, Longhorn, and Alpine to keep the enemy off balance. None of these operations resulted in large-scale engagements, but an estimated 163 tons of rice was kept out of enemy hands.

Several significant actions during the 1966–67 monsoon season were fought by the 2d Battalion at An Hoa. Operation Mississippi featured some intermittent heavy contact, but yielded only a few enemy dead. Its major focus was to relocate two thousand refugees from troublesome Antenna Valley, which thereafter became a free-fire zone. Operation Tuscaloosa in January 1967 was a bust until 2/5 imposed heavy losses on the enemy during a nine-hour firefight near Go Noi Island, a six-by-two-mile area hemmed in by major waterways on each side that was not a true island. The area was laced with hedge-rowed villages and crisscrossed by numerous drainage ditches that doubled as trench lines. The populace consisted primarily of women and children, most of whom had relatives fighting with the Viet Cong. Booby traps abounded and night ambushes or hit-and-run shootings were commonplace. In short, Go Noi Island was not a nice place for U.S. Marines.

The 2d Battalion's lead elements were caught in a horseshoe ambush while crossing the Thu Bon River. Then, after more than an hour of artillery preparation, Capt. Jerome J. Doherty's Company H pushed the Viet Cong R-20 Main Force Regiment out of a trench line. The 2d Battalion engaged in a running gunfight as it pursued the enemy into Le Bac village and finally annihilated the Viet Cong in hand-to-hand combat. Among the Marines trying to cross the fire-swept river that day was John J. Culbertson, who possessed both the skill of a sniper and a facile pen. Thirty years later he would chronicle the nameless battles fought in the An Hoa Basin as a tribute to his comrades-in-arms.

Operation Newcastle was a three-day mission just north of An Hoa during which Lt. Col. Mallett C. Jackson Jr.'s 2d Battalion accounted for 118 enemy dead in late March 1967.

Farther south, Lt. Col. Dean E. Esslinger's 3/5 and Lt. Col. Peter L. Hilgartner's 1/5 took part in Operations Desoto and Deckhouse IV, executed jointly with the 7th Marines and ARVN forces, to clear Duc Pho during January and February 1967. Contact with the enemy was rare, but many fortified positions were destroyed and plentiful food supplies were confiscated. These operations cost the 1st Battalion two dead and twelve wounded while an estimated seventeen enemy were killed and eleven captured.

Que Son Valley

In February 1967 it was discovered that the NVA 2d Division had returned to the Que Son Valley in force. The enemy headquarters, successively known as Group 44 or Front 4, had reportedly relocated to a towering mountain named Nui Loc Son. It was also believed that the NVA 3d and 21st Regiments were moving back into the valley from their base camps deep in the jungle. As will be recalled, intense fighting in and around the DMZ prevented follow-up activities after Operation Colorado, so the Que Son area was ripe for such a move by the enemy. Despite many intelligence reports that the enemy was on the move, it was not until the winter monsoon abated and more Americans arrived at Chu Lai that the Marines were able to mount Operation Union to cleanse the Que Son Valley. Fortunately, this clearing operation coincided with a significant change of tactical responsibilities.

Colonel Kenneth J. Houghton Jr.—who it will be recalled had been the 1st Marine Division Reconnaissance Company commander supporting the 5th Marines during the drive to Seoul in Korea—assumed command of the 5th Marines on 28 February. Marine Task Force X-Ray was dissolved when U.S. Army Task Force Oregon arrived at Chu Lai and was given responsibility for much of X-Ray's TAOR in April. This change shifted the Marine TAOR north into Quang Tin Province. At that time the 5th Marines headquarters once again became a tactical, rather than administrative, organization. Actually, the 5th Marines "stood up" because Operation Union was becoming a much larger operation than had been previously expected. The 1st Marines and the 1st ARVN Ranger Group initiated Operation Union, but the 5th Marines replaced the 1st Marines as the controlling headquarters on 25 April 1967 after a bitter fight near Phuc Duc 4. When Houghton took over, he had three rifle battalions (1/1, 1/5, and 3/5) under his direct control and two SLF battalions (1/3 and 2/3) operating inside his assigned area of operations. At that time, however, he had neither operational nor tactical control of either SLF unit. This situation would later lead to command and control problems.

Operation Union started off inauspiciously. Contact with enemy forces was light. Lieutenant Colonel Esslinger's 3d Battalion searched the high ground south of the valley as the ARVN pushed southwest from Thang Binh. The only major incident occurred when a surprise-firing device triggered a daisy chain of cleverly placed mines. One Marine was killed and forty-three were wounded in one of the costliest single incidents of the entire war. The 3d Battalion was then joined by BLT 2/3 from the SLF, but their joint searches turned up only scattered resistance. With nothing going on in the mountains, Houghton shifted his tactical focus to the nearby lowlands.

Colonel Houghton committed the 1/5 to the valley on 1 May. Lieutenant Colonel Hilgartner's 1st Battalion was helilifted into the mountains east of Hiep Duc against light opposition, but contact became more frequent as the Marines moved west along the Song Chang. Company D discovered a sizable enemy storage area on 5 May. Ammunition, uniforms, medical supplies, and enough assorted equipment to support an entire regiment were captured. Although no major enemy forces had yet been engaged, Colonel Houghton was certain contact was imminent.

As a result, BLT 1/3 came ashore and began pushing down from the north. The enemy was now being pressed from all sides and was forced to make a stand. This happened on 10 May when Hilgartner's Company C began to climb Hill 110 about four kilometers north of Que Son. Captain Russell J. Caswell's men took the summit, but came under heavy fire from a cane field below and some caves in the face of nearby Nong Ham Mountain. The 1st Battalion, 3d Marines, tried to envelop the enemy but was soon pinned down, and helicopter-borne reinforcements were repeatedly turned away by intense antiaircraft fire. As this was happening, Capt. Gerald L. McKay's Company A, 1/5, was mistakenly hit by American aircraft while it maneuvered through heavy growth to turn the right flank. Five Marines were killed and twenty-four were injured in this tragic "friendly fire" incident. The attack stalled at that point because Company A had to treat and evacuate its dead and wounded. Colonel Houghton recalled that this incident occurred because an SLF request for an air strike was made without his knowledge or consent. Follow-up investigations led to a change in policy whereby in the future on-scene ground commanders were granted tactical control (i.e., they could direct movements) of SLF units operating ashore.

While this was going on, Lieutenant Colonel Hilgartner led his command group and elements of Company D to the top of Nong Ham Mountain. From there they provided effective supporting fires, assisting the beleaguered Marines below. The battalion mortar platoon delivered accurate fire until the tubes became too hot to handle. Company M, 3/5, was able to land at Hilgartner's position in good order because the enemy had to take cover from the 81mm shells raining down upon them. This brief respite allowed Company D to move down to reinforce Company C. By late afternoon, the Marines in the valley were able to flush the NVA out of the cane fields where the retreating enemy were exposed to unceasing artillery and airstrikes. The day's action yielded 116 enemy dead, but cost the Marines 33 killed and 135 wounded (including those hit by friendly fire).

The 1st Battalion, 1st Marines, relieved BLT 1/3 on 12 May. The Marines of 1/1, 1/5, and 3/5 remained in continual contact over the next two days. Lieutenant Colonel Esslinger used close air support and artillery fire before 3/5 assaulted enemy positions where 122 enemy were killed on 13 May. This was the first of six successive sharp fights over the next forty-eight hours. Supporting arms continued to carry the load until Companies A and M discovered another enemy bunker complex on 15 May. Air and artillery pounded the fortifications first, then the Marines closed in against only light resistance. This was the last major battle of Operation Union. The 5th Marines killed an estimated 1,500 enemy and captured 173 suspected enemy at the cost of 110 Marines dead, 473 wounded, and 2 missing in a little less than one month. Colonel Houghton believed this was the 5th Marines's most successful effort to date in Vietnam. His combat after-action report stated "the psychological impact equaled or exceeded the material damage to the Communist effort in this area of operations."

In the wake of Operation Union, the 5th Marines manned a company-sized combat outpost atop Nui Loc Son and established the regimental command post on Hill 51, a low, narrow ridge—not the imposing mountain top that one might imagine—west of Que Son. It was obvious Operation Union had hurt the enemy, but the fight for Que Son Valley was not over and daily encounters with enemy forces still occurred. As Colonel Houghton later recalled, the enemy was unusually willing to make contact during daylight hours, a fact that proved the Communists were not willing to cede the vital Que Son Valley in spite of tremendous losses.

Typical of many campaigns during the Vietnam War, the resilient enemy had been severely bloodied during Operation Union but had not been decisively defeated. Small enemy units continued to operate in and around the valley, and the hostile population located there was still not truly pacified when the Americans withdrew years later.

The 5th Marines launched a second cleansing operation in Que Son Valley on 26 May. Operation Union II was a combined operation with ARVN forces. This time the mission was to destroy the headquarters of the 3d NVA Regiment. The fighting lasted only eleven days, but it was the most intense thus far encountered by the 5th Marines in Vietnam. Houghton's plan was for three ARVN ranger units to push the enemy into an ambush manned by the Marines of 3/5. This operation began on 26 May 1967 with a helicopter-borne assault by Lieutenant Colonel Esslinger's 3d Battalion at LZ Eagle, located about twenty miles northwest of Tam Ky. Company L landed without incident, but Company M bumped into a well-prepared enemy position. Mike Company was struck by heavy small arms fire, bracketed by mortar fire, and one helicopter was shot down. Companies L and M maneuvered to silence the enemy as Company I arrived. Colonel Esslinger called for air strikes and artillery fires to support this attack. His timely intervention allowed Company I to flank the fortifications and drive through the enemy despite fierce resistance. This fight near Vinh Huy left 171 North Vietnamese dead at the cost of thirty-eight Marines killed and eighty-two wounded, among them Lieutenant Colonel Essinger whose eye wounds were so serious he had to be evacuated. Colonel Houghton then temporarily exercised direct control over 3/5 until Lt. Col. Charles B. Webster could be brought in to take command.

Houghton switched his focus to the southeast to defeat the 21st NVA Regiment on 29 May. Lieutenant Colonel Hilgartner's 1st Battalion, reinforced by Company F of the 2d Battalion, landed at LZ Robin. The 3d Battalion came in at LZ Blue Jay. After a two-day sweep the Marines came upon an enemy bunker complex at Objective Foxtrot. These positions were pounded by heavy artillery fire and numerous air strikes, then the Marines advanced to destroy the remaining enemy by close combat— the participants sometimes wielding bayonets, K-bar knives, or entrenching tools. During the melee, the 3d Battalion was pinned down and thereafter became a base of fire to support the 1st Battalion. Companies D and F both encountered intense enemy fire as they crossed the rice paddies. When Company D was pinned down in the open, Capt. James A. Graham's Company F moved up, but his 2d Platoon was quickly pinned down by a pair of machine guns. Captain Graham led his command group in a charge to relieve the embattled platoon and personally killed more than a dozen enemy. One of the enemy machine guns was knocked out of action, but NVA reinforcements were moving in. For the out-gunned and out-numbered Marines there was no choice but to pull back.

Already hit two times by enemy fire, Captain Graham elected to remain with several badly wounded Marines who could not be evacuated. From that position the skipper covered his company's withdrawal with rifle fire and directed mortar rounds onto his own position. Graham's last radio transmission reported he was being attacked by about two dozen enemy soldiers. Captain Graham was posthumously awarded the Medal of Honor for his gallant stand in the face of certain death.

Lieutenant Colonel Hilgartner, his units under intense fire from machine guns, mortars, and rocket-propelled grenades (RPGs), asked for help. Colonel Houghton realized how serious the situation was, so he committed elements of Lt. Col. Mal Jackson's 2/5, the division reserve located at An Hoa on the far side of the Que Son Mountains. Lieutenant Colonel Hilgartner later stated that the timely arrival of the division reserve "saved the day," although Major General Houghton admitted he ordered the 2d Battalion into action without the division commander's permission when he failed to contact General Nickerson by radio. In hindsight, there can be no doubt that Houghton's decisive action, albeit outside of channels, was the key to victory.

The situation was so critical on the ground that a bobtailed two-company composite battalion led by Maj. Richard H. Esau Jr. (the 2/5 executive officer) had to make a night helicopter insertion. This ad hoc unit ran afoul of a large NVA unit on its way to administer the coup de grace to the besieged Marines. Esau incurred twenty casualties but in the process his men forced the enemy back. The severity of the action at the LZ was measured by one medical evacuation crew who counted 58 holes in their helicopter after the mission. The entire fight turned in the Marines's favor when the NVA began to evacuate their fighting holes as daylight neared. An enemy column was caught in a Marine cross fire and chopped to bits in one of the most one-sided firefights in Vietnam—several hundred enemy were killed or badly wounded without a single Marine being killed in action. The remaining enemy then became easy prey for air and artillery as they fled this killing field by running across open ground. The intensity of the fighting became statistically clear the following morning: 476 North Vietnamese bodies were found while the 5th Marines lost 71 killed, 139 wounded, and 2 missing. Lance Corporal Jose Agusto Santo became a prisoner of war, but the other man's remains were never recovered nor was he on the POW list compiled after the end of the war. This grisly accounting was possible because of an informal truce during which NVA and Marine working parties ignored each other as they collected their respective dead and wounded.

Operation Union II terminated on 5 June 1967. More than a year later, on 17 October 1968, Brig. Gen. Ken Houghton represented the 5th Marines during a ceremony at the White House. Five hundred and twenty-five Marine veterans were assembled in the Rose Garden when President Lyndon B. Johnson awarded the 5th Marines a Presidential Unit Citation to recognize its outstanding performance during Operations Union I and II. This was the first such award for the 5th Marines in Vietnam. General Houghton later recalled that former regimental commander Brute Krulak had been the driving force behind this honor. After visiting the battlefield, he told both the 1st Marine Division commander and the Commandant that during Operations Union I and II the 5th Marines was the consummate fighting force, one whose actions and operating procedures should be emulated by all other regiments in Vietnam.

When Operation Union II ended, 2/5 returned to An Hoa while 1/5 and 3/5 remained in the Que Son Valley. Operation Adair followed Union II, lasting from 15–25 June. This operation was initiated when Company K, 3/5, engaged two NVA companies about four miles south of Thang Binh. The Marines encircled the enemy and used supporting arms to reduce them. Special Landing Force Bravo, consisting of BLT 2/3, joined the fight on the eighteenth. Operation Adair gave way to Operation Calhoun a week later. The lack of enemy resistance clearly signaled that the North Vietnamese had decided to return to the mountains to regroup. This left the small-scale day-to-day fighting to local Viet Cong.

Concurrently, the Viet Cong decided it was time to interrupt pacification efforts in the An Hoa Basin and targeted the Nong Son coal mine protected by 2/5. Nong Son, the only active coal mine in South Vietnam, was in a relatively isolated area, where it was defended by 1st Lt. James B. Scuras's Company F, reinforced by a section of 4.2-inch mortars and an 81mm mortar section. The attack was well planned and carefully coordinated. Just before midnight on 3 July, a Marine listening post reported movement before it was overrun. Well-placed enemy mortar rounds blew up the ammunition dump and knocked out the 4.2-inch mortars. This barrage was followed by a wave of enemy sappers who blasted bunkers and mortar positions as they probed the Marine defenses. Private First Class Melvin E. Newlin and four others were manning a critical defensive position when the VC attacked. Although the enemy wounded him and killed his comrades, Newlin single-handedly fought off three attempts to overrun his position before he was knocked unconscious by an enemy grenade. After reviving, Newlin once again opened fire and is credited with breaking the enemy attack before being mortally wounded. He was awarded the Medal of Honor. The enemy managed to penetrate the Marine position but was unable to drive the Leathernecks out. The Marines suffered thirteen killed and forty-three wounded that night, but they returned possession of Nong Son.

Lieutenant Colonel Webster's 3d Battalion participated in Operation Pike in the coastal lowlands near Hoi An in early August 1967. During this operation 3/5 was under the operational control of Col. Herbert E. Ing's 1st Marines. The 3d Battalion was credited with inflicting more than a hundred casualties as the enemy tried to flee south. When these Communists tried to move into the area near Tam Ky, they were confronted by the newly arrived army units of Task Force Oregon (later designated the "American" Division) and pushed back into the Marine TAOR. The enemy quickly dispersed to go underground or sought the protection of the jungle-covered Que Son mountains.

The additional army maneuver battalions now under III MAF control freed the Marines to commit much larger forces to secure Quang Tin Province, specifically the troublesome Que Son Valley. Marine Task Force X-Ray was reactivated and its commander, Brig. Gen. Foster C. "Frosty" LaHue, was ordered to clean out the valley one more time. Task Force X-Ray included Col. Stanley Davis's 5th Marines and SLF Alpha (BLT 1/3). Frosty LaHue promptly launched Operation Cochise to clear the enemy away from Hiep Duc. There was only one notable action. On

16 August, Lieutenant Colonel Webster's 3/5 killed forty enemy at a cost of only three wounded. This was the only major engagement during the eleven-day operation. Most enemy contact was the result of sniper fire, and most of the Marine casualties were caused by booby traps.

The next major operation was triggered when the enemy attacked Capt. Robert F. Morgan's Company D just before dawn on 4 September. The company had been conducting a sweep near Dong Son 1 about eight miles southwest of Thang Binh astride Route 534. Enemy small arms and mortars opened up on the Marine perimeter at about 0430. Morgan quickly called in his listening posts so the Marines could safely return fire. In the interim, the enemy bracketed the Marines and then poured in unrelenting fire for almost two hours. Captain Morgan was killed as he reorganized his defensive lines at about 0620. First Lieutenant William P. Vacca took over and called for air strikes within fifty meters of the Marine lines. Lieutenant Colonel Hilgartner ordered Capt. Thomas D. Reese Jr. to move Company B from the battalion command post to reinforce Company D. This action and those that followed later became known as Operation Swift.

Company B arrived at about 0820 and was engaged by a second enemy force inside Dong Son 1. Captain Reese requested and received air-delivered tear gas to dislodge the enemy. The tactic worked. The Communists broke and fled toward the Ly-Ly River leaving twenty-six comrades behind. Things did not go as well for Company D, however. The NVA lured several medical evacuation helicopters into an antiaircraft ambush using false signals. Two UH-34s were hit and one UH-1E gunship was downed. Realizing a major fight was in the offing, Colonel Davis ordered 3/5's Lieutenant Colonel Webster to ready two of his companies for action at about 0920. Companies K and M joined the 1st Battalion at Dong Son 1 a little more than three hours later. The 1st Battalion command group was preparing to move out when Company B discovered another enemy pocket on the west end of the village. An air strike was called in, and nine more enemy soldiers were killed. By that time the fighting to the west had diminished, and it was obvious Companies B and D were firmly in control of the area.

When Lieutenant Colonel Hilgartner was alerted that another large enemy force was nearby, he ordered Companies K and M to form into a line of skirmishers and advance across open ground. It did not take the NVA long to find the range from their L-shaped entrenchment. First Lieutenant John D. Murray's Company M became heavily engaged near

Chau Lai 1 and was surrounded atop a small knoll. With his unit pinned down by intense small-arms fire and hit by more than two hundred mortar rounds, Murray called for air support. He received a tear gas drop. In the ensuing action, Marines who had earlier discarded their gas masks as useless gear learned a painful lesson when they, too, were engulfed by clouds of the choking chemicals.

During the fighting, Lt. Vincent R. Capadanno, USNR, the 3d Battalion's chaplain, made repeated trips to assist Marines wounded in the fighting. Although twice wounded—he was struck by a bullet that amputated several fingers and was hit by multiple fragments that caused leg, torso, and head injuries—he refused medical aid and continued to help others until he was struck down by machine-gun fire while trying to shield a wounded corpsman. Capadanno was posthumously awarded the Medal of Honor.

Elsewhere on the same battlefield, Sgt. Lawrence D. Peters, a squad leader from Company M's 2d Platoon, stood up in clear view of the enemy to point out targets to his men. He was hit in the leg during an enemy fusillade, but continued to lead his squad until the enemy was driven back. The heroic Sergeant Peters, who was mortally wounded later that night, was later awarded a posthumous Medal of Honor.

Companies K and M had become isolated during the fierce fighting and manned separate perimeters when darkness closed in. Company M remained on its knoll, but Capt. Joseph R. Tenny's Company K pulled back to Hilgartner's command post. Marine artillery from Que Son protected Companies B and D, while Marine air covered Companies K and M. At one point, Grumman A-6 Intruder bombers delivered five-hundred-pound bombs within fifty meters of Company M, and another time they delivered ordnance as close as sixty meters from Company K. The duel between the fearless Marine pilots and relentless NVA gunners ended when the antiaircraft guns on Hill 63 were knocked out. There were only scattered encounters with NVA troops during the rest of the night.

On the morning of the fifth, Lieutenant Colonel Webster's command group, reinforced by Company D, 1st Marines, joined Companies B and D, 5th Marines, west of Dong Son 1. In an ironic twist of fate, Lieutenant Colonel Hilgartner was commanding Webster's Companies K and M, while Webster was leading Hilgartner's Companies B and D. When the battle was over, 130 NVA lay dead. The Marines lost 54 killed and 104 wounded. Colonel Davis flew in to assess the situation, then issued orders for the 1st and 3d Battalions to continue to sweep toward the foothills on the southern edge of the basin. Hilgartner and Webster retook control of their respective organic rifle companies at that time.

At about 1515 the following afternoon, 1/5 ran into two battalions of the VC 1st Regiment near Vinh Huy 3. Company B was halted by fire and forced to maneuver in order to get out of an ambush. While so engaged, the VC hit 1st Lt. John E. Brackeen's exposed 2d Platoon with simultaneous frontal and flank assaults. During this action, Sgt. Rodney M. Davis, the platoon's right guide, covered an enemy grenade with his body to shield the rest of the platoon command group. The mortally wounded Davis thus became the first African-American Marine to receive the Medal of Honor. The platoon was able to fall back under cover of tear gas, but had to leave the dead Marines behind. Encouraged by their temporary success, the enemy then mounted an attack on the battalion position. Close air support and artillery fire kept them at bay until nightfall, when VC sappers infiltrated the Marine lines under the cover of darkness. Major Charles H. Black, the battalion operations officer, killed several intruders and then rallied nearby Marines to drive out the rest of the sappers. The enemy was gone by the early hours of the next morning, but left behind sixty-one dead. The Marines lost thirty-five killed or wounded during that night and the previous day.

The 3d Battalion was busy on the afternoon of the sixth as well. Lieutenant Colonel Webster's men claimed Hill 48 without significant resistance. He then ordered Capt. Francis M. Burke to lead Company I up nearby Hill 43. The lead platoon discovered two NVA about two hundred meters short of the objective and quickly gave chase. This turned out to be a tactical error as the pursuing Marines were led into an ambush. Company I soon encountered steady small-arms and automatic weapons fire, so Burke ordered his men to get on line and began to sweep ahead. By 1630, Burke's company was so heavily engaged it was unable to maneuver. Colonel Webster then sent Company K to the rescue. The two companies were able to form a coherent perimeter, but a few dead had to be left outside the lines and some casualties could not be evacuated until after dark. Just before dusk, an enemy force was scattered by helicopter gunships, but two others hit the Marine lines between 1900 and 2300. The Marines engaged in hand-to-hand fighting with the enemy before repulsing both assaults. Company M arrived just after 2300, but the enemy continued to press its attack until warded off by tear gas at around midnight. Only scattered sniper and mortar fire were encountered thereafter. The enemy lost about 90 men, while the Marines suffered 34 killed and 109 wounded.

The previous night's futile enemy attacks proved to be even more costly to the Viet Cong when the Marines discovered a map pinpointing company and command post locations of the VC 1st Regiment during a routine search the next morning. This intelligence windfall dictated quick action. The 1st Battalion was ordered to sweep the locations on the map after supporting arms thoroughly worked them over. Two days later, Hilgartner's Marines found ninety-one cases of small-arms ammunition, twenty-seven cases of mortar rounds, six cases of 75mm recoilless rifle rounds, and hundreds of grenades. Sample items were collected for intelligence purposes and the rest of the cache was blown in place.

Captain Eugene W. Bowers's Company H, 2/5, which was attached to Lt. Col. William K. Rockey's 3d Battalion, was on a search-and-destroy mission when it established a company defensive position to facilitate helicopter resupply on 10 September. Second Lieutenant Allan J. Herman's 3d Platoon was conducting a security patrol when it was ambushed by a reinforced NVA company. Lieutenant Herman was killed in the ensuing firefight, and the platoon was pinned down with heavy casualties. Captain Bowers quickly maneuvered his remaining units to fix the enemy and called for close air support, artillery, and helicopter gunships. Lieutenant Colonel Rockey also sent Company M to support Bowers. The two companies launched a successful assault after the NVA positions were pounded by 250-pound bombs and sprayed with tear gas. The Marines killed more than forty of the enemy. Although this was a successful action, an ominous note was sounded when it was later noted that six of the nine Marines killed in action were attempting to clear jams in their newly issued M16 rifles when they were gunned down. This was not the first problem with the troublesome M16s. Expert rifleman John Culbertson bitterly noted that they had failed earlier field trials but reluctant Marines were forced to go into the field with them even though adoption of the so-called "black rifle" was not recommended. The wisdom of this decision came under public scrutiny when problems with the M16 became so pronounced that they spurred Congressional investigations that revealed many shortcomings. The rifle was subsequently modified to become the M16A1 and new ammunition was issued, but even these measures did not inspire complete trust in the controversial weapon. Three years later, some Marines still carried unauthorized but reliable M14 rifles.

Captain Burke's Company I was attacked by two NVA companies at about 0330 on the morning of the twelfth. The attackers were first repelled by India Company and then were ambushed by elements of Captain Tenney's Company K as they fled the battle zone. This was the last big battle of Operation Swift for the 5th Marines. When Swift was terminated on 15 September, the enemy's 1967 dry-season offensive was a failure. The NVA 3d and 21st Regiments were considered combat ineffective because they had lost more than four thousand men since April, and the number of large-scale contacts had dropped to almost zero. The enemy was still present, but he no longer effectively challenged the U.S. presence.

The end of Operation Swift also marked a significant shift in enemy tactics and a change in American dispositions. By late 1967 it had become clear to both sides that the enemy could not eject the Americans from their base at Da Nang. The NVA and VC were even having trouble mustering enough combat power to threaten isolated outposts in the Que Son Valley and An Hoa Basin. The enemy therefore decided to husband increasingly scarce resources for a major push in the north and reverted to classic guerrilla warfare in southern I Corps. The VC and NVA began to avoid contact and spent their time stockpiling supplies. The new weapon of choice became 122mm (and later 140mm) Soviet-made unguided rockets. These rockets were relatively lightweight and carried a tremendous punch, but they were very inaccurate. Although rockets lacked the pinpoint accuracy of artillery and heavy mortars, they were much more mobile, were far simpler to operate, and had greater range than field guns. It took a well-trained rocket team less than an hour to set up and fire a dozen or so rockets. Because enemy rocketeers were invariably long gone by the time counterbattery fires could be brought to bear, the only solution was saturation patrolling to prevent the establishment of firing positions. The VC countermeasure to Marine saturation patrols was increasing the number and sophistication of surprise firing devices. The war south of Da Nang thus became a costly battle of attrition fought primarily by Marine squads and fire teams that spent their days looking for the enemy and their nights waiting in ambush.

After Operation Swift, General Westmoreland ordered the 1st Air Cavalry Division north to reinforce the Marines in I Corps. The army's "First Team" began replacing the 5th Marines in the Que Son Valley at the end of September 1967. The 5th Marines—now commanded by Col. Robert D. "Dewey" Bohn, who had commanded Company G, 3/5, at Inchon—

relocated to Da Nang on 4 October. The 1st and 3d Battalions moved north into the Da Nang Vital Area to patrol an area known as the Rocket Belt. There, the 5th Marines implemented saturation patrolling to prevent 122mm rockets fired by the NVA 363d Artillery Regiment from bombarding the city of Da Nang, its busy airfield, the helicopter facilities at Marble Mountain, and Division Ridge. An important secondary task was to assist the Revolutionary Development Program by conducting pacification operations. Tactically speaking, large-scale sweeps were out and small-unit activities were in. The regiment was now fighting a decentralized "squad leader's" war. The Marines spent the days "hole hunting," searching for VC and weapons caches. At night, squad ambushes were set up throughout the area. The major threat to individual Marines now became mines and booby traps or deadly ambushes. Units not beating the bush for the enemy were on alert to act as quick reaction forces that could be airlifted into the battle area on short notice.

The next operation was code-named Essex, and its purpose was to clear Antenna Valley south of An Hoa. The valley, widely known to be an NVA assembly area, ran through the Que Sons starting at Nong Son and moving in a generally east-west direction toward Go Noi Island. Allegedly the area received its nickname (Antenna Valley) because so many radiomen had been killed or wounded in action.

Operation Essex was conducted by Lt. Col. George C. McNaughton's 2/5. Antenna Valley had been evacuated during Operation Mississippi in 1966 and became a free-fire zone. In the interim, the North Vietnamese returned to occupy the area. By the end of 1967, many villages had become fortified positions protected by barbed wire and defensive trench lines. Typical of enemy thoroughness, these formidable bastions were carefully located to ensure mutual support and invariably had interlocking fields of fire. Each village was protected by nearby streambeds or open rice paddies, making a covered approach impossible. In case of attack, the NVA pattern was to defend such positions during the day and then melt away during the hours of darkness.

Operation Essex began with a helicopter assault six miles south of An Hoa on 6 November 1967. Captain Gene Bowers's Company H came under heavy fire as it approached the fortified village of Ap Bon 2. Bowers tried to maneuver his company, but each attempt was stopped by accurate enemy fire. Unable to advance, he pummeled the village with air and artillery before launching an assault. The Marines finally moved out under cover of supporting arms but were held up by barbed wire and a bamboo hedge. A deluge of enemy mortar rounds rained down on the Marines and grazing fire from heavy machine guns crisscrossed the rice paddies as they tried to pass through. When the attack faltered, the Marines sought cover behind paddy dikes.

Captain Bowers directed additional air strikes, some of which hit only a few meters from the Marines, and called for reinforcements. Lieutenant Colonel McNaughton sent Company F, the battalion reserve, to Ap Bon in the late afternoon, but Company F's attack also failed. At dusk, the harried Marines in both companies pulled back and established defensive positions about seventy meters from Ap Bon. Air force fixed-wing "Spooky" gunships circling overhead provided close-in fire support and dropped flares throughout the night to keep the enemy at bay. By 0430 it became obvious the enemy had slipped away. The Marines searched the village at dawn, discovered no enemy, and reported all bunkers and trench lines had been cleared. The fight for Ap Bon 2 had cost the Marines fifty-three casualties (including sixteen dead). Intelligence reports later indicated more than sixty enemy, including the battalion commander, had been killed at Ap Bon 2 on 6 November. There was only minor contact thereafter. Operation Essex, the last major 5th Marines operation of 1967, ended on 17 November.

The last combat operation of 1967 was Operation Auburn. Reacting to intelligence that a pair of Viet Cong local force battalions, the V-25th and R-20th, and Group 44's headquarters had returned to Go Noi Island in order to stir up trouble and to screen the movements of the 638th Rocket Battalion. Colonel Bohn decided to preempt such activities by conducting a search-and-destroy operation. Planning began on Christmas Day. The concept was for a helicopter-borne force to land at LZ Hawk to draw the enemy's attention while other Marine and ARVN forces closed the area from the north and west. To do this, a composite battalion—two companies from 2/5, one company from 3/5, and one from 2/3—supported by 2/11's artillery and the helicopters of MAG-16 would make up the assault force. On-call air support in the form of fixed-wing and helicopter gunships would also be readily available. Lieutenant Colonel Rockey of 3/5 was the task force commander.

Typical of most large search-and-destroy operations of the time, Operation Auburn started with a sharp firefight, but then quickly turned into a futile search. The assault company, E, 2/3, swooped into LZ Hawk on the morning of 28 December. The landing was initially harassed by small-arms fire, but the fight quickly turned ugly as the Marines neared

Bao An Dong village. The enemy stopped the Marine advance there, and the succeeding landing waves came under increasingly heavy fire at LZ Hawk. Company I, 3/5, was ordered to outflank the enemy but could not do so when it came under heavy fire from a former graveyard that had been turned into a field fortification by the Viet Cong. When his attempts to outmaneuver the enemy failed, Lieutenant Colonel Rockey called for supporting fires. However, he was frustrated by numerous "check fires," which stopped the artillery from shooting when friendly aircraft were overhead, a common occurrence because the battle area was within the flight path of Da Nang Air Base. Eventually, covered by the fires of the adjoining company and close-in fires by helicopter gunships, Company E was able to extricate itself from the ambush site.

Colonel Bohn, concerned over the unexpectedly fierce resistance by a force much larger than the one thought to be located there, decided to commit a second battalion. Accordingly, Lieutenant Colonel McNaughton's 2/5 was ordered in. The plan now was for 2/5's two companies and the regimental command group to land at LZ Hawk to reinforce the five companies already on the ground. Once the landing force was safely on the ground, the new arrivals would advance to seize an abandoned village from which they would then support the attack by Rockey's original composite battalion under the cover of heavy artillery fires and using close air support whenever possible. This time the attacks were successful. Rather than stand and fight, the enemy slipped away leaving only a rear-guard platoon to delay the Marine advance. Both villages were in Marine hands by noon. From then on the Marines encountered only scattered sniper fire, and almost all casualties were caused by booby traps that infested the area. Operation Auburn was neither a resounding success nor a total failure. It was, instead, typical of Marine operations throughout most of the war.

The 1st Marine Division used a break in the fighting provided by the December-January monsoon rains to redeploy some of its units north of Da Nang. On 13 January 1968, the 1st and 2d Battalions of the 5th Marines were assigned to recently reactivated Task Force X-Ray, which was going north. Brigadier General LaHue commanded Task Force X-Ray with orders to screen the western approaches to Hue City and to keep Highway 1 open between Hue and Da Nang. This move was part of Operation Checkers, a general redeployment of Marine and army forces in I Corps. The resulting shift of the 1st and 5th Marines into Thua Thien Province allowed the entire 3d Marine Division to move north to defend the DMZ, where North Vietnamese forces were gathering strength for a new offensive that threatened the major base at Dong Ha and the combat base at Khe Sanh.

Elements of the 5th Marines boarded trucks and took Highway 1 north from Da Nang past Red Beach and the Esso refinery over the Nam O Bridge into cloud-shrouded Hai Van Pass. Regimental headquarters went all the way to Phu Bai. Lieutenant Colonel Robert P. Whalen's 1/5 guarded Highway 1 south of the Hai Van Pass while Lt. Col. Ernest C. Cheatham Jr.'s 2/5 deployed to Phu Loc located astride Highway 1 near the vital Troui Bridge to keep the MSR open between Hai Van Pass and Phu Bai. Lieutenant Colonel Rockey's 3/5 remained near Da Nang to patrol the Rocket Belt and serve as an emergency rapid-reaction force.

Highway 1 was choked with military and civilian traffic as the Marines struggled to complete their redeployment before the onset of an upcoming three-day truce at the beginning of the annual lunar new year period known as Tet, the most important holiday on the Vietnamese calendar. Tet was normally a joyous festival during which families gathered to honor their ancestors, celebrate life, and express hope for the future. Western culture has no direct equivalent of Tet, which combines familial piety, religious fervor, and joyous festivities. A Vietnamese officer described Tet to the author as "a combination of Easter, Christmas, Yom Kippur, Thanksgiving, New Year's Eve, and the Fourth of July all celebrated at the same time." In the past, a short cease-fire had always allowed a welcome respite from the fighting for both sides. The truce that would usher in the Year of the Monkey was slated to begin at 1800 on 29 January 1968. In accordance with past practices, leaves were freely granted to ARVN soldiers for Tet, but the wary Americans adopted a more prudent attitude of watchful waiting by curtailing offensive activity while maintaining a strong defensive posture.

Hopes for a peaceful Tet holiday were shattered in the early morning hours of 29 January when the enemy hit Da Nang with mortar and rocket fires during a premature attack that tipped their hand. Additional attacks on U.S. and ARVN installations across the country were launched the next day. During fighting south and west of Da Nang, Lieutenant Colonel Rockey's 3d Battalion was sent into action to stem the enemy tide washing down from the hills that ringed the An Hoa Basin. In one action, Capt. Henry Kolakowski Jr.'s Company I was airlifted to a paddy abutting the Cau Do River to relieve pressure on an embattled Combined Action Platoon. Well-placed artillery and close air support disrupted enemy movements as the Marines aided South Vietnamese Regional Forces (RFs) holding the hamlet of Thon Trung Luong. Company I held off several hundred attackers during a nightlong firefight. On the morning of the thirty-first the Marines and ARVN cleared the area between Highway 1 and the coast. More than 100 Viet Cong were killed, 88 were captured, and 13 suspects and 70 laborers were detained. The 2d NVA Division faded back into the hills after suffering more than 1,000 casualties without capturing a single objective. Major General Donn J. Robertson, the commanding general of the 1st Marine Division, attributed the successful defense of Da Nang to the joint actions of 3/5, the 11th Marines, and the army's 196th Light Infantry Brigade. Unfortunately, these attacks were only the beginning of the largest enemy general offensive of the Vietnam War to date.

Hue City

Eight miles north of Phu Bai, at the juncture of Highway 1 and the Perfume River, lay the former Vietnamese capital city of Hue. This urban cultural center was actually two cites of mixed European and Oriental architecture that reflected both Vietnam's colonial and imperial past. North of the Perfume River was a walled area known as the Citadel, which was built in the eighteenth century. That majestic fortress included the historic Imperial Palace surrounded by the exotic Forbidden City. The only military base inside the Citadel was the 1st ARVN Division headquarters at the Mang Ca military complex, located at the compound's northeastern tip. Across the Perfume River was a modern French quarter that included provincial headquarters, Hue University, Thua Thien Prison, the national treasury, city hospital, and the Cercle Sportif country club. Remarkably, this enigmatic city had remained a tranquil eye in the storm of war that engulfed South Vietnam, thus far treated as an open city by both sides. As a result, Hue was neither heavily garrisoned nor well fortified by the South Vietnamese, despite the fact that it was both a vital communications hub and a provincial capital whose capture offered the enemy a bountiful military and political harvest.

Hue's blissful aloofness from the war was about to come to an end. The U.S. Marines were not the only warriors on the move in January 1968. The NVA 4th, 5th, and 6th Regiments slipped into Thua Thien Province almost unnoticed. There, they were joined by main force and local Viet Cong guerrillas. By skillfully avoiding contact and keeping a very low profile, this division-sized amalgam of VC and NVA forces was able to gather on the outskirts of Hue unmolested. The American base at Phu Bai was hit by mortar fire on 26 January, but except for Lieutenant Colonel Cheatham's 2d Battalion, which was defending Truoi Bridge near Phu Loc, there was little in the way of large-scale activity as an enemy fifth column infiltrated Hue in small groups under the cover of the Tet celebrations to covertly prepare the way for a surprise attack.

At 0223 on 31 January, an enemy flare arched across the dark morning sky signaling it was time for the unexpected onslaught to begin. The NVA 6th Regiment quickly captured the entire Citadel except for the 1st ARVN Division headquarters. The NVA 4th Regiment did likewise in the southern part of the city and was able to secure all its objectives except for the thinly held MACV headquarters compound. When the call for help went out, Task Force X-Ray responded by sending a single Marine rifle company to relieve the MACV compound. Needless to say, one company was not enough to dislodge an entrenched enemy division. When Company A, 1/1, was ambushed in a murderous cross fire at the An Cuu Bridge on the southern approach to Hue, a second call for help went out.

Lieutenant Colonel Cheatham's 2/5 was busy protecting the vital Truoi Bridge from attacks by several VC battalions. This all-metal, double-span, combination highway and railway bridge was the most vulnerable choke point on Highway 1 between Da Nang and Phu Bai, so its loss would be a fatal blow. All four of Cheatham's companies were in contact with the enemy and had their hands full when he received word that two of his units were going to be pulled back to Phu Bai. Ernest Cheatham was arguably one of the finest battalion commanders in Vietnam. Aggressive and outspoken, the hulking ex–football player displayed an unusual mix of aggressiveness, personal bravery, keen tactical insight, and compassion for his men. "Big Ernie" Cheatham did not suffer fools gladly and he railed against the upcoming move, which he felt would weaken his forces beyond the point of mission accomplishment. The only response from Task Force X-Ray was a vague one that told him in no uncertain terms to send the troops, but did not explain the situation or offer further counsel. Unknown by all hands at that time was that a landmark battle was unfolding in Hue City, and the 5th Marines was about to be committed to a desperate, monthlong fight that would rival Belleau Wood, Guadalcanal, and the frozen Chosin in historical importance.

Captain Charles L. Meadows's Company G, 2/5, accompanied Lt. Col. Marcus J. Gravel's 1/1 command group into the fight at Hue on 31 January. The relief force departed Phu Bai at 1030 and reached the beleaguered Marine company at the An Cuu Bridge late in the morning. As his Marines maneuvered to defeat the enemy, Chuck Meadows made a fortuitous discovery inside a local gas station: He found a tourist map of the city that clearly showed each street and identified all public buildings with numbers. This simple act of fate cut through the fog of war and allowed Marine commanders to coordinate their attacks using similar maps thereafter.

When the enemy pulled back, the Marine convoy, which now included more than two hundred men as well as Marine M48 tanks and army M5 gun trucks and M42 Duster antiaircraft tracked vehicles, proceeded to the MACV compound. There, at about 1445, Lieutenant Colonel Gravel reported to Task Force X-Ray by radio. He was ordered to relieve pressure on the ARVN forces fighting inside the Citadel by launching a counterattack but was denied permission to use close air support or artillery fire. Gravel protested that an unsupported attack against the Citadel would be both costly and futile, but he was told to press on.

Gravel assigned the remnants of Company A to defend the MACV compound and reluctantly told Captain Meadows to attack across the main bridge over the Perfume River. Company G's lead elements made it across Nguyen Huang Bridge under heavy fire after Cpl. Lester A. Tully wiped out an enemy machine-gun position. But the main attack stalled at the base of the Citadel's thick concrete walls, and an intense two-hour firefight broke out. The Marines had to once again cross the fire-swept bridge when they were ordered to pull back. True to Gravel's predictions, this abortive attack against well-fortified enemy positions had cost Company G one-third of its strength—five killed and forty-four wounded— without meaningful gain. The only saving grace was that Task Force X-Ray belatedly realized the enemy inside Hue were well armed and would defend their positions at all costs.

At about 0700 on 1 February, Company G jumped off to take the provincial prison, rescue a pair of State Department officials in a building nearby, and escort convoys carrying the wounded back to Phu Bai. Second Lieutenant Michael McNeil's 1st Platoon encountered heavy resistance and could make no progress toward the prison, 2d Lt. Steven L. Hancock's 2d Platoon successfully brought in the State Department personnel, and 2d Lt. William L. Rogers III of the 3d Platoon went to

Phu Bai, where he briefed the Task Force X-Ray staff on the severity of the situation in Hue and made a cogent plea for reinforcements. Captain Michael P. Downs's Company F, 2/5, was airlifted into Hue in the afternoon, bringing with it two 81mm mortars and two 106mm recoilless rifles. The Foxtrot Marines were quickly embroiled in the fighting and suffered fifteen casualties just trying to move out of the landing zone.

Colonel Stanley S. Hughes, the 1st Marines commander, was given tactical control of all the Marine forces in the southern part of the city. Company H, 2/5, and Colonel Cheatham's 2d Battalion command group moved from Phu Loc to Phu Bai. While the troops were resting, their commanders spent the evening preparing for the 5th Marines's first sustained urban combat since the liberation of Seoul in 1950. Lieutenant Colonel Cheatham boned up by reading all available materials. Major Albert J. "John" Salvati gathered demolitions, tear gas, gas masks, hand grenades, flamethrowers, direct-fire antitank weapons—including light antitank weapons (LAWs), bazookas, and 106mm recoilless rifles—and ammunition. Captain George R. "Ron" Christmas of Company H held an officers' call to discuss the upcoming movement and worked out a tactical plan for the next day's advance into Hue City.

The Marines made some minor gains in the southern part of the city on 2 February. Company G seized the university administration building, and Company F cleared the area surrounding the MACV compound. Later in the day, Company H was able to fight its way through an extended ambush to the MACV compound. However, the enemy still held most of the city when Captain Christmas's men occupied Hue University that evening.

Colonel Hughes established his regimental command post at the MACV compound and realigned his assigned units into two battalions on the morning of the third. Lieutenant Colonel Cheatham took charge of 2/5's three rifle companies just after noon. Lieutenant Colonel Gravel kept control of the reinforced company from his own battalion. Unfortunately, the 2d Battalion attacks that afternoon failed due to flanking fire by enemy machine guns that raked the streets with a solid wall of green tracers flying at shoe-top level. Smoke grenades had no effect because the NVA gunners had presighted their weapons and opened fire as soon as pyrotechnic devices ignited. No significant gains were made that day.

The battle for Hue was an abrupt transition from the rice paddy and jungle warfare the Marines had thus far encountered in Vietnam, but they quickly learned how to take back the mean streets of Hue. Tanks and Ontos antitank vehicles combined to form deadly hunter-killer teams that could destroy enemy strong points with direct fire. Recoilless rifles provided outstanding suppressive fires while flying debris from the back blast masked Marine movements more effectively than did smoke grenades. Demolition charges and 3.5-inch antitank rockets were used to breach walls so that Marines did not have to move down exposed streets. Machine guns and antitank weapons, normally parceled out to infantry maneuver units, were consolidated so they could deliver concentrated fire. Tear gas proved to be a very effective weapon because its use blinded the enemy and often flushed defenders out of covered positions.

On the evening of the third, plans were worked out by which Cheatham's Marines would attack west along Le Loi Street and Gravel's men would protect the left flank and provide fire support where practical. Ron Christmas's Company H would move parallel to the Perfume River on the right to seize the public health complex, Mike Downs's Company F was to take the treasury building in the center, and Chuck Meadows's Company G would be in support. The 1st Battalion, 1st Marines, would protect the far left flank. The area of operations was about eleven blocks long and nine blocks wide. Intermediate objectives included the treasury, the post office, the public health complex, a girls' school, and the prison. The final objective was the provincial headquarters, an easy target to spot because a red-yellow-and-blue National Liberation Front flag flapped defiantly from its flagpole. Although not mentioned in any formal attack order, capture of this hated symbol was the foremost goal in the minds of the grunts.

Lieutenant Colonel Cheatham showed up at the line of departure to direct the attack on the morning of the fourth. He used tracer rounds from his M16 rifle to point out targets for the recoilless rifle teams supporting the attack. Company H used 3.5-inch rocket launchers, LAWs, M79 grenade launchers, and M60 machine-gun fire to cover its assault on the health complex. The lead platoon rushed across the street and secured a foothold in the medical clinic after an NVA machine gun was knocked out by 3.5-inch rockets fired from the upper story of Hue University. Captain Downs's Company F had a tougher time with the heavily fortified and well-defended treasury. Major Salvati, the battalion executive officer, played an instrumental role throughout this attack. He started by directing recoilless rifle fire, then used a 3.5-inch rocket launcher to eliminate suspected enemy positions, and personally placed E8 tear-gas launchers in exposed positions. Second Lieutenant Donald A. Hausrath, fresh out of The Basic School at Quantico, led the 3d Platoon's daring charge into the treasury, which was quickly secured room by room by gas-mask-clad Marines. Luckily, most of the defenders either had already fled or were incapacitated by the tear gas. The treasury and the post office were both in Marine hands by 1700.

The Marines continued the attack the next morning. The university library and the country club were taken with relative ease, but the hospital was a tougher nut to crack. Company F supported the main attack by Companies H and G. Although initially stymied, Company G was able to enter and secure the hospital during the afternoon. Thirty NVA were taken prisoner during the room-to-room fighting. Additionally, Pham Van Khoa, the mayor of Hue, was discovered inside the hospital and led to safety. The Marines were closing in on the NVA headquarters when Lieutenant Colonel Cheatham halted the attack at 1700. Only two objectives, the provincial headquarters and the prison, remained to be taken.

These last objectives fell on Tuesday the sixth. Progress was slow at first. Tear gas fired into the headquarters compound was carried away by uncooperative winds. Although several attempts to storm the complex were repulsed by heavy fire, the Marines were able to work their way into a "dead zone" (i.e., a spot where the enemy cannot depress his weapons enough to fire into the area) located directly under the eight-foot-high wall by midafternoon. Captain Christmas directed mortar and tank fires as tear-gas canisters burst throughout the courtyard. Second Lieutenant Leo Myers's 1st Platoon blew a hole in the wall and charged across the courtyard, then knocked through the front door to clear the ground floor of the administration building. Gunnery Sergeant Frank A. Thomas rushed to the flagpole with an American flag tucked safely inside his flack jacket. Privates First Class Walter Kaczmarek and Alan McDonald cut down the Viet Cong flag, and then Old Glory was raised to a chorus of cheers from Marines who were still fighting. Columbia Broadcasting System reporter Don Webster commented for the nightly news, "There was no bugler and . . . the Marines were too busy to salute, but not often was a flag so proudly raised." Unfortunately, this small incident represented what was wrong about America's conflict in Vietnam. Hue City was not Iwo Jima, so this flag raising was a violation of protocol, which strictly prohibited solitary display of the U.S. national colors. To true Marine warriors, however, troop morale and combat effectiveness are more important than political correctness. Big Ernie Cheatham was one of those true warriors, and he put his career at risk to demonstrate that fact. At the previous night's officers' call, Cheatham gave his blessing to fly an American flag because he firmly believed the morale value of such an act would far outweigh the consequences of the dressing down he was sure to receive from senior officers more interested in diplomatic sensitivity than effective war fighting. Within two hours, the 2d Battalion held all its objectives and Lieutenant Colonel Cheatham laconically reported, "be advised we have taken provincial headquarters." He then silently prepared himself to be reprimanded for the flag raising.

In four days of close-quarters battle as tough as at Blanc Mont, Okinawa, or the Pusan Perimeter, 2/5, had inflicted more than a thousand casualties on the enemy. The NVA 4th Regiment had been broken and could offer no more organized resistance, but the fighting south of the Perfume River would continue for three more weeks. The 2d Battalion continued to conduct clearing operations as far as the Phu Cam Canal west of the city. There was little resistance when Company H secured the Le Lai military compound and its still intact armory on 8 February. Company G liberated the U.S. consul general's residence that day and freed the mayor's family two days later.

All of the missions assigned to the 2d Battalion were completed on the tenth, but Lieutenant Colonel Cheatham continued clearing operations to root out the defeated enemy on his own initiative. Companies H and F were hit by rocket fire as they swept the far side of the Phu Cam Canal on the thirteenth. Company H lost all of its officers, including Captain Christmas, in this action, and 1st Lt. William Harvey, the battalion's assistant operations officer, became the new company commander. The 2d Battalion's final action at Hue was a night march south through the city and across the Phu Cam Canal, where a sudden reversal of course caught thirty-seven enemy soldiers in the open.

Although things were well in hand south of the Perfume River, there was a bitter fight going on for the Citadel. Unable to push the enemy out, the ARVN commander called for Marines. This task was given to 1/5, which heretofore had been guarding Highway 1. Operating from four company-sized enclaves astride what the French called the "Street Without Joy," the 1st Battalion had been under constant pressure from mortar attacks and nightly probes. Major Robert B. Thompson replaced Lieutenant Colonel Whalen as commanding officer when Whalen was wounded on 1 February while leading a relief column going to the aid of some Vietnamese RFs. Thompson was ordered to bring his battalion to Phu Bai after it became obvious the battle for Hue was going to take longer than expected.

Captain James J. Bowe's Company A, 1/5, was attached to the 1st Marines at 1400 on 10 February. The company moved from Phu Bai to An Cuu Bridge by truck, and then proceeded to the MACV compound on foot. Concurrently, Capt. Fern Jennings's Company B and 1st Lt. Scott C. Nelson's Company C were alerted they would be moving into Hue in the near future.

The next morning, Company B made a helicopter landing under fire at Mang Ca, the ARVN headquarters in the northeast sector of the Citadel. The rest of the 1st Battalion made a motor march from Phu Bai to the MACV compound. Major Thompson reported to Colonel Hughes at 1600 and was ordered to move his battalion into the Citadel as soon as possible. There, the 1st Battalion would clear the southeast quadrant sandwiched between the Imperial Palace and the outer walls of the Citadel. The attack was to proceed from Mang Ca to Thuong Tu Gate. Most fire support limitations had been lifted, but the Imperial Palace was still off limits. Despite operating in the South Vietnamese sector, the 1st Battalion was to remain under American operational control, and Major Thompson reported directly to Colonel Hughes. Five M48 tanks from the 1st Platoon, Company A, 1st Tank Battalion, were attached to 1/5 at about 1700, and Company A and elements of Company B were ferried up the Perfume River to Mang Ca by landing craft within half an hour. Company C and the battalion command post arrived there on the morning of the twelfth. Captain Myron C. Harrington's Company D stayed south of the river and was attached to Lieutenant Colonel Cheatham's 2d Battalion.

The 1st Battalion departed the Mang Ca compound at about 0800 in column formation. Company A was in the lead, followed by Company C, the battalion command group, and Company B. The move had been planned as a semiadministrative one to relieve ARVN units holding positions in the vicinity of Dong Ba Tower. At about 0815, Company A was suddenly taken under heavy fire at least two hundred yards short of the planned assembly area and Captain Bowe was hit. Company B immediately maneuvered to the left and Company C attacked through Company A. The Marines reached Mai Thuc Loan Street, the proposed line of departure that ran from the corner of the Imperial Palace to Dong Ba

Tower, by 1445 but could move no farther. As darkness closed in, Major Thompson ordered a halt and radioed headquarters to request Company D be returned to his control. Colonel Hughes concurred and ordered this done the next day. The 1st Battalion lost three killed and thirty-four wounded during its first day inside the Citadel.

The next day's attack yielded only about the length of a football field before Major Thompson ordered his units to pull back so air, naval gunfire, and artillery could plaster the dug-in enemy. Concurrently, Company D's move to Mang Ca was delayed when the small-craft flotilla carrying it was engulfed by misdirected tear gas. Upon arrival at the Citadel, Captain Harrington was told his unit would lead the assault the next morning to retake Dong Ba Tower, located about midway along the Citadel outer wall.

By that time, Major Thompson's Marines had learned the same lessons as the men fighting south of the Perfume River. They were now massing fires, using tear gas to dislodge stubborn enemy, and covering their movements with 106mm recoilless rifle fire. The 1st Battalion, however, faced some unique problems. Coordination with the ARVN was difficult because of intervening command layers and language problems, maneuver was difficult within such a compressed space, and the Marines were forbidden to fire into the Imperial Palace. These factors beyond Major Thompson's direct control often held up the advance and were directly responsible for the large number of Marine casualties.

The Marines jumped off at 0800 on the fifteenth behind a rolling barrage reminiscent of those used at Belleau Wood, Soissons, and Blanc Mont. Companies B and C retook the lost ground and penetrated into the depths of their assigned sectors against light-to-moderate opposition. The preassault barrage had clearly done its work well. The attackers were also assisted by accurate 60mm mortar fire and fire from 90mm tank guns. Meanwhile, Company D ran into a hornet's nest on top of the Citadel outer wall, where the bombardment had been ineffective. Harrington's men had to take the top of the wall in close-quarters battle using rifles, grenades, and fists. Inch by inch the defenders grudgingly gave ground until the Marines held what was left of Dong Ba Tower. Major Thompson stopped the attack when Company C began taking casualties from the Imperial Palace. The fighting that day cost the 1st Battalion six killed and thirty-three wounded.

The battle for Dong Ba Tower resumed when the NVA counterattacked at 0430 on the sixteenth. The tower changed hands several times, but when dawn broke the Marines had wrestled control of this vital position from the enemy for good. The failed NVA attack was followed by a concentration of small arms and B-40 rocket attacks that pinned Companies B and D in position, but Lieutenant Nelson's Company C was able to make good progress on the left. One of the heroes that day was 1st Lt. Patrick D. Polk, who brought a resupply convoy from Phu Bai, swam across the Dong Ba Canal to deliver a case of badly needed grenades, and then volunteered to take over Company A. He immediately led a successful rescue mission to bring out several wounded men being used as bait by NVA snipers. (This incident was the real-life basis for the fictional plot of the movie *Full Metal Jacket*.) The costliest day inside the Citadel thus far resulted in twelve Marines killed and sixty wounded. That evening, Major Thompson was informed that his NVA counterpart had been killed earlier in the day and was further told that the new commander had unsuccessfully requested permission to retreat. This information confirmed that, although there was still much tough fighting ahead, the Marines now held the upper hand in their portion of the Citadel.

Company D repulsed a counterattack in the early morning hours of 17 February. Slow but steady progress was made on the left, but the right flank was still under heavy enemy fire from the Imperial Palace. Major Thompson therefore concentrated on moving down the left flank. Sixty-two replacements arrived that evening, many of them so new in country that they still wore "stateside" sateen utility uniforms and heavy black leather boots. The eighteenth was cold and dreary and although 1/5 stayed in place, the battalion still suffered four killed and fourteen wounded in a series of sharp fights in the rubble. That evening the elite ARVN "Black Panther" assault company was attached to the Marines in order to deal with the trouble coming from the Imperial Palace. The next two days saw only grinding progress against stubborn resistance as the enemy was slowly pressed back against the base of the Citadel's southern wall. As the twentieth came to an end, Major Thompson took stock of his situation: Most companies mustered only about eighty men, many platoons were commanded by sergeants or corporals, the battalion was short of ammunition and had not been fed for two days, and—most galling of all—the Imperial Palace was still off limits to Marine supporting arms. Intelligence reports indicated that the NVA 6th Regiment had been reinforced by elements of the 5th, 29th, and 90th Regiments. The latter two units were previously believed to have been at Khe Sanh. The only good news that night was that Company L was on the way.

At 2330 on the twentieth, Lieutenant Polk led a patrol from Company A to seal off the Thuong Tu Gate. This night attack met no resistance, and the Marines were able to occupy a three-story building near the gate. At dawn on the twenty-first, Lieutenant Polk spotted several NVA units gathering in the open and called for mortars. A barrage of tear gas disrupted the enemy and Marine snipers used the confusion to pick off enemy leaders. Follow-up attacks by Companies B, C, and D brought the Marines to within one block of the wall. Unfortunately, the lift of Capt. John D. Niotis's Company L was disrupted by heavy antiaircraft fire and only two platoons were able to get into the Citadel that evening.

Companies B and C suffered eight casualties at the hands of an NVA mortar attack at about 0330 on the twenty-second. Major Thompson ordered what he hoped would be 1/5's final assault to begin at 0930, but the main attack quickly bogged down. After Company L finished its move to Mang Ca in the morning, it relieved Company B in the lines at about noon. Not long after that, two Marine A-4 Skyhawks conducted a series of daring close air support missions within a hundred meters of the Marine lines. The fighter-bombers blasted the NVA out of their fortifications for good. Company L followed up the air strike with an aggressive attack that carried to the Citadel wall. Corporal James Avella of Company A raised the Stars and Stripes over Thuong Tu Gate just after 1300. The stubborn NVA had finally cracked, and the 1st Battalion stood poised to finish the job the next day.

When the final Marine attack began at 0800 on 23 February, Company A held the top of the wall and controlled the Thuong Tu Gate, Company D moved along the base of the wall to clear it of spider holes and individuals still holding out, Company L pivoted west to clear its sector as far as the Imperial Palace, and Company C was in reserve. Company B had previously returned to Phu Bai and was being refitted. The Company L attack was a masterpiece of combined arms. Air strikes hit the NVA hard as the Marines moved forward supported by armored vehicles under the cover of accurate mortar fire. The fighting continued until Company D was able to reduce the last four enemy strong points at about 1600. By dark, all objectives inside the Citadel were firmly in Marine hands.

The South Vietnamese flag was raised in front of the Citadel the next day and Hue was declared secure on the twenty-sixth, although fighting inside the city continued until 2 March. The battle for Hue was one of the toughest fights in Marine Corps history. Almost two-thirds of the Marines who fought there became casualties. When the monthlong fight finally ended, two understrength battalions of the 5th Marines had soundly defeated an entrenched, well-armed, and numerically superior foe. These units were later awarded a Presidential Unit Citation for their achievements. On a much larger scale, there is little doubt the Tet Offensive was the turning point in the Vietnam War. In the wake of what was wrongly perceived on the home front as an unprecedented military setback, the Johnson administration began to rethink the U.S. commitment to South Vietnam. On the Communist side, the Viet Cong was no longer an effective fighting force after Tet, and the NVA began to shoulder most of the fighting load after August 1968. Thus, in an ironic twist of fate, the North Vietnamese were becoming more involved in South Vietnam just as the Americans decided to pull out.

An Hoa

During March and April 1968 the 1st and 2d Battalions conducted security operations in and around the vital Hai Van Pass. The most important engagement of this period occurred when a platoon from Company D ambushed a Viet Cong battalion moving down a trail near the Nong River located a few miles southeast of Phu Bai. The ambush was sprung by a Marine command-detonated Claymore mine and was followed by a deluge of rifle fire and 40mm grenades. The outnumbered Marines made excellent use of supporting arms. Mortars, artillery, and close air support from fighter-bombers and an air force AC-47 gunship pounded the dazed enemy, who left more than two dozen dead. No Marines were killed or seriously wounded. This was one of the most successful American small-unit actions in Vietnam.

The 3d Battalion, which remained in the Da Nang Vital Area, met incoming elements of the 27th Marines on 20 February and helped familiarize the new arrivals with their assigned operating area. Six days later, 3/5 joined elements of the 3d Marines for Operation Houston, a security sweep of Highway 1 from Da Nang to Phu Bai. When Houston ended, the 3d Battalion returned to the operational control of the 5th Marines for the first time since regimental headquarters moved to Phu Bai in January.

That summer the 5th Marines returned to Quang Nam Province, and the regiment moved about twenty miles southwest of Da Nang to block the Thong Duc Corridor. The area was 2/5's former home, and the An Hoa Basin would continue to be the regiment's primary TAOR for the next two years. Key terrain in the region included the infamous Arizona (a fertile four-by-seven-mile agriculture flat between the Vu Gia and Thu Bon Rivers), Go Noi Island (a populated area along the south bank of the Ky Lam River southeast of An Hoa), the northern Que Son Mountains, and Charlie Ridge (Dai Loc slope). An Hoa Combat Base, the westernmost major facility in the 1st Marine Division's TAOR, was composed of two military cantonments. The main camp included regimental headquarters, an airstrip, artillery positions, a logistics support area, and the 1/5 and 3/5 rear areas. A smaller camp just across the road served as 2/5's home base. The main supply route—Route 534, familiarly called "Liberty Road"—ran south from Highway 4 across Liberty Bridge then turned west to An Hoa. Nearby was a proposed coal and industrial complex, an abandoned railway, and a West German–run hospital. Enemy Base Area 112 sheltered the NVA 2d Division at the west end of the Thuong Duc Corridor in the rugged jungle-covered Ong Thu Mountains not far from the Laotian border. The An Hoa Basin was important for two reasons: It offered the enemy a good avenue of approach to Da Nang, and its fertile lowlands were a primary source of food. Unnamed battles were fought and refought to control the An Hoa Basin, but the average Marine most likely remembered his time there as a daily grind against overwhelming fatigue amidst intense heat under a burning sun during which the days were punctuated by fear of the booby traps that proliferated there. By that time, such devices were inflicting more casualties on U.S. forces than enemy fire. This remained true for the rest of the war. For example, the 1st Platoon of Company H, 2/5, suffered two killed and seven seriously wounded over the course of three incidents without seeing a single enemy soldier on 22 April 1970. The An Hoa Basin was, to use a term of the times, the worst of Vietnam's "Bad Bush."

The 5th Marines, now commanded by Col. Paul G. Graham, launched a sweep-and-clear operation called Mameluke Thrust in August 1968. One platoon from Company E was pinned down by enemy mortar and recoilless rifle fire on the sixth. The rest of the company maneuvered on the right flank while artillery and close air support battered enemy positions. The Viet Cong then broke contact, leaving behind about two dozen bodies and the recoilless rifle. The Marines lost one killed and seventeen wounded. Ten days later, on 16 August, Lt. Col. James W. Stemple's 2/5 and Lt. Col. Donald N. Rexroad's 3/5 drove east from An Hoa toward a blocking position manned by BLT 2/7 of the Special Landing Force, which had come ashore for Operation Swift Play. The fleeing enemy ricocheted back and forth between the two Marine forces and lost at least fifty men during the fighting. Companies F, G, and H trapped a large NVA force near Cu Ban northwest of An Hoa at the end of September. The major fight occurred at La Phat hamlet when it took Company G more than five hours to evict a Communist platoon, an action that cost seven Marines killed and nineteen wounded. By the time Mameluke Thrust ended on 23 October the enemy had suffered more than twenty-seven hundred casualties in an almost continual series of sharp fights between the Thu Bong and Vu Gia Rivers.

During that time, the 1st Battalion was responsible for securing Dai Loc and the northern part of Duc Duc Districts. Most actions there were isolated incidents that involved individual enemy snipers or units of squad size or less, although on the night of 11–12 September two NVA companies were engaged with heavy enemy losses. The Marines countered enemy tactics by instituting a program of night operations using company-strength dual-axis maneuvers and extensive squad and platoon night ambushes. Captain (later Lieutenant General) Martin L. Brantner, the Company D commander, was awarded two Navy Crosses in eight days. The first was for his actions during a grenade duel at Lan Phouc village, and the second for holding off an all-night enemy assault at My Binh on 11–12 September.

In late September, the U.S. Special Forces camp at Thuong Duc was under attack and called on the Marines for help. This led to Maui Peak, a multibattalion operation under the tactical control of Col. Herbert L. Beckington, commander of the 7th Marines. While the main body, consisting of elements of the 7th Marines and 51st ARVN Regiment, drove west along Highway 4, Lieutenant Colonel Stemple's 2/5 moved overland in a flanking movement while Lt. Col. Rufus A. Seymour's 3/5 awaited helicopter lift. The 2d Battalion assaulted through a semicircular line of enemy fortifications on 6 October and took Hill 163 about two miles from the besieged camp. Meanwhile, 3/5 was unable to land at LZ Sparrow due to heavy antiaircraft fire and was instead diverted to an alternate landing zone about three miles away. The fighting continued until the twelfth, when Company E successfully repelled an NVA assault on Hill 163. Operation Maui Peak ended on the nineteenth with enemy losses counted at 353. Marine losses were twenty-eight dead and a hundred wounded.

In late October, Mameluke Thrust gave way to Operation Henderson Hill with the 5th Marines's new commander, Col. James B. Ord Jr., in operational control. Although the regimental headquarters coordinated the operation, the 1st Reconnaissance Battalion carried the load. Six- to eight-man reconnaissance teams were secretly inserted and then hid in concealed positions until the enemy happened by. When an enemy force or position was located, Marine spotters called for and adjusted artillery fire, naval gunfire, or close air support without leaving cover. These so-called Key Hole tactics were so successful that just over a hundred Marine patrols inflicted almost four hundred enemy casualties without suffering a single fatality. During the operation, Maj. Gen. Carl A. Youngdale, the 1st Marine Division commander, personally briefed Lieutenant Colonel Stemple before sending 2/5 into the Arizona to seek and destroy the NVA 90th Regiment, which had reportedly just arrived in the An Hoa Basin. The ensuing search by 2/5 and 3/5 turned up no sign of the phantom unit, but did find an important document titled "Winter-Spring 1968–69 Campaign." Only elements of Lt. Col. Richard F. Daley's 1/5 participated in the final phase of Operation Henderson Hill, which terminated in December.

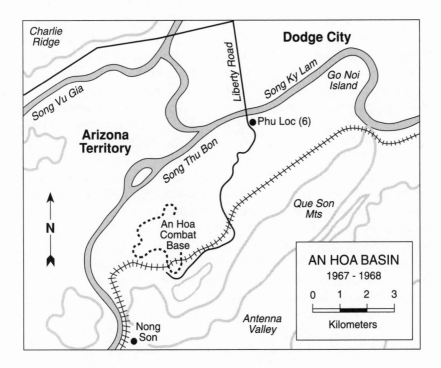

Concurrent with Henderson Hill, the 1st Marines was conducting Operation Meade River, a gigantic cordon-and-search operation by six U.S. Marine battalions to trap elements of the NVA 36th, 38th, and 368B Regiments as well as more than a hundred main force Viet Cong hiding in the Dodge City area. Dodge City was a three-by-five-mile square of tunnel-infested lowlands located east of Charlie Ridge and south of Hill 55. The plan was to mount the largest helicopter assault in Marine Corps history to seal off more than seven thousand enemy troops in a thirty-six-square-mile area. Seventy-six helicopters ferried more than thirty-five hundred Marines into forty-seven different landing zones within two hours on the morning of 20 November. The regiment's 2d and 3d Battalions participated in Meade River from 20 November to 7 December. They joined other Marine units converging on Dodge City from the north, south, and east just as an SLF battalion landing team slammed the western approach shut. There was fierce fighting as more than thirteen hundred VC and NVA repeatedly tried to break out of the trap, but after several weeks of heavy combat it was estimated that less than two hundred of the enemy made good their escape. Those who did get away slipped back into Base Area 112 to rest and refit or went underground in the Arizona.

It was quickly decided to follow Meade River with a high-mobility operation to clean out the An Hoa Basin and penetrate Base Area 112 before the NVA could recover. Brigadier General Ross T. Dwyer Jr. formed Task Force Yankee to conduct Operation Taylor Common. Task Force Yankee included the 5th Marines, three additional rifle battalions, and a field artillery group. Operating in close cooperation but not attached to U.S. units was an ARVN ranger group. In the first phase of Taylor Common the Marines would scour the Arizona to round up any stragglers from Meade River. The second phase was to establish a series of fire support and combat operations bases inside Base Area 112, moving ever westward toward the Laotian border. The major difference between a fire support base (FSB) and a combat operations base (COB) was the presence of artillery: FSBs usually housed a composite artillery battery protected by a rifle company, while COBs were manned by elements of an infantry battalion supported by organic mortars and recoilless rifles. Taylor Common used helicopter mobility to the fullest, employing helicopter insertion techniques pioneered by the 3d Marine Division. Such operations were brand-new for the 1st Marine Division, so elements of the 3d Marine Division moved to An Hoa to coordinate the helicopter insertion phase of Taylor Common. The 2d and 3d Battalions, 5th Marines, would conduct helicopter-borne operations into Base Area 112 while the 1st Battalion conducted clearing operations near An Hoa.

The first phase of Taylor Common, clearing Liberty Road south from the bridge to An Hoa, began on 6 December. The helicopter assault into Base Area 112 began five days later. Lieutenant Colonel Harry E. Atkinson's 3/5 flew from An Hoa to Hill 575 just west of the Arizona. Riflemen provided security as the engineers prepared a hilltop artillery platform and dug fighting positions. When this was done, 3/5's rifle companies patrolled the area radiating out from newly christened FSB Lance in a cloverleaf pattern. Two days later the 2d Battalion performed similar operations to create and secure Fire Support Base Pike. Other units did likewise at FSBs Spear and Mace. Saturation patrols discovered and destroyed many hastily deserted enemy camps, supply caches, hospitals, and even found an empty prison camp. By 1 January 1969, the Marines were operating from COB Broadsword and FSB Tomahawk at the far west end of Base Area 112. About a week later, 2/5 assaulted Hill 435 at the northwest edge of Base Area 112 and established FSB Saber, which isolated the northern approaches and effectively interdicted enemy supply routes from Laos and the A Shau Valley. In mid-February it was decided Base Area 112 had been neutralized, and all forces except for Companies L and M at FSB Tomahawk and FSB Maxwell respectively were ordered back to An Hoa.

While the bulk of Task Force Yankee was destroying Base Area 112, 1/5 had been conducting search-and-clear operations and saturation patrols between An Hoa and Go Noi Island. The major action there occurred on the night of 29 January 1969 when about three hundred enemy soldiers were taken under fire after they were spied crossing the Ky Lam River. The enemy ran into an ambush set by Company D, and seventy-two Viet Cong were killed in the ensuing one-sided fight.

After a three-day rest at An Hoa, 2/5 returned to the field with orders to work with ARVN units to find, fix, and destroy Viet Cong forces in the vicinity of Go Noi Island. Two days later, however, An Hoa was hit by mortar fire and enemy reconnaissance units probed Liberty Bridge, so 2/5 was reassigned to security duty on Liberty Road.

Just as things were heating up at An Hoa, the enemy resumed pressure on the Marine positions inside Base Area 112 as well. During a sapper attack on FSB Tomahawk on 1 March, Pfc. Daniel D. Bruce covered a satchel charge with his body to save his comrades from H&S Company, 3/5. He was killed by the explosion and later awarded the Medal of Honor.

Brigadier General Sam Jaskilka, who had commanded Company E, 5th Marines, in Korea, and now led Task Force Yankee, ordered Companies L and M to pull back. However, what was planned as a one-day retrograde mission turned out to be a three-day ordeal under fire. Company M was unable to be lifted out on schedule because it was heavily engaged on the ground, and Company L had to remain in place to guard a downed helicopter. Company L finally returned to An Hoa on the sixth, but Company M could not be extracted until the next day. Operation Taylor Common finally terminated on 8 March.

Eleven days after the close of Operation Taylor Common, the 1/5 command post came under enemy attack by an estimated Viet Cong company on its way to destroy Liberty Bridge, a recently rebuilt, monsoon-proof 825-foot span that was an essential link in An Hoa's MSR. The attack opened with an 82mm mortar barrage and was followed by a hail of B-40 rockets to cover the ground assault. The Marines responded with a blizzard of mortar and artillery fire and then halted the attackers with small arms. The NVA attack failed. Liberty Bridge was untouched and opened as scheduled on 30 March. Seventy enemy dead were left on the battlefield; the Marines lost seven dead and thirty wounded.

The next major operation was Muskogee Meadow, a dual search-and-clear and rice-denial operation to keep the enemy from obtaining much-needed food. All three of Col. William J. Zaro's 5th Marines battalions were involved in this operation. Lieutenant Colonel Daley's 1/5 conducted patrols, sweeps, and ambushes in eastern Duc Duc and western Duy Xuyen Districts to protect Liberty Bridge, the Seabee compound, and Liberty Road.

The leader of the 3d Platoon of Capt. Michael Wyly's Company D was an aggressive Naval Academy graduate and Basic School honor-man, 2d Lt. James H. Webb Jr. He quickly proved his leadership ability in the field and would be the company commander six months later. Lieutenant Colonel James H. Higgins's 2d Battalion was assigned to the Arizona. Lieutenant Colonel Atkinson's 3d Battalion was responsible for the defense of An Hoa Combat Base—which had recently received more than 400 rounds of combined rocket, mortar, and recoilless rifle fire—as well as security operations in the Phu Nhuan and Thu Bon Districts south of the Thu Bon River. The only major action occurred on 13 April when

Companies E, G, and H flushed a number of enemy and forced them into kill zones established by elements of the 1st and 7th Marines. This two-day running fight resulted in more than a hundred enemy dead and the capture of one 12.7mm machine gun and a short-range rocket launcher. Muskogee Meadow was considered an unqualified success after local farmers were able to harvest more than fifteen tons of rice, and the Marines captured about 27,000 pounds of enemy foodstuffs. The human cost was 162 enemy lost with 16 Marines killed and 121 wounded.

At about this time, Viet Cong and North Vietnamese political leaders ordered the onset of a new military campaign intended to ratchet up domestic pressure upon American president Richard M. Nixon, who had been elected in large measure due to his promises to end the war in Vietnam. The period from late April until mid-June 1969 saw the bloodiest fighting in I Corps except for the Tet Offensive of 1968. Reeling from criticism over the battle for Hamburger Hill and with U.S. casualties running about four hundred a week, President Nixon announced that Americans would cease offensive operations and would begin to withdraw combat troops in the near future. Both pronouncements effected the 5th Marines, but not in the way many had hoped. First, as James Webb noted, "we continued to do the same thing but stopped naming our op[eration]s." Second, it would be almost two years before the regiment finally pulled out of Vietnam.

The new Communist push brought a sudden influx of new NVA into the An Hoa Basin. Viet Cong main force units, which had previously been manned primarily by South Vietnamese volunteers led by North Vietnamese cadres, now mustered almost all NVA regulars. The Marines reacted to this serious threat accordingly. The month of May saw what has since become known as "the Battle of the Northern Arizona." According to Jim Webb's post-war discussion with former Viet Cong, the Communists felt this was the largest and most decisive battle of the war in Quang Nam Province. This action was, in fact, the continuation of an earlier action in which Webb's 2d Platoon was hit by enemy fire emanating from an "L-shaped" ambush near La Thap Village, the "gateway to Go Noi Island" which was south of Liberty Bridge and east of the Arizona on 20 April. That original skirmish resulted in a major fight in which the enemy was slowly pushed back after being hit by artillery fire and close air support. Mysteriously, the enemy suddenly disappeared. Although the fighting abruptly ended, it was obvious the enemy was still somewhere in the area. It was then decided to conduct a more elaborate "search and clear operation." On 2 May 1969, Companies B and M conducted a skillful night movement to cordon La Thap 4. Thirty-six enemy were killed and fourteen more were captured in the ensuing fire fight. Intelligence gathered from many sources, including enemy prisoner of war interrogations after the La Thap raid, revealed that the enemy was massing to attack Marine positions. Colonel Zaro immediately halted dispersed small-unit activities and consolidated his 1st and 2d Battalions for an unnamed three-day operation to clear the northern Arizona using six rifle companies: three to sweep, two to block, and one as a helicopter-borne standby reserve force.

The 5th Marines took on two NVA regiments and their attached Viet Cong auxiliaries south of Hill 65 on the ninth. The Marine main body—which included the regimental command group, five tanks, and Companies E, F, and H—moved into positions north of the Thu Bon River on the night of 8–9 May. Concurrently, Companies A and D moved southwest out of the Liberty Bridge compound into blocking positions in the eastern Arizona. Just after first light, the Marines began a carefully planned advance covered by close air support and artillery fire. Observers at Liberty Bridge reported two groups of about a hundred men each moving in the open. Pounded by intense and unrelenting supporting arms fires, this enemy movement quickly became a chaotic rout. Amtrac-mounted Companies G and K joined the Marine main body as darkness fell. The Marines then manned a night cordon around My Hoa village, with each flank anchored on the Vu Gia River. The action that followed was later cited as an outstanding example of Marine air-ground coordination by the commanding generals of III MAF and the 1st Marine Division in their respective after-action analysis.

That night the enemy probed but did not penetrate the Marine lines. On the morning of the tenth the Marines closed their noose with the assistance of aerial observers who had an excellent view of the unfolding situation. The following day was devoted to small-unit saturation patrols to find and destroy NVA survivors. The major action was fought by elements of Company H, which had to dislodge an enemy force holding a bunker-laden tree line. This fight lasted all day and featured hand-to-hand fighting. Enemy resistance was sufficiently diminished by the twelfth to allow Colonel Zaro to release his units back to their parent commands. The enemy plan to attack Hill 65 had been shattered, more than 230 NVA had been dispatched, and 2/5 was awarded a Meritorious Unit Commendation for its outstanding performance.

While the bulk of the 5th Marines was punishing the enemy in the northern Arizona and enemy attacks on Liberty Bridge and Hill 65 were foiled, An Hoa Combat Base came under increasing pressure. More than four hundred rounds of mixed rocket, mortar, and recoilless rifle fire had hit the base in the past month. Luckily, these attacks had done only minor damage and few casualties were inflicted. The NVA made a more serious attempt on the night of 11–12 May. Fourteen enemy sappers were discovered trying to penetrate An Hoa's eastern defenses. They were allowed through the outer wire to enter a preplanned kill zone where they were trapped by Marine snipers using starlight scope night observation devices. All of the enemy were killed before they could enter the compound.

Simultaneously, the Communists tried to overrun 1/5's command post at Phu Loc 6 near Liberty Bridge. Enemy sappers, supported by flamethrowers and rockets, repeatedly probed the Marine defenses but were repelled each time. The Marines fought back using mortars, grenade launchers, 106mm beehive rounds, and close-in fire support from air force "Spooky" fixed-wing gunships. Fourteen NVA were killed and one was captured. Three Marines were wounded. It turned out that this was the first of several attacks conducted during the next month by the NVA 90th Regiment in an effort to drive 1/5 out of the area.

The 3d Battalion was placed under the operational control of the 1st Marines for Operation Pipestone Canyon, another multibattalion cleansing operation to clear the enemy from Go Noi Island. On Monday, 26 May, Lieutenant Colonel Atkinson's Marines moved out of Liberty Bridge across ground churned up by the combined fires of the 1st Battalion, 11th Marines, and the heavy cruiser USS *Newport News*. There was little resistance except for the omnipresent mines and booby traps that killed ten Marines and wounded more than a hundred in the two-battalion attack force. The 3d Battalion reached its assigned blocking position along the railway berm on the thirtieth. A five-battalion combined U.S., ARVN, and South Korean sweep force began its movement to flush the enemy into the trap the next morning. This operation continued until 11 June, and during the course of the action many undernourished NVA were captured or surrendered. The 3d Battalion was released back to its parent regiment after three weeks, most of which were spent in blocking positions or protecting army and Marine bulldozers razing Dodge City and Go Noi Island. The final accounting for Operation Pipestone Canyon was 488 enemy killed and 28 captured; the Marines lost 54 killed and 482 wounded.

The 1st Battalion became involved in a weeklong fight with NVA and VC units beginning on 7 June. The battalion repulsed numerous probes and came under heavy fire from B-40 rockets, 82mm mortars, and 90mm recoilless rifles. Captain Philip A. Torrey's Company A overran an enemy battalion command post defended by two infantry companies on the eighth. The fighting lasted almost two days and resulted in more than eighty enemy dead. In the ensuing days, the NVA lost an estimated 350 troops, including a battalion commander killed during a firefight with Capt. Gene E. Castagnetti's Company B. The fighting took its toll of enemy, but it was also costly to the Marines. By the twelfth, Marine losses were fifteen killed and about ten times that many wounded, a casualty rate of almost 15 percent. The action was so successful in accomplishing its mission that Lt. Gen. Herman Nickerson Jr., the III MAF commander, sent a congratulatory message to 1/5.

In the wake of so many failed attempts to overrun Marine positions, and considering the severe punishment handed to them by the 5th Marines in the Arizona, the NVA changed tactics and began a war of attrition using booby traps instead of overt action. The Arizona, western Go Noi Island, and the Phu Nhuans were heavily sown with mines and booby traps in an effort to disrupt the Marine campaign to secure the Thuong Duc Corridor. No longer able to smell out large enemy units, the regiment conducted only one large operation and relied instead on small patrols and nightly ambushes throughout the summer. Almost all enemy contacts between the end of June and early November came as a result of small-unit operations. The general operational pattern during this time was to rotate the three battalions, with one operating company-sized formation scattered throughout the Arizona, one securing Liberty Bridge and Liberty Road, and the third guarding An Hoa or mounting independent operations of some sort.

A major exception to this rule of thumb was a 5th Marines–controlled operation to clear Base Area 116. It was believed that Front 4 headquarters and supply elements and elements of the NVA 36th Regiment were located in or around Base Area 116. This operation, known as Durham Peak, used Lt. Col. John M. Terry Jr.'s 3/5 and Lieutenant Colonel Higgins's 2/5 as well as ARVN and elements of the 1st Marines to scour the Que Son Mountains and clear Antenna Valley. The operation kicked off on 19 July with the 3d Battalion and an ARVN ranger group making a helicopter assault into the upper reaches of Antenna Valley. Company patrols swept the area and uncovered numerous bunker complexes, supply caches, and many graves. In general, enemy resistance was light because of the effectiveness of air force B-52s' preassault bombing of the free-fire zone. The Marines cautiously explored trails running toward the Que Son Mountains and ran into increasing resistance as they moved higher up. This was clearly a rear-guard action because the enemy was pulling out of the area. The combination of high winds, rugged terrain, and limited landing zones made resupply difficult, so the Marines had to make do with freeze-dried Long-Range Reconnaissance Patrol (LRRP) rations and local water supplies. A combination of poor diet, insufficient rest, and bad water took its toll as the operation continued. Malaria also thinned the Marine ranks during this period. Colonel Zaro committed his reserve on 31 July when 2/5 flew from Phu Loc 6 to Hill 848 in the center of the operational area. Enemy contact was scattered, limited to a few sharp fights of short duration. In fact, most NVA still in the area were sick or wounded and could muster little opposition. Operation Durham Peak closed in the second week of August with 2/5 and 3/5 returning to An Hoa on the twelfth and thirteenth respectively. Seventy-six NVA were confirmed dead; the Marines lost sixteen killed and sixty-eight wounded.

Contact with the enemy remained light throughout the rest of August. Colonel Nobel L. Beck became commander of the 5th Marines on the sixteenth. The 1st Battalion continued its security missions as before. The 2d Battalion, commanded by Lt. Col. James T. Bowen after 24 August, moved to Hill 65. The 3d Battalion began operations in the Arizona to clear Phu Loi and Nam An villages. Although enemy contact stepped up somewhat in September, the only significant action occurred on 11–12 September when Capt. William M. McKay's Company I engaged an estimated enemy company in the vicinity of Ham Ty 1. Major Martin J. Dahlquist Jr., 3/5's operations officer, tripped a booby trap and had to be evacuated. Captain McKay directed air strikes and artillery before Company I assaulted the NVA position on the eleventh. A subsequent search revealed a dozen enemy dead and sixteen weapons, including a carriage-mounted heavy machine gun. Company I incurred eighteen casualties when hit by mortar and small-arms fire that night. The month of September closed with the regiment pulling two days of security duty during local elections.

The annual northeast monsoon dumped forty inches of rain in the An Hoa Basin during October 1969. Flood conditions in the Arizona brought a halt to lowland operations for the first two weeks of that month. Lieutenant Colonel Joseph K. Giffis Jr.'s 1st Battalion was pulled out of the Arizona for joint security operations with Combined Action Company 29 in the vicinity of Mau Chan 2, Thu Bon 5, and Tick Lake. The 2d Battalion conducted search-and-clear operations on the high ground in Thuong Duc Valley. The rapidly rising waters of the Vu Gia and Thu Bon Rivers forced Lieutenant Colonel Terry's 3d Battalion to evacuate Liberty Bridge and Phu Loc 6. A security platoon and a four-man watch team had to be lifted from the Liberty Bridge watchtower by helicopter. Flood damage to the roads halted overland movement, so An Hoa had to depend on helicopters and C-130 transport planes for re-supply.

The enemy used the cover of the monsoon rains to move back into the northern Arizona near Hill 65. Warned that the VC Q-83 Battalion was staging to attack Dai Loc District, Colonel Beck ordered the regiment to make a hammer-and-anvil spoiling attack near Football Island. Companies A and D, 1/5, moved into blocking positions on 30 October. Company I, 3/5, secured a landing zone for 2/5 and then assumed blocking positions at the eastern tip of the Arizona. Companies G and H and Lieutenant Colonel Bowens's command group conducted a series of aggressive sweeps in conjunction with Regional Force Company 369. More than a hundred of the enemy were killed or captured in ten days of fighting.

The next major action took place from 17–21 November. The 2d Battalion slipped into the Arizona on board resupply helicopters while the 1st and 3d Battalions occupied blocking positions. Three days of complicated maneuvering forced a large number of the enemy onto Football Island in the Thu Bon River. A massive artillery time-on-target shoot in which all guns fire so their rounds will impact simultaneously covered the island, then the rifle units followed up with a thorough search of the target area. About forty enemy soldiers tried to escape on the night of the twentieth but were ambushed by elements of the 1st Battalion. Eighteen were killed and a large quantity of food, weapons, and ammunition was captured.

Lieutenant Colonel Johan S. Getson's 3/5 was split into groups Alpha and Bravo in December. Major Denver T. Dale III's Group Bravo, consisting of Company L and Company E, 2/5, continued to secure Liberty Bridge and Liberty Road. Lieutenant Colonel Getson's Group Alpha, consisting of Companies I, K, and M, conducted an uneventful five-day search-and-clear operation in the northern Que Son Mountains before returning to the Arizona. During the remainder of the month

1/5 patrolled the Arizona and utilized "Operation Butterfly" techniques to deny the enemy sustenance. Ten-man teams used detonation cord, explosives, and gasoline to destroy 760 rice seedling beds, each one capable of feeding an enemy squad for about a month. Colonel Beck labeled this "nipping Rice Krispies in the bud" and concluded that such operations, augmented by extensive patrols and ambushes, severely limited the enemy's mobility and greatly reduced his strike capability. The major action of the month occurred when a fleeing enemy soldier led Company F to an enemy force of unknown size. The resulting fight cost the enemy eight men.

The year 1970 was one of expanding responsibilities and changing tactics for the 5th Marines. The impending withdrawal of elements of the 1st Marine Division meant the remaining Americans would have to cover more territory with fewer men. By midyear, the Marines could muster only two regiments to cover an area once assigned to four regiments. The Communists, reeling from heavy losses in 1969 and well aware that the United States was on the verge of pulling out of Vietnam, prudently decided to husband its assets and dropped large-scale operations. The enemy now emphasized passive defense by once again increasing the numbers of mines and booby traps, harassing the Americans by fire rather than assault, and stepping up the propaganda campaign to win the hearts and minds of the peasant farmers who populated the An Hoa Basin.

The changing situation required tactical adjustments by the Marines. No longer regularly facing large enemy formations and forced to cover twice the ground, helicopter mobility became a force multiplier for hard-pressed Marine commanders. The 5th Marines began using "Kingfisher" tactics in January 1970. This method used an air-ground package for helicopter-borne combat patrolling. A rifle platoon mounted in three CH-46 Sea Knight medium transport helicopters flew over the operations area accompanied by OV-10A Bronco observation aircraft and supported by a four-plane section of Bell AH-1G Cobra attack helicopters. When the enemy was spotted, the Cobras would prep the target area with rockets and machine guns while the riflemen landed and moved toward the sound of gunfire. Aerial observers directed close-air and artillery fires when needed and provided information to the commanders on the ground. Once the infantry had deplaned the Sea Knights returned to pick up a second platoon, which was by then standing by at the airstrip. These tactics were ideal for taking on small enemy units that could not outrun the helicopters, lacked antiaircraft assets, and could be easily isolated for defeat in detail by superior firepower. Kingfisher patrols also minimized the booby trap threat, a factor that significantly cut Marine casualties.

The regiment began the year with 1/5 defending the Thuong Duc Corridor from Hills 65, 25, and 52; 2/5 securing Liberty Bridge and Liberty Road; and 3/5 in the Arizona. Generally, these assignments were rotated on a monthly basis. The new Kingfisher tactics proved very successful when an airborne platoon from Captain McKay's Company I was directed to a spot on the south bank of the Vu Gia River on 13 January. It turned out to be a hot landing zone, so a second platoon was flown in about a mile away. In a coordinated effort, the two platoons moved toward each other while on-call fixed-wing strike aircraft and Cobra gunships attacked targets of opportunity. This unexpectedly rapid response caught the enemy off guard, and they were soon running in every direction. In two hours of combat the Marines killed at least ten of the enemy at the cost of only two wounded in action.

As a result of the withdrawal of the 3d Marine Division and a general realignment of U.S. forces in I Corps, the 5th Marines adjusted it TAOR assignments. Colonel Ralph F. Estey had been the regimental commander since 1 February. When he lost the services of the 1st Battalion, which was placed under the direct control of the 1st Marine Division, he had to extend the operational areas of the 2d and 3d Battalions. The regiment also took operational control of Company M, 1st Marines, which provided the Combined Unit Pacification Program (CUPP) units located in the hamlets near Hills 37 and 55. This program was part of an increased emphasis on "Vietnamization," which gave local RFs ever-increasing responsibility for carrying on the war. The CUPP concept was a variation of the very successful CAP program. The major difference was that existing rifle squads instead of handpicked, specially trained Marines were assigned to CUPP units. They lived in close proximity to one hamlet and worked daily with the same Popular Force or Regional Force militia unit for an extended period of time.

The regiment's realigned tactical areas meant that 3/5 was assigned to the northern area where it was charged with defense of the Thuong Duc Valley and Highway 4 from Hills 65, 25, and 52. Lieutenant Colonel Getson's battalion ran daily saturation patrols and sent out nightly ambushes, supported the CUPP and CAP units in its area, and made an occasional foray up Charlie Ridge. Lieutenant Colonel Frederick D. Leder's 2/5 in the southern zone protected Liberty Bridge and Liberty Road, patrolled the Arizona, and occasionally swept western Go Noi Island. In essence, these two battalions were now covering the same territory that six battalions once did.

When the 1st Tank Battalion and the 26th Marines redeployed to the United States, Lt. Col. Cornelius F. "Doc" Savage Jr.'s 1/5 became the division reserve and mobile strike force. It was assigned to the Southern Sector Defense Command near Da Nang on 6 March. One company was the designated "Pacifier" intervention unit, one company manned static defense positions at Hill 34, and two patrolled northern and central defense sectors, to include defending the Cobb and Song Cau Do Bridges. Pacifier operations were like Kingfisher operations because they used similar air-ground assets, but they differed because Pacifiers conducted traditional reserve unit missions. Rather than being airborne patrols, Pacifiers were emergency reaction forces who assisted units in contact or struck preplanned targets revealed by late-breaking intelligence reports. A Pacifier package consisted of three elements: a command element (the commander and operations officer mounted in a UH-1E Huey), the ground element (several rifle platoons), and the aviation element (CH-46 Sea Knight transport helicopters and AH-1G Cobra gunships). The 1st Battalion conducted more than fifty Pacifier operations between 15 March and 21 June. Lieutenant Colonel Bernard E. Trainor, who commanded 1/5 from August to November 1970, opined that "Pacifier operations . . . successful[ly kept] the VC/NVA off balance." He further noted, "Over time the air/ground team [became such] a well-oiled machine . . . detailed orders were [not] necessary [and] common sense proved more useful than a five-paragraph order." These operations were so successful that a second Pacifier company was added in June 1970.

Because the enemy no longer employed large units in the An Hoa Basin, there were no big battles on the scale of Mameluke Thrust or the fight for the northern Arizona the previous year. Once again, most Marine casualties were the result of booby traps. This problem got so bad that some areas near Hill 65 were designated off limits after 19 April. Still the enemy did, however, sometimes try to catch the Marines off guard. At 0145 on 8 May, Company G was attacked while guarding Liberty Bridge. The enemy was repelled at the cost of twenty-one Marines and Vietnamese RFs wounded. Company E moved down from the foothills of the Que Sons and a Pacifier platoon was flown in when word of this action was passed on. These units located and killed ten retreating VC.

Companies F and H joined an RF platoon to cordon and search Le Nam 1, a hamlet located about two miles south of Liberty Bridge on 13 May. Only two enemy soldiers were confirmed dead, but twenty-four VC/NVA, including three doctors, were captured. Weapons, ammunition, and medical supplies also fell into Marine hands that day. While the fight was on, a Pacifier platoon flew in and was able to dispatch eight of the fleeing enemy. Four days later a similar operation at Le Nam 2 garnered like results. The largest single engagement of this period occurred when fifteen enemy were gunned down as they tried to escape from Football Island. Contact was so rare that the 3d Battalion listed only three killed and thirty-seven wounded during the spring of 1970, while enemy losses were estimated as twenty killed, five weapons captured, eight pounds of documents seized, and 720 pounds of rice confiscated.

Company H detected an enemy platoon moving in the open northeast of An Hoa on 31 May. Company A, 1/5, was the Pacifier reaction force that day and immediately mounted its helicopters for the short ride to An Hoa. Supported by Cobra gunships, the two Marine companies killed five enemy troops and captured one. A second Pacifier package was added on 12 June. Later that month a new wrinkle was tried. Pacifier Companies B and C, 1/5, joined Company G, 2/5, and a skeleton command group from the 2d Battalion to scour the northern Arizona for reported food and weapons storage areas on 20–21 June. Later in the week, the same units joined for a spoiling attack to break up an enemy force massing to assault Hill 55. From March to June 1970, Pacifier operations accounted for 156 enemy dead, 18 prisoners of war, and large quantities of food, weapons, ammunition, and medical supplies. Marine losses during that time were 2 dead and 21 wounded.

The 5th Marines received a new commander when Col. Clark V. Judge assumed command on 27 June, a billet he held until the 5th Marines left Vietnam. The 2d Battalion guarded Liberty Bridge, secured Liberty Road, defended An Hoa, conducted mobile search operations in the Arizona, and made several forays onto Go Noi Island. The 3d Battalion, commanded by Lt. Col. Herschel L. Johnson Jr. after 18 August, kept a rear party at An Hoa, but the forward command post operated from Hill 65 and its units outposted Hills 52 and 25 along Highway 4 to protect the Thuong Duc MSR.

The 5th Marines had been affected by the withdrawal of U.S. forces from Vietnam, but there was no immediate plan to redeploy the regiment. Thus far the changes involved tactical innovations, restructuring the TAOR, and the reduction of individual tours of duty from thirteen months to one year. The next withdrawal announcement had a much greater impact. The 7th Marines was scheduled to pull out in the fall, and the 5th Marines would follow early the next year. This schedule was somewhat deceptive, however. The Marine withdrawals were conducted under the official rubric "Operation Keystone," but harried personnel officers referred to them as "Operation Mixmaster" because of the personnel turbulence they created. Units going home were made up of "short timers" yanked from all units of 1st Marine Division. Men with longer periods of time until their rotation date took their places. This ensured individual equity with respect to time served, but played havoc with unit cohesion.

The regiment was slated to move south into the Que Son Mountains and assume the 7th Marines's area of responsibility when that unit pulled out. In July and August 1970, regimental headquarters and logistics units moved out of An Hoa, but Colonel Judge had to maintain a presence there until the 51st ARVN Regiment took over in October. The 3d Battalion's rear party moved from An Hoa to Hill 37 in July, and was followed there by the regimental forward command post in August. The 5th Marines's rear party on the other hand moved to Camp Reasoner on Division Ridge. Lieutenant Colonel Thomas M. Hamlin's 2/5 stayed at An Hoa, and Lieutenant Colonel Trainor's 1/5 remained under division control at Hill 34 while conducting an average of four Pacifier operations each week.

Trainor modified the use of Pacifier operations during his time in command. He had each unit affix a different colored patch on top of its helmets to ease command and control from the air. He normally landed only one or two platoons and kept the others airborne for effective exploitation of the situation. Units on the ground would pursue only by fire because the wily Viet Cong made a habit of drawing Marines into ambushes or minefields. These new tactics proved highly successful and minimized losses to mines and booby traps. Pacifier operations accounted for eleven enemy soldiers killed, fifteen prisoners, and four weapons in August.

The 5th Marines, less the 1st Battalion, conducted two named operations during the summer of 1970: Barren Green and Lyon Valley. The first was aimed at denying food grown near VC-controlled My Hiep village in the northern Arizona. For two days, 15 and 16 July, a reinforced platoon from 3/5 joined RFs from Dai Loc Province as they guarded

civilians harvesting about thirty tons of corn. This was no easy assignment because enemy sniper fire and booby traps killed three South Vietnamese civilians and also wounded eight RFs, five civilians, and a dozen
Marines. The civilian workers fled in fear and left most of the corn in
the fields. From 24 to 27 July, companies from the 2d and 3d Battalions,
reinforced by Company C, 1st Tank Battalion, returned to the My Hiep
area and captured a few noncombatant civilian "rice humpers" working for the VC. They also flushed a carrying party of the NVA 38th Regiment into a reconnaissance patrol ambush. Following that, 3/5 moved
to My Hiep to protect tracked vehicles as they crushed what remained
of the once lush cornfields. The Marines killed seventeen of the enemy,
captured three, and destroyed about five tons of foodstuffs during Barren Green.

Operation Lyon Valley in August was also aimed at denying food to
the NVA by blocking trails and destroying caches in the mountains
southwest of the Arizona. Companies F and H, 2/5; Company L, 3/5;
and 2/5's command group screened the northern face of the Que Son
Mountains. The local trails showed signs of hard use, but few enemy
troops were found. Company F killed three of the enemy in one firefight
in the only meeting engagement of the operation. All companies discovered numerous caches, fighting positions, and potential rocket
launching spots. The Marines lifted out of the area on 22 August, bringing with them a captured 12.7mm antiaircraft machine gun. The following day, Companies F and H snuck into the southwest Arizona without preparation fires. Only one NVA was taken, but a large amount of
food was uncovered. The Marines suffered no combat casualties during
Lyon Valley, but eleven men were felled by heat stroke or incapacitated
by accidents. The enemy lost five dead, one captured, and more than a
dozen base camps were uncovered and destroyed.

The most spectacular Pacifier operations occurred in the fall of 1970.
Company C made two insertions on 25 September. During the first, one
prisoner was taken and some medical gear captured. The company then
returned to LZ Baldy until dusk to await a meeting of the local VC cadre.
The helicopter-borne Marines descended out of the darkness and caught
the VC leaders by surprise. Four were killed and a fifth, Comrade
Nguyen Dac Loi, was captured. Loi was a tremendous intelligence find
because he was the communications chief for the espionage section of
the Quang Da Special Zone, which included Da Nang and Que Son. Loi
was eventually persuaded to lead Capt. Anthony C. Zinni's Company C

directly to the Que Son headquarters located inside a cave on an inaccessible mountainside on 5 November. Stocky Tony Zinni, an intellectual and former college athlete, was picked for the mission because he had served a previous tour of duty with the South Vietnamese Marines and was familiar with the Vietnamese language. Although Zinni was seriously wounded and had to be evacuated, Company C soundly defeated the VC C-111 Company at the cost of two killed and nine wounded. The VC lost forty-one killed. More importantly, the Marines found a well-camouflaged complex that could shelter five hundred men and included a command suite with a fireplace and running water. More than eighteen thousand pages of key intelligence documents such as unit rosters, pay records, agent dossiers, tactical maps, and photographs were captured in what proved to be the most significant intelligence find of the war in I Corps.

Imperial Lake

By the end of the summer, the U.S. withdrawals were in full force. The 1st Marine Division issued orders on 8 September for the 5th Marines to move south to replace the departing 7th Marines. Regimental headquarters was to move to LZ Baldy and take over Operation Imperial Lake on the twentieth. The 3d Battalion arrived in the Que Son Mountains on the twenty-fourth. The 2d Battalion would move as soon as it turned over An Hoa Combat Base, but this promised to be a time-consuming process because all bases had to be occupied by ARVN troops or razed before U.S. units could depart. Military Assistance Command–Vietnam and XXIV Corps orders used the term "abandon," but Marine leaders demanded that all bases be completely dismantled. The ARVN wanted only a small section of the sprawling base, so the rest of the An Hoa compound had to be dismantled by the 1st Engineer Battalion before 2/5 could leave. As it turned out, a severe weather front preceding the arrival of Typhoon Jane eventually delayed the 2d Battalion departure for almost a month.

The relief of the 7th Marines began on schedule when Capt. Buck Darling's Company G moved to LZ Baldy, where his skeleton unit assumed control of the 7th Marines CUPP units located at nine hamlets along Routes 1 and 535. The dauntless Buck Darling was on his second tour with the regiment in Vietnam, having commanded Company Cs, 1/5, in 1966. The regiment was scheduled to participate in Operation

Catawba Falls, a two-battalion effort to clear Base Area 112, before departing the An Hoa Basin. Battery D, 11th Marines, and a platoon from Company I were flown to FSB Dagger atop 1,031-foot-high Co Ban mesa to kick off the new operation. Within hours the artillery was pounding suspected enemy staging bases to announce the Marines were back. Operation Catawba Falls was, however, an elaborate ruse to cover the move of the 5th Marines from An Hoa. When the Marines boarded helicopters for the follow-up infantry assault they were flown instead directly into the Que Sons. The new 1st Marine Division commander, Major General Widdecke, who commanded the 5th Marines when it arrived in 1966, had secretly canceled the ground phase of Catawba Falls, so the move to LZ Baldy went unhampered. The riflemen of 3d Platoon, Company I, at FSB Dagger were supposed to provide close-in security, but they actually formed a work party to dump the considerable amount of trash accumulated by the heavy artillery firing schedule.

The regiment had three primary missions after moving into the Que Sons: (1) conducting offensive Operation Imperial Lake to keep the enemy off balance, (2) defending various base camps and providing quick reaction forces, and (3) protecting the populated lowland breadbasket north and west of LZ Baldy. To this end, Colonel Judge was controlling Operation Imperial Lake by the end of September. Regimental headquarters was located at LZ Baldy, and 3/5's CP was at FSB Ross when 2/5 arrived at Baldy on 15 October. Artillery batteries were located at Baldy, Ross, and FSB Ryder. Company G, 2/5, controlled the CUPP units assigned to specific villages and hamlets in the Moc Bai sector of the Que Son Valley. The 1st Battalion, still under division's operational control, remained at Hill 34 and continued its Pacifier and security missions.

Colonel Judge initiated a new tactical concept he called the "quick reaction force" (QRF). The QRF was actually a locally controlled Pacifier. Colonel Judge was given operational control of a dedicated helicopter package consisting of one UH-1E command ship, four CH-46 Sea Knights, and four AH-1G Cobras that operated from LZ Baldy. This decentralized aviation support gave ground commanders maximum flexibility and increased their ability to react to quickly changing tactical situations. In general, one QRF platoon remained on fifteen-minute alert at the airstrip with the rest of the company prepared to follow within an hour. The initial QRF concept was modified as time passed to include closer coordination with reconnaissance teams and later utilized Kingfisher tactics. The QRF concept was so successful that the 1st Marines soon adopted it as well.

The major operational obstacle during October and early November was the weather. Four tropical storms—Iris on 4 October, Joan on the fifteenth, Kate on the twenty-fifth, and Louise on the twenty-ninth—brought unusually heavy monsoon downfalls, including more than seventeen inches of rain in eight days at the end of the month. The worst floods since 1964 transformed the Quang Nam lowlands into a vast shallow lake that displaced people, ruined the rice crop, and virtually halted military operations everywhere except in the Que Son Mountains. In the 5th Marines's zone more than 350 people—including CAG, CUPP, RF and PF advisers, and the ROK Marine Corps's "Blue Dragon" Brigade headquarters—sought shelter at LZ Baldy and, for the most part, high-mobility operations were temporarily suspended because Marine helicopters were needed for rescue operations. They flew missions of mercy despite high winds, heavy rain, and poor visibility. More rain, frequent dense fog, swollen streams, and washed out roads and bridges continued to hamper operations long after the floodwaters subsided. This weather had an unusual impact on operations as well. The rising tide inundated Communist supply caches and flooded their underground hiding places. Soon, bands of displaced enemy troops moving toward high ground became easy fodder for the Marines and ARVN throughout November and early December.

Lieutenant Colonel Johnson's 3/5 relieved the 7th Marines at FSB Ross and began working the Que Son Mountains starting on 2 October. Two of Johnson's four companies were earmarked for Operation Imperial Lake, one defended Ross, and the other was a security force under the operational control of the 11th Marines to protect FSB Ryder and observation posts on Hills 425, 119, 218, and 270. Patrols from Companies L and M found many small caches of arms, food, and supplies, but encountered few North Vietnamese or Viet Cong in the process.

Lieutenant Colonel Hamlin's 2/5 at Baldy and reconnaissance teams operating from patrol bases Ranchhouse and Rainbow relieved 3/5 as the Imperial Lake search force on 18 October. Company F occupied LZ Rainbow and Company H was the QRF at Baldy. The regiment was also responsible for the lowland areas at the base of the southern Que Son Mountains. Elements of each of the three organic battalions were involved in operations in that area. Company G, 2/5's CUPP unit, secured nine villages and hamlets in the lowlands near Baldy. Additional units were also used in the valley when the tactical situation allowed. Company E, for example, killed four VC between 26 and 31 October while operating in support of Company G. However, the regiment was hard-pressed to continue Imperial Lake and still adequately patrol the valley. It thus was reinforced on two occasions by elements of the army's 23d Americal Division. From 2–15 October, Army Task Force Saint moved its headquarters to LZ Baldy while conducting Tulare Falls I, a combined search-and-clear operation that killed thirty enemy and captured twenty-one VC suspects. From 27 October to 30 November, Army Task Force Burnett reported to Colonel Judge during Operation Tulare Falls II. Colonel Ralph Estey, the former 5th Marines commander then serving as 1st Marine Division operations officer, played down interservice rivalry when he noted: "Colonel Judge doesn't have [enough] units . . . to saturate his AO . . . the [Americal] task force [does] and [army units] are welcome at any time."

The first real success of the new QRF concept occurred on 21 October. Company H's 3d Platoon was called in by a spotter team that discovered several enemy about four miles southeast of Rainbow. The QRF platoon promptly found more than a thousand pounds of rice in leaf-covered urns. Two contacts the following day resulted in four enemy dead without Marine losses. Unfortunately, the Marines prowling the Que Sons were left without resupply when the tropical storms hit. They continued operations by tightening their belts and going on short rations or, in the case of Companies F and H, no rations, for three days. A reaction force from Company F killed six NVA on 27 October, but lost one killed and three wounded. Company F added three more enemy soldiers to its toll on the thirtieth. By the end of the month, QRF operations had accounted for seventy-four VC/NVA dead and captured thirty-four weapons.

The regiment committed more resources to Imperial Lake in November. Lieutenant Colonel Hamlin was given operational control of all 2d and 3d Battalion forces (three companies from 2/5 and two companies from 3/5) in the western Que Sons and moved his forward command post from Baldy to Hill 381 located about two and a half miles south of OP Rainbow on 6 November. Concurrently, a new command element and two more companies joined Operation Imperial Lake. Lieutenant Colonel Trainor moved his forward command element and Companies A and C into the northern Que Sons for the rest of the month. Up to ten reconnaissance teams were also under the operational control of the 5th Marines at any one time. They used Hill 510 deep in the mountains as a base camp. Korean Marines and U.S. Army units also participated in Imperial Lake on several occasions. The VC and NVA avoided contact during this time.

The general pattern for Imperial Lake operations was for squads or platoons to search for suspected caches or base camps. Bunkers and caves were destroyed by C-4 plastic explosives or were seeded with heat-activated CS tear gas crystals. The most spectacular find was the previously described discovery of the Front 4 headquarters complex on 5 November, the most significant intelligence find of the war in I Corps. The enemy strayed from its base camps on occasion. Viet Cong sappers probed OP Rainbow's outer defenses on the night of 8–9 November, but there was no follow-up attack. The other major contacts in November occurred late in the month. The 2d Battalion command post was hit on the twenty-eighth by rockets and B-40 rocket-propelled grenades that cost one Marine killed and nine wounded. First Lieutenant James D. Jones, the Company I commander, was killed by small-arms fire while clearing an enemy base camp two days later.

A Marine CAP unit in the lowlands near the Ba Ben River three miles north of LZ Baldy was attacked by an enemy platoon on the fourth. The QRF, 1st Lt. John R. Scott's 2d Platoon from Company F, was quickly inserted into the midst of an enemy column. Cobra gunships raked the enemy with rockets and machine-gun fire while the Marines on the ground poured fire into the VC as they broke and ran for the dubious safety of the river. The pursuit turned into a grenade duel as the enemy retreated, and at least twenty VC were killed. The Marines lost one man killed in action.

On 22 November, Lt. Col. Franklin A. Hart Jr., the former commander of 3/7, took over 1/5 when Lieutenant Colonel Trainor shifted to the 1st Reconnaissance Battalion to replace Lt. Col. William G. Leftwich Jr., who was killed in action on 18 November. This exchange of experienced officers allowed the regiment to continue Operation Imperial Lake with little disruption because Hart was already familiar with the terrain and objectives.

Lieutenant Colonel Hamlin returned his command post to LZ Baldy on 2 December. The 3d Battalion command element relieved 2/5 on Hill 381 that same day. The 2d Battalion coordinated operations in the lowlands north and west of Baldy for the next three weeks. Lieutenant Colonel Johnson of the 3d Battalion initially had operational control of five companies, but this number was reduced to only two when 2/5 returned to the field on the eighteenth. Lieutenant Colonel Hamlin's forward command post and two companies operated in close cooperation with the reconnaissance teams from Hill 510 for the rest of the month.

Lieutenant Colonel Hart's 1/5 remained in the northern Que Sons, and enemy activity remained light until the end of the year. The major find occurred when scouts from Company L fired on eight individuals about a mile and a half south of Hill 381 on the twenty-fourth. Companies K and L then spent Christmas Eve and Christmas Day searching the area. They discovered the newly relocated Front 4 command post. They uncovered six large caves that included spare uniforms, supplies, many documents, and a sophisticated communications suite.

A Viet Cong company tried to overrun Company G's 1st Platoon at Phu Thai three miles southwest of Baldy just before dawn on the ninth. The besieged CUPP Marines and RFs fought back and called for artillery. The action continued after daybreak when the enemy, unable to penetrate the Marine wire and under heavy fire, fell back. They left more than 10 dead and a litter of weapons. The Marines lost 2 men seriously wounded, and the RFs lost 2 dead and 14 wounded. South Vietnamese vice president Nguyen Cao Ky visited the CUPP Marines that afternoon and congratulated them for their victory against overwhelming odds.

Keystone Robin Charlie, the sixth and last segment of the previously announced redeployment included the 5th Marines. This withdrawal of 124,000 Marines was scheduled to begin in January and was to be completed by mid-April 1971, at which time III MAF would be downgraded to form the 3d MAB. The 5th Marines was to be relieved by ARVN forces and elements of the Americal Division's 196th Light Infantry Brigade. The plan was to withdraw by echelon, with battalions moving through a final debarkation point at Hill 34 one at a time. The 3d Battalion would go first, beginning in mid-February, 2/5 and the regimental headquarters would follow in early March, and 1/5 would be last. Lieutenant General Robertson, who had been promoted and given command of III MAF after his tenure as 1st Marine Division commander, approved the plan on 8 February.

Although enemy forces in the region had been badly battered and their effective strength reduced to less than nine thousand by January 1971, the Communists could still launch a surprise attack at any time, so it was imperative to keep them on the run even though withdrawal was imminent. To this end, Colonel Judge continued Imperial Lake at a high tempo. The 2d Battalion operated from Baldy and 3/5 worked from Ross. Each battalion kept two companies continuously in the field for the first six weeks of 1971. The 1st Battalion, still under Major General Widdecke's operational control, rotated its companies between the northern Que Sons and Division Ridge until 8 January. Lieutenant Colonel Hart pulled his jump CP and one company back to Hill 34 at that time. The other company was placed under Lieutenant Colonel Hamlin's operational control.

The regiment kept five rifle companies and seven reconnaissance teams in the mountains until 13 February. There were a few small firefights and several cave complexes were discovered. Company H made the largest haul: ten thousand rounds of small-arms and heavy machine-gun ammunition, almost five hundred pounds of foodstuffs, and some crew-served and individual weapons. The largest fight of 1971 occurred on 25 January when a squad from Company L discovered ten enemy troops moving down a trail and mowed down nine of their number. The booty included an assortment of weapons, individual fighting equipment, and a North Vietnamese flag. The regiment accounted for eighty-five enemy dead and forty-one weapons captured in January, while suffering one killed and thirty-seven wounded during that time.

The Communist K-800 Campaign to recapture the Que Son Valley spilled over into the 5th Marines's area of operations in late January. Front 4 units moved out of the mountains and into the lowlands to attack South Vietnamese RF and PF outposts, overrun American CUPP units, destroy bridges, harass refugee settlements, and terrorize government-controlled villages. Captain Robert O. Tilley's Company G, the CUPP unit guarding the lowlands, did more fighting and inflicted more casualties than did the Marines combing the mountains in 1971. In January, CUPP 6, a Marine squad paired with the South Vietnamese 196th PF Platoon, moved into the pro-Viet Cong village of Phu Huong located about two miles south of Baldy. There, CUPP 6 was involved in twenty-eight separate incidents including a half-dozen extended firefights. The largest of these was a two-and-a-half hour battle on the night of 11–12 January. The Marines and PFs on patrol countered a VC ambush by calling for assistance from "Black Hammer," a three-ship night helicopter assault force. The Nighthawks of Marine Light Helicopter Squadron 167 used a specially outfitted Huey search aircraft that mounted a night observation device and Xenon searchlight and two armed Hueys. This specialized force, with Captain Tilley often on board the command ship, worked in close cooperation with Company G. The enemy left sixteen dead on the field of battle that night, but returned to harass CUPP 6 five more times before the end of the month. At the end of January, the CUPP Marines and Black Hammer gunships had accounted for more than sixty enemy dead, captured two NVA, and accepted ten Hoi Chanh defectors. Company F was sent in to reinforce CUPP 6 in February. This eased the pressure in the Moc Bai subsector, although there were still seven incidents that month. A series of terrorist attacks on Xuan Phouc led Colonel Judge to have Lieutenant Colonel Hamlin send his attached Company C, 1/5, into the valley as well.

The 1st Battalion revived the old Kingfisher helicopter-borne patrols under the code name "Green Anvil" during this time. A command helicopter would rove over the valley at low level to locate enemy positions or draw fire. At that point, two Cobra gunships would work over the target area and cover the QRF squad arriving in Sea Knights. These patrols were usually sent to specific areas at the direction of the 1st Marine Division intelligence section. Green Anvil operations accounted for four enemy dead and five prisoners in January. The 2d Battalion's Companies E and F made eight Green Anvil insertions in February. The largest of these actions began at 1830 on the twenty-fourth. The search Huey spotted three bunkers and some scattered equipment. Company E's 1st Platoon was met by enemy fire as the Marines landed. This resulted in a running gunfight with both the ground Marines and Cobra gunships in hot pursuit of the fleeing enemy. Fifteen VC/NVA were killed, two were captured, and many documents were seized. Green Anvil operations resulted in thirty-five enemy dead and five prisoners, plus eleven weapons and more than six thousand pounds of food and documents captured.

The 3d Battalion halted combat operations on 13 February when the battalion command post displaced from Hill 381 to FSB Ross, but Companies K and L continued operations attached to 2/5. Lieutenant Colonel Johnson formally turned over FSB Ross to the South Vietnamese two days later. That same day, the fifteenth, H&S Company and Companies I, K, and L moved to Hill 34. Elements of Company M also went to Hill 34 that day, but most of the company stayed behind to protect the engineers as they demolished FSB Ryder and OP Roundup. These detachments were lifted back to Hill 34 on the sixteenth after Company F took over the security mission.

The 2d Battalion began coming out of the field in early March. Companies F and H joined the battalion command element and Company E at LZ Baldy. Company G was released from its CUPP responsibilities and then moved to Baldy, where it was re-formed as a conventional rifle company. Seven helicopters of Colonel Judge's "dedicated package" flew over LZ Baldy for the last time on 3 March. This time they were not carrying the QRF on a combat mission, but instead flew over a ceremony marking the departure of the 5th Marines. Below them, representative platoons from headquarters and each rifle battalion passed in review before assembled dignitaries. As historian Ronald H. Spector ironically noted, "Many of [these] Marines [were] barely out of grade school when . . . the 5th Marines first landed in 1966."

The 1st Battalion continued Operation Imperial Lake until 23 March, when Lieutenant Colonel Hart pulled his forward command post and two rifle companies off Hill 510 and moved them back to Hill 34 to stand down. Company D was the last unit in the field, with two platoons searching and one platoon guarding LZ Baldy. Six Communists were killed in brief firefights, and documents, foodstuffs, equipment, and ammunition were taken during this last combat action. The regiment's last fatality in Vietnam was a Marine killed by a booby trap on 11 March 1971.

Although the Vietnam War was still slowly grinding its way toward an unsatisfactory end, the 5th Marines's tour of duty in Vietnam was over. Regimental headquarters and the 2d and 3d Battalions sailed for the United States in early March, and the 1st Battalion was ready to leave by the end of the month. Elements of the regiment had participated in more than fifty major operations and had fought in three of Vietnam's four military regions during almost five years in country. Its service was varied. Members of the 5th Marines had conducted amphibious landings while serving with the SLF and participated in many offensive, defensive, and civic action operations. The regiment's most notable combat actions were Operations Union I and II, the battle for Hue City, and Operations Meade River, Mameluke Thrust, and Imperial Lake. The regiment also pioneered or perfected many new tactics during its tour of duty. The regiment was awarded three Presidential Unit Citations, one Navy Unit Commendation, and one Meritorious Unit Commendation. It also received the Cross of Gallantry with Palm and Meritorious Unit Citation Civil Actions Streamers from the South Vietnamese government.

Postscript

Jim Webb, an infantry officer with Company D in 1969, turned out to be a modern "man for all seasons." He proved to be the most versatile—and probably the most famous—member of the Vietnam-era 5th

Marines. Webb was not only a first-class combat leader; he was also a man of high intellect, a talented writer, a selfless public servant, and an articulate defender of Vietnam veterans. Jim Webb was a highly decorated Marine who was wounded twice and earned the Navy Cross, Silver Star, and two Bronze Star medals during nine months in the field. Upon his return to the United States he was selected for early promotion to captain while serving at Quantico. Suffering from wounds that would not properly heal, he was transferred to Marine Corps headquarters, where he began to hone his writing skills. He was medically retired in 1972 and went on to become counsel to the Veterans Affairs Committee of the U.S. House of Representatives after graduating from law school. Concurrently, he wrote *Fields of Fire*, the first of several best-selling novels. His others included *A Country Such As This*, *A Sense of Honor*, and *Something to Die For*. He was recognized by the Veterans Administration as its first Vietnam Veteran of the Year and played an instrumental role in the creation of the Vietnam Memorial in Washington, D.C. As a television journalist, he received an Emmy award for his reporting of the Beirut crisis. He became the assistant secretary of defense for reserve affairs and later served as secretary of the navy during the Reagan administration. After leaving the political arena, Webb turned to screen writing and film production. His most notable success in that field of endeavor so far has been the popular movie *Rules of Engagement*. Throughout his controversial career, Webb has steadfastly remained a staunch spokesman for veterans and a vehement proponent of American military readiness.

Tony Zinni—a former Villanova University football player who led Charlie Company, 1/5, in 1970— graduated from several prestigious military schools and received two master's degrees from civilian institutions before achieving four-star rank. During the last decade of the 1990s he was considered one of America's foremost experts on military operations other than war as a result of his tours of duty as the commanding officer of the 35th Marine Amphibious Unit during security and disaster relief operations in the Philippines; deputy commander of Combined Task Force Provide Comfort, which conducted international humanitarian and security operations in northern Iraq in the wake of the Gulf War; and military coordinator for Operation Provide Hope, which performed relief efforts in the Soviet Union. He also played a leading role in U.S. operations in Somalia, serving successively as director of operations for

Operation Restore Hope, United Nations special envoy during Operation Continue Hope, and as commander of a combined task force overseeing the withdrawal of U.N. peacekeepers during Operation United Shield. Upon his return from Somalia, Zinni took over I MEF and later served as commanding general of the U.S. Central Command just prior to his retirement.

Rough and tough Big Ernie Cheatham of 2/5 went on to a distinguished career after Vietnam. As commanding general of the 1st Marine Division and commander of Fleet Marine Force Atlantic, he helped to spearhead the phoenixlike revival of America's armed forces after the troubled post-Vietnam era. According to Marine historian Allan R. Millett, Cheatham was the top choice of navy secretary Jim Webb, who wanted a proven "warfighter" to become Commandant. However, Cheatham steadfastly maintained that although he was an excellent combat leader, his forthright manner was unsuited for the Machiavellian behind-the-scenes give-and-take necessary for what was essentially a political job. That reluctance, coupled with health problems, prevented his appointment to the Corps's top post. Instead, another Marine warrior, Gen. Alfred M. Gray Jr., went on to lead the Marine Corps to one of its most spectacular victories in the Persian Gulf.

Bernard "Mick" Trainor, the former commander of 1/5 in 1970, eventually wore three stars, but he was probably most recognizable to the general public for his role as ABC's military analyst during the Gulf War. After retirement, Trainor was a special correspondent for military affairs for the *New York Times* from 1986 to 1990, and he coauthored a best-selling history of the Gulf Conflict, *The Generals' War.* Trainor is currently director of national security programs for the John F. Kennedy School of Government at Harvard University. Ron Christmas, the commander of Hotel, 2/5, at Hue City also retired as a lieutenant general. He is currently director of the Marine Corps Heritage Foundation. Marty Brandtner, the man who earned two Navy Crosses in nine days, also became a lieutenant general. His most prominent post was as the assistant operations officer on the Joint Staff during the Gulf War.

Interestingly, in late 1968 two men who rose to prominence during their time with the 5th Marines were considered by most Marines to be the leading candidates to become Commandant when Wallace Greene left. Either Silent Lew Walt, the burly combat leader who earned three Navy Crosses while leading units of the 5th Marines, or intellectual Brute

Krulak, who toughened the regiment before it was sent to Korea in 1950, was expected to be promoted by the rank-and-file. Instead, President Lyndon Johnson—perhaps wary of causing a split by selecting one of the two most popular men in the Corps—opted for a darkhorse, Leonard C. Chapman. Lew Walt did, however, receive his fourth star while on active duty; the first non-Commandant Marine to do so. Because tombstone promotions were no longer on the table, Brute Krulak retired a lieutenant general, but his son later became Commandant.

Ken Houghton received the Navy Cross, a second Legion of Merit, a second Silver Star, and two more Purple Hearts for his service as commanding officer of the 5th Marines. He went on to command both the 1st and 3d Marine Divisions as well as serving as assistant chief of staff for personnel (G-1) at Headquarters Marine Corps before retiring as a major general. Regimental commanders Chuck Widdecke, Fred Haynes, Dewey Bohn, and Paul Graham also achieved two-star rank before retiring. Terry Murray (the former Naval Academy football star who later commanded Fox, 2/5, in 1970) is currently a serving major general.

Activities of the 5th Marines have been the focus of a large body of the literature emanating from the Vietnam War, particularly regarding actions during the battle for Hue City and the nasty guerrilla warfare southwest of Da Nang. This body of work includes two of the best-selling and most critically acclaimed works of fiction about the war in Vietnam, Jim Webb's *Fields of Fire* and Robert Roth's *Sand in the Wind*. Both novels concentrate on the day-to-day life of the grunts by telling their stories through the point of view of platoon leaders and enlisted Marines. Webb's book is set in the "Arizona Territory" in 1969, while Roth's narrative travels from An Hoa in 1967 to Hue City in 1968. Each offers a moving and accurate portrayal of what the Vietnam War was like to those who had to fight it. Three memoirs by former members of the 5th Marines have also gone on to become book-of-the-month selections. Two of them, *Operation Tuscaloosa* and *Sniper in the Arizona,* chronicle the experiences of enlisted man John Culbertson and his 2/5 squad mates in the An Hoa Basin. Together they carry the reader through the latter part of 1966 and the first half of 1967. The third memoir, *Phase Line Green*, records the experiences of Nick Warr, a platoon leader with 1/5 at Hue City in February 1968. Additionally, Marine combat correspondents attached to the 5th Marines at Hue wrote two paperback novellas. They are Dale Dye, author of *Run Between the Rain Drops,* and Gustav Hasford, who wrote *The Short-Timers.* The former is noteworthy

primarily because its author has since become a well-known movie ac-
tor and is a much-sought-after technical adviser whose body of work includes what is arguably the best-received movie about Vietnam, Oliver
Stone's *Platoon.* Now a retired Marine captain, Dye teamed up with Jim
Webb for the movie *Rules of Engagement.* Hasford's book achieved fame
and went through numerous printings after it was adapted for the
screen by Stanley Kubrick as *Full Metal Jacket.*

7: Persian Gulf

Commandant Robert E. Cushman Jr. said of the Marine Corps in 1971, "We are pulling our heads out of the jungle and getting back into the amphibious business." This statement, however, turned out to be more of a future goal than immediate reality. The early and mid-1970s were troubled years for America's armed forces. Declining budgets, elimination of the draft, a European strategic focus, and widespread antimilitary sentiment after the Vietnam War caused unprecedented turmoil within the Marine Corps. Fortunately, the Marine Corps underwent a phoenixlike resurrection beginning during the tenure of Commandant Louis H. Wilson. The Marine Corps was reorganized, rearmed, once again embraced its amphibious heritage, and was "good to go" when the call to arms again sounded in 1990. The history of the 5th Marines from the end of the Vietnam War until the start of the Persian Gulf War accurately reflects the trials and final triumph of that arduous journey.

The regiment returned to Camp Pendleton's familiar rolling hills for the third time in April 1971, and once again claimed Camp Margarita as its home. President Richard M. Nixon welcomed the 1st Marine Division veterans home on 30 April. For the first half-decade after its return to the United States, however, the regiment was not truly a combat-ready unit due a postwar drawdown and high personnel turnover. The Marine Corps, just like all the other American armed services in the wake of the Vietnam War, struggled with a myriad of personnel problems that included substance abuse, racial tensions, and disenchantment with military life, which made quality recruiting difficult. Probably the only redeeming quality during this era was that the tough times guaranteed only truly dedicated Marines would stay in. The 1st Marine Division provided advanced individual training for recruits slated for service with the 3d Marine Division during the early 1970s. One battalion of the 5th Marines was manned at almost zero strength, and a second experienced a high turnover rate because it was primarily used to prepare recent graduates from the San Diego Recruit Depot for service with the Fleet Marine Force.

The commanding officers of the 5th Marines during this formative period were Lt. Col. Richard R. Burritt, Lt. Col. Max J. Hochenauer, and Col. Robert N. Burhams in succession during 1971. Colonel Burhams was followed by Cols. John F. Roche III, Jack D. Rowley, John H. Cahill, and Warren L. Ammentorp. Richard Burritt, by then a colonel, once again commanded the Fighting Fifth from July 1976 to January 1978. He was followed by Col. William J. Masterpool, Col. (later Lt. Gen.) Anthony Lukeman, and Col. Domminick R. Gannon. Colonel (later Maj. Gen.) John I. Hopkins ushered in a new decade when he took over on 16 August 1980.

The Marine Corps began to emerge from the doldrums in the mid-1970s. The 2d and 3d Battalions participated in amphibious exercise Bell Canyon in 1974. This was the first large-unit field exercise since the regiment's return from Vietnam. The Marine desert training facility at Twentynine Palms in the Mojave Desert was transformed from an out-of-the-way artillery range into the largest Marine combat training base at about the same time. That refurbished desert outpost became the site of the highly regarded Palm Tree battalion-sized live-fire exercises starting in 1977.

This expanded training coincided with a national-level in-depth review of U.S. strategy and discussion about what role the Marine Corps would play in the future. The lessons of the Vietnam War had been absorbed and it was decided to rearm and restructure the Marine Corps to facilitate its role as America's force in readiness. Events in the Middle East and a domestic energy crisis refocused Marine Corps attention away from possible operations on Europe's northern tier toward the Persian Gulf with its vast oil supplies. This redirection in strategic thought had a great impact on the 5th Marines.

The most notable event of the immediate post-Vietnam era for the 5th Marines was Operation New Arrival, the resettlement of a flood of "boat people" from Southeast Asia who had been granted political asylum between July and December 1975. Refugees from Communist repression in Southeast Asia were called "boat people" because they desperately fled their homeland in rickety craft hoping to be picked up by ships of the U.S. Seventh Fleet or to make landfall on a hospitable shore. There is no way of knowing exactly how many left Vietnam, but it is estimated that probably far less than half of the refugees reached safety. Many upon arrival in the United States were placed in temporary quarters at a gigantic tent city inside Camp Pendleton until they could be properly processed, acclimated to their new environment, and relocated to new homes. Other domestic duties performed by the regiment included riot control training and fighting wildfires that frequently swept Southern California and the western United States.

Changes in Marine Corps policy resulted in the 5th Marines starting a Camp Pendleton-to-Okinawa rotation that later became known as the Unit Deployment Program (UDP). This program was reminiscent of the pre-Vietnam transplacement rotation except that units deployed by air rather than by ship, and they served overseas for only six months instead of for more than a year. These UDP deployments were expansive, but they greatly increased unit cohesion and reduced personnel turbulence. The 3d Marine Division on Okinawa mustered two regiments: the 4th and the 9th. The 1st Marine Division provided battalions to the 9th Marines while the 2d Marine Division rotated units with the 4th Marines. Accordingly, 2/9 became part of the 5th Marines UDP rotation and served about eighteen months at Camp Pendleton under the regiment's operational control in each two-year period. The 1st Battalion, 5th Marines, replaced 2/9 on Okinawa in February 1979. That unit was, in turn, replaced by 2/5 in August and 3/5 the following February. In August 1980 the full cycle was completed when 2/9 returned to its home on the Rock for a six-month "pump." This unit rotation continued until the 5th Marines deployed to Southwest Asia in 1990.

The Marine Corps restructured its infantry battalions for increased effectiveness, better mobility, and to take advantage of new weapons systems in August 1979. The number of rifle companies was reduced from four to three, but battalion weapons companies were reintroduced in the I-series table of organization. Each of the new companies included a mortar platoon with eight 81mm mortars, an antiarmor platoon with twenty-four M47 Dragon antitank missiles, and a heavy machine-gun platoon with eight M2HB .50-caliber machine guns and eight M19 40mm automatic grenade-launchers. The long-serving thirteen-man rifle squad consisting of three four-man fire teams was replaced with an eleven-man squad consisting of a squad leader and two five-man fire teams. Forty-five newly developed 5/4-ton high-mobility, multipurpose, wheeled vehicles (HMMWVs or "humvees") replaced 149 other pieces of rolling stock in the infantry battalions.

The United States created the Rapid Deployment Joint Task Force (RDJTF) in 1980 to meet the need for a mobile strike force to intervene in the Indian Ocean area. This multiservice organization increased its area of responsibility from the Horn of Africa to include Southwest Asia and much of the Middle East as time passed. The RDJTF was dissolved on 31 December 1982, but the U.S. Central Command (CENTCOM) stood up the very next day. This new organization occupied the same quarters and was responsible for the same geographic area as was the RDJTF, but unified command status gave its commander much more influence.

The Fleet Marine Force was reorganized to include permanent MAGTFs in 1983. California-based I MAF became the Marine component command assigned to CENTCOM. This contingency had a significant impact on the Marine Corps, especially the units of the 1st Marine Division. A Maritime Prepositioning Force (MPF), consisting of squadrons of forward-deployed container ships, air-deployable Marine brigades, and appropriate naval support elements, was created. This concept enabled I MAF to deploy its fly-in element overseas within a matter of days rather than a matter of weeks. The rest of I MAF had to be ready to deploy by ship within ninety days. The 5th Marines, as part of the 1st Marine Division, was assigned to I MAF as its seaborne element.

The regiment adopted the 1038C tables of equipment and organization in the early 1980s (1/5 in September 1983, 2/5 in May 1984, and 3/5 in September 1984) as part of a Corpswide reorganization. Individual Marines dressed in woodland battledress uniforms (BDUs or "cammies") and wore Kevlar "Fritz" helmets after 1985. Marine infantrymen were armed with improved M16A2 rifles, M9 9mm Baretta pistols, M249 squad automatic weapons (SAWs), AT4 light antitank rocket launchers, and improved M60E3 medium machine guns. The regiment significantly increased its antiarmor capability by adding a tube-launched, optically tracked, wire-guided (TOW) antitank missile platoon and increasing the number of Dragons from twenty-four to thirty-two in 1984. Gone were the familiar canned C rations of earlier days, replaced by freeze-dried combat rations called Meals, Ready-to-Eat (MREs), although these new MREs were quickly dubbed "Meals Rejected By Everyone" by wags throughout the Marine Corps. One can only wonder what their World War I compatriots, who often went days without food, would have thought of such an invention.

The regiment's main mission was to prepare battalions for overseas tours on Okinawa, but each year elements of the regiment conducted battalion combined arms exercises (CAX) at the Marine Corps Combined-Arms Combat Center at Twentynine Palms, practiced amphibious operations after a month of schooling at the Landing Force Training Center at Coronado and Camp Pendleton, or participated in biannual Gallant Eagle joint exercises. The Gallant Eagle exercises were massive CENTCOM-sponsored joint training exercises that included all four services operating in four or more states. Scenarios reflected contemporary CENTCOM contingency plans and the exercises were considered rehearsals for the Bright Star combined exercises held in Egypt every other year. The 5th Marines usually conducted a simulated amphibious landing, and then became the aggressor force opposing elements of I MAF and the army's XVIII Airborne Corps during Gallant Eagles. These field exercises featured good staff training and provided an opportunity to practice live fire support coordination and field operations in a joint environment.

Thirteen permanent MAGTF headquarters were created in April 1985. After this reorganization, I MAF included two standing brigades and three independent MAUs. The 5th MAB was headquartered at Camp Pendleton and was the designated I MAF seaborne deployment force. The 5th MAB was also responsible for West Coast amphibious training. The 7th MAB was the MPF fly-in element associated with the navy MPS squadron located at Diego Garcia atoll in the southern Indian Ocean. The 1st Marines had no MAB affiliation; instead, it was the parent command of the three MAUs (the 11th, 13th, and 15th) home-based at Camp Pendleton that provided forward-deployed forces afloat in the western Pacific. The 5th Marines was the ground combat element of the 5th MAB. The regiment also continued to rotate its battalions to Okinawa and sometimes provided the Camp Pendleton air contingency force, which was under the operational control of the 7th MAB. The 7th Marines relocated to Twentynine Palms and became a mechanized combined-arms task force assigned to the 7th MAB. There were several organizational changes during the late 1980s. The beloved three-fire team, thirteen-man squad was brought back in 1986, and in 1988 Commandant Al Gray replaced the word *Amphibious* with *Expeditionary* in the title of all MAGTFs after explaining that the Marine Corps was ready to go anywhere, anytime, by any conveyance, and was not locked in to ship-to-shore movements. The 5th Marines was thereafter assigned to the 5th MEB instead of the 5th MAB.

Southwest Asia

The first day of August 1990 was an unexceptional one in the annals of the 5th Marines. Regimental headquarters was located at Camp Margarita, where Col. Randolph A. Gangle had operational control of the regiment's 2d and 3d Battalions. These battalions were involved in normal training activities and none was scheduled for overseas deployment in the near future. The 1st Battalion, commanded by Lt. Col. Christopher Cortez, was in a high state of readiness because it was the Camp Pendleton air contingency battalion and had to be ready to fly into harm's way within hours if an unexpected call to action came. This unit was not under Colonel Gangle's operational control, so it would deploy as part of the 7th MEB in case of an emergency.

The next morning, Iraqi dictator Saddam Hussein shocked the world when he unleashed his elite Republican Guard on his peaceful neighbor, the emirate of Kuwait. Saddam's armored units poured across Kuwait's northern and western borders without warning, quickly captured Kuwait City, then rushed south toward the oil-rich but nearly defenseless kingdom of Saudi Arabia. Saddam's unprovoked attack was a brutal power grab to take over Kuwait's abundant oil fields. The entire world listened in stunned astonishment as Saddam brazenly declared that Kuwait had become Iraq's "19th Province." His plans for Saudi Arabia were not clear, but a threat to the kingdom's stability was definitely implied. The United States quickly formed a worldwide coalition that offered multinational forces to defend the rest of the Arabian Peninsula against Saddam's aggression. The Americans called this strictly defensive operation Desert Shield.

In the early summer of 1990, all of I MEF's elements were located in Southern California. The 7th MEB was located at Twentynine Palms. The 5th MEB was at Camp Pendleton, where it served as I MEF's seaborne brigade. Contingency plans called for the 5th MEB to draw its ground combat element from the 1st Marine Division at Camp Pendleton. The aviation combat element, MAG-50, would use 3d MAW assets from Tustin, El Toro, and Camp Pendleton. Brigade Service Support Group 5 would use detachments from the 1st Force Service Support Group at Camp Pendleton to provide logistics support.

On 7 August 1990—the forty-eighth anniversary of the 5th Marines's landing on Guadalcanal—the 1st (Hawaii), 4th (Okinawa), and 7th MEBs all received warning orders to prepare to deploy to Saudi Arabia. Three days later, Maj. Gen. John I. Hopkins, the 7th MEB commander, assumed operational control of 1/5. Within a week, 1/5 became one of the first Marine ground combat units to land in Saudi Arabia. After four miserable days stuck in oppressively hot warehouses at the Saudi port of Al Jubayl, the Marines of 1/5 married up with prestocked supplies and equipment carried on board MPF ships and then moved out to defend what was known as the Jubayl Vital Area. The 1st Battalion was assigned to RCT 7, later designated Task Force Ripper, which was commanded by Col. Carlton W. Fulford. The 1st Battalion was initially used to secure Al Jubayl's modern deepwater port and international air facility before later manning forward positions along a terrain feature called Cement Ridge. The 1st Battalion, 5th Marines, was a mainstay in I MEF's mobile defense plans.

Back at Camp Pendleton, Brig. Gen. Peter J. Rowe, commander of the 5th MEB, received a deployment warning order on 13 October. He learned that the 5th MEB was going to Southwest Asia as an amphibious landing force embarked on board the ships of RAdm. Stephen S. Clarey's Amphibious Group 3 (PhibGru 3). No firm sailing date was set, but Colonel Gangle's Regimental Landing Team 5 (RLT 5), consisting of 2/5 and 3/5 plus assorted combat support and service support detachments, was placed under General Rowe's command at that time. The most likely mission at that time was an amphibious assault to seize the port of Ras Al Qulayah in southern Kuwait. Other operational contingencies included a variety of amphibious raids, maritime interdiction, in-extremis hostage rescues, and noncombatant evacuations.

Colonel Gangle had to make do with what was left after most of the 1st Marine Division left for Southwest Asia when he began to assemble RLT 5. The most pressing need was for combat support units. A second concern was that many men assigned to the regiment were nondeployable because they were near the end of their service contracts or had just returned from overseas. About half of 2/5 was nondeployable under existing regulations, and 3/5 had just returned from a unit deployment to Okinawa on 4 August, so few of its men were eligible for another overseas move. This problem was solved when the Commandant stopped releasing Marines from active duty and waived overseas deployment rules. This so-called "stop-loss program" immediately made previously nondeployable Marines eligible for overseas duty. President George Bush's nearly concurrent decision to call up the reserves gave the green light to activate Selected Marine Corps Reserve units and Individual Ready Reservists. Another nagging shortfall ended when General Rowe was allowed to embed the fully equipped and well-trained 11th MEU into the 5th MEB.

Regimental Landing Team 5 thus became a diverse unit composed of regulars and reservists. In addition to the regiment's organic battalions, the unit included the 2d Battalion, 11th Marines, and BLT 3/1 from the 11th MEU(SOC). Most of the rest of the regiment's combat support units came from the Selected Marine Corps Reserve. When it was at last ready to deploy, RLT 5 included Capt. Gary K. Schenkel's Headquarters Company; Lt. Col. Donald R. Selvage's 3/5; Lt. Col. Kevin M. Kennedy's 2/5; Lt. Col. Robert S. Robichaud's 3/1; Lt. Col. Paul A. Gido's 2/11; a composite reconnaissance company commanded by Capt. Erik Grabowski that included regulars and reservists from the 1st and 4th Reconnaissance Battalions; Capt. John V. Geary's Company A, 4th Tank Battalion; Maj. John W. Saputo's Company A, 4th Assault Amphibian Battalion; Capt Larry O. Christian's Company A, 4th Light Armored Infantry Battalion; Capt. James I. Maxwell's Company F, 2/25; Capt. Peter J. Massaro's TOW platoon from Headquarters Company, 23d Marines; Capt. Truman D. Anderson Jr.'s Company B, 1st Combat Engineer Battalion; Capt. John S. Sharpe's Company A, 4th Combat Engineer Battalion; and Capt. David G. Brown's 5th and 6th Truck Platoons, 6th Motor Transport Battalion. The bulk of these, except some of the recon Marines and Company B's engineers, were reservists. The regiment mustered 4,732 personnel when it sailed.

Reserve units began arriving at Oceanside on 15 November. They were assigned to their active duty commands within forty-eight hours, but the majority of the individual reservists attended a four-day Southwest Asia training program run by the School of Infantry before actually joining their new commands. The regulars were at first a little uneasy about the state of reserve readiness, but they soon discovered the reservists were highly motivated, skilled individuals who were proud to serve their country and asked only to be accepted as fellow Marines by their active-duty counterparts. General Rowe said the reservists were devoted, enthusiastic, intelligent, and noted that the only operational difficulty was familiarizing reserve units with 5th MEB standard operating procedures. Colonel Drake Trumpe, 5th MEB's chief of staff, thought the reservists were "outstanding" and said that their smooth transition from civilian life to military life validated the Total Force concept instituted after the Vietnam War. The integration of the reserves was so successful that Colonel Gangle reported by the time the 5th Marines arrived in Southwest Asia he could not tell the regulars from the reservists.

Among the problems confronting Colonel Gangle on the eve of his unit's departure for the combat zone were the lack of training time and questions about the ability of so many new units to work in harmony. The training status of the units in the regiment varied widely. The 11th MEU had been training since the summer and was certified "special operations capable" after a rigorous program that culminated with a final training exercise testing its ability to conduct eighteen different missions. The 2d and 3d Battalions, 5th Marines, and the 2d Battalion, 11th Marines, had been conducting normal training but had not had a chance to fully integrate all of the combat support attachments that made up the regimental landing team. Most of the reserve units that came on board in mid-November drilled only one weekend each month and pulled just two weeks of active-duty training each year. Luckily, elements of the 4th Assault Amphibian Battalion and the 4th Tank Battalion had participated in combined-arms exercises at Twentynine Palms the previous summer, so they were intimately familiar with the rigors of a desert environment. On the downside, the "Gulfport Trackers" of the 4th Assault Amphibian Battalion had not worked with amphibious ships during the past year.

Colonel Gangle conducted a computer-enhanced command post exercise to sharpen regimental command and control procedures. Maritime interdiction and small-unit special operations training was held in early November. The regiment then moved to the Marine Corps Combined Arms Combat Center at Twentynine Palms for a series of live-fire exercises. Unfortunately, 3/5 did not join its reserve combat support units until after the exercise was over. When that training was completed, most of the regiment's regulars were able to enjoy a final ninety-six-hour liberty over the Thanksgiving holiday while the reservists spent the long weekend training. This did not sap morale, however; in the words of one reservist: "A lost weekend was a small price to pay to defend your country. Besides, most of us realized we were about to embark upon the greatest adventure of our lives."

The largest amphibious group to sail from the West Coast since the Vietnam deployment in 1965 departed San Diego on 1 December when PhibGru 3 slipped over the horizon on its way to the Persian Gulf. The route across the Pacific led to Hawaii and the Philippines, then through the Strait of Malacca into the Indian Ocean and finally to the North Arabian Sea. The 5th Marines took advantage of the Zambales Training Facility when the task group put into Subic Bay in the Philippines on Christmas Day. Exercise Quick Thrust included advance-force operations, raids, and long-range reconnaissance insertions on the twenty-seventh. Regimental Landing Team 5 then executed a turn-away landing by surface and air-cushion landing craft while MAG-50 made a helicopter turn-away over six landing zones. The 5th Marines conducted live-fire training using small arms, crew-served weapons, light armored vehicles (LAVs), tanks, and assault amphibians on the twenty-ninth. This training period was followed by boisterous New Year's Eve celebrations during the last liberty call before departing for the combat zone on 2 January 1991.

The 5th MEB linked up with the 4th MEB in the North Arabian Sea on 13 January to form the largest amphibious task force assembled in a combat zone since the Korean conflict. Together, these units and their thirty-one amphibious ships formed the largest Marine force afloat since Exercise Steel Pike in 1964. While the regiment was en route, the amphibious plan called Operation Desert Saber was changed. Instead of landing at Ras Al Qulayah on Kuwait's southern coast, the landing site was moved north to a port and industrial complex known as Ash Shuaybah. The 4th and 5th MEBs would conduct night landings over two separate beaches. Regimental Landing Team 5 was slated for a surface landing across Red Beach at H-hour on A day (amphibious landing). The 5th Marines would then fan out to the north and west to seize the force beachhead line and become a blocking force while RLT 2 captured port facilities to support logistics-over-the-shore operations. The actual landing date was not designated at that time because the assault would be timed to coincide with the progress of I MEF's attack up the coast.

The amphibious rehearsal for Desert Saber, Exercise Sea Soldier IV, was the largest amphibious exercise since 1964. It lasted from 22 January to 2 February 1991 at Suqrah Bay, Oman, which was located outside of the Persian Gulf just south of the fleet anchorage at Masirah Island. Sea Soldier IV began when RLT 5 conducted surface and helicopter-borne demonstrations west of Ras Al Madrakah. The main event, a two-brigade predawn assault controlled by the 4th MEB's command element, began at 0400 on 26 February. In addition to the surface assault, three rifle battalions were airlifted from nine ships during the largest helicopter-borne exercise conducted by the Marine Corps in recent years. There was a twenty-four-hour field exercise followed by a week of desert training that culminated with an amphibious withdrawal exercise. The 4th and 5th MEB staffs held a command-post exercise after the initial landings that turned out to be the only opportunity for all aviation and ground commanders to get together to coordinate their plans for Operation Desert Saber. During field exercises, the Marines worked on individual skills, small-unit tactics, overland movement, and combat firing techniques. While on shore, vehicles and equipment were worked on by mobile maintenance teams. A comprehensive enemy prisoner of war (EPW) exercise tested the ability of military police and counterintelligence teams to handle Iraqi prisoners. More than sixty role players were interrogated, processed, and held in a mock EPW compound. This training was not only challenging, it was also relevant: Unit after-action reports indicated that many lessons learned during Sea Soldier IV were later put to good use in Kuwait.

When Exercise Sea Soldier IV ended, the 5th Marines reembarked and traveled north into the Persian Gulf through the Strait of Hormuz for a final training exercise before moving into the northern Gulf. The 5th MEB conducted a supporting arms center coordination exercise (SACCEX) at Al Hamra in the United Arab Emirates from 9–12 February 1991. The 5th MEB amphibious task group then sailed north to Al Jubayl for an amphibious planning conference. Elements of the 5th Marines were cross-decked to different ships during that time as well because one "big deck" amphibious assault ship, the *Tripoli,* was pulled out of PhibGru 3 to serve as a mine-clearing operations platform. Operation Desert Saber was placed on hold at that conference, and General Rowe learned that instead of leading an amphibious assault, his 5th MEB was to become the I MEF reserve on the yet-to-be-designated G day (ground assault). Thus, RLT 5 became the only major ground unit that would participate in both the amphibious deception and the ground assault to liberate Kuwait.

Meanwhile, Lt. Col. Chris Cortez's "orphaned" 1/5 was one of three rifle battalions assigned to Task Force Ripper in northern Saudi Arabia. Ripper had been creeping north since the transition from defense to offense in mid-November. This movement continued at full pace after the Marines opened a new logistics base at Al Khanjar in the middle of the barren desert. In the wake of the air war that started on 19 January 1991, 1/5 stepped up its minefield breaching techniques and increased

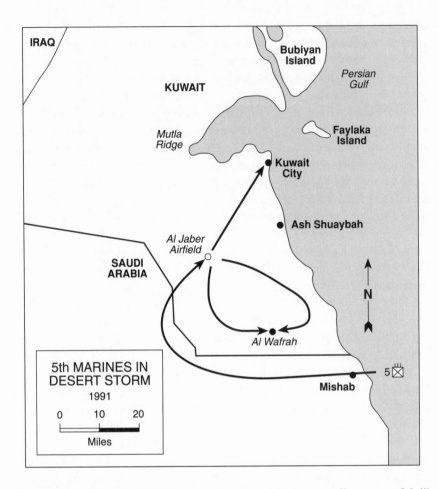

IRAQ

Bubiyan
Island

Persian
Gulf

KUWAIT

Mutla
Ridge

Faylaka
Island

● Kuwait
City

● Ash Shuaybah

Al Jaber
Airfield

SAUDI
ARABIA

N

● Al Wafrah

5th MARINES IN
DESERT STORM
1991

0   10   20

Miles

Mishab

5

live-fire training. On 23 February, the eve of G day, a well-prepared 1/5 was just outside Kuwait's southwestern heel, poised to participate in the 1st Marine Division's breach of the minefields. The ground assault was launched in the midst of an infrequent desert rainstorm and under a dense cloud of smoke from the flaming oil fields nearby. The 1st Battalion moved through a protective sand berm between the Al Wafrah and Al Manaqish oil fields accompanied by loudspeakers blaring the "Marine Hymn" at about 0410 on the twenty-fourth. Red star cluster flares announced the battalion's arrival at the first minefield a little more than two hours later. Combat engineers cleared lanes using mine-clearing line charges and tank dozers. The 1st Battalion went through the first barriers mounted on AAVs from the 3d Assault Amphibian Battalion moving behind M60 tanks from Company B, 3d Tank Battalion, to a battle position just outside the second minefield. This barrier was quickly breached, and 1/5 was on its way to Al Jaber Air Base, MEF Objective A, by 0755.

The first hours had gone far better than expected. The 1st Battalion suffered no casualties and Lieutenant Colonel Cortez's main concern was the large number of Iraqis surrendering to the Marines. Company B dismounted and handled more than five hundred EPWs until relieved of that duty by the division reserve. The first face-to-face encounter with Iraqi forces—there had been some indirect fire during the breach—occurred at about 1300 when two T-62 tanks were destroyed. Some ineffective enemy mortar fire followed that encounter. Several more Iraqi tanks were knocked out as Task Force Ripper advanced, and the number of prisoners taken swelled to more than a thousand by midafternoon. The 1st Battalion was in position to assault Al Jaber in the late afternoon, but the unexpectedly quick enemy collapse made it possible to advance the timetable. Accordingly, 1/5 bypassed this objective and headed through the burning oil fields straight for Kuwait International Airport, MEF Objective C, instead. Task Force Ripper had succeeded beyond all expectations and an Iraqi pullout from Kuwait City was imminent.

While Task Force Ripper and 1/5 were running roughshod over all opposition on the way to Kuwait City, RLT 5 became the only major Marine ground unit to participate in both the amphibious deception and operations ashore during Operation Desert Storm. When the scheme of maneuver changed from a frontal attack up Kuwait's east coast to a flank attack from the west in February 1991, it eliminated the need to seize a coastal enclave to support over-the-shore logistics and freed RLT 5 to become I MEF's ground reserve force. Insertion of the regiment was crucial because the movement of the 1st and 2d Marine Divisions to their assembly areas left the Kuwait border near the Al Wafrah National Forest almost undefended. This void meant Combat Service Support Area One at Kibrit and the road from Mishab to Al Khanjar were at risk. The gap was being filled with a small deception force known as Task Force Troy, but elements of RLT 5 would be needed to bolster this area after the outbreak of hostilities.

Colonel Gangle's orders were to relieve Task Force Troy, guard the I MEF flank in its zone, and be prepared to move on order to protect I MEF's northwest flank, secure breach sites, provide MSR security, and clear bypassed enemy positions while moving behind the 2d Marine Division. Initially, the zone of operations would be the border area directly across from Kuwait's Al Wafrah National Forest. The term *National Forest* is misleading. Al Wafrah was actually an agricultural station with its vegetation evenly spaced in neat rows rather than a dense growth of trees and underbrush as the title infers. The major threat came from elements of the Iraqi 5th Mechanized Division lurking in the oil processing and agricultural complexes near Al Wafrah. This force, believed to be the residue from an earlier Iraqi attack on Khafji, could number up to five hundred men and might possess as many as two dozen tanks and a similar number of armored personnel carriers. (After hostilities ended, this force was deemed to be an elite Republican Guard–trained commando battalion attached to the 5th Mechanized Division.) To keep the amphibious deception viable until the last minute, however, the 5th Marines would have to remain at sea until the ground attack was well under way. That meant RLT 5 would not be allowed to begin landing at the port of Mishab until midmorning on the twenty-fourth.

Colonel Gangle divided RLT 5 into four combat elements. Battalion Landing Team 3/1 was the helicopter-borne assault element, BLT 2/5 was the motorized element and helicopter-borne backup force, BLT 3/5 was a mechanized combined-arms task force, and 2/11 would furnish artillery support. Colonel Gangle's main limiting factor was a lack of transportation. Without heavy equipment transporters for rapid movement, BLT 3/5 would have to move cross-country at a slow pace to avoid vehicle breakdowns while in transit.

The first elements of RLT 5 to go ashore were airlifted into a key blocking position just south of the Al Wafrah National Forest in the afternoon on G day. The bulk of the regiment came ashore at Mishab, and then conducted a two-day, 130-mile overland end run of the Iraqi lines into Kuwait. Colonel Gangle divided his operational focus into two distinct phases. During the first phase, BLT 3/1 carried the load. It made a helicopter assault near the Kuwait border to reinforce Task Force Troy, engaged Iraqi forces in the Al Wafrah National Forest, and then moved north into Kuwait, where it was attached to the 2d Marine Division. The remainder of RLT 5 landed at Mishab and made a lengthy motor march via Kibrit, the breach sites, and Al Jaber to join I MEF. During that phase, RLT 5 conducted route security operations. These roles were reversed in the second phase. After its release by the 2d Marine Division, BLT 3/1 became the regimental reserve at Mishab while RLT 5 cleared the Al Wafrah area of enemy forces.

Landing craft moved to-and-fro carrying men and equipment from the amphibious ships to the landing beaches while helicopters raced overhead carrying more men and equipment from ships outside Mishab Harbor throughout G day. H-hour had to be delayed due to bad weather, and the difficult harbor entry and lack of dock facilities slowed operations. The RLT's off-loading operations thus did not begin until late on the twenty-fourth and lasted until 0956 on the twenty-seventh. The first unit into action was helicopter-borne BLT 3/1. Battalion Landing Team 2/5, coming off the amphibious assault ships *Tarawa* and *New Orleans* and the dock transport *Juneau*, made it ashore next. Lieutenant Colonel Gido's artillery landed from the dock landing ship *Anchorage* with the next echelon. The final evolution included the RLT 5 command element coming in from the *Juneau* and BLT 3/5 debarking from the *Mount Vernon, Vancouver, Frederick,* and *Barbour County.*

Battalion Landing Team 3/1 immediately occupied defensive positions near the border on the twenty-fourth, but the rest of RLT 5 remained in the Mishab staging area on the twenty-fifth until it formed into three convoys: BLT 3/1's support party, the BLT 2/5 motorized task force, and the BLT 3/5 mechanized task force. Colonel Gangle planned to set up near Kibrit so RLT 5 could back up BLT 3/1 or move forward to Al Khanjar as the situation required. The first convoy left in the early afternoon. The BLT 3/5 mechanized task force, including a few humvees and all RLT 5 tanks and AAVs, departed in the midafternoon on the first leg of a twenty-eight-hour journey. The AAVs and tanks could only move at about ten miles per hour and had to halt for ten minutes every hour. Although this snail's pace was frustrating, the task force moved 186 miles without a single vehicle breakdown.

Colonel Gangle's forward command element, BLT 2/5, and the artillery in the motorized convoy soon outpaced the slower moving mechanized task force. This convoy included the RLT 5 forward CP; the BLT 2/5 jump CP, three rifle companies (E, F, and G), and 2/11. It arrived at Kibrit in the afternoon on G-plus-1. There, Colonel Gangle learned the Marine offensive was moving far more rapidly than had been expected, and he was told that RLT 5 should move on immediately. On the twenty-sixth, BLT 2/5 left Kibrit and passed through Khanjar on its way to the Umm Gudair oil field where Lieutenant Colonel Kennedy established a battalion patrol base. The battalion passed through two minefields and entered the Kuwaiti desert in a scenario plucked from Dante's *Inferno.* Many enemy mines were visible, exposed by the blowing sand, against a backdrop of burning oil wells. Along the way, a D9 bulldozer wrecked by a mine explosion was lying on its side in silent testimony that 2/5 was now in the combat zone. To use a popular phrase of the day, "Kuwait wasn't Hell, but purgatory must certainly be right next door."

Kennedy arrayed Companies E, F, and G to repel an armored attack from the north after eighteen hectic hours on the road. Once the battalion settled in, motorized patrols fanned out in the rainy night to secure the MSR and protect minefield breach points. One platoon-sized patrol from Company E made its way south to the Al Wafrah oil refinery to locate some tanks and enemy soldiers reportedly in the area but came home empty-handed after a futile night of searching in the fog, rain, and cold.

The next morning, BLT 2/5 moved to Al Jaber Air Base, but was slowed by poor visibility caused by burning oil wells and a low-lying, slow-moving weather front. The wind shifted, bringing with it the residue of several hundred burning oil wells. It was literally raining oil, and the sun was so completely blocked that even night vision devices would not function. Thus, what had been only a dark smudge on the horizon in the morning became a total blackout by 1400 on the twenty-seventh. The convoy became hopelessly tangled in a huge traffic jam caused by this "darkness at noon," but finally arrived at Al Jaber Air Base just before nightfall. Al Jaber was another scene of pure destruction. Abandoned Iraqi vehicles, weapons, and equipment were strewn everywhere. The buildings and the airstrip were a shambles, thoroughly destroyed by aerial bombardment. Unexploded ordnance, particularly cluster-bomb units, lay all around. Despite these obstacles, 2/5 established a defense perimeter that evening. Search teams combed the area and took possession of four Soviet MTLB armored personnel carriers, two T-55 tanks, one T-72 tank, and one Chinese Type-531 armored personnel carrier. Uncounted tons of enemy ammunition, supplies, small arms, and documents were also confiscated.

Once ashore, Colonel Selvage's BLT 3/5 made a forty-three-mile road march along Route Green from Mishab to Kibrit in order to relieve Task Force Troy. When the plans changed, however, BLT 3/5 refueled at Kibrit and continued moving. The mechanized task force finally arrived at Al Khanjar before noon on the twenty-sixth. Colonel Selvage was then ordered through the minefield breaches into Kuwait. Intelligence reports warned that BLT 3/5 might have to fight bypassed elements of the Iraqi 6th Infantry Division on the way to Al Jaber Air Base. Battalion

Landing Team 3/5 entered Kuwait at 1505. Colonel Selvage established night defensive positions in the vicinity of Phase Line Mary and ordered patrolling to begin at midnight. Almost two hours later, at 0155, Capt. Steven Suddreth reported BLT 3/5's first contact when a TOW gunner discovered a T-55 tank in the vicinity of the police post at Phase Line Jill. Suddreth ordered him to hold his fire because the target might be a Syrian tank from the neighboring Joint Forces Command North. Daylight showed the tank to be an Iraqi T-55 that had been previously disabled by fire. The following morning, most of the task force moved to Al Jaber Air Base, but Company K and BLT 3/1's Company L, an AAV-mounted unit attached to BLT 3/5, remained behind to secure the southern flank.

While RLT 5 was moving into Kuwait, Lieutenant Colonel Cortez's 1/5, still part of Task Force Ripper, fought its way north on the 1st Marine Division's left flank. Ripper moved out at 0610 on G-plus-1. The 1st Battalion zone of action was parallel to the road to Kuwait City. The 2d Marine Division was on the left and the fiery Al Burqan and Al Magwa oil fields were to the right. The path was littered with destroyed armored vehicles, but there were a few live Iraqis still around. Marine Cobras were called in to reduce a stubborn position at 0904. A humvee-mounted TOW from 1/5 knocked out an Iraqi T-72 not long after that. Smoke and rain clouds began to obscure the battlefield by the time Task Force Ripper reached its limit of advance about ten kilometers south of Kuwait City. The major impediment thereafter was dense cloud cover that blocked out the sun. It became so dark that offensive operations had to be temporarily suspended. Nevertheless, Task Force Ripper was able to move past a major communications complex and take its final objective, a wooded area known as "the Grove" on the south side of Sixth Ring Road just west of Kuwait International Airport.

By the evening of the twenty-seventh, G-plus-3, it was obvious Saddam Hussein had been defeated. Iraqi occupation forces fled north out of Kuwait City and were being pounded by air strikes as they moved north along the roads to Basrah and Umm Qasr. To the west, the U.S. VII Corps had crushed an Iraqi armored column in the Euphrates Valley and was advancing east to cut off the last escape routes. Task Force Ripper began to stand down just after dawn on the twenty-eighth when it was learned a cease-fire was to begin at 0800. However, the Marines were authorized to engage any Iraqi units or individuals that showed hostile intent or refused to honor the cease-fire agreement.

Although a cease-fire went into effect exactly one hundred hours after the ground assault began, the Gulf War was not yet over for the 5th Marines. With operations at a standstill, it was prudent to begin moving the 5th MEB out of Kuwait so it could reboard amphibious ships and resume the role of an afloat reserve, but Colonel Gangle was also ordered to have RLT 5 sweep through the Al Wafrah National Forest and clear it of Iraqi soldiers as the 5th MEB pulled out of Kuwait. He hoped any Iraqis there would surrender without a fight, but he was not certain that would be the case. An estimated seventy to one hundred Iraqis were still inside Al Wafrah, so Gangle wisely elected to approach the sweep through the forest as a combat operation. The 2d and 3d Battalions, 5th Marines, were to clear Al Wafrah, while BLT 3/1 remained on call at Mishab and the artillery assumed positions near Kibrit. The clearing operation was to begin on 1 March and conclude as soon a possible, hopefully the next day.

Colonel Gangle issued his orders at 2300 on the twenty-eighth. He wanted BLTs 2/5 and 3/5 to clear their respective zones from west to east beginning at dawn. A captured map overlay showed Iraqi minefield positions, so he ordered BLT 3/5 to sweep the north side of the mine belt and BLT 2/5 to move in from the south. Company A, 4th Tank Battalion, and the 23d Marines's TOW Platoon were collectively labeled "Team Tank" and formed the maneuver force reserve. Several units from BLT 3/1, including LAV Detachment 11, Battery G, and AAV-mounted Company L, remained with the regiment for the clearing operations. The 2d Battalion, 11th Marines, would handle fire support. Psychological operations (psyops) helicopters announcing the cease-fire and giving surrender instructions using loudspeakers and leaflets would precede the advance.

The 5th Marines left the assembly area at 0600 on 1 March and moved to the line of departure. The 2d Battalion began moving south toward the Al Wafrah oil-processing complex at about 0700. There was a three-hour delay at Phase Line Janice while psyops helicopters crisscrossed the objective area. At about 1100, RLT 5 resumed the advance with BLTs 2/5 and 3/5 forward and Team Tank moving behind. Colonel Kennedy opted to use a battalion wedge formation with Companies E and G following a screen of LAVs while H&S Company and Company F brought up the rear. Colonel Selvage, on the other hand, used all four BLT 3/5 mechanized rifle companies on line. During the afternoon, BLT 2/5 discovered fresh food while clearing its portion of the built-up area but spotted no Iraqis. Captain Mark A. McDonald, the Company F commander, reported an explosion, possibly an RPG round, about a hundred meters behind his rearmost truck at about 1600. A burst of Iraqi small-arms and automatic weapons fire caused no casualties about an hour later. The 81mm mortar platoon marked the target using illumination rounds and a pair of AH-1J Cobra helicopter gunships swooped in. During a brief and very one sided gunfight, they destroyed several buildings and other likely hiding places in BLT 2/5's zone. The advance then continued to the edge of the forest. There, each BLT established 360-degree night defensive positions on its respective side of the obstacle barrier and Colonel Gangle requested more time to clear the forest. His request was granted, but General Rowe was emphatic that RLT 5 had to be out of Kuwait no later than 1800 on the third.

Colonel Gangle decided to use a small ruse the next day. Battalion Landing Team 2/5 would move back through the forest as if it was leaving, but BLT 3/5 would follow at a distance. The plan was for BLT 3/5 to catch the Iraqis by surprise if they tried to harass BLT 2/5 from the rear. Any remaining Iraqis who refused to throw down their arms would be forced to surrender or pushed into preplanned aerial/artillery kill zones. This action started at about 0700 on the second. Company B, 1st Combat Engineer Battalion, breached an eleven-row minefield using AAV-mounted mine-clearing line charges, bangalore torpedoes, satchel charges, and tank-mounted mine rakes to clear a lane through the obstacle belt. The job was completed at 0855 and BLT 3/5's forward elements began moving south at 0900. About three hours later, Company L, BLT 3/1, came under automatic weapons and small-arms fire. The Marines returned fire and trapped the Iraqis inside a house. An armed UH-1N destroyed that building at 1343. The surviving Iraqis broke contact and fled. Colonel Selvage ordered BLT 3/5 to halt and establish night defensive positions about nine kilometers west of the morning start line.

The advance resumed at daybreak on the morning of the third and BLT 3/5 captured a truck and detained its driver at about 0830. The regiment suffered its only combat casualties when a Marine tripped a booby trap, injuring himself and another man later that morning. Second Lieutenant Bruce S. McCaw, 2/5's motor transport officer, fearlessly drove straight into the minefield to save the wounded men. Both were evacuated by helicopter and were later treated for leg and eye wounds. Some enemy soldiers were taken under fire by 81mm mortars at about 1230.

The final combat action occurred when the RLT 5 command post was fired upon. Company L, BLT 3/1, immediately engaged an enemy force holed up in the built-up area near the Al Wafrah oil-processing complex. The buildings were destroyed or damaged by small arms, rounds from M19 automatic grenade launchers, TOW missiles, and helicopter close-in fire support. When the firefight ended RLT 5 moved back into Saudi Arabia, leaving behind farmland littered with long-dead camels, horses, and chickens whose overpowering stench lent little to the exotic ambiance. That night, the Marines collected ammunition, celebrated with bonfires made of ration cartons, played a little touch football, and boxed and banded materials for embarkation. The war was over after only eight days, hardly the trial by fire endured by the regiment at Belleau Wood or Peleliu, but the 5th Marines played a key role in one of the most successful and impressive military actions in American military history.

Sea Angel

The regiment reboarded its amphibious ships at Mishab on 3–5 March. At that time RLT 5 was reduced by about a third. Some reservists were sent home by air transport, and BLT 3/1 was detached when the 11th MEU(SOC) and its five ships broke out of the 5th MEB. The 5th Marines remained afloat in the north Arabian Sea, on call to conduct a non-combatant evacuation of Addis Ababa, Ethiopia, where rebel forces threatened the city. When that crisis abated the amphibious task group carrying RLT 5 finally set sail for home, just as Cyclone Marian thundered across the Bay of Bengal to batter the coast of Bangladesh for eight hours.

The coastal lowlands were hit by gale-force winds and swamped by tidal waves. These "winds of death" claimed 139,000 lives, killed more than a million livestock, displaced more than ten million people, and ruined more than seventy-four thousand acres of crops. Cyclone Marian also destroyed the existing infrastructure, making relief operations difficult. The major port of Chittagong was awash and could not handle incoming traffic, all roads were washed out, and electrical service was disrupted throughout the affected area. Survivors of the storm were threatened by starvation and disease. The recently elected democratic government, which only eight weeks before had ended more than fifteen years of military dictatorship, had been overwhelmed by the forces of nature. Prime Minister Begum Khaldea Zia appealed for help, and international aid and assistance was soon on the way. The United States quickly joined international humanitarian efforts to save Bangladesh.

A U.S. joint task force commanded by Marine Maj. Gen. Henry C. Stackpole III was created to provide transportation, communications, medical, and logistics support. The major problem was that although there were plenty of relief supplies available in Dhaka, they were located more than 120 miles from the disaster zone. Rapid movement of these supplies would require more helicopters and additional watercraft because Cyclone Marian had eradicated all lines of communication within the disaster area. Luckily, the perfect instrument for such operations was nearby. The homeward-bound 5th MEB was sailing through the Indian Ocean and was well suited for relief operations in Bangladesh. The areas most in need of help were the offshore islands and the coastal lowlands. The amphibious task force could easily provide badly needed transportation by using its organic landing craft, small boats, helicopters, and amphibious vehicles. Political implications were minimized because operations could be sea-based and would require only a few Americans on the shore. This would decrease the impact of cultural differences and reduce the drain on already scarce resources in the affected area.

Amphibious Group 3 arrived in the northern Bay of Bengal on 15 May 1991. General Rowe and Colonel Gangle immediately flew to Chittagong to meet General Stackpole. At the initial briefing, Stackpole explained the situation as he saw it. There were plenty of relief supplies and more were on the way. A dedicated but inexperienced democratic government was struggling to take control of the situation. Nongovernment relief agencies were at hand, but they lacked adequate communications and transportation. With these issues in mind, Stackpole told General Rowe that the focus of the Marine effort was going to be distribution of emergency relief supplies.

General Stackpole assigned the Marines a nine-thousand-square-mile area of operations that ran more than 150 miles along the coast from Chittagong at the apex of the Bay of Bengal south past Chokoria to Cox's Bazaar. This area also included South Hatia, Sandwip, Kutubdia, Matabari, and Maiskal Islands. The regiment's mission was to assist the Bangladeshi government by lifting relief supplies using helicopter, water, and surface assets, and to provide medical assistance, water production, engineer and material handling equipment, security, rations, communications, and other support on short notice. This was to be accomplished within two weeks, and a minimum "footprint" would be created by using as few Americans on the beach as possible. Choppy water, tricky currents, underwater hazards, and high winds dictated that operations after dark should be avoided because they were too risky.

All personnel going ashore had to be immunized and undergo malaria prevention measures. The Marines remained sea-based throughout the operation, so there were never more than five hundred ashore at one time. The main body of the amphibious task group remained over the horizon, steaming back and forth at a modified offshore deployment location about thirty miles from Chittagong. A two-ship LST Group closed the beach and anchored in position about eleven kilometers out to serve as forward replenishment stations. The Marines were tasked to work in support of, but not under the operational control of, the joint task force. General Rowe appointed Colonel Gangle mission commander to control operations ashore on 16 May. Rowe described Gangle as "senior and savvy" and noted that the RLT 5 staff was "a sound base around which to build an integrated mission command" because the aviation and combat service support element commanders would be too busy to effectively do two jobs at once.

The mission command element was located at Chittagong, but a second control center was opened later at Cox's Bazaar. Helicopter and small-craft landing zones were located at suitable sites up and down the coast. Intermediate supply points were maintained at each site and small relief distribution teams were scattered across the entire area of operations. Relief operations began on the seventeenth. Colonel Gangle established a mission liaison cell in the JTF (Forward) headquarters at Chittagong. This staff worked closely with the JTF, government representatives, and nongovernment relief agencies to deliver bulk supplies, distribute relief aid, and provide medical attention. Mission control centers were manned twenty-four hours a day to receive reports, constantly update information, maintain communications with forward-deployed units, and to ensure that reliable information was disseminated up and down the chain of command. The 5th Marines provided work parties, communicators, and liaison officers. Small detachments, each consisting of only two or three Marines, manned high-frequency radios at government buildings, relief storehouses, and distribution points. These sites supported government and nongovernment relief agencies.

The first day ashore set a pattern that became standard operating procedure throughout Operation Sea Angel. Helicopters and landing craft carried personnel and equipment ashore at first light. These transportation assets unloaded cargo and were directed to various pickup or delivery points by mission control centers. Tracking the wide variety of missions spread across a nine-thousand-square-mile area of operations was difficult. In mission control centers called TACLOGS (short for tactical/logistics), busy watch officers manned a bank of phones, scribbled messages, and answered questions. Area maps were dotted with colored pins and colored markers to monitor unit locations and ongoing missions. Constant updating of this information was imperative to keep decisionmakers abreast of the fluid situation and ever changing requirements. Charts detailed air and boat missions, noting the scheduled time, date, location, delivery area, and load configuration. Other charts and maps indicated the current status of assets, delivery priorities, planned routes, call signs, and radio frequencies.

Distribution teams reinforced U.S. Army Special Forces disaster relief teams already in place. The Marines coordinated resupply efforts, radioed situation reports to headquarters, and provided terminal guidance at the landing zones. American and Bangladeshi military personnel, a few relief workers, and at least one government representative manned distribution points. Marine engineers often ran reverse osmosis water purification units (ROWPUs) at these sites, which also became favorite places to set up medical treatment centers.

Air-cushion landing craft (LCACs) soon became the stars of the show. Photos of LCACs rushing over the water, kicking up a silver spray as they made their runs to the shore while carrying sixty tons at forty miles per hour, were popular with the international press, and this vision led Gen. Colin L. Powell, chairman of the Joint Chiefs of Staff, to call the relief operation Sea Angel instead of Productive Effort. The LCACs received the publicity, but LCUs, LCMs, rigid raider craft, and inflatable boats carried the bulk of the load. The nature of the terrain made small craft ideal for distribution missions, but the forces of nature put excellent seamanship at a premium. Winds reached velocities of up to fifty knots, there was a twenty-one-foot tidal rise, and ever shifting twelve-knot currents swirled between the islands and the mainland. Landing beaches were established on Sandwip, Kutubdia, Matabari, and Maiskhal Islands. Another landing beach was established at Cox's Bazaar on the mainland.

Air operations began with daily morning flights and ended when the helicopters returned to their mother ships in the evening. Ship-to-shore and shore-to-ship movements were controlled by the *Tarawa*'s tactical air control center. The general daily aviation plan was to use Sea Knights and Sea Stallions to deliver work parties, bulk cargo (e.g., large bags of rice, lentils, flour, and wheat), medical teams, ROWPUs, and livestock. Ironically, humanitarian relief was flooding into Bangladesh so fast it could not be expeditiously moved to the forward areas. This was particularly true for items too big or too delicate to be manhandled by Bangladeshi workers. Nongovernment relief workers and government officials understood the problem but were helpless to do much because they lacked the proper equipment. This was a major reason why the assets the Marines brought to Bangladesh were crucial to the success of Operation Sea Angel.

Almost every RLT 5 Marine volunteered to go ashore, but not all could be sent at one time. Colonel Gangle used a rotation system to allow as many Marines as possible to get ashore so they could see what Operation Sea Angel was all about. Working parties were organized every day to help move relief supplies. The Bangladeshis were very impressed by the Americans's efficiency, team spirit, and camaraderie. They were also awed by the robust Marines's ability to throw fifty-pound sacks around with ease. The natives began using the American "daisy chain" method of passing bags of food, building materials, and medical supplies from person to person. The Marines and the Bangladeshis were soon working side by side and became friends. Within a few days it was common practice for the Bangladeshis to give the Marines a broad smile and a distinctive thumbs-up sign when the workday ended.

The Marine intervention soon doubled the amount of incoming supplies. At first, relief efforts were limited to the vicinity of Chittagong, however, operations were rapidly expanded and soon included many of the outlying areas and offshore islands. On 19 May, Colonel Gangle ordered Lieutenant Colonel Selvage to move BLT 3/5's headquarters ashore to establish a second control center at Cox's Bazaar, a small resort city located at the southern tip of the area of operations. Its six-thousand-foot airfield and small boat harbor became the focal points for combined U.S.-British relief efforts at Kutubdia, Matabari, Chokoria, and Moheshkha.

By the time the allotted two-week period came to an end, the "situation was well in hand," and the 5th Marines sailed for home on 29 May. The amphibious task group entered the Strait of Malacca on 1 June and headed for the Philippines. (Colonel Gangle conducted a battle study of the defense of Corregidor early in World War II during a brief layover at Subic Bay.) The next leg of the journey home began on the ninth. The regiment finally debarked on 29 June, 210 days after leaving for South-west Asia. During its six months overseas the regiment had participated in extensive amphibious training, fought in ground combat, and delivered humanitarian aid to helpless people.

Postscript

The regiment was awarded a Navy Unit Commendation for combat operations in Southwest Asia and a Joint Service Meritorious Unit Award for humanitarian operations in Bangladesh. Lieutenant Colonel Christopher Cortez is currently a serving brigadier general.

8: Marching On

Even before the end of the Persian Gulf War, changes in the international balance of power were beginning to usher in what President Bush called the "New World Order." The collapse of the Soviet Union, America's most potent opponent throughout the Cold War, downgraded the threat of an international nuclear holocaust and virtually eliminated the potential for a massive ground conflict in Western Europe. The stunning victory in the Persian Gulf left America as the world's only super power, a circumstance that dictated a drastically revised national strategy. In the New World Order, the primary threats to peace became localized regional conflicts and unstable countries rather than an international conflagration between Communism and the free world. The United States was more likely to become the arbiter of a dispute between warring nations or to lend a helping hand to a disaster-struck area than it was to come racing to save a threatened ally. Likewise, the end of the Gulf War brought about a significant change in America's military posture—just as the end of World War I, World War II, and the Vietnam War had. This radical change in outlook and support impacted the Marine Corps in several ways.

There was a significant reduction in military personnel, reduced funding, and a new strategic outlook. Overall, the American military establishment was cut back by about one-third, and the U.S. military budget was similarly reduced. A new maritime strategy shifted America's focus on regional conflicts. The most likely future arenas of naval combat were no longer the oceans but the shallow, brown-water littorals of the world. This required the continual forward presence of forcible-entry units near potential trouble spots, and these small units had to be backed up by more robust rapid-deployment follow-on forces. Ironically, unlike most previous military drawdowns, this time there was no reduction in requirements. The Cold War was over and the world was generally a safer place, but peace was not universal. The Middle East, the Pacific Rim, Africa, Eastern Europe, and Latin America continued to be troublesome. The demands of the New World Order placed new emphasis on military operations other than war (peacekeeping, humanitarian interventions, disaster relief, noncombatant evacuations, etc.). In fact, the operational tempo for all U.S. services steadily increased as time passed. Ironically, bases at home and abroad were closed as America's armed forces scaled back just as new demands for overseas American presence stepped up.

Obviously, these events affected the Marine Corps. The Marines maintained three expeditionary forces: I MEF on the West Coast, II MEF on the East Coast, and III MEF in the western Pacific. By the mid-1990s, the Marine Corps had been forced to reduce manning levels across the board, eliminate many of its standing MAGTF headquarters, and reduce the 3d Marine Division on Okinawa to brigade strength. The 9th Marines disbanded and the 4th Marines consisted of rifle battalions from the 1st and 2d Marine Divisions that rotated unit deployments to the Rock. Eventually, a permanent Marine expeditionary unit was home based in the Far East to help ease the void. The Marines became, to use Gen. Charles C. Krulak's phrase, "America's 9-1-1 force." The 1st and 2d Marine Divisions maintained a full slate of unit deployments, conducted exercises and operations around the world, and provided numerous contingency alert units. Additionally, every 1st Marine Division rifle battalion was placed in the Seventh Fleet landing force queue. As part of this force-in-readiness posture, Marine units of varying sizes intervened in Somalia, Haiti, Kuwait, Liberia, Rwanda, Bosnia, and Kosovo during the last decade of the twentieth century.

The Nineties and Beyond

The post–Gulf War national euphoria had, for the most part, dissipated by the time the 5th Marines returned to Camp Pendleton in late June 1991, but their friends and families still warmly greeted these returning veterans. They certainly did not have to slink back home, as did Vietnam veterans two decades earlier. Most active-duty personnel were given short leaves and then returned to Camp Pendleton to continue their careers. Reservists and Marines retained in uniform beyond the expiration of their term of service were released from active duty. By the end of the summer, the 5th Marines, now commanded by Col. James A. Fulks, resumed normal activities. Battalions once again shuffled between Okinawa and the United States. Incoming Marines could expect to serve most of their first hitch with the same outfit and would most likely participate in amphibious training at Coronado, undergo live-fire training during combined-arms exercises at Twentynine Palms, and serve two overseas "pumps," one on Okinawa and the other a MEU(SOC) deployment. The regiment added an antiarmor platoon composed of eight M220E4 humvee-mounted TOW II launchers to each of its weapons companies in October 1992, but the number of Dragon missiles was reduced from thirty-six to twenty-four in 1995.

The regiment felt the impact of overall force reductions beginning in 1994. Two parent organizations, the 5th MEB at Camp Pendleton and the 9th MEB on Okinawa, were both disbanded. The dissolution of the 9th Marines in 1994 meant that 2/4, became the regiment's fourth UDP battalion. One of the regiment's primary missions also changed at that time. The 5th Marines thereafter became the source unit for the ground combat element of the Okinawa-based 31st MEU.

Lieutenant Colonel Patrick E. Donahue's 3/5 was the first unit to fulfill this mission. The battalion's deployment lasted from May to November 1994. The 31st MEU's main role was to fill the gap left when California-based MEU(SOC)s were in transit or made emergency deployments outside the western Pacific. The 31st MEU was also tasked with "showing the flag" and conducting many of the annual combined amphibious exercises such as Cobra Gold (Thailand), Valiant Usher (Australia), Team Spirit (South Korea), and Tandem Thrust (Guam). This means the regiment's UDP rifle battalion is usually at sea about two months out of every six-month pump, most often sailing the western Pacific on board the ships of PhiRon 11. As this was written the ships permanently assigned to Amphibious Squadron 11 and home ported at Sasebo, Japan, were the *Belleau Wood, Dubuque, Germantown,* and *San Bernardino.* While on the Rock, units of the 5th Marines are stationed at Camp Hansen. They participate in jungle training in the rugged Northern Training Area and conduct amphibious training from White Beach when not afloat.

The post–Gulf War era saw a return to the traditional Marine Corps missions of protecting American lives and property at home and abroad.

The year 1994 was a busy one for Col. Jeffery E. Scheferman's 5th Marines. The 1st Battalion was pulled away from Camp Pendleton to fight forest fires that threatened the western United States, 2/5 participated in two real-world contingencies while afloat in the Indian Ocean, and elements of 3/5 showed the flag by conducting combined maneuvers with Russian Marines for the first time. Lieutenant Colonel Brian J. Patch's BLT 2/5 was the ground combat element of the 11th MEU (SOC) from January to July 1994. During that time, Col. William C. McMullen's two-thousand-man 11th MEU (SOC) provided an afloat cover force as the last American units departed Somalia in April. The BLT was embarked on board the amphibious assault ship USS *Peleliu,* the dock transport ship *Duluth,* the dock landing ship *Anchorage,* and the tank landing ship *Frederick* for Operation Continue Hope. On 9 April, a three-hundred-man detachment from the *Peleliu* was dispatched to Burundi in Central Africa to protect more than 250 Americans, most of them missionaries or aid workers fleeing civil strife in Rwanda. The Marines participating in Operation Distant Runner were transported more than six hundred miles by air using four KC-130 transports and three CH-53 Sea Stallion heavy-lift helicopters. The crisis was precipitated when a plane carrying the presidents of Rwanda and Burundi crashed under suspicious circumstances. Widespread violence between Rwanda's warring Hutu and Tutsi tribes resulted in the killing of several European nationals. At that point, the U.S. ambassador arranged for all Americans to be transported out of the country. They traveled from Kigali, the capital of Rwanda, to Bujumbura, the capital of Burundi, by overland convoy. The Marines were used as a stand-by security force and assisted the evacuation of U.S. citizens from Burundi to Nairobi, Kenya. The security detachment returned to the *Peleliu* on 12 April.

Elements of the 5th Marines played a role in one of the most notable thaws in the Cold War when a detachment from Lt. Col. Richard D. Motl's BLT 3/5 made a port call to Vladivostok, Russia, in June 1994. Russian and U.S. Marines conducted the first combined landing exercise including units from both countries. Exercise Cooperation From The Sea involved an international humanitarian intervention scenario that practiced joint administration of an area hit by a natural disaster. Following the exercise, the American Leathernecks watched Russian training, participated in a commemorative ceremony honoring Russians killed in World War II, and inspected a Russian military base before reboarding the USS *Dubuque* for the return trip to Japan.

The regiment was called on to help solve problems at home on several occasions as well. It performed domestic disaster relief after a devastating flood struck Camp Pendleton on 16 January 1993. A four-foot wave of water swept over the banks of the Margarita River and washed out Basilone Bridge, part of Vandegrift Boulevard, and San Mateo Creek Bridge. This left the base without power or fresh water and caused extensive damage. The flood and its aftermath shut down operations for more than two months. The next year, 1/5 was awarded a Meritorious Unit Citation for its work with Task Force Wildfire from 31 July to 2 September 1994. More than twelve hundred Marines were sent to Wenatchee National Forest in central Washington to battle the largest forest fire in four decades. The National Forest Service was hard-pressed for manpower because there were twenty-six fires in eight states blazing at the same time. Task Force Wildfire was present for duty with the Tyee Incident Command within six days of notification. The Marines cut and raked fire lines in order to give individual firefighters a brief respite and freed highly skilled professional fire crews for more complex duties. The 2d Battalion was likewise called to southern Oregon to assist sixteen hundred firefighters who were battling a fifty-thousand-acre wildfire in the Umatilla National Forest in September 1995. Similar duties awaited the Marines as the new millennium dawned. The National Interagency Firefighting Center requested military assistance in the midsummer of 2000. Officials from that agency traveled to Camp Pendleton to provide classroom and hands-on training. On 5 August, a five-hundred-person task force built around 3/5 deployed to Salmon-Challis National Forest in Idaho in conjunction with U.S. Army and National Guard units to combat more than a dozen fires engulfing more than one hundred thousand acres.

By 1997, Col. Barry P. Griffin's 5th Marines still manned the 31st MEU, but the regiment had also become the 1st Marine Division's primary helicopter-borne operations force and specialized in military operations other than war as well as maintaining its traditional high state of operational readiness.

The contemporary 5th Marines remains true to its proud heritage. Regardless of whether the crisis is foreign or domestic, the modern 5th Marines—like the afloat reaction force of 1914 or the mail guards of the 1920s—is continually standing by to do whatever the president directs. Thankfully, there does not appear to be a major conflict like World War I, World War II, Korea, or Vietnam in the immediate future. As this is written, it is much more likely that the regiment will be used as an amphibious force in readiness like the original 5th Regiment in the Caribbean. A regional crisis could see the regiment become part of a naval expeditionary force much like the one that sailed to the Persian Gulf in 1991. Low-intensity conflicts and operations other than war place a premium on the lessons learned during the Banana Wars and occupation duties. Peacekeeping, humanitarian intervention, and security operations are old hat for the 5th Marines, considering its experiences in the German occupation of 1918–19, the Second Nicaraguan Campaign, North China after World War II, and Operation Sea Angel in Bangladesh. The modern regiment, just like its forebears for nearly a century, is smartly and proudly in step as the men and women of the Marine Corps march into the twenty-first century.

Appendix: Battle Honors

Since 1914 the 5th Marine Regiment has received numerous battle honors, more in fact than any other similar-sized unit in the U.S. armed forces during that period. These battle honors include those bestowed by both the United States and its allies.

The American naval service grants three awards in recognition of outstanding service by a unit: the Presidential Unit Citation, the Naval Unit Commendation, and the Meritorious Unit Commendation. The Department of Defense also grants a Joint Meritorious Unit Award to units operating as part of joint (multiservice) or combined (multinational) task forces. Foreign governments frequently honor American troops serving in their country by granting unit awards for outstanding duty performance. Additionally, service in a particular area or campaign is officially noted. Streamers attached to the unit colors (battle flag) are used to indicate these awards. Devices attached to the streamers indicate the number of awards: a silver star for five awards and a bronze star for each award less than five. Individuals who served with those organizations at specified times are authorized to wear ribbons in recognition of that service.

The following is a list of 5th Marines battle and campaign honors:

U.S. Presidential Unit Citation Streamer with One Silver and Four Bronze Stars

World War II
Guadalcanal, 1942
Peleliu-Ngesebus, 1944
Okinawa, 1945

Korea
Pusan, 1950
Inchon-Seoul, 1950
Chosin Reservoir, 1950
Spring Offensives, 1951

Vietnam
1966–67
1967
1967–68

Joint Meritorious Unit Award Streamer

Bangladesh, 1991

Navy Unit Commendation Streamer with Two Bronze Stars

Korea, 1952–53
Vietnam, 1968–69
Southwest Asia, 1990–91

Meritorious Unit Commendation Streamer

Vietnam, 1968

Other Unit Awards

World War I Victory Streamer with One Silver Star
Army of Occupation Germany Streamer
Second Nicaraguan Campaign Streamer
American Defense Service Streamer with One Bronze Star
Asiatic-Pacific Campaign Streamer with One Silver and One Bronze
Star
World War II Victory Streamer
Navy Occupation Streamer with "Asia" Device
China Service Streamer
National Defense Service Streamer with Two Bronze Stars
Korean Service Streamer with Two Silver Stars
Vietnam Service Streamer with Two Silver and Two Bronze Stars

Southwest Asia Streamer with Three Bronze Stars
French Croix de Guerre with Two Palms and One Gold Star
Korean Presidential Unit Citation Streamer
Vietnam Cross of Gallantry Streamer with Palm
Vietnam Meritorious Unit Citation Civil Actions Streamer

Sources

The main sources of information for this book are documents held at the Marine Corps Historical Center (MCHC) in Building 58 at the Washington Navy Yard. Since this was written, however, some of that material has been transferred to the Marine Corps Research Center at Quantico or the Federal Records Center in Suitland, Maryland. The main records from 1914 until 1950 were the regimental muster rolls, (herein cited as M-rolls). These valuable sources are far more than simple station lists; they document transfers, movements, combat actions, awards, casualties, and legal actions as well as providing a wealth of other information. By World War II, units began keeping annotated message logs called historical diaries, cited as HD. Unit diaries (herein cited as UD) supplanted the regimental muster rolls, and detailed historical records called command chronologies (herein cited as ComdCs) became the primary unit historical documents as time passed. Most battle narratives consist of unit after-action reports (herein cited as AAR) or special-action reports (herein cited as SAR), which can be found in area files or as attachments to unit historical diaries. Also helpful were the Reference Section biographical, geographic, subject, and unit files. The Marine Corps History and Museums Division maintains an oral history collection that features a vast number of taped and transcribed interviews (herein cited as interview). Valuable sources for the Persian Gulf War are the Battlefield Assessment Team (BAT) interviews conducted in Southwest Asia located at the Marine Corps Research Center. Photographs, maps, and artwork are used courtesy of the Marine Corps art and photographic collections, the Marine Corps University, the *Marine Corps Gazette,* and the National Archives and Records Administration.

Official sources have been supplemented with materials provided by George B. Clark of Brass Hat Publishing in Pike, New Hampshire. The author's personal collection of letters, interviews, notes, journals, artifacts, and photographs from Vietnam, Exercise Team Spirit–84 in Korea, Exercise Gallant Eagle–86, and operations in Southwest Asia were also used.

Official reference works about general Marine Corps history include Capt. William D. Parker, *A Concise History of the United States Marine Corps, 1775–1969* (Washington: Historical Division, Headquarters Marine Corps, 1970); Col. William M. Miller and Maj. John H. Johnstone, *Chronology of the United States Marine Corps,* vol. 1, 1775–1934 (Washington: Historical Division, Headquarters Marine Corps, 1965); Carolyn A. Tyson, *Chronology of the United States Marine Corps,* vol. 2, 1934–1946 (Washington: Historical Division, Headquarters Marine Corps, 1971); Ralph W. Donnelly, Gabrielle M. Neufeld, and Carolyn A. Tyson, *Chronology of the United States Marine Corps,* vol. 3, 1947–1964 (Washington: Historical Division, Headquarters Marine Corps, 1971); and *The 1st Marine Division and Its Regiments* (Washington: History and Museums Division, Headquarters Marine Corps, 1999).

Additional background, color, and context came from popular histories of the Marine Corps including: Joseph H. Alexander and Merrill L. Bartlett, *Sea Soldiers in the Cold War* (Annapolis, Md.: Naval Institute Press, 1995); Robert D. Heinl, *Soldiers of the Sea* (Annapolis, Md.: U.S. Naval Institute Press, 1962); Allan R. Millett, *Semper Fidelis: The History of the United States Marine Corps* (New York: Macmillan, 1980); J. Robert Moskin, *The U.S. Marine Corps Story* (Boston: Little, Brown, 1992); Edwin H. Simmons, *The U.S. Marines: The First Two Hundred Years* (New York: Viking, 1976); and E. H. Simmons and J. R. Moskin, eds., *The Marines* (Hong Kong: Marine Corps Heritage Foundation, 1999). Each of these excellent works fills some specific niche of Marine Corps history. Although they vary considerably in length and format, all have been carefully researched and are well written. Another valuable source was the U.S. Congress, *Medal of Honor Recipients, 1863–1978* (Washington: GPO, 1979). Two histories of the 5th Marines that served as the rocks upon which the foundation of this book was written are Maj. James M. Yingling's *A Brief History of the 5th Marines* (Washington: Historical Branch, G3 Division, Headquarters Marine Corps, 1968) and Maj. Ronald H. Spector's draft manuscript titled "A Brief History of the 5th Marines," (Reference Section, MCHC, 1985). The former is an official pamphlet covering the years 1914 to 1967; the latter is an unpublished addendum covering about another decade that includes the regiment's entire Vietnam service and its subsequent return to Camp Pendleton.

Chapter 1. Genesis

5th Mar M-rolls, 1914; Capt. Stephen M. Fuller and Graham A. Cosmas, *Marines in the Dominican Republic* (Washington: History and Museums Division, Headquarters Marine Corps, 1975); Yingling, *Brief History,* pp. 1–2.

This historical period does not appear in the official unit lineage certificate because this activation is formally considered only a provisional one and thus is not listed (Head, Reference Section, MCHC, to author, 17 Jan. 1997).

Chapter 2. World War I

Records of the Second Division (Regular); 5th Mar M-rolls, June 1917–May 1918; 5th Mar Subject File; "A Brief History of the Fifth Regiment U.S. Marines During the World War," MS, Reference Section, MCHC, ca. 1919; *History of the First Battalion, 5th Regiment, U.S. Marines* (n.p.: 1919); *History of the Second Battalion, 5th Regiment, U.S. Marines* (n.p.: 1919); *History of Third Battalion, 5th Regiment, U.S. Marines* (n.p.: 1919); American Battle Monuments Commission, *American Armies and Battlefields in Europe* (Washington: GPO, 1938); George B. Clark, *Devil Dogs* (Novato, Calif.: Presidio Press, 1999); James G. Harbord, *The American Army in France* (Boston: Little, Brown, 1936); idem., *Leaves From A War Diary* (New York: Dodd, Mead, 1925); Meirion and Susie Harries, *The Last Days Of Innocence: America At War, 1917–1918* (New York: Random House, 1997); Maj. Edwin N. McClellan, *The U.S. Marine Corps During the World War* (Washington: GPO, 1920); Laurence Stallings, *The Doughboys: The Story of the AEF, 1917–1918* (New York: Harper and Row, 1963); Capt. John W. Thomason Jr., *Fix Bayonets!* (New York: Scribner's, 1925); Frederic M. Wise with Meigs O. Frost, *A Marine Tells It to You* (Chicago: Sears, 1929).

First To Fight

"Brief History of the Fifth Regiment," pp. 1–2; McClellan, *Marine Corps in the World War;* Clark, *Devil Dogs,* pp. 1–26; Jack Shulimson, "First to

Fight," *Marine Corps Gazette,* Nov. 1988, pp. 56–61; Yingling, *Brief History,* pp. 2–4; George B. Clark, comments on draft manuscript.

Training

5th Mar M-rolls June–Dec. 1917; "Brief History of the Fifth Regiment," pp. 2–9; Ben Finney, *Once a Marine Always A Marine* (New York: Crown, 1977), p. 28; Lt. Gen. Merwin H. Silverthorn interview; Clark, *Devil Dogs,* pp. 27–41; George Clark, *His Road To Glory: The Life and Times of Hiram Iddings Bearss, Hoosier Marine* (Pike, N.H.: Brass Hat, 2000), pp. 193–97.

At the Front

5th Mar M-rolls; "Brief History of the Fifth Regiment," pp. 9–14; Clark, *Devil Dogs,* pp. 42–61; Wise, *Marine Tells It,* p. 191.

Belleau Wood

5th Regt M-rolls, June 1918; "Brief History of the Fifth Regiment," pp. 14–28; Robert Asprey, *At Belleau Wood* (New York: Putnam, 1965); Maj. Eliot D. Cooke, *We Can Take It* (Pike, N.H.: Brass Hat, n.d.); Clark, *Devil Dogs,* pp. 62–221; McClellan, *Marine Corps in the World War,* pp. 40-44; 1st Lt. Brendan B. McBreen, "2d Battalion, 5th Marines at Belleau Wood," Project Leatherneck, 1994, copy in author's collection; Maj. Edwin N. McClellan, "The Capture of Hill 142, Bouresches, and Belleau Wood," *Marine Corps Gazette,* Sept. 1920, pp. 277–313; idem., "The Battle of Belleau Wood," *Marine Corps Gazette,* Dec. 1920, pp. 370–404; Maj. Robert W. Lamont, "Over There: Key Battles of the 2d Infantry Division," *Marine Corps Gazette,* June 1993, pp. 76–83; Brig. Gen. Robert H. Williams, "The 4th Marine Brigade, Part I," *Marine Corps Gazette,* Nov. 1980, pp. 58–68; Stallings, *Doughboys,* pp. 95–113; John W. Thomason Jr., "Second Division Northwest of Chateau Thierry, 1 June–10 July 1918," n.d., copy in author's collection; Wise, *Marine Tells It,* pp. 191–206.

"Retreat Hell!" p. 29–30. This incident has been the subject of much controversy over the years because many Marine officers ignored French suggestions to retreat on the way to Belleau Wood. Fritz Wise claimed to have made the comment in his memoir, but no evidence supports his claim. Laurence Stallings, who was not present, attributed it to Buck Neville in *The Doughboys,* but other records show that Neville himself identified Lloyd Williams as the speaker. Recent scholarship, contemporary documents, and eyewitness testimony all confirm Captain Williams was the originator of that specific quote.

The Hoffman alias, p. 34. It has been asserted by some sources that Janson used the name "Hoffman" due to rampant anti-German discrimination in America. However, this is doubtful because Janson enlisted three years before war was declared. It is far more likely that he wanted to hide something in his past. This would not have been unusual because in 1914 the Marine Corps had a reputation as an "American Foreign Legion" and recruiters turned a blind eye on a prospect's past and tacitly offered anonymity in return for service. At any rate, Janson was not alone: several other Marine heroes used aliases as well.

The 3d Battalion's Assault on Belleau Wood, p. 36. An interesting sidelight on this attack brings into question an important bit of Marine Corps lore. Correspondent Floyd Gibbons described an incident that occurred when the assault wave hesitated on its way through the wheat. In vivid prose he told of, but did not specifically identify, a veteran gunnery sergeant who yelled: "Come on you Sons of Bitches. Do you want to live forever?" Over the years this quote has often been attributed to legendary Marine Dan Daly. However, this assertion does not stand up under the microscope of hindsight. Daly himself denied it, pointing out that he was a "born again Christian" who did not swear. Additionally, Daly was assigned to a 6th Regiment machine gun company that did not participate in the initial assault and was located far away from Gibbon's vantage point near 3/5's command post. The logic usually given for the selection of Daly was his past record and the ribbon bars described by Gibbons. Interestingly, this evidence argues against Daly being the one. Gibbons noted the swearing sergeant's campaign ribbons indicated long service in China and the tropics, but he does not mention a Medal of Honor ribbon. I have been unable to pin down who actually uttered those immortal words (there were no less than sixteen gunnery sergeants present with 3/5 at that time) but I am convinced that the anonymous speaker was a member of Major Berry's command.

"Devil Dogs," p. 51. Recent scholarship has revealed that this rumor was probably not true, but the nickname stuck anyway. See John G. Miller, "Devil Dogs At Belleau Wood," *Naval History,* December 1997, p. 28.

Soissons

5th Regt M-rolls, July 1918; "Brief History of the Fifth Regiment," pp. 28–34; Clark, *Devil Dogs,* pp. 222–58; McClellan, *Marine Corps in the World War,* pp. 45–47; McClellan, "The Aisne-Marne Offensive," *Marine Corps Gazette,* Mar. 1921, pp. 66–84, and June 1921, pp. 188–27; Stallings,

Doughboys, pp. 141–53; Thomason, *Fix Bayonets!* pp. 54–91; Williams, "4th Marine Brigade, Part II: Soissons," *Marine Corps Gazette,* Dec. 1980, pp. 59–64; Yingling, *Brief History,* pp. 7–8.

Casualties at Soissons, McClellan cites a higher number: seventy-nine killed in action or died of wounds.

The Marbache Sector

5th Regt M-rolls, Sept. 1918; "Brief History of the Fifth Regiment," pp. 34–35; Clark, *Devil Dogs,* pp. 259–67; McClellan, "In The Marbache Sector," *Marine Corps Gazette,* Sept. 1921, pp. 253–68; Williams, "4th Marine Brigade, Part III: The Road to Victory," *Marine Corps Gazette,* Jan. 1981, pp. 63–68; Yingling, *Brief History,* pp. 8–11.

Saint-Mihiel

5th Regt M-rolls, Sept. 1918; "Brief History of the Fifth Regiment," pp. 35–39; Clark, *Devil Dogs,* pp. 268–87; Yingling, *Brief History,* p. 9.

Casualties, p. 63. McClellan says twenty-seven Marines were killed and 143 wounded in "The St. Mihiel Offensive," *Marine Corps Gazette,* Dec. 1921, pp. 396–97.

Blanc Mont

5th Regt M-rolls, Oct. 1918; "Brief History of the Fifth Regiment," pp. 40–50; 5th Marines Subject File, "History of the First Battalion, 5th Regiment, U.S. Marines" (Washington, D.C.: Reference Section, MCHC); George B. Clark, *The 4th Marine Brigade at Blanc Mont* (Pike, N.H.: Brass Hat, 1997); idem, *Devil Dogs,* pp. 288–342; McClellan, "The Battle of Blanc Mont Ridge," pt. 1, *Marine Corps Gazette,* Mar. 1922, pp. 1–21, pt. 2, June 1922, pp. 206–11, and pt. 3, Sept. 1922, pp. 287–88; Brig. Gen. Edwin H. Simmons, "With the Marines at Blanc Mont," *Marine Corps Gazette,* Nov. 1993, pp. 35–43; War Department, *Blanc Mont* (Washington: Historical Branch, War Plans Division, General Staff, 1922); Williams, "4th Marine Brigade," Part III, pp. 64–68; Yingling, *Brief History,* pp. 9–12.

Crossing the Meuse

5th Regt M-rolls, Oct.–Nov. 1918; "Brief History of the Fifth Regiment," pp. 44–50; Clark, *Devil Dogs,* pp. 343–81; Col. Rolfe L. Hillman, "Crossing the Meuse," *Marine Corps Gazette,* Nov. 1988, pp. 68–73; Williams, "4th Marine Brigade, Part IV," *Marine Corps Gazette,* Feb. 1981, pp. 56–60.

10 November 1918, p.73. Some sharp-eyed readers may note that this date was the 143d Birthday of the Corps and wonder why that is not mentioned in the text. The fact is, the Marine Corps birthday was not officially recognized until three years later.

Watch on the Rhine

5th Regt, "History," pp. 51–55; McClellan, *USMC in WW,* pp. 56–58, 78–82; Clark, *Devil Dogs,* pp. 382–89; Williams, "4th Marine Brigade, Part IV," Yingling, *5th Marines,* pp. 12–13.

Postscript

Robert Blake, Louis Cukela, Alphonse DeCarre, Logan Feland, George W. Hamilton, LeRoy P. Hunt, Wendell C. Neville, Bennett Puryear Jr., Lemuel C. Shepherd Jr., Merwin H. Silverthorn, and Michael Wodarczyk biographical files; Laurence Stallings and Maxwell Anderson, in *Famous Plays of the 1920s,* ed. Kenneth MacGowan (New York: Dell, 1959), "What Price Glory?" pp. 55–132.

Chapter 3. Between the World Wars

Quantico

5th Regt M-rolls, July 1920–Dec. 1925; Lt. Col. Kenneth J. Clifford, USMCR, *Progress and Purpose: A Developmental History of the U.S. Marine Corps, 1900–1970* (Washington: History and Museums Division, Headquarters Marine Corps, 1973), pp. 30–35; Yingling, *Brief History,* pp. 13–14.

Nicaragua

5th Mar M-rolls, Jan. 1926–Dec. 1933; Heinl, *Soldiers of the Sea;* pp. 260–290; Neil McCaulay, *The Sandino Affair* (Durham, N.C.: Duke University Press, 1985), pp. 71–73; Millett, *Semper Fidelis,* pp. 236–263; Ivan Musicant, *The Banana Wars* (New York: Macmillan, 1990), pp. 285–361; Bernard C. Nalty, *The United States Marines in Nicaragua* (Washington: Historical Branch, G3 Division, Headquarters Marine Corps, 1968); Simmons, *U.S. Marines,* 112–17; Yingling, *Brief History,* pp. 13–19.

The Fleet Marine Force

CO, 5th Mar, FLEX 3 Rpt, 26 Feb. 37; 5th Mar M-rolls, Sept. 1934–June 1942; Clifford, *Progress and Purpose,* pp. 41–58; Jeter A. Isley and Philip

A. Crowl, *The U.S. Marines and Amphibious War* (Princeton, N.J.: Princeton University Press, 1951), pp. 45–70; Lt. Col. Frank O. Hough, Verle E. Ludwig, and Henry I. Shaw Jr., *History of Marine Corps Operations in World War II*, vol. 1, *Pearl Harbor to Guadalcanal* (Washington: Historical Branch, Headquarters Marine Corps, 1958), pp. 11–56; Henry I. Shaw Jr., *Opening Moves: Marines Gear Up For War*, Marines in World War II Commemorative Series (Washington: History and Museums Division, Headquarters Marine Corps, 1991); Holland M. Smith, *Coral and Brass* (Washington: Zenger, 1979), p. 19; Yingling, *Brief History*, pp. 19–21.

Chapter 4. World War II

Hough, Ludwig, and Shaw, *Pearl Harbor to Guadalcanal;* Henry I. Shaw Jr. and Maj. Douglas T. Kane, *History of Marine Corps Operations in World War II*, vol. 2, *Isolation of Rabaul* (Washington: Historical Branch, Headquarters Marine Corps, 1963); Henry I. Shaw Jr., Bernard C. Nalty, and Edwin T. Turnbladh, *History of Marine Corps Operations in World War II*, vol. 3, *Central Pacific Drive* (Washington: Historical Branch, Headquarters Marine Corps, 1966); George W. Garand and Truman R. Strobridge, *History of Marine Corps Operations in World War II*, vol. 4 *Western Pacific Operations* (Washington: Historical Division, Headquarters Marine Corps, 1968); Benis M. Frank and Henry I. Shaw Jr., *History of Marine Corps Operations in World War II*, vol. 5, *Victory and Occupation* (Washington: Historical Branch, Headquarters Marine Corps, 1966); Frank O. Hough, *The Island War* (Philadelphia: Lippincott, 1947); Isely and Crowl, *U.S. Marines and Amphibious War;* Robert Leckie, *Strong Men Armed* (New York: Random House, 1962); George McMillan, *The Old Breed: A History of the First Marine Division in World War II* (Washington: Infantry Journal Press, 1949); Samuel Eliot Morison, *Two Ocean War* (Boston: Little, Brown, 1963); S.E. Smith, ed., *The United States Marine Corps in World War II* (New York: Random House, 1969); Ronald H. Spector, *Eagle Against the Sun: The American War with Japan* (New York: Free Press, 1985).

Call to Arms
Shaw Jr., *Opening Moves.*

Guadalcanal
5th Mar M-rolls, July-Dec. 1942; Brig. Gen. Samuel B. Griffith, *Battle For Guadalcanal* (Annapolis, Md.: Naval and Aviation, 1979); Eric Ham-

mel, *Guadalcanal: Starvation Island* (New York: Crown, 1987); Jon T. Hoffman, *Once A Legend: "Red Mike" Edson of the Marine Raiders* (Novato, Calif.: Presidio, 1994), pp. 165–232; Hough, Ludwig, and Shaw, *Pearl Harbor To Guadalcanal;* Robert Leckie, *Challenge for the Pacific* (New York: Doubleday, 1965); John Miller Jr., *Guadalcanal: The First Offensive,* U.S. Army in World War II (Washington: Center for Military History, 1968); Henry I. Shaw Jr., *First Offensive: The Marine Campaign for Guadalcanal,* Marines in World War II Commemorative Series (Washington: History and Museums Division, Headquarters Marine Corps, 1992); Merrill B. Twining, *No Bended Knee* (Novato, Calif.: Presidio Press, 1996); Yingling, *Brief History,* pp. 21–25; Maj. John L. Zimmerman, *The Guadalcanal Campaign* (Washington: Historical Division, Headquarters Marine Corps, 1949).

New Britain
5th Mar M-rolls, Dec. 1943-Apr. 1944; Lt. Col. Frank O. Hough and Maj. John A. Crown, *The Campaign for New Britain* (Washington: Historical Branch, Headquarters Marine Corps, 1952); John Miller Jr., *CARTWHEEL: The Reduction of Rabaul, U.S. Army in World War II* (Washington: Office of the Chief of Military History, 1959); Bernard C. Nalty, *Cape Glouster: The Green Inferno,* Marines in World War II Commemorative Series (Washington: History and Museums Division, Headquarters Marine Corps, 1994); Shaw and Kane, *Isolation of Rabaul;* Yingling, *Brief History,* pp. 25–32.

Peleliu
5th Mar M-rolls, Sept.–Dec. 1944; 1st Lt Brendan B. McBreen, "2d Battalion, 5th Marines Land At Peleliu," copy in author's collection; Garand and Strobridge, *Western Pacific Operations,* pp. 51–Brig. Gen. Gordon D. Gayle, *Bloody Beaches: The Marines at Peleliu,* Marines in World War II Commemorative Series (Washington: History and Museums Division, Headquarters Marine Corps, 1996); Maj. Frank O. Hough, *The Assault on Peleliu* (Washington: Historical Division, Headquarters Marine Corps, 1950); McMillan, *Old Breed;* E. B. Sledge, *With the Old Breed at Peleliu and Okinawa* (Novato, Calif.: Presidio, 1981), pp. 420–21; Yingling, *Brief History,* pp. 30–34.

Okinawa
5th Mar M-rolls, Apr.-June 1945; Okinawa Area File; Col. Joseph H. Alexander, *The Final Campaign: Marines in the Victory on Okinawa,* Marines

in World War II Commemorative Series (Washington: History and Museums Division, Headquarters Marine Corps, 1996); Roy E. Appleman, *Okinawa: The Last Battle,* U.S. Army in World War II (Washington: Office of the Chief of Military History, 1948); Benis M. Frank, *Okinawa: Touchstone to Victory* (New York, Ballantine, 1969); Frank and Shaw, *Victory and Occupation;* Maj. Charles S. Nichols and Henry I. Shaw, *Okinawa: Victory in the Pacific* (Washington: Historical Branch, Headquarters Marine Corps, 1955); Capt. James R. Stockman, *The 1st Marine Division on Okinawa* (Washington: Historical Division, Headquarters Marine Corps, n.d.).

Occupation Duty
5th Mar M-rolls, 1 Jan. 1946–15 Dec. 1949; Thomas B. Allen and Norman Polmar, *Code-Name Downfall* (New York: Simon and Schuster, 1995); James M. Davis, *Top Secret: The Story of the Invasion of Japan* (Omaha: Ranger Publications, 1986); Frank and Shaw, *Victory and Occupation,* pp. 397–407, 521–635; Henry I. Shaw Jr., *The U.S. Marines in North China, 1945–1949* (Historical Branch, Headquarters Marine Corps, 1962); Yingling, *Brief History,* pp. 39–41.

Ammunition Dump Fight, pp. 196–197. All of the Marine dead were enlisted men from Company C, 1/5: Pfcs. Salvatore L. Dinenna, John P. Peloro, Alford E. Perkey, and Pvts. Joseph D. Pavraznik, and Frank C. Spencer.

Postscript
Leland Diamond, Gordon D. Gayle, Harold D. Harris, and Lewis W. Walt biographical files; Dennis Carpenter, *Anyone Here a Marine?* vol. 2 (Great Neck, N.Y.: Brightlight Publications, n.d.), pp. 30–31.

Chapter 5. Korea

Roy E. Appleman, *Ridgway Duels for Korea* (College Station: Texas A&M University Press, 1990); idem, *South to the Naktong, North to the Yalu,* U.S. Army in the Korean War (Washington: Office of the Chief of Military History, 1961); Andrew Geer, *The New Breed: The Story of the U.S. Marines in Korea* (New York: Harper Brothers, 1952); Robert Leckie, *Conflict: The History of the Korean War, 1950–53* (New York: G. P. Putnam's Sons, 1962); Billy C. Mossman, *Ebb and Flow: November 1950–July 1951,* U.S. Army in the Korean War (Washington: Center of Military History, 1990); Matthew B. Ridgway, *The Korean War* (Garden City, N.Y.: Doubleday, 1967).

Pusan

5th Mar UD, June–Sept. 1950; 1/5 SAR, 9 Sept. 1950; John Chapin, *Fire Brigade: U.S. Marines in the Pusan Perimeter,* Marines in the Korean War Commemorative Series (Washington: History and Museums Division, Headquarters Marine Corps, 2000); Geer, *New Breed,* pp. 1–102; Lynn Montross and Capt. Nicholas A. Canzona, *U.S. Marine Corps Operations in Korea, 1950–1953,* vol. 1, *The Pusan Perimeter* (Washington: Historical Branch, Headquarters Marine Corps, 1954); Yingling, *Brief History,* pp.43–45.

Inchon and Seoul

5th Mar HD, Sept.–Oct. 1950; 3/5 SAR; Col. Joseph H. Alexander, *The Battle of the Barricades: U.S. Marines in the Recapture of Seoul,* Marines in the Korean War Commemorative Series (Washington: History and Museums Division, Headquarters Marine Corps, 2000); Robert D. Heinl, *Victory at High Tide* (New York: J. B. Lippincott, 1968); Lynn Montross and Capt. Nicholas A. Canzona, *U.S. Marine Corps Operations in Korea, 1950–1953,* vol. 2, *The Inchon-Seoul Operation* (Washington: Historical Branch, Headquarters Marine Corps, 1957); Edwin H. Simmons, *Over the Seawall: U.S. Marines at Inchon, 1950,* Marines in the Korean War Commemorative Series (Washington: History and Museums Division, Headquarters Marine Corps, 2000); Yingling, *Brief History,* pp. 45–47.

The Frozen Chosin

5th Mar UD, Oct.–Dec. 1950; 1/5 SAR for 21 Nov.–10 Dec. 1950; Roy E. Appleman, *East of Chosin* (College Station: Texas A&M University Press, 1987); Geer, *New Breed,* pp. 192–374; Eric Hammel, *Chosin: Heroic Ordeal of the Korean War* (New York: Vanguard Press, 1981); Robert Leckie, *March to Glory* (New York: World Publishing, 1959); Lynn Montross and Nicholas Canzona, *U.S. Marine Corps Operations in Korea, 1950–1953,* vol. 3, *The Chosin Reservoir Campaign* (Washington: Historical Branch, Headquarters Marine Corps, 1957); Yingling, *Brief History,* pp.47–50.

The East-Central Front

5th Mar UD, Jan. 1951–May 1952; Paul N. McCloskey Jr., *The Taking of Hill 610* (Woodside, Calif.: Eaglet Books, 1992); Lynn Montross, Maj. Hubard D. Kuokka, and Maj. Norman W. Hicks, *U.S. Marine Corps Operations in Korea, 1950–1953,* vol. 4, *The East-Central Front* (Historical

Branch, Headquarters Marine Corps, 1961); Yingling, *Brief History,* pp.50–55.

West Korea
Lt. Col. Pat Meid and Maj. James M. Yingling, *U.S. Marine Corps Operations in Korea, 1950–1953,* vol. 5, *Operations in West Korea* (Washington: Historical Division, Headquarters Marine Corps, 1972); Yingling, *Brief History,* pp. 55–56.

Post-Korea
5th Mar UD, May 1952–Dec. 1962; Clifford, *Progress and Purpose,* pp. 79–94; Parker, *Concise History,* pp. 85–92; Heinl, *Soldiers of the Sea,* pp. 600–02; Millett, *Semper Fidelis,* pp. 518–58; Yingling, *Brief History,* pp. 56–58.

Postscript
Robert D. Bohn, Victor H. Krulak, Oliver P. Smith, and Lewis W. Walt biographical files.

Chapter 6. Vietnam

Fleet Marine Force Pacific monthly operations summaries; 5th Mar UD; 5th Mar ComdCs; "The 5th Marines in RVN," Unit Files, Reference Section, Headquarters Marine Corps, n.d.; Gunther Lewy, *America in Vietnam* (New York: Oxford University Press, 1978); Michael MacClear, *The Ten Thousand Day War: Vietnam, 1945–1975* (New York: St. Martin's Press, 1981); Maurice Matloff, ed., *American Military History,* Army Historical Series (Washington: Office of the Chief of Military History, 1969), pp. 619–48; Millett, *Semper Fidelis,* pp. 559–606; Moskin, *U.S. Marine Corps Story,* pp. 619–96; Edward F. Murphy, *Semper Fi—Vietnam* (Novato, Calif.: Presidio Press, 1997); Bernard C. Nalty, *The Vietnam War* (New York: Barnes & Noble Books, 1998); Douglas Pike, *Viet Cong* (Cambridge, Mass.: MIT Press, 1966); idem., *PAVN: The People's Army of North Vietnam* (Novato, Calif.: Presidio Press, 1989); Edwin H. Simmons, *Marines: The Illustrated History of the Vietnam War* (New York: Bantam Books, 1987); idem., Simmons, *U.S. Marines,* pp. 264–97; U.S. Marine Corps, *The Marines in Vietnam, 1954–1973: An Anthology and Annotated Bibliography* (Washington: History and Museums Division, Headquarters Marine Corps, 1974); Gen. Lewis W. Walt, *Strange War, Strange Strategy* (New York: Funk and Wagnalls, 1970); Gen. William C. Westmoreland, *A Soldier Reports* (Garden City, N.Y.: Doubleday, 1976); Capt. Robert H. Whitlow,

USMC, *The Advisory and Combat Assistance Era, 1954–1964* (Washington History and Museums Division, Headquarters Marine Corps, 1977); Yingling, *Brief History*, pp. 58–62; Spector, 5th Mar draft, pp. 93–98.

Special Landing Forces

Ralph F. Moody and Benis M. Frank, "Special Landing Forces in Vietnam, 1965–1969," copy in author's collection; Jack Shulimson, *An Expanding War, 1966*, U.S. Marines in Vietnam (Washington: History and Museums Division, Headquarters Marine Corps, 1982), pp. 128–36; Jack Shulimson and Maj. Charles M. Johnson, *Landing and Buildup, 1965*, U.S. Marines in Vietnam (Washington: History and Museums Division, Headquarters Marine Corps, 1978), pp. 193–203; Edwin H. Simmons, "Marine Corps Operations in Vietnam, 1965–1966," *Naval Review* (Annapolis: U.S. Naval Institute, 1968), pp. 2–35.

Chu Lai

5th Mar AAR "Operation Colorado," copy in author's collection; Shulimson, *Expanding War*, pp. 161–76, 211–20; Simmons, "1965–1966," pp. 2–35.

Que Son Valley

5th Mar AAR "Operation Union," copy in author's collection; John J. Culbertson, *Operation Tuscaloosa* (New York: Ivy Books, 1997); idem, *Sniper in the Arizona* (New York: Ivy Books, 1999); Gary L. Telfer, Lt. Col. Lane Rogers, and V. Keith Fleming Jr., *Fighting the North Vietnamese, 1967*, U.S. Marines in Vietnam (Washington: History and Museums Division, Headquarters Marine Corps, 1984); Edwin H. Simmons, "Marine Corps Operations in Vietnam, 1967," *Naval Review* (Annapolis: U.S. Naval Institute, 1969), pp. 112–41.

The M16 Controversy. During the course of several discussions about Vietnam, Marine sniper John J. Culbertson described the "black rifle fiasco" in the earthy terms of a pissed-off grunt when he used words to the effect that "Someone in authority must have had shit for brains to send men into the field with a rifle that would not shoot." He also opined that callous disregard for America's fighting men became obvious when civilian and military higher-ups denied the obvious after being shown indisputable proof the rifle was no good and was costing lives. Many Vietnam veterans remain convinced to this day that the M16 was chosen solely for political reasons. Luckily, I encountered relatively few problems with my own M16A1, which had a chrome receiver with a manual cartridge-assist lever and fired ammunition using slower-burning powder. When researching this problem, I was often reminded of the infamous controversy when the navy's Bureau of Ordnance refused to accept overwhelming evidence its torpedoes were faulty during the first two years of World War II. My father was a submarine officer who often related his experiences at that time. Interestingly, the current U.S. infantry rifle, the M16A2, is virtually a brand-new weapon whose parts are, for the most part, not interchangeable with either of the older model M16s.

Hue City

Tom Bartlett, "Hue City, Tet '68," *Leatherneck,* Apr. 1988, pp. 24–29; Capt. George R. Christmas, "A Company Commander reflects on Operation Hue City," *Marine Corps Gazette,* Apr. 1971, pp. 34–39; Maj. Ron Christmas, "A Company Commander Remembers the Battle for Hue," *Marine Corps Gazette,* Feb. 1977 pp. 19–26; Eric Hammel, *Fire in the Streets: The Battle for Hue, Tet 1968* (Chicago: Contemporary Books, 1991); Eric Hammel, "Mean Streets," *Old Breed News,* Aug. 1996, pp. 16–19; 1st Lt. Brendan B. McBreen, "2d Battalion, 5th Marines at Hue," Camp Pendleton: Project Leatherneck, n.d.; Keith W. Nolan, "Battle at Hue City," U.S. Naval Institute *Proceedings,* April 1982, pp. 51–58; idem., *Battle For Hue: Tet, 1968* (Novato, Calif.: Presidio Press, 1983); Jack Shulimson, "Marines Mark 25th Anniversary of Pivotal Battle for Hue," *Fortitudine* (winter 1992–93): pp. 9–11, 24; idem., Lt. Col. Leonard A. Blasiol, Charles R. Smith, and Capt. David A. Dawson, *The Defining Year: 1968,* U.S. Marines in Vietnam (Washington: History and Museums Division, Headquarters Marine Corps, 1997), pp. 83–111, 141–213, 328–49, 414–56; Brig. Gen. Edwin H. Simmons, "Marine Corps Operations in Vietnam, 1968," *Naval Review* (Annapolis: U.S. Naval Institute, 1970), pp. 292–320; Simmons, *Marines in Vietnam,* pp. 93–100; Ronald H. Spector, *After Tet: The Bloodiest Year in Vietnam* (New York: Free Press, 1993); Spector, 5th Mar draft, pp. 103–107; Nicholas Warr, *Phase Line Green* (New York: Ivy Books, 1997).

Results of the Tet Offensive, p. 318. For more information about how and why the American media misinterpreted the Tet Offensive see Peter Braestrup's *Big Story* (Novato, Calif.: Presidio Press, 1994).

An Hoa

Col. Noble L. Beck, "Rice Krispies Nipped in the Bud," *Marine Corps Gazette,* May 1970, p. 50; Lt. Col. Charles K. Breslauer, "Battle of the Northern Arizona," *Marine Corps Gazette,* Jan. 1977, pp. 47–55; Ronald J.

Brown, Vietnam Journal, author's collection; Graham A. Cosmas and Lt. Col. Terrance P. Murray, *Vietnamization and Redeployment, 1970–71*, U.S. Marine Operations in Vietnam (Washington: History and Museums Division, Headquarters Marine Corps, 1986), pp. 77–82; Simmons, "Marines in Vietnam, 1968," *Naval Review* (Annapolis: U.S. Naval Institute, 1970), pp. 292–320; idem., "Marine Corps Operations in Vietnam, 1969–1972," *Naval Review* (Annapolis: U.S. Naval Institute, 1973), pp. 194–223; Charles R. Smith, *High Mobility and Standdown, 1969*, U.S. Marine Operations in Vietnam (Washington: History and Museums Division, Headquarters Marine Corps, 1988), pp. 80–125, 173–216; Spector, *After Tet*, pp. 236; 309–10; Spector, 5th Mar draft, pp. 108–18; Lt. Gen. Bernard E. Trainor, "Pacifier Operations in Vietnam," *Marine Corps Gazette*, June 1986, pp. 36–37.

Imperial Lake

Cosmas and Murray, *Vietnamization and Redeployment, 1970–1971*, pp. 89–124, 186–262.

Postscript

Ernest C. Cheatham, Kenneth J. Houghton Jr., Terrance P. Murray, and Anthony C. Zinni biographical files; conversations with John J. Culbertson; Michael R. Gordon and Bernard E. Trainor, *The General's War: The Inside Story of the Conflict in the Gulf* (Boston: Little, Brown, 1995); Gustav Hasford, *The Short Timers* (New York: Bantam, 1979); Robert Roth, *Sand in the Wind* (Boston: Little, Brown, 1973); Robert Timberg, *The Nightingale's Song* (New York: Simon and Schuster, 1995); Jim Webb, *Fields of Fire* (Englewood Cliffs, N.J.: Prentice Hall, 1978).

Chapter 7. Persian Gulf

5th MEB ComdCs, July 1972–June 1991; Spector, 5th Mar draft, pp. 117–18.

Martin Binkin and Jeffery Record, *Where Does the Marine Corps Go from Here?* (Washington: Brookings Institution, 1976); Maj. Ronald J. Brown, Gallant Eagle–86 Journal, author's collection; Millett, *Semper Fidelis*, pp. 607–35.

Southwest Asia

5th MEB SAR "Desert Storm"; 5th MEB staff interview; 5th Mar ComdCs, July 1990–June 1991; 1/5 ComdCs; 2/5 ComdCs; 3/5 ComdCs;

Ronald J. Brown, Southwest Asia Journal, author's collection; Col. Randolph A. Gangle interview; Brig. Gen. Peter J. Rowe interview; 1st Lt Brendan B. McBreen, "2/5 in Desert Storm," Project Leatherneck, n.d., author's collection; Lt. Col. Ronald J. Brown, *With Marine Forces Afloat during Desert Shield and Desert Storm,* U.S. Marines in the Persian Gulf, 1990–1991 (Washington: History and Museums Division, Headquarters Marine Corps, 1999); Lt. Col. Charles H. Cureton, *With the 1st Marine Division in Desert Shield and Desert Storm,* U.S. Marines in the Persian Gulf, 1990–1991 (Washington: History and Museums Division, Headquarters Marine Corps, 1993); Lt. Col. Dennis P. Mrozcowski, *With the 2d Marine Division in Desert Shield and Desert Storm,* U.S. Marines in the Persian Gulf, 1990–1991 (Washington: History and Museums Division, Headquarters Marine Corps, 1992); Col. Charles J. Quilter II, *With the I Marine Expeditionary Force,* U.S. Marines in the Persian Gulf, 1990–1991 (History and Museums Division, Headquarters Marine Corps, 1992). Brig. Gen. Edwin H. Simmons, USMC (Ret.), "Getting Marines to the Gulf," and "Getting the Job Done," *Naval Review* (Annapolis, Md., U.S. Naval Institute, 1991): pp. 50–64, 94–96.

Sea Angel
Lt. Col. Donald R. Selvage, "Operation Sea Angel: Bangladesh Disaster Relief," *Marine Corps Gazette,* Nov. 91, pp. 89–97; Charles R. Smith *Angels From The Sea: Relief Operations in Bangladesh,* 1991 (History and Museums Division, Headquarters Marine Corps, 1995); Lt. Gen. Henry C. Stackpole III, "Operation Sea Angel: Marine Corps Relief Operations in Bangladesh," MCHC Seminar, 30 Jan. 1992, and "Angels From the Sea," *Naval Review* (Annapolis, Md. U.S. Naval Institute, 1992): pp. 128-132

Chapter 8. Marching On
5th Mar ComdCs, Jan. 1992–Dec. 1998; CMC annual reports 1992–99; TO/E 1027G; Tom Clancy, *Marine: A Guided Tour of a Marine Expeditionary Unit* (New York: Berkeley Books, 1996); Staff, "Floods Devastate Camp Pendleton," *Marine Corps Gazette,* Feb. 1993, p. 7.

Index

Swain, Harold W., 235
Sweeney, William E., 208, 211
Sweet, Walter, 49
Syngman Rhee, 203

Taillfontaine (France), 52
Taking Hill 610 (Book), 277
Taku (China), 193
Talasea (New Britain), 143, 145, 146, 148, 284
Talbot, Ralph, 81
Tam Ky (Vietnam), 288, 294
Tampico (Mexico), 2
Tanambogo (Solomons Islands), 106
Taplett, Robert D., 206, 207, 209, 210, 212, 217, 225, 227, 229, 234, 235, 236, 237, 243
Tarawa, 110, 151, 206
Target Hill (New Britain), 138
Taylor, William A., 180
Telpaneca (Nicaragua), 98
Tenny, Joseph R., 299, 302
Tenaru (Ilu) River (Guadalcanal), 118
Tentative Manual for Landing Operations, 103
Terry, John M. Jr., 328, 330
Tet Offensive (Vietnam), 308, 318, 325
Texas A&M University, 206
Thang Binh (Vietnam), 292, 298
Tharau, Herman, 28-29, 60
Thayer, Sydney Jr., 75
The General's War (Book), 347
The Short Timers (Novel), 348
Thiaucourt (France), 61, 63
Thomas, Frank A., 312
Thomas, Gerald C., 250
Thomason, John W. Jr, 34, 53, 54, 56, 69, 74, 81, 82, 98
Thompson, Robert B., 313, 314, 315, 316, 317
Thong Duc Corridor (Vietnam), 289, 318, 320, 332
Thu Bon River (Vietnam), 290, 319. 320, 324, 330
Thua Thien Province (Vietnam), 284, 305, 307
Thuong Tu Gate (Vietnam), 314, 317
Tientsin (China), 193, 195

Tigny (France), 53
Tilley, Robert O., 343
Tobin, John L., 206, 211
Toktong Pass, (Korea), 239, 241
Tokyo (Japan), 192
Tompkins, Rathvon M., 272
Torcy (France), 31, 33, 35, 42, 49
Torrey, Philip A., 328
Toul (France), 60, 63
Toulon Sector (France), 25
Tracy, James K., 89
Trainor, Bernard E., 333, 335, 340, 341, 347
Triangle Farm (France), 27, 30, 35, 38
Truman, Pres. Harry S., 51, 155, 192, 200
Trumpe, Drake, 358
Truoi Bridge (Vietnam), 308
Tschirgi, Harvey C., 269, 272
Tulagi (Solomons Islands), 116, 118, 119, 121, 125
Tully, Lester A., 309
Turnage, Allen H., 103, 106
Turrill, Julius S., 11, 19, 25, 27, 31, 33, 34, 35, 47, 50, 53, 57, 60
Twentynine Palms (California), 273, 355, 356, 359, 379
Typhoons
  Jane, 337
  Joan, 339
  Kate, 339
  Louise, 339

Ulithi Atoll (Pacific), 177
Umurbrogol (Peleliu), 151, 152, 161, 162, 167, 168, 171, 172
Ungok (Korea), 263
Unit Deployment Program (UDP), 353
United Arab Emirates, 361
United Nations Command (UNC), 205, 207, 210, 233, 234, 244, 248, 249, 250, 254, 256, 270, 271
Uskurait, Robert H., 283
Uris, Leon, 276
Ushijima, Mitsuru, 176, 186
Usseldange (Luxembourg), 77
Utley, Harold H., 94
Uttfield (Luxembourg), 77